As I note in Chapter VIII, 80 percent of
all books sold in the US today are published
by just 5 multinational corporations.

This makes book publishing in smaller concerns
an increasingly difficult challenge. If you find anything
remarkable in these pages, please consider writing a review
at your favorite on-line book retailers.

And thank you for opening this book.
I think you will find it well worth the time to read.

—Joseph N. Abraham MD

"I've always believed society to be a fundamentally rational thing, but what if it wasn't?
What if it was built on insanity?"

—Jon Ronson, *The Psychopath Test*

Winner: World History
Independent Press Award

Winner, World History
NYC Big Book Awards

Winner, Current Events/Social Change
New Generation Indie Book Awards

Gold Medal
Non Fiction Authors Association

Short List, Grand Prize
Eric Hoffer Book Award

1st Runner Up, Legacy Nonfiction
Eric Hoffer Book Award

Bronze Medal, Historical Nonfiction
Readers' Favorite Awards

Finalist
Montaigne Medal

Finalist, Historical Non-Fiction
New Generation Indie Book Awards

Finalist, Best New Non-Fiction
American Book Fest

Finalist, Adult Non-Fiction
The Wishing Shelf

Honorable Mention, Nonfiction
Paris Book Festival

Honorable Mention, Nonfiction
New York Book Festival

Honorable Mention, General Nonfiction
Hollywood Book Festival

". . . concise, compelling, and challenging exploration of how humanity became what it is."

—*Publishers Weekly*

". . . the book's scientific analysis, which spans Darwin's concept of evolution to cutting-edge psychology, is a welcome addition to historical conversations. . ."

—*Kirkus Reviews*

". . . reviews the historical precedent for accepting corruption and violence from our authorities. Why do we excuse an act, unforgivable if committed by an ordinary citizen, if executed or ordered by a leader?"

—*The Los Angeles Review of Books*

"In 10 chapters, Abraham traces the last 10,000 years from the era of kings and conquerors to the modern world and its own ugly truths."

—*New Orleans Times-Picayune*

"[Abraham] provides insight into historical patterns of power and dominance at all levels of government, religion and corporate existence."

—*Baton Rouge Morning Advocate*

"The term 'must-read' has been so overused. But *Kings, Conquerors, Psychopaths* is a must-read. . . a must-own. . . and, most of all, a **must-ponder**."

—Joe Gandelman, *San Diego Jewish World*

★★★★★ ". . . this may be the most important book you will ever read."

—Robin Levin, *The Death of Carthage*

★★★★★ "This book is a must-read. . . I believe that this book will stand the test of time and scrutiny."

—Journalist Carol Beggy, co-author of the award-winning *Boston* book series; co-author of *Ted Kennedy: Scenes from an Epic Life*

★★★★★ ". . . this is only my third [5-star rating] of the year. . . . It was simply outstanding. . ."

—Stephanie Verhaegen, *Bookfever* book blog

"A detailed and engaging examination of our haunted past and threatening future. Read it and weep."

—John Mack Faragher, Howard R. Lamar Professor Emeritus, Yale University, *Daniel Boone*; *A Great and Noble Scheme*; and *The American Heritage Encyclopedia of American History*

"It's always easier to turn away from the horrors of history, but Abraham forces us to look, and look carefully. Using wide-ranging research and an unflinching eye for detail, he reminds us that it's only through the stories of the past that we can understand where we've come from, what we've become, and how we can even hope to effect change."

—Candice Millard, *New York Times* best-selling author of *The River of Doubt* and the Edgar Award-winning *Destiny of the Republic*

"Abraham makes an insightful, novel argument based on both a keen clinical eye, and an exhaustive review of the literature, for understanding the historical and genetic roots of this problem, and why we should be aware of the potential dictators all around us."

—James Fallon, *The Psychopath Inside*, Sloan Scholar, Senior Fullbright Fellow, NIH Career Awardee, UCI Medical School Professor Emeritus

"Psychiatrists are known for their ability to see what is covertly behind the overt words. Though his name is not mentioned, I could see that the title of this timely book could be: *Kings, Conquerors, Trumps!*"

—H. Steven Moffic, MD, sole designee "Hero of Public Psychiatry" by the American Psychiatric Association; Editorial Board, *Psychiatric Times*; author, *Psychiatry, a Problem-Oriented Approach*; *Psychiatry and Ethics*; co-author, *The Dangerous Case of Donald Trump*

"The book never mentions Trump, but he's on every page."

—Anonymous academic referee

". . . [a] survey of the ways in which power is attained, exercised, and often mythologized throughout human history serve as a stark reminder of how fragile and vulnerable to exploitation our modern democratic societies are, and how important it is for all of us to educate ourselves and our fellow citizens to sustain and improve the all-to-human structures and systems required for effective self-governance."

—Review, *Math Values* (Mathematical Association of America)

"... provides unique and important insights for our world at large. This book is a must-read for any American concerned about the future of our society."

—Jim Engster, *NPR* affiliate *WRKF*, Baton Rouge

"... fascinating and frightening not just as an explanation to understanding the people who have transformed mankind, but what it portends for the future, which just might not be so kind."

—Steven Sabludowsy, *BayouBuzz.com*

"For those who want their minds expanded and blown: Dr. Abraham is the man."

—Pearson Cross, *NPR* affiliate *KRVS*, Lafayette, Louisiana

"Detailed, engaging, and provocative examination of our shared history."

—Marcus Hedahl, United States Naval Academy

KINGS, CONQUERORS, PSYCHOPATHS

KINGS, CONQUERORS, PSYCHOPATHS

From Alexander to Hitler to the Corporation

JOSEPH N. ABRAHAM, MD

Cover design by Eleanor Renée Rogers

© 2020 Hidden Hills Press
A section of Metaphysical Properties, LLC
All rights reserved
ISBN 13 (paper): 978-0-578-68059-0

Second edition printed 2020 by Hidden Hills Press
First edition printed 2018 by the University of Louisiana Press

For Pretty Lady,
Son,
and Pretty Girl

Contents

Acknowledgments IX

Prologue: **Fantasy and Horror** XV
War is not gallant heroism, it is horror: it is the sadistic dismembering of soldiers and civilians.

Chapter I: **Kings** 1
Kings were gangsters running national protection rackets: they extorted money from their subjects, monopolized high-profit resources, and dealt brutally with any resistance.

Chapter II: **Conquerors** 15
Conquerors are serial killers who prey upon nations. They commit murder, theft, and enslavement against millions for fabulous wealth.

Chapter III: **Psychopaths** 81
Conquerors meet the diagnostic criteria for the 'dark tetrad': criminal psychopathy, narcissism, Machiavellianism, and sadism. Kings and conquerors do not need to personally meet the psychiatric criteria for these disorders, because successful conquest and monarchy always do.

Interlude: **Genetics, Eugenics, Genocide** 117
Human genetic behavior is ruts, not rails. It is a mistake to categorize people by their genetic characteristics, but ignoring our genetic influences leaves us more vulnerable to them.

Chapter IV: **The Breeding Programme** 127
Through rape and polygamy, on one side of our family tree we are all descended from the conqueror and his armies; on the other side, we are descended from their victims. Through both lineages we have been selected to ignore doubt and independent thought, on risk of torture and death. Survival under king and conqueror required that we not only agree, but that we blindly believe anything the monarch said, however illogical or outrageous.

Chapter V: **The Noble Classes** 141
Those atop the noble hierarchy were 'important' people. By default, the rest of us were unimportant and expendable. Through his lieutenants, the king designed civilization as a rigid caste system

of subjugation, subordination, and exclusion. Despite the rapid expansion of egalitarian ideals in recent centuries, the world still struggles against authoritarian factions who work to pull us back toward hierarchy and oppression.

CHAPTER VI: PRIVILEGE & THE DOUBLE STANDARD................... 149
'Privilege' means 'private law', a legal double standard: the king and nobility demand a middle class morality of the commoners, while they pursue a criminal anti-morality of exploitation and evil.

CHAPTER VII: THE AUTHORITARIAN PERSONALITY....................... 155
Millennia of cultural and genetic selection under king and conqueror leave us vulnerable to blind loyalty, and many of us still believe any lie or hypocrisy the despot presents. This explains political and religious fanaticism, blind obedience to political strongmen, and the resulting cult of personality.

CHAPTER VIII: THE ATROCINO... 197
King and conqueror have morphed into modern business and political leaders, who continue to exploit us and expend our lives for power, wealth, and narcissism.

CHAPTER IX: THE MODERN WORLD 209
For 10,0000 years under the king, progress was slow and serendipitous. After 1776, as the oppression of the noble classes was gradually eliminated, diffuse prosperity and independent thought grew rapidly. That liberation, with the attendant expansion of intellectual and economic participation, allowed genius and progress to explode, giving us the modern world.

CHAPTER X: THE UGLY TRUTH 243
Without the slaughter, torture, and terror of the conqueror, we would still be neolithic hunter-gatherers. That was the horrific cost of civilization.

EPILOGUE: RESPONSE.. 255
Equality and democratic participation are still the only real antidotes to the psychopaths and narcissists who struggle for monarchy and monopoly around the globe. If progress is to continue, it is essential that we have an educated and engaged electorate. Without it, we will revert to the brutality of the past.

ENDNOTES 277

INDEX 297

Acknowledgments

Many of the scholars who helped with this book are recognized in the footnotes. I like that arrangement—I suspect that more people read footnotes than acknowledgments.

There is one person who has contributed far more to this book than any other. Mathé Allain has been my mentor, and one of my very best friends, for four decades. Many of the ideas and historical observations in the following come from anecdotes she shared with me, from films she dragged me to see, or from books she suggested. The conversation with Eugen Weber described in Chapter VI took place at her home. Many of the ideas here I worked through in conversations with her. (That should not, however, be interpreted as her endorsement for everything in the book; she can be a demanding critic and a feisty intellectual adversary.) Some of the more memorable influences I gained from our discussions were the story of the vase at Soissons; the film *Ridicule*; and Yourcenar's *Memoirs of Hadrien*. Perhaps the most influential was the film *Medea* starring Maria Callas in her only non-musical role. In it, Jason and the Argonauts are not portrayed as dashing defenders of virtue, but as all ancient heroes really were: marauders, thieves, murderers, and rapists.

Mathé led me to one of the more important ideas here in a passive way, however. Before I met her as my professor for Louisiana French Literature at the University of Louisiana, I heard her frequently praised by other students. As a result, I had expected the sort of martinet that we will meet in Chapter III, the character of Charles W. Kingsfield Jr., played by Richard Houseman in the film *The Paper Chase*: domineering, demanding, and even degrading. Instead, she was gracious, generous, and patient. That got me to wondering why we expect 'important' people to act like Kingsfield.

Mathé was also one of the early pillars for the Center for Louisiana Studies, which was founded as both a research center and a press, and which eventually generated the University of Louisiana Press. And so she literally influenced this book from cover to cover.

The second person I need to thank is someone who, strangely enough, I have not met as of publication. You will encounter James Fallon several times in these pages. I contacted him a few years back with my thesis, and he has been an enthusiastic supporter ever since. He has repeatedly offered me priceless advice and encouragement.

Vaughan Baker and Amos Simpson were also mentors, friends of Mathé, and early supporters, editors, and intellectual contributors to the Center for Louisiana Studies/UL Press. (They were also guests at the small dinner party with Eugen Weber.) Amos was easily the most influential history teacher I had. His enthusiasm for history was contagious, and inspired my lifelong interest in history. Without that influence, this book would probably not have been written. Amos passed away before being able to give me input, but Vaughan has offered much helpful feedback, intellectual counterpoint, and encouragement.

Steve Giambrone is the crotchety philosopher in the anecdote about *The Lion King*. He is actually not crotchety at all, and he and his wife Amanda are some of my favorite people to sit, drink, and laugh with. Steve has read parts of this, suggested corrections, and questioned some ideas on philosophical grounds.

Much of this book was sparked by a 1978 discussion with Darryl Felder while I was taking his class in invertebrate zoology. At the time I was trying to understand why the Cajun and Creole culture was so different from other cultures I had experienced, and how the University of Louisiana shared many of those differences. Darryl compared it to another university and said, "They're a hierarchy. This place is more of a network." That set me off thinking about this thesis.

John Mack Faragher (Yale), Geoffrey A. Parker (University of Liverpool), and Jack Palmer (University of Louisiana-Monroe) all agreed to serve as referees, although as things worked out, I did not have to ask them for their time. John Mack Faragher, however, agreed to read the manuscript, which was a large contribution as he has a demanding editing and publishing slate. Jon Ronson generously allowed us to use his quote on the cover.

There are any number of people who agreed to look at advance copies of this, including: Tom Zoellner; Richard Florida; Lylah Alphonse; Ruth Wedgwood; Larry Hollier; Elizabeth Taylor; Liam T. A. Ford; Jerry Rosenblum; Don Asmussen; William Kaufman; Julie Scelfo; Amanda Hess; Susan Gregory Thomas; James L. Franklin; Peter Keough; Carol Beggy; Christian Caryl; Peter Goldman; Rand Hyden; Hank Saroyan; and Tex Sample.

George Wooddell helped with sociological approaches, and Cary Heath advised me on several economics questions. I am particularly indebted to Jan Swift and her sharp eyes.

Acknowledgments

I must also thank my referees; one of whom, May Waggoner, was one of my early French professors and an occasional grocery store conversant. I owe her a quiet date for tea.

And I also need to thank Mary Duhé, who laid out the printer's files for the original UL Press edition, and who updated those files for this edition.

If we had read more widely we should not have completed the book —which perhaps might have been the better course.
—H. Munro & Nora K. Chadwick[1]

A poem is never finished; it is only abandoned.
—Paul Valéry (attributed)[2]

Go, litel bok; go, litel myn tragedye.
—Geoffrey Chaucer[3]

Prologue:
Fantasy & Horror

> *The only thing that I can remember about Alexander the Great was that at age twenty-six he wept because there were no more people to murder and rob. That is the epitome of Western Civilization.*
>
> —Kwame Ture (Stokely Carmichael)[*]

> *Where have all the good men gone, and where are all the gods,*
> *Where's the street-wise Hercules to fight the rising odds?*
> *Isn't there a white knight upon a fiery steed?*
> *Late at night I toss, and I turn, and I dream of what I need:*
> *I need a hero!*
>
> —Jim Steinman and Dean Pitchford[1]

In libraries and bookstores, works of unrestrained imagination are often grouped together under 'fantasy and horror.' To begin to understand the thesis of this book, we will need to use imagination in a different but more restrained way so that we might separate fantasy from horror. By doing this, I hope to present a vicious but inescapable conclusion. So I ask the reader to use her imagination for a moment to consider an extreme but very real horror. It will be unpleasant, but it is essential for what follows.

Imagine picking up a meat cleaver and hacking another person to death. At first, you try to do it quickly, cleave his head open if you can, split his face in two, or open his chest or his belly. But if you can't do that, chop off anything you can reach: fingers, hands, feet, limbs. Keep chopping until he can no longer defend himself, or no longer chooses to, and then kill him.

---

[*] "Western Civilization has been anything but civilized. It has been more barbaric, as a matter of fact. We are told that Western Civilization begins with the Greeks, and the epitome of that is Alexander the Great. The only thing that I can remember about Alexander the Great was that at age twenty-six he wept because there were no more people to murder and rob. That is the epitome of Western Civilization. And if you're not satisfied with that, you could always take the Roman Empire: their favorite pastimes were watching men kill each other or lions eating up men—they were a civilized people. The fact is that their civilization, as they called it, stemmed from the fact that they oppressed other peoples. And that the oppression of other people allowed them a certain luxury, at the expense of those other people." Kwame Ture, *Stokely Speaks: From Black Power to Pan-Africanism* (Chicago Review Press, 2007).

Move on, and murder more people in the same way. At first, focus on men who are armed but who may be at a disadvantage in their weapons and their training. Once there are no more armed men to kill, move on to unarmed men. And then, start on the women and the elderly. Don't omit the children: chop up the toddlers and the babies. Spare no one.

If there is time, however, and you are so motivated, rape the women, young and old, even the little girls—or if you have the preference and your fellows tolerate such things, rape the handsome young men and small boys. Then kill them. Feel free to kill them slowly, torturing them and watching them scream in pain and beg for mercy. When your sadism is sated, chop them to death, too.

Next, imagine enjoying it. Imagine enjoying it so much that it becomes your main goal in life, so that you spend your career working, planning, and victimizing as many people as you can in this manner. Then imagine that it becomes so important to you that you sit down and cry when you realize that there is no one left to slaughter.

Then consider the man who takes the wealth he has stolen from these victims and invests it to create an industry of systematic mass human butchery and theft. He expends his fortune in much the same way that billionaires today assemble sports franchises, recruiting team members, supporting them financially, outfitting them with impressive team uniforms and expensive equipment, and then constantly training them to be as efficiently brutal and lethal as possible. When his team is large enough and the members are well-trained enough, he leads them out to pursue human slaughter as a great, exciting, and highly profitable sport.

What sort of people would admire these butchers? What society would revere these men as celebrities, even gods? Who would bow down to people like this?

We would. We have just imagined virtually all of world civilization and our shared origins. With those imaginings, we have considered the source for many modern obstacles to cooperation, collaboration, and progress.

• • •

On March 16, 1968, a group of U.S. soldiers carrying out orders under Task Force Barker entered two hamlets of Son My Lai in Vietnam and proceeded to carry out exactly this sort of slaughter. In a small improvement from the foregoing, however, the soldiers used guns rather than cleavers. They slaughtered perhaps five hundred babies, children, women, and elders, gang raping some of the young women, even girls as young as ten, before killing

Prologue xvii

My Lai Massacre, photos by Ronald L. Haeberle for the U.S. Federal Government. Left: My Lai Family. Note the young girl, about thirteen years old, buttoning her shirt. As the photographer walked up, one of the soldiers was attempting to rape her. After the photographer took these pictures, he heard gunfire. They were all executed.

Below: These are two brothers, the younger one has been shot, the older one is holding him. Both were executed after this picture was taken.

My Lai Road. Note the babies and toddlers among the dead.

them.² Not one male of fighting age was discovered in the massacre. The absence of fighting men magnified the horror. But it was also, perhaps, an insight into the horror: Why would a peaceful farming community contain no young men?

It was no matter. The international outcry was red-hot.

But there was nothing new in it. In a now-hackneyed phrase, Hannah Arendt once brooded about "the banality of evil."³ She was referring to one particular Nazi bureaucrat, but I will argue that, unknowingly, she also indicted civilization, humanity, and life itself. Because the fact is, the savagery may change, the body counts may change, and the historical contexts may change, but war and conquest do not: the horror does not change, nor do the outcomes. Fortunately, and precisely because of the awareness of the Holocaust and of My Lai, we have begun to change. Those changes are something we will attempt to understand so that we can build on them and avoid relapse.

This book is based on things that were always in front of us, obvious things which we have overlooked. I will argue that subconsciously, but for powerful historical reasons, we overlook the horrible realities of civilization. My thesis defending that comprises five essential insights: Conquest is murder and theft; Conquerors are vicious criminals; Vicious criminals become kings; Kings designed civilization; And we are the products of that civilization.

For ten thousand years, kings and conquerors forced us to suffer as their victims or to serve as their enforcers and victimizers. Survival under the king required that we submit and obey on pain of death. That insight is of pressing importance today. Kings and their replacements are gradually disappearing, but our training and breeding are still with us. We still blindly follow authoritarian demagogues. And new demagogues are appearing.

It is only in the past half-millennium that we have begun a dialogue that allows us to question our dysfunctions under the king. One of those inherited dysfunctions is a broad inhumanity. Until recently, there was little concern for the suffering of anyone outside of the nobles and one's own small circle of family and friends. Street children dying of hunger and exposure, citizens in distant lands slaughtered for the king's ambition, petty criminals and independent thinkers undergoing torture and dismemberment—these were of no concern. Justice was whatever the king and the nobles dictated justice to be. It was unheard of that commoners were considered important. They could be dispensed with, quickly or slowly, whenever it suited the monarch's ambitions or his personal desires.

We will return to that lack of concern repeatedly and see that, however the particulars may change, what happened in the Holocaust and in My Lai was very old. Those two events, however, changed everything. Between them, naïve civilians were roughly awakened with a sample of the realities of conquest and life throughout civilization. In that wake-up call, the romance of the hero's war tectonically crashed with the splatter-film of the butcher's war.

...

After the publication of *On the Origin of Species*, Charles Darwin knew he had a serious problem. He had laid out a theory of how living things might change over time through competition for limited resources, neatly summed up in Herbert Spencer's phrase, "survival of the fittest." That concept, however, was at risk of being toppled by a feather. Specifically, a peacock's feather: in many species, males grow ornaments and weapons, fight, and behave in ways that *decrease* their survival. That should not happen.

But Darwin also understood that organic competition was more than survival, it was equally reproduction. If an organism dies too early, it does not reproduce; and if an organism survives but does not reproduce, it has still failed. To address this problem, Darwin published his secondary theory of 'sexual selection.'[4] Darwin proposed a Victorian concept, that although the males' costly traits and behaviors diminished their survival, those burdens also allowed males to exploit females, copulate with more of them, and leave more offspring. Since the 1960s, the field of sexual selection has exploded with a proliferation of theories and explanations.

In the 1990s, I published what seemed a simple insight into the problem. If natural selection is competition for limited resources, when males die, that leaves more food and other resources for females and their young. I suggested that by reversing Darwin's Victorian and unfortunately sexist approach, if we consider that females are as ruthless as males, there was another possibility. Perhaps females are sabotaging males as a way of eliminating competition, thereby providing more resources for their offspring.[5]

The validity of that idea is secondary. The fascinating aspect has been the reaction of colleagues. Outside of those working in sexual selection and allied fields, scholars generally respond with some variation of, "That has to be true." If it is true, however, it challenges research and theory in sexual selection. On the other hand, however, if it is not true, it threatens the central concept of competition for limited resources, which means it challenges natural selection.

So it presents a double bind for scholars within the field of sexual selection. Their reactions, including those from some of the most distinguished modern evolutionary biologists, have been surprising: they will not discuss it. Many of them have told me I am mistaken but will not tell me where the mistake lies. When I attempt to elicit an explanation, most of them discontinue the conversation.

The few who do continue the discussion, however, present an interesting pattern. They do not explore the hypothesis but suggest that I look at research which supports the theories to which they subscribe. It slowly occurred to

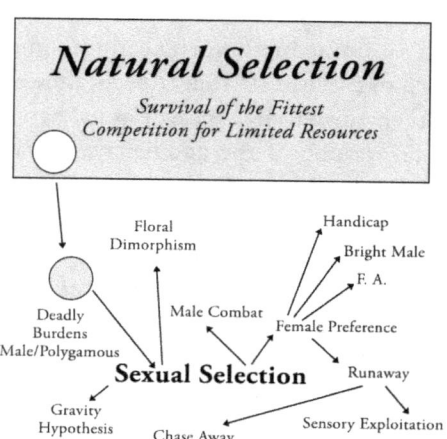

me that these two responses are what some religious fundamentalists also do when challenged—they either ignore the problem, or they sidestep the question by quoting their preferred scripture.

As I thought about these phenomena more, I became increasingly intrigued. Why would a professionally trained scholar reject alternate explanations without a fair consideration? In pursuing the problem I eventually abandoned several unpublished papers and began reading and reflecting on the problem of human intellectual recalcitrance.

Along the way, I came across the writings of Thomas Kuhn and Bernard Barber, who independently detailed how prominent scientists frequently reject new analyses or experimental data when it challenges their traditions or their own research.* My interest further grew with the rise of a particularly disturbing political intolerance, one that denies logic, facts, and even clear evidence, in favor of what partisans prefer to believe.†

While I was pursuing my reading, I heard the modern historian Eugen Weber give a talk on how honor had changed between the ancient and modern worlds. We will return to that talk in Chapter IV, but I realized that the concept of honor could not have changed. There must have been two expressions of honor throughout history, and that those different concepts broke down among social classes. As I continued to read and reflect, it struck me that there might be connections among the hypocrisies of fundamentalists, scientists, political partisans, and the historical social classes.

It seems that a resistance to logic is a common human foible. At some time or another, all of us, from the major scholar down to the small child, fall prey to authority, self-service, or both. My central question for this book became: Why do we have a great capacity for logic within certain contexts but refuse to apply that capacity in other contexts? This book is the result of a couple of decades of reading, thinking, and writing about these patterns.

---

* Kuhn's book is slender, but a difficult read. Barber's article, however, is brief, quite easy to read, and can generally be found as a .pdf file on the Internet. (The web locations for the paper have proven inconstant. An exact Internet search for the title will generally return locations where the paper is currently available.) Kuhn, however, considers the more extensive patterns of scientific resistance, and he also provides prescriptions for addressing the problem. Thomas Kuhn, *The Structure of Scientific Revolutions* (University of Chicago Press, 1962); Bernard Barber, "Resistance by Scientists to Scientific Discovery," *Science* 134, no. 3479 (September 1, 1961): 596-602.

† That accelerating phenomenon convinced me to shorten my reading and research by several years and to push my publication date up in time for the 2018 U.S. election cycle. Hence the wistful epigraphs in the front matter.

⋯

As I worked on this book, a question frequently nagged me: Why me? I'm an evolutionary biologist and a physician. This book focuses on the grand scope of human civilization, and it seemed that it would have been more appropriate that a historian, political scientist, or even philosopher write this book.

A few thoughts have occurred to me. First, emergency medicine requires a certain dark paranoia. I do not have the safety buffer of patient rechecks and I cannot pursue the lengthy, thorough workup that the primary care physician can. I can't miss anything big, and I typically have only one bite at the apple. So for any patient who has worrisome symptoms or major risk factors, I am constantly fretting, "What is the worst thing that could be happening here? What do I need to consider?" Brooding over the worst of life is key to this book. A practiced negativity, even a professional cynicism, from years in the ER helped with these insights.

Second, the evolutionary biologist deals with the idea of constant, enormous death, and from it, the implication of great horror. We will explore this in our consideration of the 'lovely deathscape' in Chapter IV; only a minority, sometimes a tiny minority, of living things survive to maturity. Historically, and even today in many parts of the world, this has also been true for humanity. As we will see, the great bulk of people through civilization died early deaths, which means that in previous times the annual death tolls must have been staggering. I began wondering about what happened to all of the people who died and about what might be missing from the historical record.

Third, and following from that question, in Chapter II we will meet a woman who as a history graduate student produced important investigative research; and she gave me another insight into why a scientist might write this book. The emphasis in historical research is on primary resource materials. History is a difficult field in which too often the historian tries to understand the past by working with only scraps and bits of information. To gain what accuracy is possible, the historian seeks the greatest fidelity in the research materials she has and tries not to stray too far into conjecture. So it is important in historical research to stay as close as possible to first-person accounts. For this reason, much of historical research focuses on positive data.

The aforementioned graduate student, however, found herself surrounded by negative data. She grew concerned about what was missing, at what should have been there but was not, and that proved key. She nevertheless confirmed her suspicions with positive information gained from interviewing survivors and other witnesses.

Prologue

As a scientist and a physician, I constantly focus on negative data. In the sciences, we work with universal concepts and use logical extensions of our laws to probe areas we cannot directly investigate. For instance, in evolutionary biology, we might know that a certain plant existed in one period and a second, related plant appeared at a later time. Using the constantly repeating patterns of biology, we project reasonable assumptions into the negative gaps. Those will be accepted by our colleagues until new theory or new data give us cause to reconsider.

In medicine we do the same. We often look for what is missing. It might be a missing symptom that is important to the diagnosis, or it might be a test that should be different in a suspected disease. But we also work from negative information when something is missing in the patient's story, *i.e.*, in the patient's 'history.' It is not unusual for me to be talking to a patient and to get the feeling that something isn't quite right, something is missing, either in the patient's presentation, her story, or in my analysis. Emergency physicians, perhaps, are more attuned to negative data than other clinicians. As noted, in the ER there is constant pressure to work fast without missing anything critical. With that, patients often do not trust you as they would their own doctor, and so they may withhold information. Negative information is a constant consideration, and we have to extend known patterns into unknown areas. At the same time, the patterns we work from include shocking and heinous things: carnage, abuse, neglect, exploitation. We have to include the entire range of human possibility in our considerations, which means we constantly consider things that most people avoid thinking about or are even unaware is a possibility.

Much of this book is based on negative data, and I became convinced that much of what we are missing is shocking and heinous. Historically, we know little of the horror in most wars—or as we shall see, of the horrors in peacetime—but we know that there is no way that war could be anything but horrific. In what histories exist, however, the patterns are consistent and predictable. And the violence I see in the emergency department are small pixels that imply much about the enormous tableaux of conquest and war.

Which brings us back to the bizarre aspects in human illogic. We have largely missed what was right in front of us, what even brief consideration would suggest must be true. In Chapter II we will consider the misrepresentation, and even whitewashing, that is common in the contemporary records, and along the way we will briefly note scholars who argue against the apparent, the inescapable, and even the documented when it does not fit their purposes or their ideology. In subsequent chapters we will then show that we are all like the scientists: at times, we all reject the most obvious evidence and logic in favor of some preferred authority.

Why does this illogic exist? Where did it come from? The explanations I will offer are, again, products of taking what little we do know, adding to it logical insights that seem inescapable, and using those to penetrate the enormous parts of human history that are unknown. By projecting recurrent historical patterns into the vast negative gaps of recorded civilization, we will better understand suffering and misery today around the globe.

...

Probably all of us at one time have been enthralled with someone only to look back later and wince or even shudder at the object of our attentions. He or she was not at all the admirable person we had imagined and in fact was perhaps cold, vain, manipulative, or even sadistic. If we were lucky enough to escape without major injury, we may give a tilt of the head and sigh in relief. We are baffled that we were so caught up in our projections about who we thought we were seeing, blinded by their confidence, beauty, fame, talent, or success, that we missed large flaws right in front of us.

By the end of this book, we shall see that virtually all of us have been taught, and have typically accepted, this same distorted view of the conquerors and kings of history. Most of us will be shocked with both our blindness and with the obvious flaws that become apparent only with our awakening. How could we have been so completely wrong about people we admired so thoroughly?

Not everyone will awaken, however. Ironically, as noted in the preceding, this will include many of the people who have studied these historical characters most intensively. They will object to the thesis here, perhaps angrily and adamantly. Because they are the authorities on these people, their objections will have the weight of example and experience.

This may create confusion for many readers: on the one hand there are examples and cogent arguments; on the other are respected authorities who argue against what seems logical or even inescapable. That is a key point of this book. This is the confusion of civilization, and it is imperative that we escape it. I recommend that when trying to resolve the tension, return to the central five points we noted. It does not seem that they can be refuted.

Which leads to another point. We certainly must take care to listen to people who have intensively studied their topics. But we should never completely defer to anyone. At some point we have to rely on our own logic and intelligence to analyze the world around us, which requires that we be skeptical of authority.

As we shall see, failing to exercise our own autonomy and failing to question authority is what got us into this mess in the first place.

Chapter I:
Kings

So look again, without the respect owed to a classic, and you will discover that The Iliad, *Chapter I, presents two gang-leading thugs, Achilles and Agamemnon, facing each other down, trading threats and insults over loot and women; and the whole poem turns about plunder and pride and the sport of killing, the struggle for preeminence and face.*

– Eugen Weber[1]

Legend: A lie that has attained the dignity of age.

– H. L. Mencken

Popular tradition has it that in 1929, Al Capone hosted his top lieutenants at a posh supper, and in what appeared to be a pep talk, he considered the game of baseball. He even pulled out a baseball bat to make his point. And then he really made his point: he beat three of his henchmen to death with the bat.

This story resembles a historical anecdote regarding Clovis I of France, the king who unified the Franks and the key figure for converting the nation to Christianity. In the looting after the Battle of Soissons in 468 CE, one of Clovis's men took a precious vase from the church. Remigius, the bishop who baptized Clovis—St. Rémy, as he is known today—sent word to Clovis that if only one thing could be restored from the looting, he would ask for the vase to be returned. Clovis went to the soldier who had stolen it, and as king, claimed the vase for himself as his share of the booty. The soldier simply smashed the precious vase. Clovis said nothing.

Some months later during an inspection, when Clovis happened across the same soldier, he snatched the man's ax from his hand, declared it filthy, and threw it to the ground. As the soldier stooped to pick it up, Clovis bashed in his head, declaring, "As you did to the vase of Soissons, so I do to you."

Another of the crimes attributed to Capone was the St. Valentine's Day Massacre in the same year as the baseball dinner. Turf struggles between Al Capone and the Northside Irish Gang had become increasingly fractious. On the night of St. Valentine's Day, men in police uniform showed up at a warehouse where seven members of the Northsiders were staked out. The seven were lined up against a wall and executed with submachine guns.

This bears resemblance to another historical event, the St. Bartholomew's Day Massacre of 1572. That massacre erupted during the French Wars of Religion, one of many struggles where individual conscience, and even the soul, were claimed as the king's empire. Catherine de' Medici invited Protestant Huguenot leaders to the marriage of Catherine's niece and the Huguenot King Henry III of Navarre. Catherine and her son Charles IX demonstrated their hospitality by assassinating the Huguenot leaders. That attack rapidly spread into a killing spree among the Parisians, who by some estimates slaughtered as many as one hundred thousand Huguenots.

These are only brief anecdotes, but they suggest that the king and the gangster worked in similar ways. Their power derived from deceit, cunning, and lethal force.

Because in truth, kings are highly successful gangsters. Some may object that kings cannot be compared to gangsters, and there is validity to this complaint—as we will see, gangsters are often less brutal than kings, in both scope and methods. Consider, for instance, that there is no evidence that Capone ever clubbed his henchmen to death, nor is there proof that he was involved in the St. Valentine's Day Massacre. The brutalities of Clovis and Catherine, however, are points of historical record.*

• • •

We inherit traditions of the king as we read about him in our legends and fairy tales, in the likenesses of King Arthur and King Aragorn: virtuous, brave, kind, generous, honest, wise, and egalitarian. The king's children, the princes and princesses, also comprised these attributes and were charming and sumptuously sexy as well. And the knights who served the royals were valiant, dashing heroes, enforcers of fairness and justice, and protectors of the weak.

There has been no such king in history.† Rather than Arthur or Aragorn, the reality is closer to Michael Corleone or Tony Soprano, only again, much worse.[2] As we shall see, kings were ruthless gangsters with vast holdings, their

---

* To be fair, there is much debate over Catherine's role in the St. Bartholomew's Day Massacre. But it should be remembered that she was an early fan of Machiavelli's *The Prince*, and the book became the model for her womanly thugishness. If she were innocent on St. Bartholomew's Day, she was guilty on sufficient other occasions so that I have not badly maligned her here.

† This is only a mild overstatement. Any king who was not ruthless and vicious soon lost his kingdom to usurpers or to revolution. Modern ceremonial kings and queens may fit the fairy tales, but they aren't really monarchs; *vide infra*.

blue-blooded princes and princesses were typically cruel, vain, and self-absorbed, and the knights of yore were thugs who, much like the paramilitary squads who serve third-world dictators, were feared wherever they went. We have been immersed in the king's cult of personality for so long that we struggle to separate fact from fairy tale.

We think that the kings, princes, and knights were 'heroes.' That is a double misconception. The original heroes were half human, half god, and the 'godly' portion was largely ungodly by modern standards. The foremost Western hero, Hercules, is illustrative: He killed his music tutor Linus; He killed his own family by the Greek princess Megara; And, while in his marriages, he carried on affairs with various men and women. Other gods and heroes behaved similarly.

The ancient kings, however, certainly behaved as ancient gods did: they were vain, bloodthirsty, treacherous, and hypersexual. Not surprisingly, many ancient rulers desired to be deities. Pharaoh and other ancient kings insisted that they were gods, and Roman emperors were often proclaimed as gods after death.

With the advent of Christianity, however, Western nations changed the narrative. The king was no longer a god, but chosen by God. *Dieu et mon droit* is the English justification for royal power: "God and my right."

...

Compare the gangster and the king. A racketeer assembles criminals and thugs from the lower strata of society and calls them his gang. A king assembles soldiers, many also from the lowest strata of society, and calls them his army. The criminal organization includes lower-level 'associates' and upper-level 'made' men, who are further broken down into ranks such as *soldati*, *capi*, and others. The king's army is likewise split into infantry and officers, and he further ranks them in tiers with various titles.

The gangster gains control of a territory by pushing aside other criminals and even the police. He calls it 'muscling in.' The king does the same thing with countries and nations and calls it 'conquest.' The gangster will call his territory his turf; the king will call his territory his realm.

The gangster has a central meeting place, stocked with weapons, in a location providing a good view of approaching threats that can readily be defended; it will serve as his headquarters. The king, with his larger holdings, will have numerous such 'safe houses,' similarly situated and similarly stocked, which are his castles.

The mobster collects 'protection money' to support his operations, as well as his opulent lifestyle. The king does the same but calls it 'taxes.' Neither contribution is voluntary, and both mobster and king deal ruthlessly, even lethally, with those who do not contribute their expected share.

The mobster holds a monopoly on high-profit activities such as gambling, narcotics, and prostitution. The king also holds monopolies in high-profit activities such as toll roads, harbors, mines, and with time, the selling of peerages.

Finally, the mobster does not eliminate violence and crime within his turf; rather, violence and crime become his monopoly. The king, likewise, holds a monopoly on violence and crime. The fundamental activity of both king and gangster is extortion through lethal and sub-lethal intimidation. The business of the gangster and the king, in effect, is chronic, persistent theft, subjugation, and exploitation.

•••

Before the appearance of our egalitarian priorities, 'government' simply meant the king/ruler,* his appointed nobles, and perhaps the clergy of his religion. The same is true of the mobster on his turf. He is the government; if he becomes powerful enough—witness Prohibition gangsters and modern Latin American drug lords—even the official government defers to him.

One defining characteristic of king and crime lord is the aforementioned use of lethal response. Modern democracies hold life sacred and in general reserve lethal force as a reaction to other lethal force. The king, in contrast, used lethal force casually. He deployed it not only in battle, but also in eliminating enemies and in punishing criminals, even minor criminals. The gangster also uses deadly force casually and in many of the same situations. One use for deadly force that unites king and gangster, and which modern governments constitutionally prohibit, is to kill those who criticize, disrespect, or mock the king or kingpin. This, we will see, is diagnostic of his underlying and uniting dysfunctions.

Another characteristic of the king and the gangster is the use of *sub*-lethal force. In the modern world, torture, terror, and intimidation are anathema, as shown in the reaction to the My Lai Massacre. In contrast, the king regularly used terror to maintain and expand control. That terror included torture, wholesale slaughter to avenge the offense of one or a few people, and the horrors of conquest. The principle industry of the king and the gangster are terror and murder to support an industry of profit by theft. The king and gangster declare these activities immoral and illegal for everyone else,

---

* For the purposes here, I will use the English term 'king' to refer to all rulers or sovereigns.

however. In so doing, they set up a double standard: it is within the king's right to kill, torture, and rob his subjects, but the subjects may not do these at all. The mobster insists on the same.

So what actually separates the king from the rest of humanity is not his virtue, but his evil. There is one difference between ruler and ruffian, however: the criminal works in secret. Witness Capone reportedly bludgeoning his henchmen and the St. Valentine's Day Massacre, both private executions. The king, on the other hand, often enforces his power through public spectacle as we saw with Clovis and Catherine. Consider the ancient punishment of drawing and quartering:

> The greatest and most grievous punishment used in England for such as offend against the State is drawing from the prison to the place of execution upon an hurdle or sled, where they are hanged till they be half dead, and then taken down, and quartered alive; after that, their members and bowels are cut from their bodies, and thrown into a fire, provided near hand and within their own sight, even for the same purpose.[3]

This was not always the order of torture. To be quartered was to be torn limb from limb, often by four horses running at top speed. The victim did not usually survive this, and so there are some descriptions in which disembowelment and castration preceded the quartering.[*] And we will consider other methods of torture used by various monarchs throughout history in order to maintain royal control.

'Control' is another key insight. The trend in modern democracies is to exert less control over citizens, particularly in their private lives and in their freedoms of expression, conscience, and faith. The opposite is true for the king and sometimes for the crook. Consider that the Latin word for 'control' is *imperium*. Kings ruled an *empire* where they controlled not only crime but also many public and private behaviors as well. In a key contrast with the modern democracy, both king and gangster seek to expand control over their citizens.

This, again, is accomplished through intimidation. The king and the gangster make it clear what will happen to anyone infringing on their criminal enterprises or disobeying their commands. But this should not surprise us. Even a brief reflection shows that there is no way to maintain a monopoly

---

[*] For instance, Dr. John Story was the first to be hanged from the triangular tree at Tyburn; he was hanged, disemboweled, then decapitated. A. Skirboll, *Thief-Taker Hangings: How Daniel Defoe, Jonathan Wild, and Jack Sheppard Captivated London and Created the Celebrity Criminal* (Rowman & Littlefield, 2014), xv.

Tyburn Triple Tree Drawing, hanging, and quartering; note the Tyburn Triple Tree in the background. Execution of Edmund Campion, Alexander Briant, and Ralph Sherwin. *Engraving by Giovanni Battista Cavalieri: "You must go to the place from whence you came, there to remain until ye shall be drawn through the open city of London upon hurdles to the place of execution, and there be hanged and let down alive, and your privy parts cut off, and your entrails taken out and burnt in your sight; then your heads to be cut off and your bodies divided into four parts, to be disposed of at Her Majesty's pleasure. And God have mercy on your souls."* Richard Simpson, *Edmund Campion: A Biography* (John Hodges, 1896), 436.

on power except through intimidation and terror.*

There is nothing to suggest that such vicious men would have any talent for wise, progressive governance. In fact, they typically had no talent for leadership outside of warfare. A central theme of this book is that their leadership was toxic. Their sole priority was maintaining their power, prerogative, and wealth. With few exceptions, they led their countries nowhere and often suppressed or even executed anyone who attempted progress. Their modern descendants, we will see, continue that dysfunction.

• • •

Years ago I was visiting a friend and his young son as they watched the Disney animation *The Lion King*. When the shaman Rafiki presents the lion cub Simba to the other animals, they all rejoice and bow before him, just as people do for newborn royalty today. My friend, a rather cynical professor of philosophy, muttered a snarky, "Oh goody, another predator." Which is what the king is. Just as with the lion on the savanna, the king is not elected. He does not hold power by universal acclaim, and his position is not the product of virtue, generosity, nor high-mindedness.

Like the king, the lion grabs control and holds territory by the liberal use of intimidation and terror. He freely kills any occupying his territory. The males, the 'kings of the jungle,' fight to the death for property, and in an apt pun, for pride. And if the usurper wins, he quickly murders all of the cubs.†

---

* When I was in medical school in New Orleans in the 1980s, I heard from a reliable source that the local mob held a monopoly on arcade and vending machines in the city. The men who collected the money drove around in a floor-model, four-door sedan and carried no weapons. Reportedly, they didn't even lock the car doors when they went in to collect at various businesses. At one point, a couple of hoods robbed them. The collection men stood aside and let the robbers take all they wanted. When the muggers went back to their own neighborhoods, however, their friends and families adamantly insisted that they take their money elsewhere and never come back, because they were going to end up dead. The way I heard the story, the stolen money made it back to the mob's offices even before the collection men had time to return and report it. The thieves even emptied their pockets to add to the haul, begging that they not be punished. Lethal and sub-lethal force are very effective.

† The battle of male lions is an example of sexual selection, as discussed in the prologue. Victorian Darwinian interpretation is that the victorious male somehow dominates and exploits ten or so females. This does not stand to analysis. The females represent several multiples of the weight of the males; the males could not survive a challenge from them. On the other hand, if the few males keep out other males, then there is more food and other resources for the females and their young. So the question becomes, who is exploiting whom?

This harsh reality does not conform to our legends, our fairy tales, nor obviously, our animated films. Likewise, neither did the king conform to the legends and fairy tales told about him by his subjects. Despite the injustice and inequality, and ample evidence of the king's cruelty and avarice, his subjects served, defended, and praised the king. They would have found my comments here to be highly offensive, even treasonous. This is the culture we have inherited, an ancient tradition of codependency with the mobster king.

⁂

There is a famous full-length portrait of Henry VIII of England, painted by Hans Holbein the Younger. As Eugen Weber urged us in the introductory quote for this chapter, "Look again..." Overlook the iconic nature of the painting, forget the romance and the legends, ignore the artistic mastery. Intellectually dissect what is actually there.

Consider the heavy gold jewelry and the enormous, flashy gems; note Henry's neck chain with the letter 'H' worked into it repeatedly. Then compare this to modern gang-bangers who flaunt multiple, heavy, customized gold chains as markers of wealth, success, and status. Look at the heavy finger rings, and think of mobsters who sport the same things.

Consider the jeweled short sword at his side. Think about what a sword really is; forget the popular movies where the hero swings a sword, there's a splash of blood, and the foe falls dead. A sword is the cleaver we considered in the prologue; it is not so much Errol Flynn as Freddy Krueger. So imagine that Henry sports a gilded and bejeweled meat cleaver at the ready; or to bring it into the modern, imagine he carries a gold-plated, diamond-studded pistol or Tommy gun. The sword appears as elegant jewelry, but it is a not-so-subtle warning and a threat of violence. Of course, it would be the rare sixteenth-century gentlemen who went out in public without his hanger at his side; but again, that culture of common weapon-toting reminds us of the lawless behavior of gangsters.

Notice the codpiece. Not only is it prominent, Henry's clothing is arranged to accentuate it. Compare that to the frequent groping and readjustment of genitalia by many criminals, and even athletes, in public. Then look at the padded, heavily exaggerated torso and shoulders and the tight leggings showing off the calves of which Henry was so proud; these also emphasize his virility and power. Examine the fine embroidery, the rich fabrics, and the costly furs, every detail meant to express Henry's wealth and status.* Compare them to gangsters and gangstas in expensive fur coats, clothes made in garish colors and patterns, or even compare it to a zoot suit.

Consider the whole ensemble; put aside our traditions of a romantic, dapper king. It appears to be a parody of wealth and power. It corresponds to the tacky outfits that the bumptious nouveau riche might wear in a Hollywood comedy.

Granted, we have taken Henry out of his historical context, and we could argue that the modern gangster is simply mimicking earlier monarchs. I will argue that both of them are the inheritors and perpetrators of even earlier traditions, particularly the dysfunction of taking wealth that might be invested in growth and progress, and burning it in ruinous ostentation instead. And as we shall see, we have inherited the same problems in our turn.

• • •

The Fabergé jewelry made for Tsar Nikolai II draws large crowds whenever it is displayed. Perhaps the most celebrated piece among them is the Coronation Egg, which encloses a small, bejeweled coronation carriage. It is important to remember that this is not a cake decoration; it is the miniature of a real coronation carriage in which the Tsar rode to officially assume the throne.

It is similar to the coronation carriage of Elizabeth II of England, which she inherited from earlier kings. Both carriages look as if they came from a midway calliope or a Mardi Gras parade; they do not look like transportation for someone who is serious about governance. What reasonable person would buy such things, much less ride in them with a straight face?†

Translate both carriages to the present day. Imagine that we see someone riding in a top-end limousine, trimmed with gold, elaborate *Rococo* flourishes, and other ostentatious decorations. I think most of us would immediately assume that the passenger is either a gangster, or a dictator or plutocrat from some third world country.

---

* In preparing this manuscript for publication, I re-examined the portrait more carefully. It will probably not show up in the reproduction here, but the belt holding Henry's sword is a cloth band with frayed edges, which appears to be simply torn rather than hemmed or embroidered. It would be interesting to learn more about that aspect as it seems unlikely that the smallest detail was left unconsidered.

† To get an idea of how our ideas are changing from the monarchies of past, compare both of these to the wedding carriage of Charles and Diana, a much simpler and more tasteful affair. The royal couple are still traveling in an expensive and impractical carriage, of course, but in this situation we have more of the feel of a celebration, something closer to a dress-up ball than tasteless ostentation. It is also interesting to note that the Gold State Coach in which Elizabeth II rode is an uncomfortable ride. Hannah Furness, "'Not very comfortable': Queen Remembers Her 'Horrible' Coronation Coach Journey," Telegraph.co.UK: January 7, 2018.

Fabergé Coronation Carriage

Elizabeth's Coronation Carriage, The Gold State Coach, built for the English Crown in the 18th century, carried Queen Elizabeth II to her coronation.

Charles and Diana's wedding carriage

Next, consider the coronation portrait of Elizabeth II. The crown on the table to her right comprises over two pounds of gold and priceless jewels. It is so heavy that when she is required to appear with it for occasions of state, she wears it privately for several days prior just to master the feat of balancing it on her head without breaking her neck. Then look at the other items that accompanied Elizabeth at her coronation: the warrior's mace, the king's orb, and the ermine-trimmed cape the size of an area rug. All of it is over the top. At some level, even Elizabeth is aware of their impracticality and ostentation—she is never seen with anything remotely like them except when she absolutely must.

If we translate her regalia into modern fashions, if we imagine someone wearing garish clothes and displaying cumbersome accessories made of only the most expensive materials, then I think we would make the same assumption that we did for the outrageous automobile. We would conclude we were looking at some criminal or dictator, petty or pasha.

No head of an advanced nation would ever appear in such things outside of major ceremonial occasions. They would add not gravity to his appearance, but silliness. Consider, however, for much of history (and even today) these sorts of tasteless, pretentious, and even tacky costumes were not only acceptable, they were the pinnacle of fashion. Again, earlier monarchs were more like gangsters than modern heads of state.

• • •

Modern royalty, of course, differ greatly from these characterizations: they project culture, graciousness, and elegance. But then, today they hold largely ceremonial positions. They have none of the historical power that their titles suggest.

Many of the men who have replaced the historical kings are vicious despots in developing countries, embarrassments in the modern world. Just as was true for ancient kings, modern dictators hold power by brutal force, ruthlessly crushing any opposition and extracting great wealth from their countries and subjects. If we wish to understand ancient kings, monarchs such as Elizabeth II of England, Akihito of Japan, or even Pope Francis are not to whom we should look. We must study their predecessors and compare them to modern monsters.

As we will see, however, not all of the erstwhile royal replacements live in the third world. Some of them live in the advanced countries: authoritarian kleptoplutocrats still scheme to acquire power, foster inequality, and undermine the modern democracy. They struggle to regress their governments toward third world dictatorships and to take us back into feudal economies. Although such men typically dress in bespoke suits and travel in tasteful jets and limousines, their apartments and other possessions often reflect the garish tastelessness of the dictator and the gangster.

Of course, we do not think of modern dictators as kings, and we do not give them the title. We also do not compare the titans of capitalism to thugs; we do not consider them to be gangsters.

But we should. It is only because of our fairy tales that we do not.

Chapter II:
Conquerors

> *Never think that war is not a crime.*[1]
> –Ernest Hemingway

> *War, the horror of mothers.*
> –Horace

Adolf Hitler is considered one of the greatest villains in human history. His offenses are notorious: the tortured deaths of 4–6 million Jewish civilians,[2] 2–6 million Polish civilians, 2–4 million Soviet prisoners of war,[3] as well as countless Roma, homosexuals, handicapped, critics and dissenters, and many others.* Numbers alone, however, sanitize the gruesome realities of starvation and forced labor in the concentration camps, the summary executions and campaigns of terror against civilians, the mass executions in the gas chambers and the ovens, and the horrific medical torture on prisoners, including young children. Hitler also caused many other deaths on and off the battlefield, many of them German but the bulk of them Soviet. In fact, as the axle of the Axis, we could arguably attribute at least partial responsibility to Hitler for all of the fifty to eighty-five million WWII deaths, about 3 percent of the 1940 world.

Hitler fancied that he was fashioned after the great conquerors of history: Alexander of Macedon, Julius Caesar, and Napoléon Bonaparte. Those beliefs add insult to injury. Hitler was a monster. The other three are hailed as great men.

The real problem, as we shall see, lies in our concepts of greatness.

Napoléon

Napoléon disseminated the revolutionary ideas of the Enlightenment across Europe, including popular sovereignty and representative government,

---

* I owe a profound debt of gratitude to Matthew White for his book and the companion website, *Necrometrics.com*. Although there are some errors and omissions in both, these are the only resources I found that lay out, with references, a brief, broad overview of the body counts from many of the worst wars and persecutions from selected periods in history. Both are highly recommended as a starting point for anyone interested in holocaust/genocide/massacre studies. Matthew White, *The Great Big Book of Horrible Things: The Definitive Chronicle of History's 100 Worst Atrocities* (W.W. Norton, 2012).

freedom of religion, a uniform legal code, economic and educational reforms, and meritocratic appointments and promotions within his army and his administration. There were also scientific advances and an elevation of the scholar's status: Napoléon arrived in Egypt with a second army of scientists and historians. It is not surprising that innovation under his Empire produced far-reaching technical advances such as the modern ambulance,[4] widespread inoculations, food canning, and others.

Napoléon was also a remorseless butcher.*

Consider the 1799 siege of Jaffa, near present-day Tel Aviv. Napoléon sent in negotiators. The city protectors summarily executed them and displayed their heads on the ramparts. When the French broke through the walls, the troops began complete annihilation. A French doctor described the carnage:

> The soldiers cut the throats of men and women, the old and the young, Christians and Turks... father and son one on top of the other (on the same pile of bodies), a daughter being raped on the cadaver of her mother, the smoke from the burnt clothes of the dead, the smell of blood, the groans of the wounded, the shouts of the victors who were quarreling about the loot taken from a dying victim.[5]

After the sack of the town, women whom the troops found attractive were captured as sex slaves, and the soldiers bartered them for loot and wagered them in card games; apparently these included pre-pubertal girls.[6] Unfortunately, the soldiers began quarreling over their captives. To solve the problem, Napoléon ordered the girls and women rounded up, taken back to town, and executed.[7]

After the sack Napoléon ordered any surviving citizens to be executed, and over the next few days, two to three thousand children, women, and men were marched to the beach and slaughtered. To conserve bullets, on the second day the officers ordered the soldiers to mount bayonets and execute the civilians manually. The same doctor describes the aftermath, "Among the victims, we found many children who, in the act of death, had clung to their fathers."

---

* This chapter took over two years of research and writing. This segment on Napoléon, however, was relatively quick because of Philip Dwyer's outstanding scholarship. Dwyer generously corresponded with me, made suggestions, and offered corrections. Much more helpful than those, however, was his excellent paper on the atrocities of Napoléon. It is a rare joy in research to find a single, brief resource that carefully lays out almost all of the arguments and meticulous documentation that a scholar needs to make a point. Readers are encouraged to read the full paper, P.G. Dwyer, "'It Still Makes Me Shudder': Memories of Massacres and Atrocities during the Revolutionary and Napoleonic Wars," *War in History* 16, no. 4 (2009): 381. Available online at *http://wih.sagepub.com/content/16/4/381.full.pdf*.

Unlike the sack of the city, however, these executions were orderly. One witness reports, "They did not cry, they did not shout, they were resigned."[8]

I begin this examination of Hitler's models with Napoléon rather than Alexander or Caesar in order to present this graphic description of conquest at Jaffa.

The surprise is that we are surprised. Many laymen, and at least some professionals, uncritically accept a romantic concept of war, that it is a face-off between our dashing and courageous men, who nobly give their lives to protect us from their evil and cowardly men. They also embrace the misconception that combat is largely limited to rural settings where disciplined men stoically and heroically fight to the death. These are certainly what our legends, novels, art, and movies typically portray.* Even among historians, the view is occasionally encountered that Napoléon's battles—and war in general—were relatively civil affairs, some even claiming that in the Napoléonic wars there is "little evidence that soldiers attacked civilians."[9]

Again, our popular traditions suggest that military combat is little more than armies vying to obtain new territories, something like an enormous version of the board game *Risk*; it is just a real estate transaction with weapons. That approach does not stand to analysis. The goal of conquest is fabulous wealth, and there is little profit to be had from a defeated army. A defending army, after all, is not defending itself; it is defending a nation, it is defending civilians. So the idea that civilians are simply unfortunate collateral damage makes no sense. Citizens, their wealth, and their future value are the sole objective of invasion.

Looting is the quickest source of wealth; it seems probable that in the earliest stirrings of civilization, invaders were raiders, much as the Vikings were millennia later. With the growth of civilization and the expansion of safe trade routes, slave trading became an additional source of wealth. The slowest but the greatest and most sustainable source of wealth is permanent government, which derives riches from subjugation and taxation. This last is really a 'fractional slavery': king and country own part of your life.† This was

---

* The pervasiveness of our romantic myths is critical to young men boldly volunteering their lives in war. Mark Twain blamed the U.S. Civil War on Sir Walter Scott's heroic portrayals of warfare. Mark Twain, *Life on the Mississippi* (Osgood & Co, 1883). For more on this topic see: Scott Horton, "How Walter Scott Started the American Civil War," *Harper's Magazine*, July 29, 2007.

† Serfdom is a step above slavery. Indentured servitude is a step above that; it is a temporary form of serfdom. Even in the advanced countries, indentured servitude still exists—ironically, in the military. Unlike all other employment contracts that are backed by civil law, every service member from recruit to flag office is under a contract for a period of years with noncompetitive pay, but also with modest housing, reasonable subsistence, healthcare, entertainment, and other social provisions. In contrast to other employment contracts, however, the military contract is backed by criminal punishment.

a significant innovation that became the pattern for modern government. Even in the advanced countries, we remain time-shared slaves. Our freedom primarily consists of the right to choose how we serve our bondage and of democratic feedback that allows us to negotiate the terms of that bondage.

It is interesting that the transition from looting, to slaving, to taxing, is a parallel of agricultural development: hunting, herding, farming. I will argue the two are basically the same process, that the conqueror domesticated humanity. Regardless of the stage of domestication, however, when the conqueror invades he robs civilians of their wealth, their freedom, and their lives. He may claim any number of reasons for his conquest, including protection, ideological conversion, liberation, trade preservation, or others. It does not matter. Those arguments are rationalizations, or at best secondary concerns, for a simple reason: without profit, conquest is impossible. Without obscene levels of profit, it is unattractive.

In former periods and cultures, no justification was given for conquest; the conqueror explained to no one. The emergence of humanism and egalitarian considerations, however, put modern culture at odds with older historical traditions, which insist that conquest is a glorious and lofty goal, and praise conquerors as great and admirable men. The resulting dissonance created the need for a peculiar historical hypocrisy: we have rationalized conquest by ignoring the obvious motivation. For instance, the annihilation at Jaffa was 'justified' because the defending Turks executed Napoléon's emissaries. The rationale for slaughtering an entire city is that it was a reasonable response for a handful of executions, decided upon by only one or a few city leaders.

In the same way, we often excuse the invader's larger brutality as nothing more than pragmatism: viciousness discourages future resistance. That strategy is effective, but that rationalization suggests that the horror is warranted, justified.* It ignores the fundamental consideration: it was the conqueror who took up sword, invaded foreign lands, and pursued slaughter and subjugation for nothing beyond greed, power, and fame. The conqueror is a thug. Rationalizing his crimes is a variation on blaming the rape victim. If she fights back, the rapist claims he is perfectly justified in torturing and murdering her. It is a variation of the exploiter's defense: "Now see what you've made me do?!"

The preceding presents a central problem: Why do we focus on the conqueror's achievements while justifying his atrocities or even denying them altogether?

---

* W.T. Sherman's comment is illustrative: "War is the remedy that our enemies have chosen, and I say let us give them all they want."

Graphic as the descriptions of Jaffa are, they are only a quick sketch of war. To understand conquest, we must multiply these horrors for each assault; multiply that carnage again for each campaign; then multiply it yet again for each war. We must then take that result and factor it worldwide, perennially, over ten thousand years of civilization.

Consider that Jaffa was only one of the many cities, towns, and villages that Napoléon ravaged and obliterated. There is no reason to believe that there was anything unusual in the carnage of Jaffa. In the limited area of Calabria, Italy, the French army destroyed over twenty-five cities and villages. One of them was Lauria, a town of nine thousand people. It was set on fire, and as the children, women, and men came screaming from the conflagration, they were shot or bayoneted.[10]

Particularly brutal was the Peninsular War against Spain and Portugal. In Spain, Maurice de Tascher, a relative of Empress Joséphine, described the 1808 assault on Córdoba:

> The Cathedral and the sacred lives within it were not spared, which made the Spanish look upon us with horror, saying out loud that they would prefer we violated their women than their churches. We did both. The convents had to suffer all that debauchery has invented, and the outrages of the soldier given up to himself.[11]

Portugal was particularly hard-hit. There is a chilling comment from one of Napoléon's generals, François de Kellerman, who announced, "Beja revolted. Beja no longer exists."[12] Around the Lines of Torres Vedras, an estimated fifty thousand civilians died from exposure, starvation, and disease while trapped by the British and French armies.[13] By the time Napoléon ended the Peninsular War, the population of Portugal had dropped by five hundred thousand or more, roughly 15 percent of the country's pre-war population.[14]

Napoléon could be equally callous and ruthless toward his own men as he was toward his victims. As all conquerors do, he sent vast numbers of young men to die in battle for his wealth and fame. And as many conquerors have also done, in defeat he abandoned his men—and the camp followers comprising many of those soldiers' families—to torture, exposure, starvation, and death while he safely escaped. Those that Napoléon left behind in Russia suffered horribly in the mud and snow of winter. They were trapped without supply lines, with little ammunition, and with almost no horses. Along the withdrawal route, fleeing soldiers and sutlers ignored the constant pleas for food, clothes, medical attention, and transportation from the sick and injured who had fallen out, or who were thrown out, from earlier convoys. Many of those abandoned were eventually captured by Cossack and other troops, who subjected them to grisly tortures.[15]

These are a sampling of the atrocities under Napoléon's conquests. As one sergeant reported, "If I were to list all the villages that we pillaged and burnt, I would never finish."[16]

Overall, the Napoleonic Wars are estimated to have claimed the lives of perhaps 2.5–3.5 million combatants and from 759,000 to 3,000,000 civilians. These numbers seem an underestimation, however. Before the twentieth century, civilian deaths were generally underreported because they weren't considered important.* In addition, as we will see, in most conquests the civilian/combatant death ratio is much higher. The underreporting of the horror of conquest is another point of this chapter.†

Ironically, one of the chief victims of the French Emperor was France: the loss of so many young Frenchmen left the country reeling for decades.[17]

Alexander The Great

Alexander was the first great conqueror of Western civilization. He assumed the throne of Macedon at the callow age of twenty and in a brief twelve years conquered vast lands, including Egypt and Persia, the superpowers that dominated Western antiquity. As he did so, Alexander founded numerous cities and libraries throughout his captured kingdoms. Perhaps the most important of these was the Egyptian city of Alexandria, where his successors built the greatest intellectual repository of the ancient Western world, the Library of Alexandria. He disseminated Athenian and Greek culture throughout his lands, where they commingled with the learning of the Near East, producing 'Hellenistic' traditions. After the fall of Rome, these eastern records were preserved by Islamic scholars and in a few surviving Western monasteries. When the classical texts re-emerged in the late medieval period, they gave us the foundations for much of the modern world.

Nevertheless, Alexander was a sadistic cutthroat.

---

* With the possible exception of the classic Romans, who glorified death and slaughter. Below I report Caesar's own numbers, but hundreds of thousands of people slaughtered in a day or two, using swords and lances, raise doubts.

† As we shall see, in many wars, perhaps in most wars, non-combatants bear the brunt of the casualties. E. Ellis, *The Napoléonic Empire* (Palgrave Macmillan, 2003).

One of his earliest challenges as king was to deal with an uprising in nearby Thebes. His counselors urged negotiation, but he instead chose to respond ruthlessly:

> So it was that many terrible things befell the city. Greeks were mercilessly slain by Greeks, relatives were butchered by their own relatives, and even a common dialect induced no pity. In the end, when night finally intervened, the houses had been plundered and children and women and aged persons who had fled into the temples were torn from sanctuary and subjected to outrage without limit.
>
> Over six thousand Thebans perished, more than thirty thousand were captured, and the amount of property plundered was unbelievable.[18]

After subjugating the Greek peninsula, Alexander set out to conquer the rest of the known world. Two years into his career, after breaking the siege of Tyre, Alexander's forces slayed a reported six thousand fighting men in the city, crucified another two thousand, and sold into slavery thirty thousand survivors, including children and women.[19] Or at least most of the children: from contemporary records, we assume that the babies and toddlers were abandoned to die of thirst, hunger, exposure, or as food for wild animals.*

One of Alexander's greatest victories was at Persepolis, in which he avenged Darius's and Xerxes's genocidal attempts on Greece.[20] Alexander unleashed his troops to pillage the city and ordered the inhabitants slain,[21] perhaps over a million people.† Unlike his treatment of his fellow Thebans, however, he

---

* The typical fate of small children is suggested by Xenophon, *Agesilaus*, 1.21 "[Agesilaus] would often warn his men not to punish their prisoners as criminals, but to guard them as human beings; and often when shifting camp, if he noticed little children, the property of merchants, left behind—many merchants offered children for sale because they thought they would not be able to carry and feed them [The dealers often failed to find a buyer and consequently abandoned these captured children.]—he looked after them too, and had them conveyed to some place of refuge." The passage suggests that Agesilaus's actions were not the usual result for abandoned children.

† Plutarch, XXXVII. I could find no estimate of the population of ancient Persepolis, but the Fortification Tablets say that in 467 BCE, no fewer than 1,348 people were employed in the treasury alone. Persepolis was also celebrated as "the richest city on earth." By way of comparison, Athens/Attica at the time is estimated at three to four hundred thousand and contemporary Carthage was perhaps seven hundred thousand. Tertius Chandler, *Four Thousand Years of Urban Growth: An Historical Census* (St. David's University Press, 1987). It seems certain that Persepolis would be larger than these two; the Achaemenid Empire contained seventeen to thirty-five million people and stretched from western India, to the Black Sea, and into northern Egypt. Ian Morris and Walter Scheidel, *The Dynamics of Ancient Empires: State Power from Assyria to Byzantium* (Oxford University Press, 2009). So an estimate of one million for the capital city seems reasonable and perhaps even conservative.

Chehel Minar

granted amnesty to Persians who sought sanctuary in the temples. From the slaughter, Alexander plundered treasure enough that it took a reported ten thousand carts and five thousand camels to carry it away. He and his men then burned the palace and razed the city, destroying untold records and artifacts of ancient history and learning, leaving to posterity only a few ruins and the *Chehel Minar*, the 'Forty Columns,' in the wilderness.

Later, after his conquest of Massaga, Alexander complimented the opposing Indian archers as outstanding warriors, and he invited them to join his army. However, as they went to camp outside the city—or according to Alexander's apologists, to desert—he ordered his men to surround and slaughter them all, seven to nine thousand soldiers with their children and wives.[22]

Estimates are, that in his brief twelve years of campaigning, Alexander slew perhaps 200,000 fighting men (40,000 of them Greeks) and an additional 250,000 civilians, just under 500,000 souls;[23] but this obviously omits the considerations of Persepolis. Although these numbers might seem small to the modern reader, at its height Alexander's dominions, the entire Kingdom of Macedon, may have comprised only four million people.[24] This would put the lethality of conquest at 12 percent, which is in line with other ratios we will see.

As noted, apologists argue that the conqueror's brutality is an expedient to successive conquests. Given the family dysfunctions from which Alexander emerged and the choices in his personal life, however, it is doubtful that his barbarism was merely objective pragmatism.

For instance, as Alexander's mother Olympias aged, his father Philip added a new wife, Cleopatra Eurydice.[25] At the wedding banquet, a quarrel erupted between Philip and Alexander. Philip drew his sword and charged his son, intent on killing him. Fortunately for Alexander, his father was so drunk he tripped and fell to the floor. Alexander's response is telling: unfazed, he merely quipped to his friends, "He aims to cross the continents, and he can't cross the floor."[26]

Alexander's mother Olympias was equally vicious. Two years after his marriage to Eurydice, Philip was assassinated by one of his own bodyguard, and Alexander became the new king; more than one historian has speculated that Alexander and his mother plotted the assassination. At one point during the Persian campaign, Alexander sent word to his mother to "take care of my enemies." She used the instruction to exact revenge on Eurydice. In varying accounts, she either stabbed Alexander's half-sister Europa as she lay at her mother's breast and then had Eurydice hanged; or she had Eurydice roasted alive on a bronze oven with her infant son, Caranus.[27] In response to his mother's viciousness, scheming, and hectoring, Alexander simply mused, "She charges a high price for nine months' rent."[28]

At one point in his campaigns, in a scene that echoed his father's inebriated attempt at filicide, Alexander murdered his close friend Cleitus the Black in a drunken rage even though Cleitus had been a loyal general and had saved Alexander's life in the Battle of Granicus. Among the enemy soldiers crucified after the Siege of Tyre, Alexander included his own doctor for failing to save the life of one of his friends.

As noted, Alexander was also a sadist. In his Asian campaigns, he was intrigued by a Persian tradition of torture and execution. King Darius described his treatment of Fravartish (Phraortes):

> ... Fravartish was seized and led to me. I cut off his nose and ears and tongue and put out one of his eyes. He was kept bound at the entrance to my palace; all the people saw him. Afterward I impaled him at Ecbatana, and the men who were his chief followers, those at Ecbatana within the fortress, I hung out [*i.e.* flayed them and displayed their skins]... [29]

Later, Darius punished one Tritantaechmes in a fashion similar to Fravartish.

When Alexander captured Artaxerxes V (Bessus), who had attempted to usurp Alexander's position as king of the Persian empire, Alexander copied the torture. He had Artaxerxes's nose and ears cut off and then had him crucified;[30] alternate accounts relate other gruesome punishments, including tying him to bent trees and tearing off his limbs one at a time.[31]

Despite Alexander's atrocities in Persepolis, he held Darius in high regard, perhaps as an equal. He had Darius's corpse adorned as a prince and sent the macabre gift to Darius's mother; he then accepted Darius's brother as one of his intimate friends.[32] This generous behavior—from Alexander's perspective, at least—toward Darius and his family contradicts his claim that revenge was his motivation for destroying Persepolis. If he sought revenge, Darius would have been loathed as his chief target. Instead, his behaviors suggest that any explanations for conquest beyond greed, power, and bloodsport were nothing more than rationalization.

Julius Caesar

Alexander conquered the known world, meaning that he conquered the more civilized realms to the east and south, where the plunder and profit were greatest.* Julius Caesar and the Romans conquered many of those lands as well. However, the Romans were willing to take the longer view, subjugating and enslaving the lands to the north and west, tribes that generally lacked well-developed writing, engineering, international trade, and sustainable administration.† These considerations help to explain why Caesar, perhaps, was a bit more restrained than Alexander and left more infrastructure in place. First, he represented Roman imperial and financial interests in addition to his personal ambitions. Second, those Roman interests were more experienced with the profits of conquest and more focused on long-term rewards.

Through these conquests, Caesar and the Romans brought the classical tradition to much of Europe, which was pivotal. Without Caesar's conquest of Gaul and other Roman conquests across Europe, the modern world would not exist.

Caesar was nevertheless a fiend. He murdered vast populations, on and off the battlefield, and enslaved equally large numbers.[33]

Consider Caesar's defeat of the Helvetii and allied tribes in 56 BCE. First, Caesar ambushed some of them as they crossed the Saone River. After most of the group had crossed, he and his troops attacked the stranded remnant and slaughtered everyone, children, women, and the small force of warriors

---

* This is a common observation, but it's an oversimplification. Before he died, Alexander sent instructions back to Greece that next he wanted to move into the western coast of north Africa.

† It is fortunate that classical scholarship spread in both directions; when Rome collapsed a few centuries after Julius, much of the former Macedonian Kingdom was subsumed under Islam, which preserved much of the Classical traditions that exist today.

attempting to protect them. A few weeks later, in a brief nine-hour battle, he and his army slew the rest. By Caesar's own account the slain comprised 258,000, of whom only 92,000 were warriors. This means his troops slashed, dismembered, impaled, or otherwise slaughtered 166,000 children, women, and elders.[34] It should be noted that in these attacks, Caesar was not merely the commanding officer at some remove; he often mounted horse and participated in the carnage.[35]

Caesar later committed genocide against the Tencteri and Usipetes clans as well. The tribes had earlier proven treacherous, and when they subsequently sued for peace, Caesar seized their ambassadors and set his troops upon their camps in a surprise attack. As the clansmen mounted a disorganized attempt to defend their families, the children, women, and elderly attempted to escape on foot. Caesar ordered his cavalry to chase those fleeing and slaughter them all. In this particular attack, by Caesar's own account, the two tribes comprised some 430,000 people. He notes no survivors nor captives.[36] Some Romans were shocked by the carnage, but the Senate simply offered a *supplicatio*, a day of thanksgiving to the gods.[37]

These attacks were part of Caesar's famed conquest of Gaul. Plutarch describes the onslaught:

> For although it was not full ten years that he waged war in Gaul, he took by storm more than eight hundred cities, subdued three hundred nations, and fought pitched battles at different times with three million men, of whom he slew one million in hand to hand fighting and took as many more prisoners.[38]

If these numbers are to be believed, Caesar killed one million people in a region that contained perhaps six to eight million before he invaded, about the same 12 percent we have noted previously.[39] Once again, however, the majority of the tortured, mutilated, murdered, and enslaved were non-combatants: babies, children, women, and the aged.[40]

The enslaved bring up a consideration about the suffering the conqueror creates, something that goes beyond the casualties. Who suffers more: those crushed, impaled, dismembered, and incinerated to death in a relatively quick manner? Or the survivors, particularly the children, who are torn from their families to suffer through a lifetime of dehumanizing pain, abuse, drudgery, and exploitation?*

---

* It is interesting that many of the machines that opened the way for the Renaissance were actually Roman inventions. The Romans did not make much use of them, however, because slave labor was so cheap.

The Old Testament

The Old Testament is the foundational document for three of the great religions: Judaism, Christianity, and Islam. Its stories are icons of Western tradition: Adam and Eve; Abraham and Isaac; David and Goliath; Moses parting the Red Sea; the Wisdom of Solomon; Noah's Ark; and many others. For over two billion people around the world, it represents God's promises to humanity.

It is unimportant whether one believes that the Old Testament accurately describes historical events; it is one of humanity's seminal documents on virtue. As such, it both reflects the mores of early Judaism, and instructed and guided concepts of morality and justice for centuries thereafter. Strict adherents even today argue that the Old Testament is a literal description of how God expects us to live.

Part of my thesis here is that we are willing to view the horror of conquest as acceptable. Old Testament fundamentalists show that horror can be declared sacred as well.* This can be seen in all large cultures. We noted the thanksgiving the Romans offered the gods when Caesar committed genocide against two Germanic tribal nations. In the next section we will see the Greeks willing to sacrifice their own children not for victory in combat, but simply for the opportunity to wage war. After that, we will see Christians justifying their own heinous crimes with religious arguments. On top of those, every army appeals to their divine beings for success, every army thanks their deities in victory, and as we will see repeatedly, every civilization invokes its gods as justification for oppression and slaughter.

Very early in the Old Testament, Cain murders his brother Abel, an ominous beginning. Soon after, Moses ordered the Levites to slay their sons and brothers (and, we assume, their daughters and sisters) as punishment for nothing more than idolatry; three thousand were killed.[41] Even long-standing personal bonds proved no impediment for Moses. He lived among the Midianites for forty years, and one of his wives was the daughter of the famed Midianite priest Jethro. Moses nevertheless sent the Israelites to attack the Midianites, where they killed all of the men in battle. When they returned with the surviving children and women, Moses reprimanded them and ordered: "Now therefore kill every male among the little ones, and kill every woman that hath known man by lying with him. But all the women children,

---

* The Old Testament was not the only religious tradition glorifying conquest. In Norse mythology, Valhalla and Fólkvangr were reserved for those who died bravely in battle.

that have not known a man by lying with him, keep alive for yourselves."⁴²
The spared pre-pubertal girls were distributed among the soldiers. The priest Eleazar was allotted thirty-two of the hapless girls as "God's share."

The New Testament 'Prince of Peace,' Jesus, was named for an Old Testament conqueror, Joshua, the hero who razed Jericho.* When the walls fell, Joshua ordered every child, woman, man, and beast within to be slain. His army later killed twelve thousand children, women, and men of Ai and impaled their king.⁴³ Joshua continued these massacres in town after town: Makeddah, Libnah, Lachish, Eglon, Hebron, Debir, Hazor, and other cities and kingdoms.⁴⁴

There is a good deal of slaughter in the Old Testament as well as sex and torture and greed and betrayal, but the great King David adds an aspect of duplicity as well. His lusting for Bathsheba and his arranged death of her husband, Uriah, pose problems for religious scholars. But consider David's long years of fighting and killing Philistines. As a youth, he began with Goliath. Then in order to marry Saul's daughter, David is ordered to kill one hundred of the Philistines and bring back their foreskins. For good measure, David gratuitously adds another hundred foreskins—and dead men—to the sum.⁴⁵

When Saul tries to have David killed, however, David does not go into hiding. Instead, he flees into the service of the hated Philistine King Achish. This is more than self-preservation: David takes with him his six hundred best warriors with their families and pledges their service to the Philistine king as well. Achish accepts David and his troops and gives him the town of Ziklag.

David repays him by raiding Achish's allies⁴⁶ and then lying to his host that he had instead raided the Israelites and their allies. To ensure that Achish does not discover the treachery, David murders all of the inhabitants in the raided settlements:

> ⁷ And the time that David dwelt in the country of the Philistines was a full year and four months.
>
> ⁸ And David and his men went up, and invaded the Geshurites, and the Gezrites, and the Amalekites: for those nations were of old the inhabitants of the land, as thou goest to Shur, even unto the land of Egypt.
>
> ⁹ And David smote the land, and left neither man nor woman alive, and took away the sheep, and the oxen, and the asses, and the camels, and the apparel, and returned, and came to Achish.
>
> ¹⁰ And Achish said, "Whither have ye made a road to day?" And David said,

---

* Both are linguistic interpretations of the Hebrew *Yĕshúʿa*.

"Against the south of Judah, and against the south of the Jerahmeelites, and against the south of the Kenites."

¹¹ And David saved neither man nor woman alive, to bring tidings to Gath, saying, "Lest they should tell on us, saying, 'So did David, and so will be his manner all the while he dwelleth in the country of the Philistines.'"⁴⁷

When the Philistines later march into battle against Israel, David begs to fight with Achish against his own country. Achish's generals object, and David is sent away. After the Philistines conquered the Israelites, however, David reverses his loyalties yet again. When a young Amelekite brings Saul's crown and armband to David and describes how Saul had ordered the young man to kill him, David has the Amelekite executed precisely for the young man's obedience to Saul.⁴⁸

David later slaughters and subdues many other tribes and kingdoms. These are generally described as defensive actions against armies that attacked Israel. Given David's previous behaviors and treacheries, it is likely that at least some of these were initiated by David as a pretext for expanding his wealth and power.

Ancient Greeks

The first intellectual triumphs of Western civilization emerged from ancient Athens. After the Greeks defeated the Persians, particularly in the Battle of Marathon, Athenian culture exploded and gave us much of the foundations for Western civilization: philosophy, ethics, democracy, geometry, mathematics, biology, literature, theatre, poetry, art, sculpture, and architecture.

Despite the heights of their culture, the Athenians were remorseless killers. Much as with the Old Testament, it is unimportant for our considerations here whether *The Iliad* and *The Odyssey* are true. They reflect and influence Greek approaches to warfare and justice. Early in *The Iliad*, Agamemnon sacrifices his daughter Iphigeneia simply to gain favorable sailing winds to Troy. Apparently, the Greek warriors were impatient about weather. After the sack of Troy, Achilles's ghost demands the same fate for the Trojan princess Polyxena, again for favorable winds.

During the Trojan War there were the usual horrors of the battle, the siege, and the eventual sack of the city. When Odysseus returns to Ithake, however, we can see the warrior's craft in detail, and this again shows that our romantic notions are wide of the mark. Before Odysseus deals with the suitors for his wife's hand, he and his son, Telemachus, take care to sadistically punish an inconsequential goatherd: "As for Melanthius, they took him through the cloister into the inner court. There they cut off his nose and his ears; they drew out his vitals and gave them to the dogs raw, and then in their fury they cut off his hands and his feet."[49] Odysseus then hanged his hapless slave girls who had submitted to sex with Penelope's suitors. Given the inferior station that Greek women held—remember, even as queen of Ithake, Penelope was unable to eject the suitors from her own home—and the even lower station that women slaves held, the girls likely had no choice in the matter.

Given myths such as these, it is unsurprising that viciousness is present in Athens from its earliest history. The first event that can be reliably dated in Athens was an attempted coup by Cylon in 632 BCE. He and his followers seized the Temple of Athena, but after a siege, Cylon escaped the Temple with his brother and deserted his followers. The Archons promised protection to those remaining so long as they left peacefully. When they complied, they were summarily executed.[50]

There is a peculiar hypocrisy to Athenian atrocities. After asserting independence by throwing off the yoke of the Spartan tyrant Hippias and after repulsing the Persians, Athens used her success to subjugate other city states and deny them the same freedoms that she prized. In the Peloponnesian War, the small island of Melos sued to be recognized as neutral. Athens declined and insisted that Melos join her coalition. The subsequent negotiations are still studied today in political science and other classes as 'The Melian Dialogue.' The best-known quotation of the deliberations is a Machiavellian ultimatum delivered by Athens:

> Instead we recommend that you should try to get what it is possible for you to get, taking into consideration what we both really do think; since you know as well as we do that, when these matters are discussed by practical people, the standard of justice depends on the equality of power to compel, and that in fact *the strong do what they have the power to do, and the weak accept what they have to accept.*[51] [Italics added.]

The Melians politely but firmly rejected the Athenians' demands. Athens attacked, and Melos eventually surrendered unconditionally. As Thucydides grimly describes it, "...[the Melians] yielded themselves to the discretion of the Athenians, who slew all the men of military age, made slaves of the women and children, and inhabited the place with a colony sent thither afterwards of five hundred men of their own."[52] As a protest to this Athenian action, Euripides wrote *The Trojan Women*. In describing the rape and slaughter the women of Troy endured, Euripides has Hecuba's youngest daughter taken from her to be sacrificed. Then her son is taken as well, and his body is returned by a sympathetic Greek. After the play premiered, Euripides was exiled from the city.

Traditional tensions also existed between Athens and nearby Aegina. The Athenians had suffered attacks from the Aeginetans and early in the Peloponnesian War Athens took pre-emptive action:

> During the summer the Athenians also expelled the Aeginetans with their wives and children from Aegina, on the ground of their having been the chief agents in bringing the war upon them. Besides, Aegina lies so near Peloponnese, that it seemed safer to send colonists of their own to hold it, and shortly afterwards the settlers were sent out. The banished Aeginetans found an asylum in Thyrea, which was given to them by Lacedaemon, not only on account of her quarrel with Athens, but also because the Aeginetans had laid her under obligations at the time of the earthquake and the revolt of the Helots. The territory of Thyrea is on the frontier of Argolis and Laconia, reaching down to the sea. Those of the Aeginetans who did not settle here were scattered over the rest of Hellas... Meanwhile the Athenians landed, and instantly advanced with all their forces and took Thyrea. The town they burnt, pillaging what was in it; the Aeginetans who were not slain in action they took with them to Athens ... the Aeginetans captured were all put to death... [53]

The description suggests that the Athenians executed the Aeginetan children and women along with the men.

When Mytilene revolted in 428 BCE, the Athenian council voted to kill all the men and enslave the women and children. The day after a trireme had been launched to carry out the sentence, the council reconsidered its decision. In a much-celebrated debate, Diodotus urged that the death sentence be overturned in an argument based not on compassion or justice, but on simple pragmatism. Diodotus carried the day, and in a famous episode, a second trireme, dispatched at full speed, overtook the first and canceled the general slaughter. Instead of annihilation, only one thousand leading citizens were executed, and the island kingdom was crippled and heavily taxed.[54] It is not clear whether Athens was too harsh or not harsh enough: the Mytileneans revolted again some years later.

At another point in the Peloponnesian War, the Athenians attacked nearby Euboea. As Thycydides sanitizes it, they "reduced the whole country." Then in a phrase that glosses over the implications, he adds of a major city in Euboea, "the citizens of Hestiaea the Athenians ejected from their homes and appropriated their territory."[55] It was a harsher sentence than the modern reader might realize: in the ancient world, there were few options for refugees, and it is unlikely that the Histiaeans departed with much more than the clothes on their backs.

In 413 BCE of the War, the city of Mycalessus was destroyed by Thracian troops under the command of the Athenian general Diitrephes. The children, women, and men were slaughtered. For good measure, the troops raided the local school and slaughtered the young students there as well.[56]

Toward the end of the Peloponnesian War, the Athenians decided to amputate the right hands of all captured soldiers.[57] Fortunately they did not get the opportunity to carry out the penalty.

The Athenians were hardly unique, and other city-states were as brutal or more so. Sparta was the perennial rival and enemy of Athens. If Athens was liberal, Sparta was conservative; if Athens was philosophy and the arts, Sparta was brutality and war. It was Sparta who threw imperfect newborns into a pit to die; who abandoned boys to survive in the wild at the age of twelve and encouraged them to raid and murder the enslaved Helots as they did so; and who forced the survivors of those trials into homosexual tutelage with a mature soldier as part of their indoctrination into the army.

Not surprisingly, Sparta was as vicious and murderous toward other nations as they were in their internal affairs. Sparta routinely started wars with neighboring states to distract her citizens from domestic conflicts. When faced with political upheavals, the Spartan leadership created some pretext for war, defeated the enemy, and came home happy. Wealth is not the only way to profit from slaughtering people.

Thebes was a frequent victim of these murderous rages, or at least it was until the Thebans chose Epaminondas as general. He lengthened the Theban spear, modified the classic phalanx, and shocked the classical world by defeating Sparta. On the long march home, one of the soldiers sniped to the wounded Spartan King Agesilaüs II, "Isn't it funny how good they've gotten with all the training we've given them?"[58]

Spartan brutality was a constant in the Peloponnesian War. When the Spartans caught anyone on the seas, military or merchant, Athenian ally or neutral, they summarily slew them.[59] At one point in the war, the Spartans asked the brutalized Helots to name who among them had helped most in war effort. Two thousand men were named and rejoiced that they were to be rewarded. The reward for their valiant service was execution.[60]

Athens vs. Sparta are historical stereotypes of democratic deliberation vs. oligarchic bigotry. Politically and socially they represent extremes of civic conduct. In warfare, however, both were brutal, and the distinctions between them blurs. This leaves us with the conclusion that regardless of the form of government or the high-mindedness of the domestic culture, conquest is always murder and theft on a national scale. Conquest permits no other possibility.

ROMANS

As we have noted, the Romans expanded the gifts of civilization into new lands. But they also took horror to a new level present in few other—if any—large peacetime cultures. The Theatre of Marcellus hosted arts and high culture in ancient Rome and held perhaps twelve thousand people. In contrast, the Colosseum, built for entertainment where men and beasts fought to the death, held eighty thousand. There are 230 currently known amphitheater ruins across the former Roman Empire, and more are regularly excavated—each of them hosted its own gladiatorial games.[61] In the other nations we consider in this chapter, citizens knew little of the horrors perpetrated by their armies. Not so the Romans; in Rome, carnage was celebrated. Ancient Rome was a culture that elevated horror to the literally spectacular.*

There are *bas reliefs* from Pompeii that show scenes from the gladiatorial games. It is chilling to see the defeated man—or woman, because women also fought to the death—holding up a questioning hand to the spectators, with the victorious fighter standing behind him/her; both await the crowd's decision whether the defeated is to be spared or executed.[62] If the crowd gives the thumbs-up, the victor quickly kills the defeated.†

Death and carnage were relatively minor considerations for the Romans. The head of a household could execute his children and slaves with impunity. Non-citizens also suffered diminished protections.

In some circumstances even the wealthiest citizens and Senators could be murdered. During Sulla's Reign of Terror, the record states that nine thousand powerful Romans were assassinated. In this account, the Senator Catiline exacted revenge on one of his enemies:

> ...[Catiline] flogged Gratidianus through the streets to the tomb of the Catulus clan. There his arms and legs were smashed with rods, his ears cut off, his tongue wrenched from his mouth and his eyes gouged out. He was then beheaded and his corpse was offered as a sacrifice to the spirit of [Catiline's] father. In a grim postscript, an officer fainted at the horror of what he was seeing

---

* At times the public could become part of the carnage. An amphitheater in Fidenae collapsed and killed anywhere from twenty thousand to fifty thousand spectators, although the number might have been as low as 4,200. Suetonius, *Tiber*, 40; Tac. Ann, IV.63; Philip Smith, *A Dictionary of Greek and Roman Antiquities*, ed. William Smith (John Murray, 1875), 82.

† Despite current usage, the thumb represented the sword. It was used as a signal to the swordsman, not a sentence for the condemned. 'Thumbs down' meant to lower the sword. 'Thumbs up'—or more accurately, a thumb thrust outward—meant to drive in the sword.

Conquerors

Plates from François Mazois showing schematics of the bas reliefs from Pompeii of scenes from gladiatorial games.

and was himself executed for disloyalty. Catiline was then said to have carried Gratidianus's severed head "still alive and breathing" (according to Cicero in one of his more fanciful flights of rhetoric*) into Rome to present to Sulla.[63]

Some scholars question the viciousness of this account. Their objections return to a major point of this book, that the realities of conquest and historical government are frequently glossed over and even denied. There are several reasons this description is reasonable. First, consider the gory entertainment the Romans witnessed on the arena. Just as modern fans celebrate a particularly brutal hit in football, rugby, or boxing, we must assume that Roman spectators would find excitement in grisly injuries such as these. Second, as a seasoned military officer, Catiline was comfortable with human dismemberment. Finally, Catiline was simply a nasty piece of work. He was suspected of murdering his first wife, who was possibly the sister of the above-described victim, Gratidianus. He was repeatedly tried but acquitted for various scandals. Once he was acquitted of adultery with Cicero's sister-in-law, a Vestal Virgin, which if true would be revealing about Cicero's brutal indifference to both social norms and human suffer-

---

* Decapitation does not produce instantaneous brain death. The face may express pain and emotion for several seconds until the loss of blood pressure causes fainting, and complete brain death may not occur for ten minutes or more. After the loss of consciousness, lower centers of the brain may remain active for several minutes. Some patients experience seizures with a loss of consciousness, and some report dreaming. Either of these may cause facial movements. So there is no reason that the face of a beheaded victim could not continue to move for some minutes.

ing: liaisons with Vestal Virgins constituted acts of treason and required that the woman be scourged and entombed alive. Finally, Catiline twice attempted to overthrow the Roman Republic and died leading an army in his second attempt.[64]* So the preceding description of Catiline's behavior is not only plausible, it is also perhaps predictable.

The assassinations under Sulla continued with abandon. A complaint finally emerged from the Senate, not of the injustice nor even of the scale, but of the protracted time frame. Sulla was urged to publish the entire list of his enemies, have them dispatched, and let people go about their business. By the time it was over, only two hundred senators remained, too few to carry on essential affairs of state.[65]

Warfare under the Romans, of course, differed little from other conquest; all conquest is horror and butchery. But again, in Rome carnage was institutionalized and triumphantly memorialized. Near the Colosseum stands the Column of Trajan. Wrapping it is a frieze of over six hundred feet, much of which glorifies the slaughter of Trajan's conquests. It is arguably the largest and most detailed celebration of bloodshed in the world. First runner-up would be the nearby Column of Marcus Aurelius, with a frieze of 523 feet. (At 224 feet, the Bayeux Tapestry, although from a different conquering culture, also deserves mention.) Rome, unlike most other cultures, glorified viciousness.

Consider Marius in the Jugurthine War of north Africa and the incident at Capsa:

> ...long before dawn, he [Marius] reached a hilly spot of ground, not more than two miles distant from Capsa, where he waited, as secretly as possible, with his whole force. But when daylight appeared, and many of the Numidians, having no apprehensions of an enemy, went forth out of the town, he suddenly ordered all the cavalry, and with them the lightest of the infantry, to hasten forward to Capsa, and secure the gates. He himself immediately followed, with the utmost ardor, restraining his men from plunder.
>
> When the inhabitants perceived that the place was surprised, their state of consternation and extreme dread, the suddenness of the calamity, and the consideration that many of their fellow-citizens were without the walls in the power of the enemy, compelled them to surrender. The town, however, was burned; the Numidians, such as were of adult age, were put to the sword; the rest were sold, and the spoil divided among the soldiers.

---

* To his credit, his army died fighting, and Catiline's body was found in the vanguard.

> This severity, in violation of the usages of war, was not adopted from avarice or cruelty in the consul, but was exercised because the place was of great advantage to Jugurtha, and difficult of access to us, while the inhabitants were a fickle and faithless race, to be influenced neither by kindness nor by terror.[66]

Even though the city surrendered without resistance, Marius nevertheless razed it and slaughtered and enslaved the citizens. Note the apology in the last sentence, suggesting that this was simply a strategic decision: because the inhabitants were unregenerate, they were useless as allies. This would appear to be more of the victimizer's rationalizations, with perhaps some racism added in. First, the Numidians were not so fickle nor faithless that they abandoned their fellow citizens trapped outside the city walls. Second, if the Capsans were in reality as perfidious as the chronicler suggests, then they would have been of no use to Jugurtha either and could have been left in peace. Finally, for all of their supposed incorrigibility, "influenced by neither kindness nor by terror," this character flaw did not decrease their profitability as slaves. With that, we will see below that commerce, and therefore civilization, is impossible without a middle class morality of accountability and personal responsibility. If there is a city to attack, then there is a large population within who are dependable and conscientious. So the Numidians could not have been fickle, nor faithless. The victimizer frequently accuses others of his own unethical motives and then uses those accusations as an excuse for pre-emptive action. Clearly Marius, like other conquerors, is simply blaming the victim here.

In the Second Punic War when Scipio Africanus broke the siege in Iliturgi, Spain, "No one thought of taking men alive, no one thought of booty, although every place was open for plunder. They slaughtered the unarmed and the armed alike, women as well as men; cruel anger went even so far as to slay infants."[67]

Local cities took note of this. Castulo immediately capitulated. Not so Astapa; they piled their most valued possessions in the middle of the town, ordered their wives and children to sit upon them, and ringed them with piles of wood. As the men fought to their deaths, their families were burned alive along with their valuables.[68]

As noted, the Romans did not reserve their savagery for foreigners. Just as we witnessed with Sulla's Reign of Terror, when occasion presented itself the Romans slaughtered one another with equal alacrity and viciousness. The suicide of Nero precipitated civil war and the Year of the Four Emperors, in which dictators rose and fell in rapid succession: Galba (assassinated), Otho (suicide), Vitellius, (executed by) Vespasian.

The same year that he executed his emperor, Vespasian took Cremona in the Battle of Bedriacum, which had been held by Vitellius's troops:

> Forty thousand armed men burst into Cremona, and with them a body of sutlers and camp-followers, yet more numerous and yet more abandoned to lust and cruelty. Neither age nor rank were any protection from indiscriminate slaughter and violation. Aged men and women past their prime, worthless as booty, were dragged about in wanton insult. Did a grown up maiden or youth of marked beauty fall in their way, they were torn in pieces by the violent hands of ravishers; and in the end the destroyers themselves were provoked into mutual slaughter. Men, as they carried off for themselves coin or temple-offerings of massive gold, were cut down by others of superior strength. Some, scorning what met the eye, searched for hidden wealth, and dug up buried treasures, applying the scourge and the torture to the owners… In an army which included such varieties of language and character, an army comprising Roman citizens, allies, and foreigners, there was every kind of lust, each man had a law of his own, and nothing was forbidden.[69]

In addition to executing his own emperor, Vespasian is famous for initiating the Roman response to the Great Jewish Revolt of 66-69 CE. Soon after, in 70 CE, his son Titus responded to the continued resistance and the chronic nuisance of the Sicarii and other Zealots by destroying Jerusalem. After Titus captured the ancient city, the Jewish historian Josephus describes the bloodshed and suffering:

> But when they went in numbers into the lanes of the city with their swords drawn, they slew those whom they overtook without and set fire to the houses whither the Jews were fled, and burnt every soul in them, and laid waste a great many of the rest … they ran every one through whom they met with, and obstructed the very lanes with their dead bodies, and made the whole city run down with blood, to such a degree indeed that the fire of many of the houses was quenched with these men's blood … And now, since his soldiers were already quite tired with killing men, and yet there appeared to be a vast multitude still remaining alive, Caesar gave orders that they should kill none but those that were in arms, and opposed them, but should take the rest alive. But, together with those whom they had orders to slay, they slew the aged and the infirm … but of the young men he chose out the tallest and most beautiful, and reserved them for the triumph; and as for the rest of the multitude that were above seventeen years old, he put them into bonds, and sent them to the Egyptian mines. Titus also sent a great number into the provinces, as a present to them, that they might be

destroyed upon their theatres, by the sword and by the wild beasts; but those that were under seventeen years of age were sold for slaves ... Now during [this process] ... there perished, for want of food, eleven thousand.[70]

Josephus reports that between the siege and the sack, Titus murdered 1.1 million children, women, and men and sold 97,000 survivors into slavery.[71]

These are a few examples, but Roman history is dizzying with such atrocities: 300–400,000 burned to death in the city of Seleucia,[72] a reported 160,000 Pontics killed in the First Mithridatic War,[73] perhaps 300,000 Pontics and 100,000 Armenians killed in the Third Mithridatic War,[74] an estimated one million dead slaves in the three Servile Wars,[75] and well over three million slaughtered on the arena for nothing more than macabre amusement.*

There is, however, one additional person who will become important for upcoming considerations. When asked about the atrocities of Roman emperors, many readers immediately think of Nero or Caligula, who were certainly vicious. It is puzzling, however, that the outrages of Caracalla are not more widely recognized. Gibbon described him as "a monster whose life disgraced human nature," and "the common enemy of mankind."[76]

After the death of Caracalla's father, the Emperor Septimus Severus, Caracalla and his brother, Geta, inherited shared empire. Disagreements erupted between the two, and Caracalla arranged a meeting with his brother and their mother. During the meeting Caracalla's troops burst in and assassinated Geta, and he died in his mother's arms. Although this gave Caracalla complete empire, it was not enough. Insensitive to both his late father's wishes and his mother's loss, he implemented a *damnatio memoriae* upon his brother: Geta's image was removed anywhere it appeared, on por-

---

* There are no records of the total number of deaths on the arena, but in addition to the gladiators who fought to the death, there were also criminals and other 'undesirables' executed there. For instance, recall the preceding passage from Josephus, that Titus sent 'a great number' of the Jerusalemites to the arena; this was not an unusual punishment for enemy captured in battle, and the Romans were frequently at war. With that, the Roman appetite was large; Trajan sent a reported ten thousand gladiators into the arena after an important victory (Dion. Cass., LXVIII, 15). Granted, not all gladiatorial battles ended in death, as the public had the option of sparing a downed fighter; but it is telling of Roman appetites that Augustus outlawed the *sine missione* games, where the rules mandated death for all defeated gladiators (Suetonius, *Augustus*, 45). Finally, as noted there were well over 230 amphitheaters across the Roman Empire, and the gladiatorial games lasted for seven hundred years. Not all of those amphitheaters were active for the entire seven hundred years, but if we conservatively assume just one death per arena, per month, for seven hundred years, that modest assumption alone yields almost two million deaths. This easily supports estimates by some scholars of 3.5 million deaths and suggests it was probably much higher.

traits, busts, and coins. He then ordered perhaps twenty thousand of Geta's friends and supporters assassinated.[77]

The Alexandrian Egyptians, somehow missing Caracalla's savagery in all of this, staged a lampoon of the emperor over his actions. Caracalla sailed to Egypt, announcing that he wished to worship the god Amun and pay tribute to Alexander's victories. Herodian relates Caracalla's real intent:

> The emperor therefore joined the Alexandrians in celebrating and merrymaking. When he observed that the city was overflowing with people who had come in from the surrounding area, he issued a public proclamation directing all the young men to assemble in a broad plain, saying that he wished to organize a phalanx in honor of Alexander similar to his Macedonian and Spartan battalions, this unit to bear the name of the hero. He ordered the youths to form in rows so that he might approach each one and determine whether his age, size of body, and state of health qualified him for military service. Believing him to be sincere, all the youths, quite reasonably hopeful because of the honor he had previously paid the city, assembled with their parents and brothers, who had come to celebrate the youths' expectations. Caracalla now approached them as they were drawn up in groups and passed among them, touching each youth and saying a word of praise to this one and that one until his entire army had surrounded them. The youths did not notice or suspect anything. After he had visited them all, he judged that they were now trapped in the net of steel formed by his soldiers' weapons, and left the field, accompanied by his personal bodyguard. At a given signal the soldiers fell upon the encircled youths, attacking them and any others present. They cut them down, these armed soldiers fighting against unarmed, surrounded boys, butchering them in every conceivable fashion. Some did the killing while others outside the ring dug huge trenches; they dragged those who had fallen to these trenches and threw them in, filling the ditch with bodies. Piling on earth, they quickly raised a huge burial mound. Many were thrown in half-alive, and others were forced in unwounded. A number of soldiers perished there too; for all who were thrust into the trench alive, if they had the strength, clung to their killers and pulled them in with them. So great was the slaughter that the wide mouths of the Nile and the entire shore around the city were stained red by the streams of blood flowing through the plain.[78]

Caracalla then unleashed his troops on the larger city for several days of indiscriminate slaughter, where an additional twenty thousand people perished. This was the price for mocking the Emperor of Rome.

CHRISTIANS

It is fascinating that a gentle, peaceful religion founded by a moralist peasant carpenter became a justification, even a vehicle, for atrocity throughout most of its history.

Christians spent their first three hundred years scurrying as the hunted. We noted that Titus destroyed Jerusalem in 70 CE. In the city were perhaps a few of the surviving Christianity founders along with those they had groomed to replace them. When the Jerusalemites died, that left the disciples of Paul—who was a later arrival, a Hellenized, Romanized, Christian Jew—as leaders of the church. More than one critic objected that with Paul, Christianity became harsher, more authoritarian, and lost some of Jesus's gentleness and tolerance. For instance, Thomas Paine noted that because of Paul, "... the church has set up a system of religion very contradictory to the character of the person whose name it bears. It has set up a religion of pomp and of revenue in pretended imitation of a person whose life was humility and poverty."[79] Even today, less tolerant sects of Christianity read primarily from Paul and the Old Testament. They largely ignore Jesus's moral teachings and parables, particularly those focusing on sacrifice and humility such as related in the Beatitudes and the Parable of the Sheep and the Goats.*

The peacefulness of Christianity faced new challenges when Constantine crashed the internal affairs of the Church. Not surprisingly, those problems grew when Constantine's successors declared Christianity to be the state religion of Rome. In much the same way that Cain's murder of Abel is an unfortunate part of early Judaism, Constantine's meddling in early Christianity was perhaps not the best for the Church. In the Eternal City, Christianity was surrounded by the Roman tradition of violence and horror. Much Christian atrocity over the centuries is arguably a legacy of Constantine and his sons.

It must be remembered that the Roman emperor was not drawn to Christianity for any philosophical or spiritual appeal, but simply because when he adopted the standard with the Christian symbol comprising the Greek letters *chi+rho*, he was victorious in conquest and slaughter. Nothing in Constantine's life suggests that he embraced Christianity in any personal way. Love of family is central to Christian teaching, but Constantine slaughtered his own

---

* I have become increasingly aware of this over the years. I have conservative Protestant friends who have asked me to bless a meal before eating. Although I am not particularly religious, I very much like Jesus's teachings on service and humility, and draw from those for the blessing. They have not asked me to bless another meal.

family as remorselessly as he did his enemies. Among those he had assassinated were his wife, Fausta; his father-in-law; one nephew; two brothers-in-law; and quite a few other members of his personal circle. Of particular interest, concurrent with his preparations for the pivotal Council of Nicaea, Constantine ordered his eldest son, the Caesar Crispus, tried and executed—probably along with Crispus's wife, Helena, and their toddler son*—even though by existing accounts, Crispus had served his father as a loyal and able general.[80]

The Council of Nicaea failed to definitively resolve the divinity of Jesus among the various churches. The Arrians rejected His divinity and rioted, and over three thousand Arrians were put to the sword. Within a few years after the Romans adopted Christianity, more Christians were slaughtered—by fellow Christians—than had died under three centuries of Roman persecution.[81]

Then Constantine's descendants took up Jesus's cross in one hand and Constantine's sword in the other. As noted, Constantine had had his wife Fausta murdered—in a hot bath, either suffocated, drowned, or scalded to death[82]—but she was nevertheless successful in ensuring empire for her three sons by him,† and they eventually ascended to leadership a few years after Constantine's death. Conflict quickly erupted among the sons, however, in part because of divergences among their religious beliefs. Constantius II eventually established complete control and began a Christian tradition of persecuting, torturing, and executing those who did not follow his preferred orthodoxy.

For many of these grisly activities, Constantius employed Paulus Catena ('The Chain'), who tortured and murdered untold numbers of victims at Scythopolis. "He was skilled in the work of bloodshed, and just as a trainer of gladiators seeks profit and emolument from the traffic in funerals and festivals, so did he from the rack or the executioner." The rack was a slow, sadistic torture in which the joints of the arms and legs are slowly dislocated and the tendons and muscles are stretched until they rip.

Paulus ordered executions for offenses as minor as wearing the wrong religious amulet. Only brief descriptions exist, so there is no reliable measure of the number of victims or the full scope of the horror. However, it is recorded that his victims suffered "mangling of their bodies"; it is known that the tried were brought to Scythopolis from across the realm, "noble and obscure

---

* Constantine ordered a *damnatio memoriae* against his son, grandson, and daughter-in-law, just as Caracalla ordered of his brother Geta after he had him assassinated. This leads scholars to suspect all three were executed.

† Crispus was her stepson.

alike"; the atrocities were such that Paulus was accused of "supplying as if from a storehouse many kinds of deception and cruelty"; and the victims were described as comprising "numbers without end."[83]

These early Roman influences dogged the Church throughout her history, generating a tradition of cruel and lethal intolerance that permeated the Middle Ages, and eventually erupted as the Inquisition.[84]

The sadism of the Inquisition need hardly be touched upon here, the stories are endless and endlessly horrifying: the aforementioned rack, the stake, the spiked wheel, the slow *garotte*, the burning of feet in the stocks, the 'pear' for tearing women apart vaginally, the slow, spiked Iron Maiden replete with lances positioned to gouge the eyes, and many others. The numbers of people incinerated, maimed, dismembered, impaled, or otherwise tortured to death are estimated anywhere from the thousands to the hundreds of thousands; those who were tortured and survived doubtless numbered many more. An insight into the scale comes from Napoléon's Spanish campaign. At least some Spaniards welcomed the relatively brief Napoleonic atrocities because it put an end to three centuries of the Inquisition.[85]

Beyond the chronic persecutions and tortures under Christianity, there were unceasing Christian wars. In the previous chapter we covered Clovis I and the Soissons vase, Catherine de' Medici, and the St. Bartholomew's Day Massacre. Clovis was yet another conqueror, and after his conversion he became a conqueror lit by zeal. At one point he captured Saxon rebels and gave them a choice: Christianity or death. When they would not convert, he had 4,500 Saxons beheaded in a single morning.[86] The St. Bartholomew's Day Massacre was part of the French Wars of Religion, in which from two to four million died.[87]

There are over seventeen centuries of post-Constantinian Christian atrocities, and many of the stories are poorly recorded, if recorded at all. There is no way to cover the entirety, but we will finish with a brief consideration of some of the nastiest monsters in Christian history: the Crusaders.[88]

In 1098, the *Franj* (as the Arabs called the Franks) besieged Ma'arra. After two weeks, the citizens agreed to surrender, if their lives would be spared:

> The Frankish commander promised to spare the lives of the inhabitants if they would stop fighting and withdraw from certain buildings. Desperately placing their trust in his word, the families gathered in the houses and cellars of the city and waited all night in fear.
>
> The *Franj* arrived at dawn. It was carnage. For three days they put people to the sword, killing more than a hundred thousand people and taking many prisoners...

"In Ma'arra our troops boiled pagan adults in cooking-pots; they impaled children on spits and devoured them grilled." The inhabitants of towns and villages near Ma'arra would never read this confession by the Frankish chronicler Radulph of Caen, but they would never forget what they had seen and heard.[89]

A similar accusation was made of Crusaders who camped at Civitot:

Rather than maintain a sensibly discreet profile, ravening Latin mobs soon began to trawl the surrounding countryside in search of plunder, allegedly subjecting the region to savage rapine: "acting with horrible cruelty to the whole population, they cut in pieces some of their babies, impaled others on wooden spits and roasted them over a fire [while] the elderly were subjected to every kind of torture."[90]

To be fair, almost all nations have described invaders and other adversaries in the worst terms, and cannibalism is a frequent charge. Accordingly, some scholars have rejected the accusation of cannibalism because the Arab chroniclers do not verify it. That argument, however, raises an even larger problem: Why would the invaders fabricate such accounts of themselves? The fact that the Crusaders were so brutal and horrific in their campaigns leaves one to suspect that the charges of cannibalism just might be true.

Consider that in 1099, the Egyptian garrison in Jerusalem surrendered and were allowed safe passage. Not so the inhabitants. They were slaughtered, and reportedly more than seventy thousand were murdered in the al-Aqsa mosque. Neither were the Jews spared: as they huddled in the synagogue for safety, the Franj burned them alive.

In 1168, the *Franj* seized Bilbays, and without provocation slaughtered the children, women, and men, Muslim and Christian alike. In 1191, Richard the Lionheart took Acre. Saladin tried to negotiate release of the captured soldiers; Saladin had released Crusaders under similar circumstances four years before, and he assumed Richard would reciprocate. But Richard roped his captives together before the city walls, 2,700 soldiers with three hundred children and women of the soldiers' families, and turned his men loose on them with swords, lances, and stones.

Then there was Reynauld of Châtillon. When the Christian patriarch of Cyprus refused to finance his raid on Cyprus, Reynauld had him tortured, had honey smeared in his wounds, and hung in the sun for the insects. In 1156, Reynauld easily conquered Cyprus, and he unleashed his troops on the inhabitants. The crops were destroyed, the livestock slaughtered, everything in the island was looted or demolished. "Women were raped, old men and children slaughtered; rich men were taken as hostages, poor ones were beheaded." Reynauld did not stop there. On his way out, he gathered all of the Greek Christian clergy and had their noses and ears cut off and sent them to Constantinople. His atrocities were so offensive that Saladin chose to personally execute Reynauld himself.

Overall, the Crusades claimed perhaps nine million lives on both sides;[91] at the time, the entire population of Western Europe was perhaps only twenty-five million, and of western Asia, twenty million.[92] This would represent over double the 12 percent casualty rate we have seen in other conquests.

Victorian English

At its height in 1922, tiny England controlled one-fourth of the Earth's land surface and about the same proportion of its people. At the same time, Britannia also controlled much of the seas. England of the nineteenth and early twentieth centuries was an imperial superpower without precedent and perhaps without successor. The majority of this great empire was added under Queen Victoria by 'right of conquest,' which as we have seen, is a euphemism for slaughtering, robbing, and enslaving people.

Which is striking, because the popular view of the Victorians is exactly the opposite. Victoria was a dowdy matron, devoted to her family and friends, and her rigid public morality dominated the period. We cannot imagine

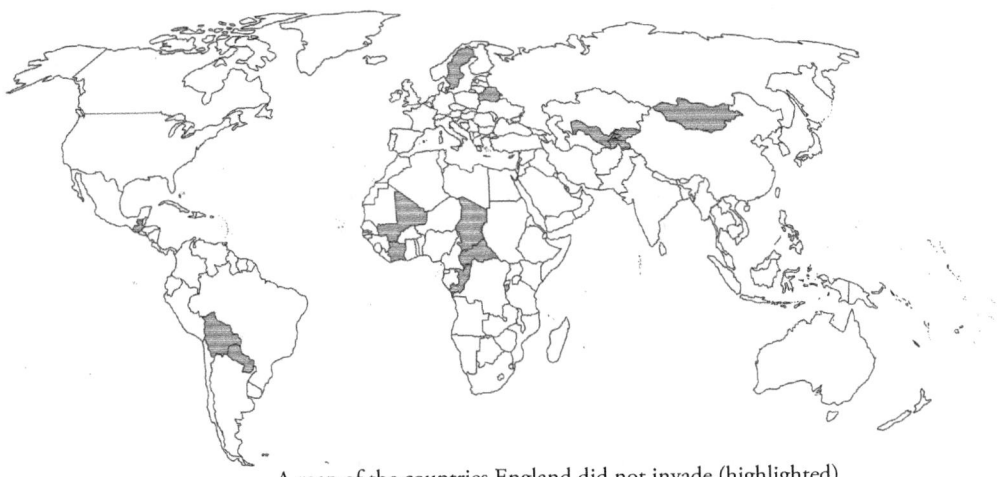

A map of the countries England did not invade (highlighted)

prudish Victoria quietly witnessing the murder of even one innocent person; and yet, she led a nation that murdered millions of innocents in her name.

In India, the Great Sepoy Rebellion of 1857 drew a vicious response from the British. In response to the grisly Bibighar Massacre of 120 English children and women, the British unleashed their forces on Delhi. The retribution left over one hundred thousand dead. Although in some places the order was to spare the women and children, in others it was to leave no one alive. "In one neighbourhood alone, Kucha Chelan, some 1,400 unarmed citizens were cut down. 'The orders went out to shoot every soul,' recorded one young officer. 'It was literally murder.'"[93]

During the Rebellion, the British employed a ghastly public spectacle, in which the accused was 'blown from a gun':

> The prisoner is generally tied to a gun with the upper part of the small of his back resting against the muzzle. When the gun is fired, his head is seen to go straight up into the air some forty or fifty feet; the arms fly off right and left, high up in the air, and fall at, perhaps, a hundred yards distance; the legs drop to the ground beneath the muzzle of the gun; and the body is literally blown away altogether, not a vestige being seen.[94]

This British brutality cowed the Indians sufficiently that twenty years later they quietly suffered the Madras Famine of 1877, one of the deadliest in history: between ten and thirty million Indians—children, women, and men—died of starvation and disease. It rivals the body counts from Hitler, Stalin, and Mao. Unlike active military operations, however, this was a massacre of omission, an intentional neglect that was nevertheless backed by military force. Guided by dogmatic ideology—in this case, social Darwinism—the Viceroy of India, Lord Lytton, allowed the famine to proceed unaddressed while exporting surplus grain from other parts of the subcontinent back to England. Beyond dogmatic ideology, the other consideration in his decision was simple greed: at one point Lytton finally agreed to a tax to help the starving, but only if it were regressive. It was critical that the fortunes of wealthy Englishmen, and even Indians, remain almost completely untouched.[95]

The Victorian English are often accused of racism, with justification. Actions during the Boer War against Dutch settlers in South Africa, however, proved that they did not reserve atrocity for non-whites. When the British destroyed the homes and villages of suspected Boer fighters, they often dispatched the women and children to "Camps of Refuge," concentration camps. A sadistic aspect of this relocation was that care was often taken to divide families so that children would be separated from their mothers and siblings. In the camps there was inadequate water and waste removal. There was

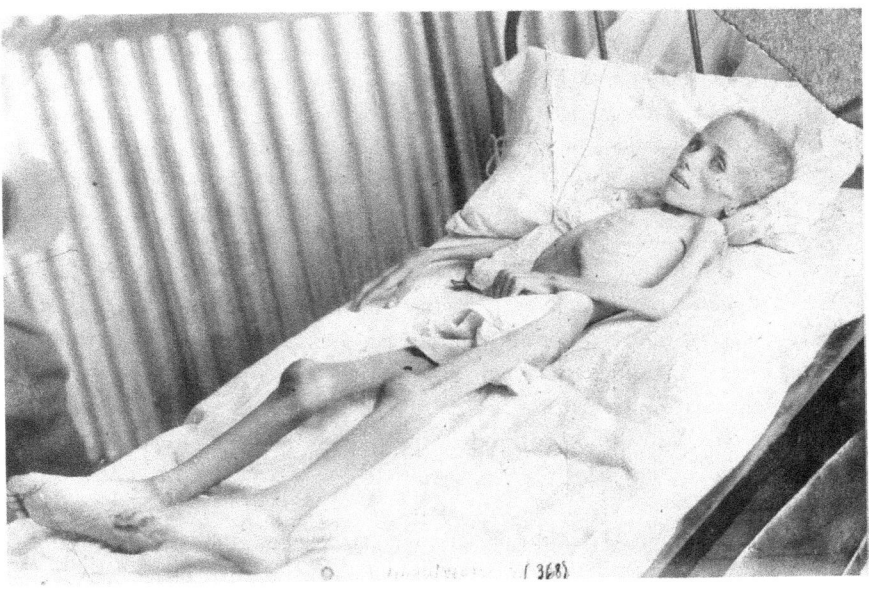

Lizzie van Zyl with her doll days before her death

also insufficient food; in the camps housing the families of the most-wanted Boers, nutrition was provided at the starvation level.

And starve they did. Over one hundred thousand children and women were incarcerated, over half of them Boers. Of the estimated 28,000 Boers who died, 22,000 were children. But as noted, the Victorians had ensured that as the children succumbed slowly and fearfully, they did so alone, without comfort from their mothers and siblings.[96]

The mascot for the Boer atrocity was six-year-old Lizzie van Zyl who wasted away from malnutrition in one of the camps. Her case provides several insights for our considerations here, particularly the practice of the victimizer blaming the victim. Emily Hobhouse was a tireless worker for the incarcerated Boers; in the appalling picture of Lizzie, it is hard to tell that she is even a child, but one can see her clutching a doll that Hobhouse had given her. Hobhouse sent this picture of Lizzie back to England where it was received with outrage. Hobhouse described Lizzie's maltreatment by the medical staff in the camp:

> Dr. Pern says the child was "quite an idiot." Unhappily neither Dr. Pern nor the nurse could speak Dutch, and the child could speak no English; to me she could talk quite sensibly about her doll, and her desire that the other children shall have dolls like the one I brought her...[97]

Mrs. Botha told one very pathetic story about Lizzie. She was in the hospital one day, probably visiting her own daughter, when the child began to cry very sadly, "Mother, Mother" she cried. "I want to go to Mother!" Mrs. Botha went up to her to comfort her and try to stop her heart-broken wailing and was just beginning to tell her she should soon see her mother when the nurse in charge broke in very crossly: "There, there, don't trouble about that child, Mrs. Botha. The sooner we are rid of her the better. She is such a nuisance we are all longing to get rid of her."[98]

Lizzie died a few days later, just after her seventh birthday.

There were many defenders of the English actions in the Boer War. Several books, articles, and tracts supporting the British efforts in South Africa were written by a Dr. Doyle, a physician who had served at Blomfontein in the War. He responded to the picture of Lizzie by, again, blaming the victims:

> It is worthy of record that the portrait of an emaciated child has been circulated upon the Continent and in America as a proof positive of the horrors of the concentration system. It is only too probable that there are many emaciated children in the camps, for they usually arrive in that condition. This particular portrait however was, as I am credibly informed, taken by the British authorities on the occasion of the criminal trial of the mother for the ill-usage of the child. The incident is characteristic of the unscrupulous tactics which have been used from the beginning to poison the mind of the world against Great Britain.[99]

Hobhouse took Doyle to task for his comments:

> Doyle, on p. 106 of his recent pamphlet referring to this case, says he was "credibly informed that the portrait of the child was taken by the British authorities on the occasion of the criminal trial of the mother for ill-usage of the child." It would be interesting to know where Dr. Doyle got this information; it is a serious thing to allege against an absent and defenseless woman. I notice Dr. Pern makes no mention of any such trial.[100]

At least partly because of his defense of British activities in South Africa, in 1902, Edward VII knighted Doyle, giving him the title for which he is known today, Sir Arthur Conan Doyle.

In addition to the preceding military and bureaucratic atrocities of conquest, there were also private English massacres. In Australia,[101] New Zealand, and Tasmania,[102] the British colonists systematically engaged in night raids where they located natives by their tribal fires, surrounded them, and discharged their weapons into the compact group. After the gunwork, they often charged in and killed survivors with bayonets. One scene is described by Australian author Henry Melville:

> A mob of some score or so of natives, men, women, and children, had been discovered by their fires, and a whole parcel of the Colonists armed themselves, and proceeded to the spot. These advanced unperceived, and were close to the natives, when the dogs gave the alarm; the natives jumped up in a moment and then was the signal for slaughter given, firearms were discharged, and those poor wretches who could not hide themselves from the light thrown on their persons by their own fires, were destroyed. The writer recollects the description of one of these scenes, as given by an eye-witness. "One man," said the informant, "was shot, he sprang up, turned round like a whipping-top, and fell dead;—the party then went up to the fires, found a great number of waddies and spears, and an infant sprawling on the ground, which one of the party pitched into one of the fires."[103]

Attacks by civilians present a consideration that will become important in the next chapter. Presumably many of the men who committed these massacres were otherwise middle class, church-going, family men; they hardly resembled vicious criminals. In fact, they likely resembled many of our neighbors and friends today. That raises an important question: If civilians prosecute these sorts of atrocities, how can we believe that the professional soldiers who made up Victoria's army, or any army, were more humane in their conquest of so much of the globe?

They weren't. Victorian and later British massacres were heavily under-reported. Given the size of English global conquest, it is striking that descriptions of British atrocities are not readily available. In the *Encyclopedia of Genocide*,[104] the Delhi Massacre of the Great Sepoy Rebellion is not noted, nor is the Amritsar Massacre of 1919 at Jallianwalla Bagh, in which the British began shooting into a religious festival of mixed Sikhs, Hindus, and Muslims, killing 1,500 children, women, and men. As for atrocities of the Boer War, the *Encyclopedia* mentions them only in passing, and they are not indexed under 'Great Britain'—supporting my thesis, very little is—but rather, indexed under 'Boer,' the victims. That is curious.

To support the assertion of under-reporting, I offer the odd case of the 1882 'Missing Massacre' of Alexandria. This was a follow-up to the well-documented Alexandria Massacre of June 11, 1882, in which about fifty people were killed, of whom only four were "British-born":* two military personnel; and two businessmen who fatuously waved pistols at the rioting crowds, an ironic reminder that Darwinian selection isn't exclusive to the poor and disenfranchised. Despite the small loss of British lives, the riot fed into British ambitions, particularly the desire for expanded empire and profits, control of the Suez Canal, and concerns over a local warlord.† So the first Massacre gave the British a pretext to deploy fifteen British warships off the coast of Alexandria. A month to the day after the riot, the Royal Navy commenced three days of bombardment on the ancient city.[105]

There are famous photographs of the aftermath, showing large portions of the city reduced to rubble. Except for the odd Englishman or two loitering in the foreground, the pictures contain nobody. Quite literally, no body: no victims, no rescuers, no survivors recovering possessions, no one beginning to rebuild. Equally odd, the salient Western research on the bombardment apparently never describes the civilian casualties. It's not just that they don't enumerate them; I could find no academic consideration that anyone might have died amid such widespread destruction.‡

We will return to British whitewashing below. The photographs of razed Alexandria, however, could serve as a metaphor for our popular concepts of armed conflict. Reflect on Conan Doyle's flimsy rationalizations when confronted with photographic evidence: rather than question the British Empire, he impugns a starving child's mother, a mother who had been deliberately torn from her daughter by the same British whom Doyle defends.

---

* At first, the English wanted to know how many British citizens were killed; they quickly amended that to "British-born" citizens, an unfortunate testament to Victorian priorities.

† The warlord was Ahmed Arabi, and historians debate whether he was really a threat to the English. Indeed, after the Alexandria Bombardment, although many of his men were executed, Arabi was exiled to Sri Lanka where he was treated with deference.

‡ Special thanks to Kenneth Cuno at the University of Illinois for his help with this. In addition to other literature I cite here, he suggested Juan Ricardo Cole, *Colonialism and Revolution in the Middle East: Social and Cultural Origins of Egypt's Urabi Movement* (Princeton University, 1993); and M. W. Daly, *The Cambridge History of Egypt*, vol. 2, *Modern Egypt from 1517 to the End of the Twentieth Century* (Cambridge University, 1998). I could find no mention of casualties in either work, although there was a mention of "tales of horror" in *The Cambridge History* on p. 232. In a modern source, I did find this comment: "About 60,000 Egyptians fled the slaughter. No one found it possible in the aftermath of the butchery to estimate with any accuracy how many died in the bombardment and the subsequent fires." Giovanni Bonello, "Maltese Spark that Led to Alexandria Bombardment," *Times of Malta*, June 5, 2011.

The 1882 "Missing Massacre": Alexandria bombardment and its aftermath

Our traditions of defending the victorious invader do not hold up to even brief consideration. Throughout history there has been chronic, recurrent conquest. Without slaughter and indiscriminate destruction, conquest is impossible. And despite our romantic, popular notions, invading armies do not delicately avoid civilians. War is hardly a refined activity.

And yet, the popular view of history, and of conquest, is very much like these photographs of Alexandria: despite the enormous destruction apparent everywhere, our popular assumptions and traditions persist that the outcome of warfare is quiet, serene, orderly. No gore. No suffering.

No bodies.

AMERICANS

It is interesting that in the United States today, the word 'colonist' often carries a lofty, near-sacred meaning. To the Europeans of the eighteenth century, however, it was the equivalent of 'bumpkin' or even 'redneck.' Consider "Yankee Doodle," a song the Americans commandeered from British troops. 'Doodle' at the time referred to a fool or a simpleton, and the song was meant to ridicule the American rustics who were ignorant of civilized behavior. So when some of those colonists announced that they were reviving the long-lost Roman republican form of government, there were jeers and peels of laughter from the European nobility and upper classes.

Which is why it is all the more remarkable that the backwards colonists succeeded. They not only succeeded; they redesigned government, and they redesigned the relationships among government, church, markets, and the free flow of information. Their daring experiment, and the evolution and expansion of it, became the model for much of the modern world.

Eventually Americans produced what was arguably the high point of western civilization: the Marshall Plan. This chapter addresses the predictable but ghastly gore of conquest and its aftermath. The Marshall Plan, however, was unprecedented and represented a sort of anti-conquest. Never before had a conquering army sought to rebuild its foes as independent, autonomous nations. The anti-conquest nature of the Marshall Plan is also demonstrated by its violation of the necessary reasons for conquest that we gave before: in place of looting, there was rebuilding; in place of slavery, liberation; and in place of taxation, funding. The reasons for the Marshall Plan were more complicated than simple high-mindedness of course,[106] but the wisdom of it nevertheless ushered in the *Pax Americana*, giving us a world where no two modern democracies have yet warred with one another.*

---

* Some have argued that the Marshall Plan was a clever, devious scheme for economic colonization. I remember being button-holed by a French scholar who said that the only reason the United States instituted the Plan was to sell American wares to Europe when it was rebuilt. First of all, she was correct, except for the word 'only': there were possibly as many reasons for the Marshall Plan as there were people who supported it. Second, I don't think Europe would have declined the U.S. aid, even if such a mercenary goal had been made patent at the time. Third, I doubt that many people in 1947 could predict results that far into the future, and even if they could, few would believe them: the two previous post-war aid packages the U.S. had sent to Europe had generated no clear results. Ironically, conservatives of the day, including many industrialists, thought the Marshall Plan was yet another waste of taxpayers' money. Beyond those, the results belie the accusation. It is true, the United States now sells to the world. But the world also sells to the United States, and overall the world economy is growing and prospering. With few exceptions, even those countries that resist the American model have enjoyed a rapid expansion of their economies in the past seventy years.

U.S. behavior, however, has not always been so admirable, before or since.

The New England Puritans—here we turn yet again to Christians—are popularly portrayed as devout and humble believers who came to the New World in a pious bid for religious freedom. In truth, they were every bit as autocratic, and at times even more intolerant, as the kings and popes they so bitterly despised. The greed, exclusiveness, and duplicity of the Puritan leadership, even when dealing with fellow believers, is shocking. The Massachusetts church leaders argued that no church should exercise control over another, but then they meddled constantly in the affairs of the other churches. The Massachusetts authorities believed that everyone was free to worship as they saw fit; at least they were until their religious views disagreed with those of Massachusetts. Although every person was compelled to attend church, only an elite few were admitted as members of the church, and those few used their positions to acquire wealth. It eventually emerged that the Massachusetts charter allowed the entire voting body to make law. The magistrates, however, had kept the charter hidden and kept that provision a secret so that they might arrogate all power to themselves. Perhaps the most revealing action was that the Massachusetts magistrates sent an assassination squad to murder Roger Williams, founder of Rhode Island, for disagreeing with them on doctrine but not on practice. This casual deployment of lethal punishment against dissenters and other undesirables would finally explode with the Salem witch trials a few years later.[*]

The Puritans' behavior toward the Native Americans was also ruthless and vicious, and they were often as rapacious and cruel as any other conqueror. The Puritans claimed that the Native Americans were their brothers in Christ, but they nevertheless slaughtered, enslaved, and otherwise exploited them. At one point, unknown natives killed a small number of traders. The Pilgrims decided the Pequot were the culprits and attacked their settlement and burned their food stores, leaving them to starve. The Pequot subsequently took the Saybrook Fort, and the English stormed the compound and set fire to the wigwams:

---

[*] Williams is easily one of the most overlooked individuals in U.S. history: as we will see, he was almost definitely the originator of freedom of expression; although a Puritan, he was the one who proposed and argued for separation of church and state, albeit on theological, not civil, grounds; he first introduced real democracy to the colonies; he and his followers introduced suffrage for women, probably the first in the modern world; and he alone among the Puritans practiced complete tolerance for dissenting viewpoints, and he suffered for it. Finally, he was the only one of the Puritans who actually practiced what he preached, going out and teaching the Gospel to the Native Americans. Barry, John M., *Roger Williams and The Creation of the American Soul: Church, State, and the Birth of Liberty* (Viking, 2012).

> ...many were burnt in the Fort, both men, women, and children, others forced out, and came in troopes to the Indians, twentie, and thirtie at a time, which our souldiers received and entertained with the point of the sword; downe fell men, women, and children... [107]

> ...therby more were burnte to death then was otherwise slaine; it burnte their bowstrings, and made them unservisable. Those yt scaped ye fire were slaine with ye sword; some hewed to peeces, and very few escaped.* [108]

Only seven men were taken captive, and possibly another seven escaped out of four to seven hundred people. Some of the Puritans who were inexperienced in warfare balked at the horror and questioned whether the slaughter conformed to Christian teaching. A leader dismissed their concerns by citing the activities of King David.

Some weeks later, another two hundred Pequot surrendered to the Narragansett; the Narragansett turned them over to the English colonists, expecting humane treatment. The Puritans slaughtered all of the men but two and enslaved the children and women.

This is the beginning of a long litany of U.S. horror and abuse toward Native Americans, including centuries of massacres, disease, and forced resettlement—perhaps none so well known as the Trail of Tears. For brevity, let us skip to mid-nineteenth-century California. Some of the settlers there frequently set out on night and early morning raids, in much the same way as did the Victorian British colonists noted above, to hunt down Native American tribes and slaughter them without provocation or notice.[109] The aftermath of one such attack, the 1860 Wiyot massacre in Humboldt County, is described:

> Amidst the wailing of mutilated infants, the cries of agony of children, the shrieks and groans of mothers in death, the savage blows are given, cutting through bone and brain... A few escaped—a child under the body of its dead mother, a young woman wounded who hid in the bushes...

> Here was a mother fatally wounded hugging the mutilated carcass of her dying infant to her bosom; there a poor child of two years old, with its ear and scalp torn from the side of its little head. Here a father frantic with grief over the bloody corpses of his four little children and wife;

---

* Note the words 'yt' and 'ye.' The 'y' character in this case is not a modern 'y,' but an updated version of the Old Norse/Old English rune the *thorn*, þ. Hence it is pronounced as 'th': 'ye olde taverne' is pronounced *'the* old tavern.'

there, a brother and sister bitterly weeping, and trying to soothe with cold water the pallid face of a dying relative. Here, an aged female still living and sitting up, though covered with ghastly wounds, and dyed in her own blood; there, a living infant by its dead mother, desirous of drawing some nourishment from a source that had ceased to flow.

The wounded, dead and dying were found all around, and in every lodge the skulls and frames of women and children cleft with axes and hatchets, and stabbed with knives, and the brains of an infant oozing from its broken head to the ground.[110]

Within forty some-odd years, massacre, starvation, and disease reduced the California Native American population from an estimated two hundred thousand to perhaps only thirty thousand.[111] Again, this is far beyond the 12 percent typical of conquest, but this was not conquest. It was an attempt at genocide.

Some years later, an expedition of cavalry in the Montana Territory stealthily surrounded a Blackfeet encampment by night. The tribe was led by Heavy Runner, and it was not the tribe the cavalry sought. In fact, Heavy Runner's tribe had been promised protection by the federal government. Many of the tribe were suffering from smallpox. Bear Head, a boy captured before the assault by "seizers" (*i.e.*, the troops), relates what he witnessed:

A seizer chief up on the bank shouted something, and at once all of the seizers began shooting into the lodges. Chief Heavy Runner ran from his lodge toward the seizers on the bank. He was shouting to them and waving a paper writing that our agent had given him, a writing saying that he was a good and peaceful man, a friend of the whites. He had run but a few steps when he fell, his body pierced with bullets. Inside the lodges men were yelling; terribly frightened women and children, screaming—screaming from wounds, from pain as they died. I saw a few men and women, escaping from their lodges, shot down as they ran. Most terrible to hear of all was the crying of the little babies at their mothers' breasts. The seizers all advanced upon the lodges, my seizer still firmly holding my arm. They shot at the tops of the lodges; cut the bindings of the poles so the whole lodge would collapse upon the fire and begin to burn—burn and smother those within. I saw my lodge so go down and burn. Within it my mother, my almost-mothers, my almost-sisters. Oh, how pitiful were their screamings as they died, and I there, powerless to help them!

Soon all was silent in the camp, and the seizers advanced, began tearing down the lodges that still stood, shooting those within them who were still alive, and trying to burn all that they tore down, burn the dead under the heaps of poles, lodge-skins, and lodge furnishings; but they did not burn well.

At last my seizer released my arm and went about with his men looking at the smoking piles, talking, pointing, laughing, all of them. And finally the seizers rounded up all of our horses, drove them up the valley a little way, and made camp.

I sat before the ruin of my lodge and felt sick. I wished that the seizers had killed me, too. In the center of the fallen lodge, where the poles had fallen upon the fire, it had burned a little, then died out. I could not pull up the lodge-skin and look under it. I could not bear to see my mother, my almost-mothers, my almost-sisters lying there, shot or smothered to death.[112]

The troops that day slaughtered an estimated 170 people, 50 of them children under the age of twelve. There were almost no men of fighting age; they were away hunting buffalo.[113]

A decade later, a sizable Pennsylvania militia company sought Native Americans who had been attacking white settlements. They did not find warriors, but at Gnaddenhütten, Ohio, they found about one hundred Native American converts to Moravian Christianity. The militia at first offered the natives safe passage but then condemned them to death. The Native Americans sang hymns, prayed, and said their good-byes as they awaited their deaths. All of them, including about thirty children, were killed with a cooper's mallet and scalped, except for two boys who managed to escape, one of whom had survived the scalping.[114]

In one of the most notorious events, a volunteer cavalry comprising 675 troops attacked a Native American encampment at Sand Creek, Colorado in 1864. The Arapaho and Cheyenne tribes there flew an American flag presented to them by Abraham Lincoln, and below it flew a white flag signaling their non-aggressive intentions and their desire for peace.[115]

Both flags were ignored. The commanding officer at the scene, U.S. Army Colonel John Chivington, was a Methodist preacher and an opponent of slavery. Despite his Christian profession and his personal beliefs about slaves, he told his men, "Damn any man who sympathizes with Indians." He ordered his men, "Kill and scalp all, big and little; nits make lice." Over 160 Native Americans were slaughtered, most of them children and women. Twenty-four-year-old Robert Bent gave the following testimony:

After the firing the warriors put the squaws and children together, and surrounded them to protect them. I saw five squaws under a bank for shelter. When the troops came up to them they ran out and showed their persons to let the soldiers know they were squaws and begged for mercy, but the soldiers shot them all. I saw one squaw lying on the bank whose leg had been broken by a shell; a soldier came up to her with a drawn sabre; she raised her arm to protect herself, when he struck, breaking her arm; she rolled over and raised her other arm, when he struck, breaking it, and then left her without killing her. There seemed to be an indiscriminate slaughter of men, women, and children. There were some thirty or forty squaws collected in a hole for protection; they sent out a little girl about six years old with a white flag on a stick; she had not proceeded but a few steps when she was shot and killed. All the squaws in that hole were afterwards killed, and four or five bucks outside. The squaws offered no resistance. Every one I saw dead was scalped. I saw one squaw cut open with an unborn child, as I thought, lying by her side. Captain Soulé, afterwards told me that such was the fact. I saw the body of White Antelope with the privates cut off, and I heard a soldier say he was going to make a tobacco-pouch out of them. I saw one squaw whose privates had been cut out. I heard Colonel Chivington say to the soldiers as they charged past him, "Remember our wives and children murdered on the Platte and Arkansas." He occupied a position where he could not have failed to have seen the American flag, which I think was a garrison flag, six by twelve. He was within fifty yards when he planted his battery. I saw a little girl about five years of age who had been hid in the sand; two soldiers discovered her, drew their pistols and shot her, and then pulled her out of the sand by the arm. I saw quite a number of infants in arms killed with their mothers.[116]

Then there was this chilling testimony from Major Scott J. Anthony:

There was one little child, probably three years old, just big enough to walk through the sand. The Indians had gone ahead, and this little child was behind, following after them. The little fellow was perfectly naked, travelling in the sand. I saw one man get off his horse at a distance of about seventy-five yards and draw up his rifle and fire. He missed the child. Another man came up and said, "let me try the son of a b-. I can hit him." He got down off his horse, kneeled down, and fired at the little child, but he missed him. A third man came up, and made a similar remark, and fired, and the little fellow dropped.[117]

Even famed Native American fighter Kit Carson was scandalized by the brutality:

...jist to think of that dog Chivington, and his dirty hounds, up thar at Sand Creek! Whoever heerd of sich doings 'mong Christians! The pore Indians had the Stars and Stripes flying over them, our old flag thar, and they'd bin told down to Denver, that so long as they kept flying they'd be safe enough. Well, then, one day along comes that durned Chivington and his cusses. They'd bin out several days huntin Hostiles, and couldn't find none nowhar, and if they had, they'd have skedaddled from 'em, you bet! So they jist lit upon these Friendlies, and massacreed 'em—yes, sir, literally massacreed 'em—in cold blood, in spite of our flag thar—yes, women and little children, even! Why, Senator Foster told me with his own lips (and him and his Committtee came out yer from Washington, you know, and investigated this muss), that thar durned miscreant and his men shot down squaws, and blew the brains out of little innocent children—pistoled little papooses in the arms of their dead mothers, and even worse than this!—them durned devils! and you call sich soldiers Christians, do ye?[118]

Chivington later testified that the action was a battle against armed men and that very few women or children were killed. There were three separate Congressional investigations into the incident, and the actions were censured, but no punishment accompanied the criticism. During one part of a Congressional investigation with Chivington in Denver, there were actually cheers from the public of, "EXTERMINATE THEM, EXTERMINATE THEM!"[119]

American atrocities were not limited to Native Americans. In 1901, a few decades after Sand Creek, General Jacob H. Smith launched the Balangiga Massacre on Samar Island, Philippines. In response to guerrilla action that killed

Balangiga Massacre

fifty-four American troops, the general ordered his men to kill all males over the age of ten. Estimates are that about 2,500 boys and men were murdered.[120]

In 1950, American forces in the Korean War slaughtered some four hundred civilians at No Gun Ri.* Many of the victims were herded into concrete tunnels beneath a railroad bridge and killed with machine gun and rifle fire. Over the next two days, the U.S. troops monitored the bodies, shooting anyone that moved, as the victims were also assaulted by air attacks. No military report was filed from the attacks. Of the victims, over two-thirds were children, women, and elders.[121]

Then there is the atrocity we covered in the prologue. In 1968, a group of U.S. soldiers entered two hamlets of Son My Lai in Vietnam and slaughtered over five hundred babies, children, women, and elders. As noted, not one male of fighting age was discovered in the massacre.

The My Lai episode is significant for several reasons. First, the assault was apparently halted because of the actions of a friend of mine, the late Hugh Thompson. Thompson was an Army helicopter pilot called in for air support at My Lai and he, with his two crew, stood down fellow soldiers on the ground to protect and rescue civilians. He then returned to headquarters and angrily complained to his superior officers, after which hostilities quickly ceased.

Second, Thompson's action is possibly unprecedented in warfare.† For those of us wishing to understand the horror of war and how to stop it, Thompson's actions deserve serious study. We are left with two critical questions: Why him? Why then?

Third, the Army tried to whitewash the slaughter, and the public almost did not find out about the atrocity. The journalist who took the damning photographs did not release them for some months and did so only when pressured by a friend.

Fourth, Thompson's resistance appears to have created a turning point in history, which creates a turning point for the thesis of this book: in response to the public outcry over My Lai, the militaries of the advanced countries have changed their attitudes toward, and rules about, the conduct of war. These considerations will become important in later chapters.

---

* Pronounced *noh gool lee*.

† In April 2013, I spoke with a historian at the USNA Stockdale Center for Ethical Leadership, asking if Thompson were the first soldier to protect foreign civilians against his own troops and live to tell the tale. He said that, as far as he knew, he was.

• • •

Currently, the standard research on holocausts, massacres, and atrocities tends to focus on Western conquerors. This is hardly chauvinism; it is no great honor to have bloodthirsty forbears. More probably, scholars focus on their own cultures out of familiarity and ready access to research materials. The main objective of this chapter, however, is to show that horror is quite common in cultures of any size. To support that assertion, we will take a cursory glance at conquerors and kings outside of the European tradition.

Ashoka

A major conqueror of old, one who illustrates several concepts important in these pages was Ashoka, the Indian king who unified most of modern India in the third century BCE.[122] His ardent conversion to Buddhism and his pursuit of peace, kindness, and generosity heavily influence Indian culture even today. The icon on the flag of India is the Ashoka Wheel, and the state emblem of India is the Ashoka Capital, comprising four outward-facing lions (see pg. 154).

In much of his life, however, Ashoka was as vicious, sadistic, and ambitious as the worst of history. In order to usurp the throne from his half-brother, Ashoka lured him into a pit of hot coals where he horribly burned to death.[123] He then murdered his other ninety-nine brothers, sparing only one.[124]

One of Ashoka's earliest acts was to command his ministers to cut down all of the fruit and flower trees and spare the useless thorn trees. When they would not, he beheaded five hundred of them by his own sword.

He was apparently an unattractive man with rough skin. When some of his harem mocked his ugliness by pruning the branches and flowers from his namesake, the ashoka tree, he burned them to death—again, five hundred of them—possibly by wrapping them in searing sheets of copper.[125]

At that point his advisers suggested that he find someone to commit his atrocities for him. His ministers located Girika, a man so vicious that he killed his own parents when they would not give him permission to be the king's torturer. Together, Girika and the king built 'Ashoka's Hell,' a seeming palace, beautiful in design on the inside and out, but ensuring a sadistic, lethal fate for anyone who stepped into it, even inadvertently. The tortures inside mimicked an Asian description of hell: victims were forced onto a hot metal floor, and molten metal was poured down their throats; they were held onto a burning floor and slowly chopped into geometric forms; or they were crucified on a hot floor and then impaled through the heart.[126] Added to those were giant mortars for pounding people to pulp, scythes for cutting and chopping them to pieces, and other untold tortures. Reportedly, one of Ashoka's concubines and a handsome young man were taken there and pulverised to death for nothing more than a pleasant conversation. It is reported that thousands were tortured and executed there.[127]

One of Ashoka's spiritual turning points came after his victory at Kalinga, where 100,000 were slain, many more died of other causes and 150,000 were deported.[128] When Ashoka considered the number of dead, saw the pain, the suffering, and the motherless children, he was moved to compassion, and he committed to Buddhism.

But his commitment to Buddhist ideals at that point was questionable.* When a Jain drew a picture of the Buddha bowing to the founder of Jainism, Ashoka flew into a rage. He ordered the execution of not only the artist, but also of all Jains in the offender's country—eighteen thousand people—along with him.[129]

---

* Some have suggested that the reports of Ashoka's earlier behaviors are not true, presumably in order to defend his religious prominence. Drekmeier in particular speculates that Ashoka's earlier reputation was probably an exaggeration and compares the conversions of Ashoka and St. Augustine. The comparison is unconvincing: Augustine was a spoiled youth whose sins were comparatively minor, largely those of carnality and pride; he certainly never murdered or attempted conquest. Charles Drekmeier, *Kingship and Community in Early India* (Stanford University, 1962); Sailendra Nath Sen, *Ancient Indian History and Civilization* (New Age International, 1999).

When a second man later committed the same offense, Ashoka ordered the man burned to death with his family inside their home. He then put a bounty on the heads of all Jains; this continued until the lone brother that Ashoka had spared was mistaken for a Jain and beheaded for the reward. Thereafter, Ashoka committed fully to Buddhist tenets.[130] Or so it is reported.

At some point later, Ashoka's new queen made advances to her step-son, Ashoka's much-beloved son Kunala, but he rebuffed her. In revenge, she tricked Ashoka into ordering Kunala's eyes plucked out.[131] Kunala submitted to this sentence with Buddhist acceptance and stoicism and then requested that his father be merciful to the queen. Ashoka was not. He had her burned to death and ordered the execution of every person in the city where Kunala's eyes were removed.[132]

Atahualpa

Atahualpa is often portrayed as the major victim of the viciousness of Pizarro, but Atahualpa easily gave as good as he got. His parents married after his father, Huayna Capac, conquered his mother's Kingdom of Quito. At one point in the battle, the deaths from both sides were so numerous that fighting had to be carried out while standing on the bodies of the dead and dying. When his father's troops surrounded the Quiteños on the lakeshore and began to slaughter them, the bloodletting turned the water red; the lake was thereafter renamed Yahuarcocha, or 'blood lake.' Huayna Capac was not entirely without admiration for his enemy, however. One of the opposing captains proved so valiant that after his soldiers caught him, Huayna Capac was considerate enough to have his skin made into a drum.[133]

After Huayna Capac's death, Atahualpa and his half-brother, Huascar, accepted the divided kingdom as per their father's will and lived in uneasy peace for a few years. Huascar claimed superiority over his half-brother because Huascar was pure Inca—his parents were, after all, siblings—and he despised Atahualpa as a bastard, even though at least some histories report that the Queen of Quito was one of Huayna Capac's lawful wives.

Civil war eventually erupted between the brothers. In one of the battles, Atahualpa's troops captured an important general from Huascar's army. The general was tortured to death, and Atahualpa had his skull made into a guilded drinking cup. He was still using the cup when the Spaniards captured him.[134]

When Atahualpa's troops finally defeated and captured Huascar, the victorious emperor sent his relative, Cusi Yupanqui, with orders that all of his brother's family and friends were to be executed:

He [Cusi Yupanqui] then caused poles to be fixed on both sides of the road, extending not more than a quarter of a league along the way to Xaquixahuana. Next he brought out of the prison all of the wives of Huascar, including those pregnant or late delivered. He ordered them to be hung to these poles with their children, and he ordered the pregnant to be cut open, and the stillborn to be hung with them. Then he caused the sons of Huascar to be brought out and hung to the poles.[135]

Thereafter, all of Huascar's nobles and friends were also executed, most by hanging, but at least one was buried alive.

Soon after, the Spaniards captured Atahualpa and gained control of his kingdom. Atahualpa bought time from his captives by providing them with an estimated six metric tons of gold and twelve tons of silver, over $300,000,000 at today's rates.[136] While captive, Atahualpa ordered the execution of his half-brother, in an attempt to protect his throne.

It was all for nothing. The Spanish soon garroted Atahualpa. Thereafter, one of Atahualpa's generals, attempting to usurp the throne, murdered Atahualpa's sons along with their regent. The Incas were apparently keen on percussion: the regent's bones and organs were carefully extracted, and his skin was incorporated, apparently whole, into a two-headed drum.[137]

Genghis Khan

Genghis, or Chinghis, Khan was a conqueror without rival in the history of the world. Up until the last century, he conquered more of the world than anyone had, ever. Unlike modern armies, however, Genghis's thirteenth-century horde* deployed almost no heavy weaponry, traveled without railroads or ships, and possibly fought without benefit of gunpowder.† He built his empire with little technology beyond the compound bow, the sword, and a few siege machines.

---

* Horde is from the Mongolian *ordu*, which designates a large group or a military section; the Urdu language derives its name from the same source. The Golden Horde, which came later, possibly gets its name from a confusion between the Mongolian words for 'gold' and 'central.'

† It is curious that the Mongols may not have used gunpowder. The Chinese had invented the compound over two centuries before. According to May, "While it is true that the Mongols never met a weapon they did not find a use for, there is no concrete evidence that the Mongols used gunpowder weapons on a regular basis outside of China." Timothy May, "Gunpowder and Firearms: Warfare in Medieval India," *Humanities and Social Sciences Online*, retrieved January 29, 2018, https://networks.h-net.org/node/12840/reviews/13288/may-khan-gunpowder-and-firearms-warfare-medieval-india.

This was largely possible through a rich Mongol culture of skilled horsemanship; that, and a generous supply of fast ponies. Warfare is hard on horses, and they generally die at much faster rates than their riders. The advance units of the Mongol army traveled light and fast (up to sixty miles a day), often by supplying each rider with two or more horses. Levity and speed were key to Genghis's success; defenders often had little time to respond to the arrival of Genghis's quick-moving shock troops.

But to those few primitive tools, we must add Genghis's intellect. Although illiterate, he constantly learned from his previous battles and improved his strategy. And he carefully studied his adversaries. By deploying spies and interrogating captured soldiers and civilians, Genghis carefully collected information about his opponents. His interests in the economic, social, political, and psychological aspects of his enemy, as well as the foe's military capabilities, allowed him to exploit weaknesses and opportunities that lesser conquerors might miss.

Genghis's intelligence included not only keen analysis but social innovation. Anticipating Napoléon by a half-millennium, Khan built his army on meritocratic principles, which not only produced more competence and efficiency in his ranks but also fostered fierce loyalty among his troops—few places in the thirteenth-century world provided any real opportunity for commoners to advance. This, in turn, helped Genghis recruit yet more troops from the armies he conquered.

He also understood the critical importance of that loyalty. When Genghis added foreign troops, he separated them out among units of his army so that their loyalty would always be to him and his officers. By the same reasoning, when troops within an opposing army betrayed their fellows in order to assist Genghis, he had them executed. He reasoned that if they were disloyal to their own comrades, then he could not trust them either.

Unfortunately, all of this intellectual and cultural excellence targeted human slaughter, where he was equally innovative. In the assault on Samarkand, Genghis deployed the strategy of gathering up local civilians and using them as body shields for his troops. The defenders had to pick their poison: waste arrows killing their own people, or allow Genghis's men to gain access to the city walls.

Naturally, the horror and slaughter continued after the battle. Frequently, once Genghis had set aside survivors who were valuable as slaves, soldiers, or craftsmen, he slaughtered everyone else—children, women, men. After the capture of Urgench, each of the 50,000 Mongols was assigned the task of executing twenty-four survivors—1.2 million people.* The Khwarazmian empire was a particular annoyance, and Genghis ordered the obliteration of the kingdom: citizens, cities, towns, royal buildings, and even farmland. After Genghis's victory in the Battle of the Thirteen Sides, the surviving enemy troops were 'measured against the linchpin': the soldiers walked past a very large wheel, and any who were taller than the axle's linchpin were beheaded.

In the Battle of Nishapur, Genghis's son-in-law Toghachar was killed. When the city was captured, the retribution was fierce:

> They then drove all the survivors, men and women, out on to the plain; and in order to avenge Toghachar it was commanded that the town should be laid waste in such a manner that the site could be ploughed upon; and that in the exaction of vengeance not even cats and dogs should be left alive.
>
> A daughter of Chingiz-Khan, who was the chief wife of Toghachar, now entered the town with her escort, and they slew all the survivors save only four hundred persons who were selected for their craftsmanship and carried off to Turkestan, where the descendants of some of them are to be found to this day.
>
> They severed the heads of the slain from their bodies and heaped them up in piles, keeping those of the men separate from those of the women and children. After which, when Toli decided to proceed to Herat, he left an emir with four hundred Taziks to dispatch in the wake of the dead all the survivors that they found.
>
> Flies and wolves feasted on the breasts of the *sadrs*; eagles on mountain tops regaled themselves with the flesh of delicate women; vultures banqueted on the throats of *houris*.†

Genghis continued this pattern across Asia and into Europe. The only positive seems to be that the efficiency and rapid movement of Genghis's conquests reportedly made the heinous luxury of deliberate torture unusual.‡ But it by no means eliminated torture. There was the execution of Inalchuq,

---

* Needless to say, many historians question this total. By this point, however, the reader may have come to suspect that many of our historical estimates of slaughter have been low.

† *Sadr* is chest, or bust; *houri* is a beautiful woman, probably a virgin. John Andrew Boyle, *Genghis Khan: The History of the World Conqueror* (Manchester University, 1997).

‡ We would probably do well to avoid statements such as, "The Mongols did not torture, mutilate, or maim." War is all three. Jack Weatherford, *Genghis Khan and the Making of the Modern World* (Broadway Books, 2005).

who had molten silver poured in his eyes and ears. There was also the execution of Prince Mstislav and his generals after the capture of Kiev, who were dispatched by placing floor planks over them. The victims suffocated as the Mongols sat atop the boards for a victory feast.

As with all conquest, the death tolls under Genghis's campaigns are widely disputed. In China alone, the numbers range anywhere from a dubious low of three million up to a high of sixty million.[138] One author suggests a population drop of over 80 percent, from sixty million to ten million.[139] An objective approach is through census figures: taxes are essential to any government, and accurate and effective taxation requires an accurate census.* The Jin of northern China recorded 7.6 million households before the arrival of the horde; Genghis's subsequent census in 1234–6 CE reports only 1.7 million households. This suggests a population drop of at least 75 percent, and possibly more, as slaughter is not a per-household event: there were not only fewer households, but also arguably fewer people within surviving households. This approach adds credibility to the highest estimates.

Even those, however, represent mortality estimates only for northern China. In the whole of Genghis's conquests, the total is much higher. His captured territories extended from the Pacific coast through the bulk of Asia and into western Europe. Some scholars have argued that the higher death estimates are not credible or that they are not even possible.[140] First, my intention in this chapter is to lend credibility to such numbers. For instance, consider that Julius Caesar reportedly killed over a million people in Gaul. Modern France comprises an area of about 640,000 km², which allows for a very rough comparison: Genghis's Mongols conquered over 24 million km², about thirty times as much territory as Caesar captured. Extrapolating that land ratio to Caesar's death toll yields an estimated 37 million potential dead by Genghis. We need to remember, however, that northern China alone may have suffered a drop larger than that. In addition, we considered that Rome penetrated the less populated areas of Europe where there were fewer large cities.† Genghis, in contrast, conquered many densely populated urban centers of Asia. Given those observations, the higher casualty estimate of 60 million deaths becomes not only credible, it may also be conservative yet.

---

* In fact, there is much evidence that writing—and therefore much of civilization—is largely the product of the king's early need and greed for accurate accounting.

† The Battle of Alesia, which concluded Caesar's Gallic campaigns, is one of the better-known sieges in the conquests. During the siege the city swelled to perhaps eighty thousand people, many of them refugees from the local environs. Given that, it would seem that Alesia was probably less than sixty thousand people under normal circumstances, much smaller than the cities of Egypt and Asia.

Shaka Zulu

Shaka, or Shaka Zulu, was the king who led the Zulu nation to a brief period of dominance in south Africa. He changed warfare in the region, and his conquests began a domino effect, continued by his successors, that resulted in the *Mfecane*, a great shuffling of peoples, tribes, and power across the southern half of Africa.

Shaka accomplished this, predictably, through horrific and indiscriminate human slaughter. It is estimated that in his twelve years in power, between one and two million people were killed.

By and large, the conquerors we have seen to this point committed their butchery primarily in pursuit of wealth or power; Shaka's behavior suggests that he was motived by an intense sadism as well. He once had his men strip off their sandals and dance on thorns. Those who objected, or who even failed to keep the rhythm, were executed. He buried entire regiments of his own men alive.

And of course, he took them to war. Previously, war among the tribes of the region was largely a ceremonial affair, more bravado than butchery. In traditional warfare, the men of much of sub-Saharan Africa boasted and insulted each other while women and children watched nearby. In his battle against the Butelezi, Shaka changed all of this. He had trained his men to suddenly sweep around the flanks of his opponent and kill everyone. When some of the Butelezi men fled into the spectators, Shaka's men pursued and killed them as well, along with the children, the women, and the aged.[141]

Shaka committed slaughter against his own people as casually as his enemies, at times for no reason at all. Europeans regularly witnessed him giving the sign toward some person or persons, who were instantly executed, no explanation given, no questions asked. Once Shaka reportedly ordered the execution of sixty boys under the age of twelve, before he had eaten his breakfast.[142]

The method of execution was often brutal:

> It has often excited my pity, admiration, and astonishment to witness the fortitude and dignified calmness with which a Zoola will go forth to execution and receive his death blow. No fetters or cords are ever employed to bind the Zoola culprit; he is left at liberty to run for his life or to stand and meet his doom. Many do run, but few escape; for, alas! every man they meet is an enemy; many stand and meet their fate with a degree of firmness that could hardly be imagined.
>
> The cruel and barbarous manner by which criminals are put to death, is shocking to humanity. There are no regular executioners; that would be

superfluous where every one appears to have a savage gratification in the horrid and revolting employment, and all are ready to carry out the most sanguinary orders of the king or an enraged chief. The victim is first stunned by a blow on the head with a club, which, when well directed, terminates his sufferings at once; but it often happens that he is merely stunned, and the moment the wretched man falls to the ground, a sharp pointed stake (which is already prepared) is introduced behind and thrust up the abdomen, and being in this manner skewered, he is thrown into the nearest thicket or jungle.[143]

When Shaka's mother died, the king was overcome with grief, and over the course of the next few hours, perhaps sixty thousand of his subjects gathered around him. Shaka then ordered some of them executed. This precipitated a mélée in which people were executed while they were executing others. Anyone who was not crying convincingly enough, who stopped for food, water, or rest, or who for any reason stood out from the others, was executed. An estimated seven thousand were dispatched over the next few hours.

Then Shaka ordered girls and women executed so that they could be buried with his mother, to serve her in the next world. He also had the arms and legs of ten young maidens broken, and they were buried alive with the others. Thereafter, he set a guard of twelve thousand men to guard her grave for the next year.

Perhaps those who died quickly and early in the mourning period suffered the least. Over the next year, Shaka ordered no farming; milk was not to be consumed, it was all to be spilt on the ground; and no sex, any woman found pregnant was to be executed with her husband. The loss of farming and milking ensured the starvation of untold thousands, and the execution of pregnant women with their spouses left behind countless orphans.[144]

His power and bloodlust rampaged unchecked. At one point, he became curious about pregnancy and ordered one or more pregnant women cut open alive so that he might examine their viscera and the unborn child. In this, Shaka may have finally gone beyond the pale: two of his half-brothers assassinated him soon after. Ironically, they murdered him with his own invention, the *iklwa* short spear,[145] so named for the grisly sucking sound it made when yanked from a victim's body.

• • •

We opened this chapter with Hitler's atrocities. But while Hitler led Germany during WWII, Joseph Stalin ruled Russia and the Soviet Union, and Mao

Zedong controlled China. In the Soviet Union Stalin murdered, by weapon or starvation, over twenty million people. That's fewer than those who died in Hitler's battles, but we must remember that Stalin overwhelmingly killed his own people: Russians, Ukrainians, Poles, and others. As for Mao, he was responsible for the deaths of an estimated forty million of his fellow Chinese.

Then there are the second-tier monsters of the twentieth century.

Idi Amin

Dictator Idi Amin was reviled as 'The Butcher of Uganda.' He created a reign of horror resulting in the torture and murder of anywhere from one hundred thousand to five hundred thousand people in a country of only ten million. The stories are chilling. Amin was widely reported to indulge in cannibalism of his victims. One wife was found dismembered and sewed back together, with arms sewed to her hips, thighs to her shoulders. His political prisoners were often forced to kill one another with pickaxes and hammers, with the survivors executed by bayonet or bullet. Early in his career, his men executed soldiers from rival ethnic groups by driving them into a barracks and dynamiting them; mowing them down with machine guns; or hacking them to death. His vengeance was unrestrained; he murdered an archbishop, the Chief Justice of the Supreme Court, and any number of journalists and editors. So many dead victims were dropped into the Nile for the crocodiles to eat that their bodies clogged the intake pipes of the Kampala hydroelectric plant. Even though he held office for only eight years, Amin set a pattern of repression and brutality that continued, and expanded, in Uganda over the next several dictators who succeeded him.[146]

Kim Jong-il

North Korea is perhaps the most secretive and impenetrable nation in the world, currently ruled by the third member of the Kim dynasty, Kim Jong-un, who was preceded by his father, Kim Jong-il, and his grandfather, Kim Il-song. All three make for fascinating, horrifying case studies of dysfunctional, oppressive, and narcissistic dictators. The country is so secretive, it is not clear how many have died under the three dictatorships, but the estimates vary widely, from half a million to six million. During the 1995–98 famine, North Korea admitted that 250,000 perished; experts believe the numbers are much higher. There are so many children orphaned from executions and starvation that the railroad companies hire men with shoot-to-kill orders to stop their thieving. There are rumors that the stews sold near the railroads are made from the orphans' corpses.

The regime achieved a level of totalitarian fanaticism not often seen in the modern world. Citizens are executed for trying to escape the country but also for sundry minor offenses such as adultery, prostitution, resisting arrest, or simply disorderly conduct. Four students were reportedly executed for streaking while drunk. Jailings are common for infractions as minor as sitting on newspapers on which a picture of Kim Jong-il is displayed. Entire families are jailed for the behavior of an ill-mannered child. Punishment for organized resistance is meted out over 'three generations': parents, grandparents, siblings, cousins, nieces, and nephews are all punished.[147]

The sheer audacity of Kim Jong-il's cult of personality, however, was remarkable even by historical standards. In his very first attempt at golf, he reportedly hit five holes-in-one and scored a 38-under-par score of 34.[148] His first attempt at bowling yielded a perfect score of 300. He coached the coach during the 2010 World Cup via an 'invisible cell phone'—a technology Kim invented himself.[149] The short, pudgy man fancied himself an irresistible ladies' man, and North Korean media claimed that he was an expert on both film and the Internet, in a country that has few theaters and little electricity.

Reportedly, he also never urinated or defecated.[150]

Pol Pot & the Khmer Rouge

In a brief four years, one of the most chilling modern regimes emerged in Cambodia/Kampuchea, which obliterated the social and political fabric of the country. The Khmer Rouge—'Red Cambodians'—arose so quickly, and operated so secretively, it was some time before outsiders could even identify that the leader of the totalitarian regime was Pol Pot.

The Khmer Rouge operated under such strict ideological fervor that there was simply no room left for decency. Families were ripped apart to live separately and herded together to die.[151] Children were indoctrinated not only to spy on and to inform on their parents, but also when necessary, to execute them as well. Parents who were tortured might also be forced to watch their own children slowly tortured first.[152]

There was an overt loathing of anything hinting of education, intelligence, independent thought, or the exotic. Anyone standing out for any reason was killed along with their families. No one was spared, even babies were smashed against trees or impaled: "The Pol Pot soldiers have evil powers...; some of them had *gōn krahk* (roasted fetuses) which gave them power... I saw the

Khmer Rouge throw babies up in the air, and impale them on knives...; they cut the livers out of the children they killed...; oh god, they were so evil."[153]

One man describes confronting a former high-ranking guard named Lor at the infamous prison, Tuol Sleng:

> First of all, I wanted to know what happened to the little children who were taken from their mothers. I could hear both the mothers and children crying and screaming when this happened. I asked Lor, "Where did you take the children? Where were they taken care of?" He replied, "There wasn't any plan [to care] for them. They were taken away and killed." I didn't know that they had been killed! I imagined that the children had been cared for at some center. I couldn't believe it. Some of the children were newborns, others four or five months old, others five or six years old. They killed them all!

On a particularly busy day, the execution schedule from Tuol Sleng lists the names of eighty-five children who were "smashed."[154]

Children were torn from their families when they were six and raised by young soldiers. "The result was tragic: there was no play, no grooming, no growing up for children from six years of age who boarded in the dormitories. Their lives were Dickensian, they were political orphans with no proper care or teachers. Some saw and partook in unspeakable cruelty. All were denied affection."[155]

The children were taught obedience and brutality. By the time they were adolescents, they were remorseless automatons:

> Pran says he was always most afraid of those Khmer Rouge soldiers who were between 12 and 15 years old; they seemed to be the most completely and savagely indoctrinated. "They took them very young and taught them nothing but discipline. Just take orders, no need for a reason. Their minds have nothing inside except discipline. They do not believe any religion or tradition except Khmer Rouge orders. That's why they killed their own people, even babies, like we might kill a mosquito. I believe they did not have any feelings about human life because they were taught only discipline."[156]

And because the Khmer Rouge had executed almost all of the educated classes, these children were thrown into no-win situations as replacements for the murdered professionals, with predictable results. "The answer was this class of barefoot children, nervously trying to repair broken mechanical parts, memorizing how to thread wires in a dynamo."[157]

In those brief four years, it is estimated that over two million people— an estimated 25 percent of the total population—died, about 12 percent of them murdered, the other half dead from starvation and disease.

OTHERS

The examples in this chapter are only a brief sample from history of the atrocities committed in the name of conquest—there are many others. At the inception of the twentieth century, King Leopold of Belgium caused the deaths of an estimated eight million in Congo, with countless tortures and maimings, as he extracted gold, diamonds, and other wealth from the country. There were the massacres of the Armenians at the hands of the Turks, perhaps 1.5 million people. The Russian Civil War preceded Stalin's massacres and cost, it is believed, nine million lives. In WWII we must also consider the Japanese, who were responsible for perhaps thirty million deaths.[158] There were about five million dead from the First Chinese Civil War, 2.5 million in the Second. Over four million died in the Second Indochina War, to which Americans contributed through their involvement in Vietnam.

There are many others: Ethiopia, 2 million; Nigeria, 1 million; Bangladesh, 1.3 million; Sudan, 1.9 million; the Mexican Revolution, 1 million. It seems endless. And pointless.

Unless we are prepared to argue that somehow human brutality suddenly worsened in the past century despite the growth of human knowledge and the expansion of social progress in recent centuries, then we are left with a repulsive conclusion: twentieth century atrocities, Hitler included, were the continuation of horror throughout civilization.

Evil is, indeed, banal.

• • •

In 1995, a young American graduate student arrived in London to examine the colonial archives of a brutal uprising in 1950s Africa. She was highly impressed with the measured and civilized response of the British toward the rebellious tribes, particularly how the British used detention camps to re-educate the detainees via civics classes and vocational training. She was so impressed, in fact, that she decided to focus her dissertation on the high-minded British management of the problem.

This, perhaps, is a caution against putting too much lipstick on pigs. Had the British not portrayed themselves in such glowing terms, the graduate student might have turned her attentions elsewhere. But she did not, and when she arrived in Africa to examine the colonial documents there, she gradually became aware that something was wrong. The meticulous British had destroyed troves of colonial records, bonfiring the overlapping archives from three dif-

John Harris and Edgar Stannard are photoed with Bompenju, Lofiko (brothers of Nsala, next page), and a third person, holding the severed hands of Lingomo and Bolengo, who have allegedly been killed by sentries of the Belgian ABIR. Picture captured by Alice Seely Harris in Baringa.

ferent departmental offices. She was puzzled as to why many of the surviving records still remained classified fifty years after the end of colonial rule.

Her concerns only grew, and what emerged after a decade of research was Caroline Elkins's *Imperial Reckoning: The Untold Story of Britain's Gulag in Kenya*.[159] As is often the case with strong investigative research, much of the truth emerged from what was missing. The official detainee numbers seemed low when compared to the lists of names in other records. There were not nearly enough women listed. No records clearly outlined the chain of command, nor was there so much as an inventory of all the detainee camps. What records did remain revealed almost no complaints nor major problems; overwhelmingly, the surviving documents were flattering. With time, Elkins slowly pieced together that, despite the official reports, twenty thousand people were not detained in Kenya. Instead, almost the entire ethnic nation of 1.5 million Kikuyu were incarcerated in concentration camps.

Then she began interviewing the survivors and even some of their British oppressors. They described indescribable horrors of beatings, torture, rape, murder, and the use of tools and machines to crush breasts, injure and kill women vaginally, to rip the testicles from men, and to rend people into lifeless gobbet. In some camps there was even an apparent campaign of infanticide: large numbers of infants and toddlers who were given 'immunizations'

Nsala of Wala in Congo looks at the severed hand and foot of his five-year-old daughter, 1904

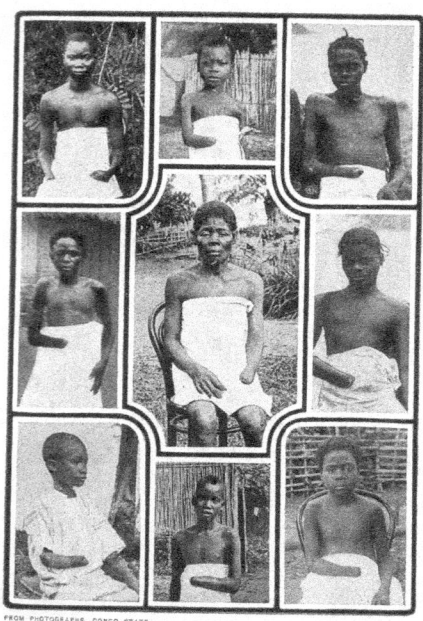

Mutilated children from the Belgian Congo

died within a few days. Mixed in with these stories were the mundane horrors: children and adults living in filth and privation behind barbed wire, slowly starving to death and succumbing to thirst, exposure, disease, and simple despair.

Because so few records remain, there is no way to know how many Kenyans died. But when compared to nearby populations, the country appears to be missing some 130–300,000 Kikuyu, many more than the officially reported eleven thousand combatant deaths.[160]

The book was a revelation to historians and an advancement in historiographic investigation. Surviving Kikuyu are filing claims against the British government for reparations. And for her efforts, Elkins won the Pulitzer Prize.

Imperial Reckoning exposes a recurring pattern. The slaughter of Koreans at No Gun Ri was not originally recorded nor reported, and the story emerged only after decades. The slaughter at My Lai came to light only after some months and only at the urging of outsiders. There is the Missing Massacre of Alexandria, in which it is inescapable that tens, perhaps hundreds of thousands of Egyptians died, but no deaths were reported or recorded, and for which scholars have ignored the obvious lapse. And there is the omission of British atrocities from *The Encyclopedia of Genocide*. British cover-ups continued even into the 1960s when Iain Macleod, Secretary of State for the Colonies, directed that the governments of former colonies should be prevented from getting any material that "might embarrass Her Majesty's government" or that could "embarrass members of the police, military forces, public servants or others eg police informers."[161] The three British examples raise questions about what other Victorian massacres remain hidden, given the Victorians' unrivaled conquest of the world. Those in turn beg the question about under-reporting of atrocities in all conquest. White-washing is a recurrent, constant obstacle to assessing the full impact of conquest and governmental oppression.

We noted the body counts from twentieth-century conflicts—but only those that claimed one million or more lives. As the size of the slaughter diminishes, the records decrease geometrically. In coming chapters, we will cover speculations that, in the medieval period at least, it is possible that more people died from raiding than warfare. It is quite possible that the smaller skirmishes, and the 'collateral damage' of killed civilians, claimed more lives than the big wars for which we have better body counts.

Even if we limit our considerations to major warfare, we must still wonder: How much of the atrocity and horror throughout history is permanently missing? We have no record for many, probably the overwhelming majority, of wars throughout civilization: Troy was havocked not once, but on at least nine occasions; the walls of Jericho fell over twenty times. Those, however, are among the few cities for which we can estimate, because our historical records have ensured that they have been meticulously excavated. How many cities disappeared, but unlike the *Chehel Minar*, left no durable markers to suggest that they ever existed? How many forgotten cities were repeatedly razed, but never recorded, and therefore never excavated?

How many modern cities are built over literal holocaust: lives and civilizations reduced to a slender layer of ash, buried deep in the archaeological record?

⋯

Currently in U.S. political and military circles, there has been much talk about the fact that, up through WWII, the United States had never been defeated. Since then, however, she has never clearly triumphed in any major conflict. Many argue that to resolve the problem, the U.S. needs to invest more heavily in military capability.

This seems an unlikely solution. The men and women who serve today are as brave, intelligent, and well-trained as any who have ever served. The brass may not always make good decisions, but when one reads the histories of WWII, WWI, the Civil War, and really, any of our wars, it emerges that many of our generals and senior officers have often seriously blundered, and many were simply incompetent. As for our financial investment in military capability and technology, in a subsequent chapter we will see that not only are the United States armed forces without rival in the world, but also all other nations reflect a small fraction of our investment, power, and capability.

The real problem is the changing nature of warfare. It is tempting to say that warfare has *recently* changed for the worse, but this chapter makes it clear that if it has changed, it is moving back to what it always was.

But even that is inaccurate. For a few recent centuries, warfare in Europe became codified; it was conducted as a 'civilized' bloodsport, largely among relatives in the royal families, and it followed rules, traditions, and accepted customs. In the Civil War, Union forces sent a message to General Robert E. Lee that his son Rooney had been captured but was safe. Early in WWI, Grand Duchess Marie-Adélaïde of Luxembourg delayed a German column by simply parking her automobile across the road. Also in WWI, pilots registering a 'kill' might send a bottle of champagne to the fallen pilot's mess tent. For a brief time, war was a gentleman's game of human slaughter, where land was wagered like poker chips. Except for that brief slice of time and place, however, warfare has been very much what the advanced countries face in modern conflicts: terror.

And the conqueror, as we have seen, responded to focused guerrilla terror with much greater terror and widespread military horror. Recall that when the Sicarii and other Jewish rebels resisted Roman rule, Titus destroyed the entirety of Jerusalem. Over the next century, the Jews attempted two additional uprisings against Rome; both were also savagely crushed. This put an end to Jewish uprisings for a couple of centuries. We saw similar retributions from Napoléon and other conquerors. We covered some of the British retaliations in India, and American retaliations against the Native Americans and in the

Philippines. Massive horror and lethal force are very effective in subjugation. People stop fighting back, and they conform to authority. At least they do for a while; with time and forgetfulness, they may try again.

So throughout history, the successful response to terrorism has been widespread horror, even annihilation. The My Lai massacre was typical of military responses against any community suspected of resisting the conqueror. Slaughtering insurgents' families is the time-tested method for dissuading opposition.

The problem today is that we no longer have the stomach for that level of brutal suppression; egalitarian ideals won't allow for retaliation against uninvolved noncombatants. So what has changed over the past 240 years of increasingly democratic warfare is the American warrior and the warriors of the developed nations. We have become more humane, more middle class, and more civilized. By and large, soldiers from the advanced countries are no longer allowed to be terrorists.

But all other soldiers were. And our adversaries today still are.

• • •

I have a friend who once surprised me by announcing that the Holocaust did not happen. He noted (accurately enough) that there weren't even six million Jews in 1930s Germany. He also insisted that Zyklon B is an insecticide (which was its original intended purpose) and that it was not used to kill Jews, but only to de-louse them.

I have had modest success in getting him to expand his considerations. I pulled up Internet numbers that showed that the majority of the Nazis' six million Jewish victims were from countries other than Germany, and he dropped that objection. I haven't yet had any luck getting him to reconsider his thoughts on Zyklon B.

I should note that in many ways he is an admirable person. He is a single father, intensely devoted to his children. He is very loyal to his friends, he is highly skilled and knowledgeable in his profession, and he is compassionate toward his patients. It's just that he lives in a deep red state, he talks with very few people who don't share his views, and he and his closest friends almost exclusively get their news from the alt-right media. In addition, he's never met a Jew.

There is a great deal of scholarship focusing on the Holocaust, its horrors, and how it was unprecedented. I am not disagreeing with any of that work; my concerns are pragmatic. I worry that by focusing on what was unusual and unique about the Shoah, rather than what was common and perennial in so many historical persecutions, we inadvertently provide aid and comfort to the enemy. Our position invites Holocaust deniers to scoff and to take an unexpected next step: it is absurd to believe that something is unique in history, so it is more likely that it never happened at all.

This book is an impassioned argument for a more inclusive, tolerant, and humane perspective. Which is important, because *ex*clusion, *in*tolerance, and *in*humanity were the starting point for the Nazi atrocities. I can see no path to a better world that does not emphasize the universal and shared humanity among us, in both war and peacetime, throughout history.

So rather than respond to the Holocaust deniers with more facts, more documents, and more photographs, I choose a different tack. I agree that Hitler was certainly a fiend, but I argue that he was, unfortunately, a very usual fiend: the scope of his crimes may have been new, the virulence of his racism may have been new, but his cruelty and malice were very old. That is a critical insight, because we do not need to search far to find those who seek to replace him, and continue his horrors. The depressing, redundant carnage, and the extended length and breadth of this chapter, were important: we need to recognize that Hitler is still among us, biding his time and slowly sapping away at the walls of the modern citadel.

I have other concerns. We can certainly count bodies in the horrors of history. But what metric have we to compare the horror and the suffering that each victim endured? It is not a peripheral question. I insist it is central; it is the conqueror who only counts the discounted lives. The moralist and the humanist, on the other hand, always begin with the individual and the humane, even the mundane. From there, she[162] builds out in an effort to create compassion and justice.

The late historian Eugen Weber once asked whether Nazi anti-Semitism, "was not mainly about Jews, any more than football is about the ball that gets kicked around?"[163] I would add to his consideration President Kennedy's insistence, "*Ich bin ein Berliner.*" Nazi Germany made it clear that law, patriotism, contribution, and public participation are insufficient to completely protect any of us. I argue that the most durable protections are cultural traditions that include the recognition that we are, all of us, Jews; and Congolese, Cambodians, Ukrainians, Mexicans, North Koreans, Poles, Somalis, Rwandans, and countless others. Identifying the universal in the Holocaust means we identify the universal in us all: the shared humanity, the empathy, the compassion.

And the horror. Because when the conqueror returns, we all become Jews among Nazis. If we do not work together to stop persecution of everyone, sooner or later all of us, each in turn, become the victims. As ancient tombstones announced, *Hodie mihi cras tibi*: "Today it's me, tomorrow it's you."

The ancient Romans terrorized children with their version of the boogieman, "*Hannibal ad portas!*" "Hannibal is at the gates!" Today we must constantly terrorize ourselves by repeating, *Hitler ad portas*. That, perhaps, is the highest purpose of Holocaust studies: to teach us that Hitler and a long line of would-be Hitlers are always at the gates. We are always one demagogue away, we are always one angry, jaded electorate away, from letting Hitler slip back inside the walls of civilization, assemble his brutalizers, and resume his slaughter.

To these concerns, we must also add the worry that just as we all are potential Jews, we are all potential Nazis as well. We will look at this in subsequent chapters, but the problem is as psychiatrist Robert Simon noted in the title of his book, *Bad Men Do What Good Men Dream*.[164] To protect ourselves and each other, we must become aware that we are all recovering alcoholics, we all have the potential to relapse into Nazism. The solution is that we recognize and constantly guard against the pitiless and the evil within ourselves as well as in others. That is our best hope for ending Holocausts once and forever.

Because right now, the dangers and the realities are pressing. All over the world, right-wing demagogues are emerging. If we are to prevent further Holocausts, it is critical that we focus upon the depressing commonness of evil. The banality of evil extends far beyond Adolph Eichmann and the Nazis. We need to be clear that the Holocaust was unique in the particular. But in the general, it was the constantly recurring nightmare of civilization.

That, I believe, is the solution to Holocaust denial: we must recognize the recurrence of human persecution. Horror is our past. If we do not embrace that fact, it will also be our future, over and over, until we finally do learn to understand and to control it.

Or until we disappear from the planet.

• • •

I have tried here to dispel the romance of our traditions and to lay out a more accurate view of the conqueror. But that presents a problem of semantics. First of all, the romance still exists. The word 'conqueror,' and in some quarters the even sketchier equivalent, 'conquistador,' still carry lofty, respectable connotations, and we often conflate them with justice, honor, compassion, wisdom, and other virtues.

Enlarging the problem, successful conquerors become kings, and as we have seen here and in the preceding chapter, the king must continue the conqueror's viciousness in order to retain his power and prerogative.

The term 'king' also poses problems. It is an English term and is tied to Western traditions. We need to include all rulers, sovereigns, monarchs, *etc.*

Then there is the problem that not all invaders became kings. Some raiders, such as the Vikings, comprised smaller gangs who simply looted towns and villages and then returned home or moved on to other victims. So we need a term that will allow us to consider raiders with conquerors, and both of them with monarchs.

But we must exclude many modern monarchs. As we noted, Elizabeth II, Akihito, or Pope Francis hardly qualify as vicious, avaricious monarchs, although their predecessors did. Those earlier monarchs are indistinguishable from the dictators and political strongmen of today. The fact that we believe the two are different and give them different names is an example of my thesis here: we have culturally white-washed the king's repulsiveness and have repainted him as a fairy tale. Review the portrait of Henry VIII; everything in the painting, and the painting itself, is designed to hide the thuggish reality. The reason we differentiate between king and dictator is because the modern version demolishes our romantic traditions.

So we also need a word that includes raiders, conquerors, vicious monarchs, and modern dictators, but excludes the modern monarch who has no interest in conquest. To address this problem I introduce the term *atrox*, Latin for 'horrible' or 'cruel,'* from which we derive, appropriately enough, the word 'atrocity.'

⋯

I anticipate that some critics will object that I have cherry-picked from the worst atrocities of history, and so we should not draw conclusions. My examples are indeed cherry-picked but in the other direction. I began by focusing on the 'best,' by examining those conquerors and cultures whom we most esteem. I moved on to the 'worst' only once the pattern was established. If there is still doubt that the pattern holds with all conquerors and successful kings, I invite the reader to simply perform an Internet search by combining the name of an earlier monarch for whom we have any reasonable history with the words 'atrocities,' 'torture,' 'assassination,' 'execution,' 'war,' or similar. It

---

* The Latin root *atro-* means 'dark,' as in 'dark matter'; but it could also relate to the dark triad and the dark tetrad we will address in the next chapter. It is interesting that darkness also relates to the color black and to nighttime, favored by criminals and terrorizing soldiers alike.

makes no difference whom we examine. As we noted, for all of the cultural and intellectual differences between ancient Athens and Sparta, in conquest the differences became moot.

We must reconsider our traditions. Consider what a conqueror represents: he is not a Washington, fighting to escape a distant king; he is not an Eisenhower, defending his country and the modern world against a fiendish coalition; he is not even a Robert E. Lee or one of many other Confederate generals, conflicted men, uncomfortable with secession, and perhaps even opposed to war itself. There is no room for romance here: conquerors are murderers and thieves on a national level. They were not like the worst of our criminals, men furtively skulking toward carefully-chosen targets, attacking in secret, and victimizing a few dozen people. No, conquerors are much worse. They march through the streets, torturing and slaughtering in broad daylight, and brazenly victimizing millions. They are the worst criminals in history. As we will see throughout this book, other interpretations are romance and rationalization. They ignore the obvious facts.

Or worse, they ignore the *defining* facts. I cannot see how the five points I introduced in the prologue are not axioms: Conquest is murder and theft; Conquerors are vicious criminals; Conquerors become kings; Kings designed civilization; And we are the products of civilization.

This presents four problems that we will pursue for the remainder of this book:

1) How and why have we rationalized and whitewashed the conqueror's crimes for ten thousand years?

2) How did we arrive at the illogic of praising and even idolizing history's worst criminals?

3) How did the conqueror's criminal dysfunctions affect his subjects and his realms, and how do they continue to hobble us today?

4) How might we begin to escape ten thousand years of codependency with history's worst criminals?

We face the problem of the emperor's new clothes: for millennia we have been immersed in a culture that has trained us to ignore logic and even the naked facts before us, to defer to authority and tradition and join the king's cult of personality. As such, critics of the narrative here may find themselves in a thicket. If they object to my thesis while ignoring the five points above, they will be defending tradition and dogma in the face of confounding logic and overwhelming evidence. They will find themselves caught in the uncomfortable irony of demonstrating the behaviors they wish to refute.

Chapter III:
Psychopaths

> *I've always believed society to be a fundamentally rational thing, but what if it wasn't? What if it was built on insanity?*
>
> –Jon Ronson

> *We are mad, not only individually, but nationally. We check manslaughter and isolated murders; but what of war and the much vaunted crime of slaughtering whole peoples?*
>
> –Seneca

> *Q: How many psychiatrists does it take to change a light bulb?*
> *A: Only one. But it takes a very long time, and the light bulb has to really want to change.*

> *A man is brutally beaten and robbed in broad daylight. As he lies unconscious and bleeding, a psychiatrist rushes up to him and exclaims, "My God! Whoever did this needs help!"*

> *Psychopaths build castles in the sky.*
> *Neurotics live in them.*
> *Psychiatrists collect the rent.*

Psychiatrists are the butt of many jokes, which is unfair and unhelpful. Psychiatrists are not intellectually inferior to other physicians. And the suffering of the psychiatric patient is a real problem, for the patient and for society.

Psychiatry is a complicated field of study and one that is not often given to simple, straight forward diagnostics. The diseases in mental health can be difficult to define and distinguish, and are therefore controversial. In addition, the course of therapy is unpredictable. This is unlike the rest of medicine: take this antibiotic for ten days and the infection will be cured; undergo this surgery and in two months you will back to normal. When psychiatrists change light bulbs, the time frame and the outcome are less predictable than with other specialties.

So we belittle mental hygienists for attempting to solve pressing but complex and confusing problems. In effect, we ridicule *them* for *our* ignorance.

This illustrates two problems that are important for our thesis. First, humanity has a tendency, even a need, to operate within simple and even simplistic paradigms that offer direct and immediate solutions to our problems. Often those simple solutions call for compulsory force and authoritarian control in order to support that directness and immediacy. Second, and from the first, we ridicule those who attempt to address complex systems that have no clear solutions and where brute force is unhelpful.

The vernacular contains many examples of the problem. People who consider complex, cerebral issues are 'highbrows,' 'longhairs,' 'stargazers,' 'bookworms,' 'nerds,' and 'geeks.' They are 'ivory tower' thinkers who 'lack common sense.' When they turn their attention to the complexities of emotional suffering, we criticize them as 'bleeding hearts' (note psychiatrist joke #2, above). The common classes, and even many in the professional classes, regard those who suggest that there are problems which are complex, escape easy solutions, and must be approached with pragmatism rather than simple ideology, are feeble, foolish, and sentimental. Again, we ridicule the wise for our ignorance; we laugh at the curious for our stupidity.* It presents an irony: ridiculing the study of insanity constitutes yet another insanity.

And so we ridicule ourselves into a corner. Many of the problems we face today—political, social, economic, commercial, cultural—involve highly complex systems that can be improved only with exactly the sort of patience, wisdom, and long-term commitment that mental hygiene requires. As we will see in this chapter, many of our most pressing problems arise from mental illness, and by deriding the psychological professions, we are excluding the best insights and strategies we have for healing our world and ourselves.

The problems of mental health are the problems of society. Mental illness is a difficult, confusing field where concepts necessarily evolve constantly and where diagnosis and therapy comprise great inconsistencies and differences of opinion. We must stray briefly into the weeds for these disagreements because by comparing the variations, we will be able to better understand the historical sources for some modern problems and be able to focus in on the probability clouds that surround the essential concepts.

• • •

---

* Ignorance means, "I don't know," which is inescapable. There will always be things we do not know. Stupidity, however, means "I don't know, and I don't want to know." That illogical approach is one of the things this book attempts to understand.

Early explorers returned from far-off lands with descriptions of magical horses, including the centaur, the unicorn, and the leviathan. The centaur is believed to have originated with the first horse riders, raiders out of the steppes of Asia who appeared to primitive peoples as half-man, half-horse. The rhinoceros is often speculated to be the inspiration for the unicorn, the fantastic horse with a horn in the middle of its head. The leviathan, on the other hand, is traditionally believed to refer to the whale or the crocodile, but a different interpretation is that it is the fearsome 'river horse,' or hippopotamus, possibly conflated with the rhinoceros.*

None of these are truly horses of course, although the centaur involved a horse, and the rhinoceros is a distant relative. The ancient people describing them were using the words they had, drawing on existing vocabulary to relay new information. This is almost always the case with new words and concepts. As we consider the etymologies of our words, we find that earlier people were constantly re-purposing older ideas and words to describe new experiences and concepts.

But there is really no other way to discuss new ideas except in terms of previously understood ones. Even a completely new word, one without an etymology—'blatant' seems to have been invented by Edmund Spencer from no clear precedent—still must have a definition, and that must be built from previously understood concepts.† The argument can be made, in fact, that any lengthy argument or exposition (including this book) retrofits older concepts to build new ones and then builds a string of new ideas into a new perspective or theory.

I will do what other explorers must do—re-purpose existing concepts. For our considerations, the older ideas will be taken from mental health and will be applied to historical figures. Specifically, I will re-purpose the diagnostic terms 'psychopathy,' 'narcissism,' 'Machiavellianism,' and 'malignant narcissism' in ways that the psychologist and psychiatrist may find imprecise and perhaps even objectionable.

I request great latitude. First, the psychiatric categories that I use may not

---

* Job 41 has the most complete Biblical description of the leviathan. Not all of those descriptions fit the hippopotamus, but neither do they fit any other living animal; although the 'plates' on the leviathan's back and the impenetrability of its hide might refer to the rhinoceros, which sports a very thick, tough skin. Unless the leviathan refers to a purely mythical creature, the hippopotamus seems a likely candidate.

† Lewis Carroll's "The Jabberwocky" might seem to violate this, but the neologisms Carroll generated often have no definitions. They have no agreed meaning, in part because they are not built from pre-existing words and ideas.

be perfect fits, but they are the best fits available. My hope is not to lay out definitive concepts for the practice of mental health, but to point to historical patterns that are related to our modern concepts and which overlap with them. People who have deeper understanding of these concepts are welcome to take these ideas, refine them, and re-purpose them yet again.

Second, new ideas must be handled gently. If early ideas are to become more useful and more accurate, they must be fostered and indulged at their birth so that they might develop and adapt as more useful tools with time.

Finally, even if I am not accurate in my usage of these terms, I believe that mental health professionals will recognize in the historical patterns an ancestry, perhaps even an ontogeny, for modern mental problems and gain insights into how they have become so widespread and harmful today. I am digging at a sort of psychiatric archaeology: I want to look at the possible origins of the modern psychiatric diagnoses from which I borrow. So although I am re-purposing older words, it is also possible to flip the perspective: I am suggesting that the modern problems are a re-purposing of older behaviors; and that perhaps the older behaviors have adapted to fit new realities.

Serial Killers

Serial killers are relatively rare; the FBI estimates that twenty-five to fifty are active in the United States at any one time. One of the nastiest was David Parker Ray, who operated in the U.S. Southwest in the 1990s. Ray went beyond rape and murder. He invested $100,000 soundproofing a trailer and outfitting it with chains, blades, saws, and homemade devices for sexual torture. He called it his 'Toy Box,' giving Ray the name he is remembered for: 'The Toy Box Killer.'

After he was arrested, investigators found an audio tape Ray made about one of his victims, a woman from whom he had previously contracted gonorrhea. He offered her $100 if she would let him tie her up for sex, and she agreed. He graphically describes the first steps for torturing the woman to death:

> She cooperated completely until I brought out a tube-tied breathing gag and a roll of duct tape.
>
> That cunt did not want to be gagged. But I got it in her mouth and put several wraps of duct tape around her head to hold it in place. To be double sure, I wrapped duct tape under her chin and over the top of her head several times so she couldn't open her jaws. She still wasn't too upset, just pissed off because I gagged her. I moved across the trailer, pulled the latches, and

let the bondage table down. That bitch took one look at the table and the rack that had been concealed behind it holding whips, harnesses, dildos and other devices related to bondage [snicker].

She came unglued!

She really got upset. I sat down beside her and told her in no uncertain terms what I thought of a whore who gave me the clap. About the aggravation, the problems with the girlfriends, the doctor bills, trips to the hospital, and that there was going to be a hell of a lot more retribution than just spanking: payback's a real motherfucker [snicker].

She just sat there trying to get loose and shaking her head back and forth— like No, no, no, but it was really Yes, yes, yes. I picked her up and sat her on the table, pushed her over on the middle of it, and positioned her on her back with her feet and arms pointed up. I held her that way and locked the chain around her neck that was attached to the table. That settled her down a little bit, but not much. A rope from the ceiling ring was tied to her ankles so she couldn't kick. The wrist bindings on the upper corner of the table consist of an adjustable chain that is attached to the corner of the table with a handcuff on the other end. Releasing one rope at a time, I secured her arms up to the upper corners of the table. Her legs were folded back, spread well apart, and also chained to the upper corners. That little whore was bouncing her ass all over the table while I finished strapping her down. I buckled table straps across her upper chest, her rib cage and her belly. Two more table straps were buckled over each side and pulled tight, holding her ass firmly down on the table. Two more straps went across the back of each knee, holding her legs securely down. That position gets uncomfortable as hell for a woman after a while, but it works pretty neat for me.

She was absolutely and totally immobilized. Couldn't move any part of her body at all except her head.[1]

His description continues with even more gruesome details. It is estimated that Ray torture-murdered sixty women in similar ways. There is no way to be sure; despite his conviction and imprisonment, no remains have been located. Ray was as shrewd as he was evil.[*]

Ray's Toy Box recalls Ashoka's Hell. We assume that the hell-master, Girika, enjoyed sadistic torture in much the same way as Ray does here, and when he wished, Girika was free to rape his victims repeatedly before he killed them. The interests of Ray, Girika, and Ashoka are comparable to the tortures used by Alexander, Catiline, and Torquemada. And every king: sadistic punishment was employed by virtually all monarchs and nobles before

---

[*] Ray died of a heart attack only a year into his sentence.

the modern period, through the rack, the *strappado*, drawing and quartering, and others. That is why this disturbing passage, brief and limited, is necessary. Like the descriptions of warfare in the previous chapter, we must abandon our romantic ideas and consider what torture really looks like.

Ray enjoyed total control, 'domination' of his victims. As noted, 'empire' means 'control.' Similarly, 'domination' comes to us from the Latin *dominus*, 'lord' or 'master,' the term for a nobleman. And for a slave owner. For most of history, there was little difference between the master of the realm and the master of the slave. 'Serf' and 'servant' are both variations of the Latin *servus*, 'slave.'* Domination and control are what the atrox and his men pursue, figuratively and literally, with people, cities, and nations. Ray desired to be what every king was, or could be if he wished.

Control is a major motivation for the most disturbing crimes. Consider that many rapists never achieve erection; for most sexual predators, rape is not about sex, but control, domination. Ray took this to the next step, combining rape with total bodily control. His victims could not resist, speak, or move. They could only suffer and conform to the fantasy that Ray wished them to be.

The desire for control and conformity unites the serial killer with the atrox. Conquerors are serial killers who prey on nations. The two are separated only by magnitude and brazenness: serial killers work covertly and victimize dozens. The conqueror attacks in broad daylight and publicly dominates, tortures, and murders millions.

Psychiatrist Michael Stone, host of the former forensic television series *Most Evil*, developed a scale of evil based on his study of murderers over years. His scale ranks notorious criminals, not only by their crimes, but also by their motivations. Manslaughter in self-defense is given a low rank; murder motivated by anger increases the ranking; those who kill out of emotionless practicality, perhaps to hide other crimes, are ranked higher; rape and sexual perversion fall above those; and torture is the strongest consideration. Combinations of these comprise different levels, and the highest level is reserved for people like David Parker Ray, who pursue them all: premeditated torture-murder with sexual domination. The same scale might be applied to conquerors. At the low end might appear a reluctant warrior like Dwight D. Eisenhower; on the same level as David Parker Ray might be Idi Amin.

---

* Strangely, slavery could be better than serfdom because a slave represented an economic investment. One example of the value of slaves comes from nineteenth-century New Orleans, where only the Irish were allowed into the hold of a ship for loading and unloading freight. The bowels of a ship in those days were dangerous places, and the shipowners had no economic interest (nor any other interest) in the well-being of the Irish.

Another serial torturer-murderer Stone considers is Jeffrey Dahmer, who raped, murdered, and dismembered at least seventeen young men and also committed cannibalism, but who acted out of curiosity as well—he dissected his victims and explored their internal organs. This compares to the accounts of cannibalism by the Crusaders and others, and of curious human dissection by Shaka Zulu.

Stone also examines John Wayne Gacy, the 'Killer Clown' who often appeared as 'Pogo the Clown' at children's parties, parades, and charitable events. Despite those laudable activities, Gacy sexually assaulted and murdered over thirty teenagers and young men in the Chicago area in the 1970s.

Homosexuality is a normal variant, but it is the homo*sadism* and the male objectification of Gacy, Dahmer, and so many conquerors that is striking. Male objectification and homosadism are often pronounced in warfare and military culture: the ideal of the uniformed and uniformly handsome, muscular, hirsute-less and beardless,* young soldier, who fearlessly and obediently charges forward to be ripped into meaty 'hunks.' †

Consider the photo of the Nazi soldiers at the Nuremberg Rallies. The soldiers are dressed identically, marching in step, and perfectly arranged; they are even the same height. The picture gives the impression that if the men were turned around, they would all be identical clones of the Aryan ideal.

This concept is picked up in the film franchise *Star Wars*, where the 'storm troopers'—frequent references to the Nazis appear in the film series—are indeed clones of one mercenary soldier. These images illustrate the atrox's desire to objectify us all and reduce us to idealized, interchangeable playthings.

---

* Beardless soldiers are illustrative. Alexander required that his soldiers shave, and at times Romans, Egyptians, and others have perpetuated those traditions. The arguments given for this decision are that an enemy could grasp a beard, or that beards carry lice. Those arguments seem to be countered by the many armies and soldiers throughout history who grew beards; if there were any major tactical advantage, it seems that beardlessness would have been more widespread.

† It is interesting that the objectifying and even dehumanizing term, 'a hunk,' is used by both heterosexual women and homosexual men to describe a tall, muscular, handsome young man.

The need for power that is inherent in sexual assault, and the sadism typical of the worst serial killers, is also reflected in conquest and totalitarian governments. The sadistic killer's desire for conformity and uniformity of his victims is standard military issue, as are dominance and submission. This is reflected in the objectification and homoeroticism that often appear in twentieth-century war propaganda, particularly during WWII. Nazi art is striking for these themes, but they can also be seen in U.S. propaganda as well, particularly as reflected in the art of J.C. Leyendecker and McClelland Barclay.* Conquerors objectify both their enforcers and their victims. The undercurrent of homosadism, however, warrants further consideration.

Returning to the rankings in *Most Evil*, Stone explores the crimes of Josef Mengele, the Nazi doctor who often decided who lived or died in the death camps. Mengele performed sadistic medical experiments on some of those he temporarily spared, including lethal, agonizing 'research' on children.

Hitler and the Nazis are the undercurrent of Stone's decades of work, as they are for much of this volume. They are also the *parti pris* for modern work on holocaust, genocide, massacre, and atrocity studies. It is one thesis of this book, however, that while Hitler expanded our awareness of evil, he did not invent it. Hitler's violence emerged from a long history of chronic violence and oppression; if Hitler was the worst, he was still one of the many convulsions in the thread of horror that runs through conquest and empire in all large pre-modern civilizations, and which continue today.

• • •

Scholarship into the evil of Hitler and the Nazis has often come from historians, ethicists, legal scholars, and many others in the humanities. Psychologists, sociologists, and anthropologists have added scientific approaches, and I wish to add to that latter scientific tradition by considering the dynamic between Hitler and his followers from biological and even medical perspectives. Before we can begin that, however, we must consider some confusions in our understandings of mental health.

---

* Barclay's art was largely heterosexual in its eroticism and often objectified women. His occasional work that appears to be homoerotic may simply reference the classical 'ideal.' That ideal of the athlete/soldier, however, reflect Greek and Roman ideals, cultures where homosexuality was acceptable; and among the Spartans it was, as we have seen, mandatory. This tradition, and the emergence of Alexander as the first major Western conqueror, add other reasons to speculate about the homosadistic aspects of our military traditions.

Psychopathy

Consider the term 'psychopath.' Perhaps because of Alfred Hitchcock's iconic film *Psycho*,[2] in popular usage the concept of psychopathy has become associated with uncontrolled violence and has also become conflated with 'psychotic,' a disease where the patient loses touch with reality and often hallucinates. To the layman, a 'psychopath' is someone who suffers from deranged thinking and who is given to out-of-control rage.

In contrast, the pure psychopath is completely rational, even hyper-rational, and he exhibits a self-control, particularly under pressure, that most normal people cannot approach. In fact, a key diagnostic for the psychopath is his 'low arousal state': the psychopath's resting pulse and blood pressure are both low and remain so when normal people would feel stress or panic. For this reason, people with psychopathic traits can provide strong leadership in chaotic situations. Various authors have noted that some psychopathic traits may be desirable in the field commander and the trauma surgeon.[3]

A low arousal state also helps the psychopath to lie convincingly, which is useful for a criminal, but also in a leader: the ability to calmly redirect the attention of people away from panic toward action, even by coloring the truth or outright lying, can help focus, unify, and motivate a group.

The psychopath, however, experiences diminished emotions in all dimensions, diminished fear and nervousness, but also diminished love and empathy. This means that he often lacks the moral dimension that empathy provides. Some authorities argue that almost all of the psychopath's dysfunctions can be explained by his low emotional responsiveness.

Unfortunately, psychopaths are not a uniform and homogeneous group. They are also subject to complex diagnostic criteria that frequently change, and to different interpretations that can disagree with one another. To use these criteria in order to understand the atrox, we must consider the variations among a few major approaches.

Cleckleyan Psychopathy

The problem of psychopathy had been discussed by various mental hygienists since the early nineteenth century, including scholars such as Philippe Pinel, Emil Kraepelin, and Kurt Schneider. Modern scholarship on the disease, however, was influenced by the American psychiatrist Herv Cleckley. In 1941, he published *The Mask of Sanity*, describing a group of unusual patients he had attempted to treat.[4] These were men and women who were irresponsible in their personal lives but who were nevertheless frequently charming. They often came from respected families and performed adequately in school, but broke their friends' and families' hearts by recurrent profligacy, dishonesty, and crime, most of it petty. They were sexually careless as well and were often indiscriminate and fleeting in their liaisons. Of particular importance for later considerations, they were generally nonviolent, and did not plan major crimes, although they might participate in them if recruited.

Cleckley published fifteen criteria for the diagnosis:

:: Superficial charm and good intelligence

:: Absence of delusions or other signs of irrational thinking

:: Absence of nervousness or neurosis

:: Unreliability

:: Untruthfulness and insincerity

:: Lack of remorse and shame

:: Inadequately motivated antisocial behavior (*i.e.*, the commission of social offenses and small crimes, but without typical motivation; the psychopath might steal a car but then abandon it out of boredom or distraction)

:: Poor judgment and failure to learn by experience

:: Pathologic egocentricity and incapacity for love

:: General poverty in major affective reactions (*i.e.*, emotional blunting in all dimensions: anger, fear, joy, depression, etc.)

:: Specific loss of insight

:: Unresponsiveness in general interpersonal relations

:: Fantastic and uninviting behavior with drink and sometimes without

:: Suicide threats rarely carried out

:: Sex life impersonal, trivial, and poorly integrated

:: Failure to follow any life plan.

In reading *The Mask of Sanity*, the impression is that many of Cleckley's psychopaths were likable scoundrels who were of limited danger to society.

Hare's Psychopathy Checklist

In 1980, psychologist Robert D. Hare published the *Psychopathy Checklist* (PCL), an assessment tool built from Cleckley's work. Hare's experiences with criminals and his study of criminology led him in 1991 to update the assessment to the PCL-R, the Psychopathy Checklist-Revised.

Hare's work focuses on different patient populations from Cleckley's. Cleckley's psychopaths were generally referred to care by family and friends, who provided a social safety net. Hare's psychopaths were major criminals, generally from unstable or abusive backgrounds.

The PCL-R criteria:

:: Glib and superficial charm

:: Pathological lying

:: Lack of remorse

:: Callousness

:: Poor behavioral controls

:: Impulsiveness

:: Irresponsibility

:: Parasitic lifestyle

:: Sexual promiscuity

:: Early behavior problems

:: Lack of realistic long-term goals

:: Many short-term marital relationships

:: Failure to accept responsibility for own actions#

:: Denial#

:: Grandiosity#

:: Need for stimulation#

:: Cunning and manipulating#

:: Juvenile delinquency#

:: Revocation of conditional release# (*i.e.*, parole violation)

:: Criminal versatility#

Note the last eight, marked with hashtags. These are characteristics that do not appear in Cleckley's criteria. The characteristic of grandiosity seems to run counter to Cleckley's requirement that the psychopath be free of delusions and other irrational thinking. It also seems to add a narcissistic dimension.

'Cunning' suggests a malicious, long-term goal, which requires planning. Cleckley's psychopaths certainly manipulated others, but most of them would not be considered 'cunning.' Rather, they seemed to largely live in the moment, had a low commitment to societal norms, and were unconcerned with the consequences of their actions. As for 'Failure to accept responsibility' and 'Denial' when confronted with their mischief, Cleckley's patients often freely admitted their involvement.

On the other hand, the 'Need for stimulation' fits very well with Cleckley's patients.

The PCL-R is an important advancement in the field, but there are two points to remember. First, Hare is looking at criminal psychopaths, which are a subset of the problem. Second, and again, we must remember the slipperiness of diagnostic certainty in the behavioral sciences.

APA ANTI-SOCIAL PERSONALITY DISORDER

In 1980, the year that Hare published his first PCL, the American Psychiatric Association published the third edition of the *Diagnostic and Statistical Manual of Mental Disorders* (DSM-3). In it, 'psychopathy' was renamed 'Anti-Social Personality Disorder' (ASPD).

The DSM-5 criteria is the most recent version:

> A) A pervasive pattern of disregard for and violation of the rights of others, occurring since age fifteen years, as indicated by three or more of the following:
>
> :: Failure to conform to social norms with respect to lawful behaviors as indicated by repeatedly performing acts that are grounds for arrest;
>
> :: Deception, as indicated by repeatedly lying, use of aliases, or conning others for personal profit or pleasure;
>
> :: Impulsivity or failure to plan ahead;
>
> :: Irritability and aggressiveness, as indicated by repeated physical fights or assaults;
>
> :: Reckless disregard for safety of self or others;

:: Consistent irresponsibility, as indicated by repeated failure to sustain consistent work behavior or honor financial obligations;

:: Lack of remorse, as indicated by being indifferent to or rationalizing having hurt, mistreated, or stolen from another.

B) The individual is at least age eighteen years.

C) There is evidence of conduct disorder with onset before age fifteen years.

D) The occurrence of antisocial behavior is not exclusively during the course of schizophrenia or a manic episode.

The DSM-5 has added to ASPD the criterion of "reckless disregard for safety of self or others," which fits well with the two preceding diagnostic frameworks. It also introduces, however, "irritability and aggressiveness," which seems to violate the concept of the low arousal state. The pure psychopath may fight for amusement or when cornered; but as we will see below, many psychopaths prefer a revenge that is as cold as their emotions.

WHO Dissocial Personality Disorder

In 1992, the World Health Organization (WHO) published the *International Statistical Classification of Diseases and Related Health Problems*, tenth edition (ICD-10). That reference offers another set of criteria and changes the name to 'Dissocial Personality Disorder', or DPD.

DPD is characterized by at least three of the following:

:: Callous unconcern for the feelings of others;

:: Gross and persistent attitude of irresponsibility and disregard for social norms, rules, and obligations;

:: Incapacity to maintain enduring relationships, though having no difficulty in establishing them;

:: Very low tolerance to frustration and a low threshold for discharge of aggression, including violence;

:: Incapacity to experience guilt or to profit from experience, particularly punishment;

:: Marked readiness to blame others or to offer plausible rationalizations for the behavior that has brought the person into conflict with society.

Note that the WHO has added, 'a very low tolerance to frustration and a low threshold for discharge of aggression, including violence.' This, as with 'irritability and aggression' in the DSM-5, seems to contradict the low arousal state. The WHO also includes "a readiness to blame others"; as noted, Cleckley's psychopaths would lie charmingly, but they also frequently admitted freely what they had done, either unconcerned with the consequences or relying on their charm to get them out of Dutch.

PSYCHOPATHIC PERSONALITY INVENTORY

In 1996, researchers Scott Lilienfeld and Brian Andrews generated another scale, the Psychopathic Personality Inventory:[5]

:: Machiavellian Egocentricity

:: Social Potency

:: Cold-heartedness

:: Carefree Non-planfulness

:: Fearlessness

:: Blame Externalization

:: Impulsive Nonconformity

:: Stress Immunity

One new consideration in the PPI is "Machiavellian egocentricity." It corresponds with Hare's 'cunning and manipulating' assessment in the PCL-R. The problem is in the name. Machiavelli's *The Prince* described ruthless but strategic leaders who had the patience and discipline to pursue long-term plans. As such, it seems to counter other items on the PPI list, 'Carefree Non-planfulness' and 'Impulsive Noncomformity,' although these latter two fit well with Cleckley. We will return to Machiavellianism.

SNAKES: BABIAK AND HARE

In 2006, Paul Babiak teamed up with Robert Hare to publish *Snakes in Suits*, looking at psychopaths in the workplace.[6] It was an important advance but presented a problem: there are several aspects of the PCL-R assessment that would prevent psychopaths from climbing the corporate ladder. These include poor behavioral controls; impulsiveness; early behavior problems; lack of realistic long-term goals; juvenile delinquency; revocation of conditional release; and criminal versatility. As a result, few of the corporate 'psychopaths' in the book would score the minimum 75 percent on Hare's PCL-R, and many might not score 65 percent. To address this difference the authors explain that psychopathy is a continuum. This nevertheless introduces an inconsistency between corporate snakes and criminal psychopaths.

Babiak and Hare also talk about problems inherent in corporations and other organizations that overlap with psychopathic behaviors. In effect, organizations can meet the psychopathic criteria, and that will be critical to our later discussions.

Babiak and Hare are correct; the diagnosis of psychopathy is a continuum. Cleckley looked at this, recounting patients who seemed normal at first but who experienced a shallow emotional life that showed up only with time and therapy.

Such people show up in all areas of medicine and in all walks of life.[7] Most of us have encountered those who might initially seem pleasant and engaging but whom we later decided to avoid. They often run low-level scams and attempt to manipulate and exploit the people around them, even their own spouses and children. With even minor power they can become sadistic and petty. When they are denied something they want, they may become vindictive. Many of them will hold their tongues in the moment but extract revenge anonymously at a later time. In a reflection of the psychopath, their families seem pleasant enough, but beneath the surface are often various dysfunctions, neuroses, and character disorders.

Then there are the patients I occasionally see, street people or recluses who show up in the emergency room when they are so sick they cannot avoid it. They seem to have no connection to others and no desire to interact with anyone else. They are not shy, they are simply cold and disinterested.

The problem is, none of the preceding completely fits the diagnostic categories we have discussed, and as we will see, many also exhibit crossover into other mental health problems.

Moral Psychopaths

These inconsistencies became more interesting after I stumbled across one of the most remarkable people I have encountered. I discovered James Fallon (the neuroscientist, not the comic) while researching the psychopathy of kings and conquerors. Fallon gave a talk to the Oslo Freedom Forum on 'The Mind of the Dictator,' in which he lays out arguments that are very similar to what I propose here: dictators fit many of the criteria for psychopathy. In the talk, he notes that there is a person in the room who meets many of the diagnostic criteria for psychopathy. Unfortunately, Fallon runs out of time before he identifies the culprit. Which was a shame, because the psychopath in the room was him.[8]

I pored over Fallon's book, *The Psychopath Inside,* in which he discusses his condition, and then he and I corresponded by email.[9] Fallon certainly does not meet many of Cleckley's or Hare's criteria: he is *emeritus* from the University of California-Irvine School of Medicine, where he is an NIH Career Awardee, a Senior Fulbright Fellow, and a Sloan Scholar. His students and co-workers are fond of him; by chance I encountered one of his colleagues (in Rome of all places) who told me that Fallon is well-liked and highly respected in the medical school.

But family and friends dropped puzzling comments about him over the years; his wife once compared him to the film character Hannibal 'The Cannibal' Lecter. Finally, professional colleagues sat him down and suggested that he seriously consider that he just might be a psychopath.

All of these present a conflicting picture, as do other odd aspects of Fallon's personality. In his book and his frequent media appearances, he lays out the arguments against himself, with quite a bit of self-deprecating humor, which certainly goes against the grandiosity noted in some diagnostic criteria. He is also, by all accounts, devoted to his family and loved by them, and he is generous to friends, colleagues, and even strangers. He has certainly been encouraging of my work and has been more than generous to me with his time and support.

His commitment to others runs counter to typical psychopathic behaviors; but his commitment is atypical, and perhaps reflects his psychopathic attitudes. Fallon reports that he is committed to his family and friends, not so much because he loves them, but because he enjoys them and "finds them interesting." As is true for the psychopath, Fallon is excited by risk and danger. Previously, he had occasionally exposed family members to dangerous situations simply because he thought they would think it fun. With experience and reflection, however, he realized that most other people do not enjoy these things and that he might have seriously harmed someone.

Fallon also admits that he has the tendency for cold vengeance typical of many psychopaths. If he feels that someone has intentionally violated some basic rule of decency, he exacts vengeance in a manner that ensures his anonymity and which arrives much later, perhaps years after the offender's violation.

The foregoing is hardly convincing, and more than one expert insist that Fallon is not a psychopath, that he instead fits some other behavioral category. His critics argue these things, understandably, because he doesn't fit their criteria. But in addition to the behavioral oddities, Fallon's brain scans reveal the cerebral anatomy of a violent criminal. He also carries the 'warrior gene' that correlates with aggressiveness and violence. Added to those, there is a thread of criminality running through his family, including one notorious relative, the ax murderer Lizzie Borden. This evidence presents a conflict between objective evidence and subjective analysis: there is strong, modern objective criteria which link Fallon to psychopathy, but practitioners applying subjective criteria of established patterns—patterns, which we have seen, do not always agree—argue that he does not qualify. We should dismiss objective data with great reluctance and only in the presence of strong contradicting evidence.

A single example cannot define a class. Fallon might simply be a sport of nature. After thinking and reading, I may have identified another example of a moral psychopath. That would be Oskar Schindler, the hero of Steven Spielberg's film *Schindler's List*.

Schindler's psychopathy is no hard sell. He came out of a highly dysfunctional home, and his father was possibly a severe psychopath, narcissist, or both, a drunk who raped and impregnated his own sister-in-law. When Oskar was young he was known as 'Schindler the Crook,' and as an adult he experienced frequent brushes with the authorities; once he was jailed under a potential death sentence.

Schindler was a spend-thrift who enjoyed high living but quickly lost interest in different jobs and projects, often after investing great time and money. He was a notorious skirt-chaser who secretly maintained a second family. His wife recognized his womanizing and compulsive lying, but she nevertheless allowed him to charm his way out of trouble and repeatedly back into her heart.

Schindler also enjoyed risk-taking. Once he intentionally threw a speedster race, apparently because he enjoyed the thrill of the race more than the thrill of winning. In fact, his entire campaign to save Jews under the noses of the Nazis was a death-defying effort that the psychopath might very well enjoy. In one example, Nazi officers came to inspect Schindler's sweatshop. After loudly maligning his Jewish employees to the Nazis, Schindler could be seen embracing the officers with tears in his eyes. Some interpreted this as heartfelt compassion for the Jews he was saving and his embarrassment at the things he was forced to say. If we accept the premise that Schindler was a psychopath, however, sadness or regret should not be within his emotional arsenal. Other than physical pain, I can imagine only one situation in which the pure psychopath would cry: mirth. It is possible that Schindler was trying to keep from laughing at his own audacity in hoodwinking the 'master race.' Few but a cool psychopath could have pulled off such a bold swindle without being caught.

Schindler presents other conflicts and contradictions. In his sweat shop, he initially exploited many of the same Jews he would later save. He permitted some of the Jewish women to be prostituted at Nazi orgies. But eventually—around when he turned thirty-five, which as we shall see in a later chapter, may be significant—moral intent emerged from him, and his choices became as striking as his psychopathy. His priorities and principles changed, and he began treating his Jewish employees—slaves, really—better. And then he began actively working to save their lives. But even his morality contained a reckless disregard that perhaps reflects psychopathy. As he protected his Jewish workers, he was taking deadly risks that imperiled him, his family, and his friends as well. That, of course, is true for anyone who risks herself to help others. What separates Schindler, however, was his seemingly blithe disregard for the risks and his cavalier attitude through it all.

There are two curious anecdotes that support these points. First, when asked why he risked his life to save so many Jews, Schindler supposedly gave the odd response, "If you saw a dog going to be crushed under a car, wouldn't you help him?" This sort of practical, dispassionate answer is not in line with the responses from the other people who struggled, sacrificed, and often died to save the victims of the Nazis. Many of them could not even speak of the evil they witnessed; they would certainly never compare their experiences with saving animals, much less a single animal. Comparing the horrors of the Holocaust to a dog in the path of a car is not without logic, but it makes for a rather jarring—and to our thesis, a cold-hearted—comparison. Such responses, however, would be in line with the expected thinking of the psychopath.

Second, there is the fate of the golden ring Schindler's Jewish employees gave him in gratitude for saving their lives. It was handcrafted by one of them from the dental work of another. It was inscribed with a Talmudic passage, "He who saves a single life saves the entire world."

Years later, Schindler traded the ring for schnapps. Most of us could not imagine being so cavalier with a gift that carried such emotional meaning for the givers and that would have carried even more emotional meaning for the normal recipient.

Schindler possibly represents another moral psychopath. It would be hard to deny either his psychopathy or his morality. Obviously, the life histories of Oskar Schindler and Jim Fallon could not be more different. But both seem to exhibit a morality, even a heroism, based on something other than human emotion or obedience to authority. Fallon and Schindler seem to represent distinct points on some continuum.

The Four-legged Stool

The two men beg the question, What does the term 'psychopath' mean? Fallon describes himself as "psychopath light."* He is also one of a growing number of scholars who believe that psychopathy is probably not a useful term, that we are dealing with several different psychological and behavioral traits, which in turn stem from several factors. Fallon describes those factors as a 'three-legged stool' comprising genes, life experiences, and anatomy/physiology.†

His metaphor can be extended. Rather than a three-legged stool, however, perhaps the basis for the expression of criminal psychopathy—and the basis for all of the human condition, for that matter—could be viewed as a four-legged stool. Ironically, in generating his metaphor Fallon is demonstrating the fourth leg: intellect. Influencing the first three legs is a fourth comprising logic, analysis, and mental discipline.

That insight, perhaps, helps explain Fallon. He seems to pursue morality, not because of emotion or tradition, but because it makes sense. This should not entirely be a surprise. The earliest stirrings of the Western intellectual tradition are mathematics and philosophy, both of which are attempts to analyze reality without reference to emotion or tradition. In fact, we could argue that this is the point of mathematics and philosophy, to analyze life and the world around us, independent of how we feel or what we have been taught.

For many intellectuals, philosophers and scientists among them, a major driver is the enjoyable pursuit of logical order. This also includes the professions. In fact, a calm, unemotional demeanor, particularly under fire, is part of the definition of 'professional.' So adding to the confusion about mental health diagnoses, we see that our very highest pursuits share characteristics with psychopathy; at her best, the philosopher, scientist, engineer, jurist, and entrepreneur take on the cold, calculated, and unemotional approach of the worst criminals. It is simply that the professional—again, a trauma surgeon or field commander—has different goals than the criminal.

This reflects my own puzzles as an emergency physician. In the normal course of my life, I am a bleeding heart. That vulnerability was severely challenged by two dying children that I have seen in the emergency room. The first was early in my career. It was a gruesome case, and I lost my emotional composure; or more accurately, I lost my unemotional composure. Fortu-

---

* As with beer, rather than illumination.

† For example, many psychopaths suffered head trauma in childhood, and various brain diseases generate behavior that is consistent with personality disorders.

nately, there were two pediatricians in the hospital who quickly took over the case, but it was moot: the child was already gone.

The second happened after I had more experience. It still puzzles me how unemotional I was. The whole time, I was almost completely analytical and procedural. In fact, I performed a procedure that I had only practiced on a mannequin, but I accomplished it without any nervousness. When the helicopter arrived from the large urban center, the trauma nurses complimented me for my thoroughness but gently pointed out that the child was dead.

On rare occasions when I have handled a minor emergency in public, friends have been surprised at how cool I was. I am always a bit puzzled by their reactions, but when I think about it, I realize that I am a bit surprised at myself as well. I realize that I blocked out distractions and calmly focused. In a way, I stop fully being me.

Sometimes I enter a similar state when I am working or thinking at home. This often happens when I am writing, particularly when the ideas are flowing freely. If my wife or kids come in and talk to me, it takes a moment for me to 'awaken' so that I can focus on them, include them in my considerations, and respond appropriately. If I have to respond before I shift my focus, I can be quite brusque and even rude.

The point of my observations is that it would seem that we can learn to turn off parts of our brains when we need to focus. When that happens, perhaps our brains mimic the neural function of the psychopath, and we become intermittent psychopaths. Brain scans might show that when we are focused on a problem, the centers for empathy and other functions dial back or perhaps switch off entirely.

Returning to Fallon's ethics, I have corresponded with him about his moral compass, and he agrees logic drives much of his concept of ethics, and illogic is uncomfortable to him. Discomfort, of course, suggests an emotional response, but the brain pathways for this discomfort probably take a different route, and/or impact other brain centers, than those supporting responses to emotions, or authority.

That insight gives new explanations for Fallon's apparent contradictions. Note that he did not stop exposing his family to risk because of fear or other emotion; it was the result of a dispassionate analysis. Intellect may also explain Fallon's drive to revenge injustice. Hard psychopaths seek vengeance for personal affronts. Fallon seeks vengeance for social affronts, and he seems less interested in protecting himself than in protecting others. It suggests that Fallon is offended by those who insult order, logic, and collegial behavior.

On a television program where Fallon was the main guest in a discussion of psychopathy, a clinical psychologist dismissed Fallon's claims of psychopathic traits.[10] Others in the audience seemed skeptical that Fallon shares characteristics with the worst criminals. Interestingly enough, an audience member who seemed to understand Fallon's condition was a woman with Asperger's, a disorder given to strict, logical use of thought and language. Logical intensity is possibly what connects her to Fallon, and she gives us a glimpse, perhaps, into how Fallon functions.

There are other suspects for the moral psychopath. Kemal Mustafa Atatürk proved repeatedly that he could be brutal and merciless, in war and peace. He sent men to die in battle without hesitation; but he also had Turks beheaded over sartorial choices, particularly for wearing the outlawed fez.[11] Like many brutal conquerors, Atatürk built around him a cult of personality that continues to dominate modern Turkey today. Nevertheless, he instituted a seemingly contradictory culture of democratic anti-totalitarianism, avoided religious and political ideologies in favor of pragmatism, and took 'moral' steps that seem to run counter to the decisions of other kings and conquerors. One of the more remarkable departures was his approach to minorities. He liberated women, and although he forced minorities to assimilate, he did not launch the persecutions and genocides typical of many despots. It is worth considering that Atatürk may not represent only a moral psychopath, but also possibly a moral atrox.

Then there is a particular breed of soldier, reflected in leaders such as George Washington, Robert E. Lee, George Marshall, and Dwight Eisenhower, but really seen at all ranks and ratings, and particularly within the special forces. These people seem to be able to deploy lethal force without losing their moral compasses away from the battle. Democratic military leaders seem to be committed to the well-being of their troops and also concerned about the young men among the enemy. Despite these human concerns, they nevertheless commit fully to the brutality of warfare. Adding to the confusing bleed-over between normality and psychopathy, these men are often aloof ciphers to their friends, colleagues, and even within their own families.

Psychopathy of Anger

A friend of mine, a devoted father and husband and a conscientious employee, served a tour of duty in Iraq a few years ago. He described how one day his vehicle hit an IED.

"You must have been terrified," I noted.

"When I calmed down, yes," he responded. "But when it happened, I jumped out of the vehicle, and I wanted to kill someone."

Note that my friend lost more than his compassion in the explosion; he also lost his fear. It would be interesting to know what happens to the brain centers when someone is overcome by extreme anger. I wonder if brain scans would show a shift in localized activity similar to the neural function of the psychopath, that the subject is experiencing intermittent psychopathy. Certainly something changed in my friend's brain with the attack, and changed back later to the more common emotion of fear.

Probably all normal people lose some of our compassion and some of our fear when extremely angry. Certainly we can all remember times when we harmed someone we love out of anger, something for which we felt deep regret in retrospect, but for which we felt no remorse at the time. In the next chapter, I will suggest that such confusions may represent conflicts between genetic drives and our higher intellectual processes.

INTERMITTENT/FACULTATIVE PSYCHOPATHY

The film *Japanese Devils*[12] presents interviews with WWII Japanese soldiers who admitted to committing or witnessing torture, rape, mutilation, massacres, bio-experiments, and, once again, cannibalism. There has been severe criticism and rejection of the charges in the movie, mostly from Japanese sources.[13] Like the arguments of Holocaust deniers, critics insist that the charges are too outrageous to be believed. The response to this, as we have seen, is that they are not outrageous: they are the mundane horror of war. Critics also point out that the soldiers in the film were Chinese prisoners of war and suggest that they had been indoctrinated by their captors. It begs the question: Were they Manchurian Candidates with implanted information? Or were they merely typical human beings who have been forced to consider what soldiers have always done?

From the preceding chapter we can see that many, perhaps all, people can vacillate between peaceful compassion and vicious brutality. Throughout much of history, nation-states had no large standing army. The same soldiers who went to war and hacked children, women, and men to death returned home and fostered trusting relationships with yet other children, women, and men.

There are two twentieth-century incidents that thread through this book. The first is the atrocities of the Nazis, particularly toward their civilian targets. The other is the My Lai massacre. As we will see, in both instances many of the people who carried out the slaughter were not fully 'evil'; they committed evil within certain contexts. Most soldiers return to civilian activity and never harm another person for the rest of their lives.

Atrocity in war is the extreme expression of intermittent psychopathy, but one that is critical for the thesis here. We need to understand the origins of some critical problems in the modern world, so that we might avoid lapsing back into perennial slaughter.

Sociopathy

I have asked a number of psychologists, psychiatrists, and criminologists to distinguish between psychopathy and sociopathy; I particularly asked it of those I encountered at a large symposium on forensic psychiatry. The only consistent answer I received was, there is no difference. One of the more interesting responses, however, was that psychopathy is what the patient experiences internally, and sociopathy is how the patient's psychopathy expresses itself in the lives of others.

Having said that, there are professional approaches that classify sociopathy as 'secondary' psychopathy, *i.e.*, psychopathy that is not innate, but the product of severe abuse or neglect. Under this framework, a critical distinction for sociopathy is the inconsistency or absence of the low arousal state. Sociopaths can become outraged when frustrated. Otherwise, they are also cold and unfeeling of those around them.

Narcissism

Just as with psychopathy, narcissism has a long history of clinical consideration and research. And just as with psychopathy, there are various diagnostic tools/lists that do not always agree. For our considerations, it will be enough to cover a basic understanding, and the DSM-5 diagnostic definition of narcissism is sufficient:

:: Grandiosity with expectations of superior treatment from others

:: Fixation on fantasies of power, success, intelligence, attractiveness, etc.

:: Self-perception of being unique, superior, and associated with high-status people and institutions

:: Needing constant admiration from others

:: Sense of entitlement to special treatment and to obedience from others

:: Exploitative of others to achieve personal gain

:: Unwilling to empathize with others' feelings, wishes, or needs

:: Intensely envious of others, and the belief that others are equally envious of them

:: Pompous and arrogant demeanor

Note that various diagnostic criteria for narcissism and criminal psychopathy show overlap; for instance, both have a blunted ability for empathy. Both manipulate others for personal gain.

But a key difference is that whereas the psychopath is often cold-blooded in his emotional range, the narcissist can be extreme in his emotional responses, particularly when he feels offended. Another difference is that narcissists obsess over loyalty. Perhaps because they retain some emotional capacity, they can apparently develop something like compassion for the people who are loyal to them, although they will still abandon and sacrifice their supporters for personal protection or sufficient gain.

There is one diagnostic criterion that is missing from the above list and which might serve as a strong indicator of narcissism: a lack of self-humor. The narcissist is almost incapable of laughing at himself. This was demonstrated in the preceding chapter, with Caracalla's revenge upon the Alexandrians.

MACHIAVELLIANISM

In 1513, at the height of the Renaissance, Florentine diplomat, writer, and savant Niccolò Machiavelli published one of the more controversial products of Western civilization, *The Prince*. His slender book is both reviled by moralists and meticulously pored over by historians. It is ironic: at the nascence of modern humanism, Machiavelli argued for an inhumane and brutal approach to political and social management.

What makes Machiavelli so controversial is that he does not advocate any personal preference in his prescriptions; he does not argue, for instance, that 'might makes right.' Personally he was not a brutal man and seemed to regret what he advocated. He simply reported his observations as to what was effective in governance and war without reference to ideology or personal preference. In effect, he takes a dispassionate approach, a clinical, philosophical, or scientific view. That dispassionate approach made Machiavelli the 'father of modern political science.'

Machiavelli studied effective rulers and reported what worked and what did not. What he claims—and what the historical record and the previous chapter support—is that brute force, shrewdly applied in a timely manner, works. Kindness, generosity, and even basic human decency, Machiavelli tells us, are not of much value, or certainly not as much as commonly thought.

Shakespeare read Machiavelli and incorporated the latter's insights into his plays. As a keen observer of the human condition, Shakespeare anticipated the diagnosis of Machiavellianism by three hundred years. Consider Shakespeare's tragedy *Othello*; the Moor may be the protagonist, but the pivot is Iago, who brilliantly and coolly manipulates everyone around him and drives Othello to murder his beloved Desdemona. Iago is a notorious example of the Machiavellian personality and a few other behavioral dysfunctions as well.

A modern theatrical interpretation of the Machiavellian is the character Chad in Neil Labute's disturbing 1997 movie, *In the Company of Men*. Chad manipulates his temporarily assigned supervisor, Howard, to destroy the life of Christine, a beautiful but vulnerable deaf woman. Chad does this both for his professional advancement and for revenge on Howard, but also simply for his personal amusement. His game succeeds, and he wrecks the lives of both Christine and Howard.

If we consider only Iago and Chad, however, we miss much nuance and the larger considerations. In the 1950s, Richard Christie, together with Robert Agger and Frank Pinner, began exploring the concept of the Machiavellian personality. They were interested in a type of behavior they had witnessed of powerful and/or influential people who seemed to be emotionally unattached to colleagues and subordinates, goal-oriented rather than ideology-oriented, and less concerned with conventional morality than others.

In 1970, Christie and Florence Geis published a self-assessment of twenty questions to identify the Machiavellian personality.[14] The test has great consistency and repeatability in clinical practice and correlates well with contemporary and historical phenomena.

The questions permit five responses: Strongly Disagree; Disagree; Neutral; Agree; Strongly Agree. The questions are arranged so that the normal response is sometimes 'Agree' or 'Strongly Agree', (roman type, below) and sometimes 'Disagree' or 'Strongly Disagree' (italic type).

1. *It is possible to be good in all respects.*
2. *Honesty is the best policy in all cases.*
3. *Most people are brave.*
4. *Most people who get ahead in the world lead clean, moral lives.*

5. When you ask someone to do something for you, it is best to give the real reasons for wanting it rather than giving reasons which carry more weight.

6. *People suffering from incurable diseases should have the choice of being put painlessly to death.*

7. *It is wise to flatter important people.*

8. *Generally speaking, people won't work hard unless they're forced to do so.*

9. *Never tell anyone the real reason you did something unless it is useful to do so.*

10. One should take action only when sure it is morally right.

11. *It is hard to get ahead without cutting corners here and there.*

12. *It is safest to assume that all people have a vicious streak and it will come out when they are given a chance.*

13. *The biggest difference between most criminals and other people is that the criminals are stupid enough to get caught.*

14. There is no excuse for lying to someone else.

15. *Most people forget more easily the death of their parents than the loss of their property.*

16. *Anyone who completely trusts anyone else is asking for trouble.*

17. Most people are basically good and kind.

18. *The best way to handle people is to tell them what they want to hear.*

19. P.T. Barnum was wrong when he said that there's a sucker born every minute.

20. All in all, it is better to be humble and honest than to be important and dishonest.

Christie and his colleagues designed their tests from characteristics that seemed to fit *The Prince* and from their professional experiences. Their final version of the questions is the one printed above, which constitutes the 'MACH IV.' These questions were selected because they correlate well with one another: they constitute a *syn-drome*, Greek for things that 'run together.'

The test has become the gold standard for the diagnosis of Machiavellianism. That creates conceptual problems, however. Unlike the other disorders we have considered, the MACH IV only identifies, but does not describe, key dysfunctions. Because of this, it is not surprising that various scholars, practitioners, and laypersons give different descriptions of the underlying condition, supplying lists of characteristics that vary in length and content. Both laymen and professionals frequently describe the Machiavellian personality as immoral, narcissistic, materialistic, duplicitous, desirous of fear and respect, cruel, or even sadistic. These descriptions, however, conflate Machiavellianism with other problems, particularly with narcissism and sadism.

Many Machiavellians do exhibit those characteristics, but these inconsistent aspects take us wide of the mark. It is critical to understand that Christie and his friends did not start their investigations with vicious and/or unethical people. To the contrary: their first, informal explorations of Machiavellian characteristics comprised discussions with the high-level scholars around them, inquiring about their colleagues' major professors and other mentors. They found that among the most productive graduate faculty, individuals who were largely aloof and demanding taskmasters seemed to be over-represented. These were the first considerations of the Machiavellian personality. This points up the problem with including other disorders with the diagnosis: these mentors were dedicated scholars who were generally ethical and high-minded.

Christie then described other people he encountered who seemed Machiavellian, not in criminal or unethical enterprises, but in government, academic administration, and appropriate to our topic, in the military. This reintroduces the military leaders we covered under psychopathy, people who might be quite proper within their personal lives but who were willing to commit to the slaughter of warfare, even for causes that they may have doubted. As noted, effective combat leaders typically present the paradox of being respectful of their troops in person, but completely disrespectful of them, their bodies, and their lives, in battle.

Scholars may reject modern military leaders as Machiavellians, but that leaves a challenge: How do we exclude someone from the category of Machiavellianism whose success depends upon manipulating and coercing others to go out, slaughter others, and be slaughtered? It would seem that other examples of Machiavellianism pale by comparison.

Consider that if we could administer the MACH IV to various modern wartime commanders, they might not score as Machiavellians. But this only points up a problem with self-assessments: What are we to do when a subject's internal dialogue reflect one set of criteria but his actions strongly reject those criteria? The general may not be a Machiavellian in his private thought and conduct, but as a successful warrior, he must be. Warfare is always Machiavellian.

As a demonstration, take the twenty questions of the MACH IV and preface them with the phrase, "Against an enemy in warfare...." If this modification does not produce a perfect score, the person taking the test probably should not be commanding troops in a battle environment. War is the fullest expression of the worst of humanity, and part of our hypothesis here is that other Machiavellians may be derivatives of the military commander, particularly the conqueror.

This contradictory consideration of effective combat leaders returns to the recurrent theme that when it comes to conquest and warfare, we subscribe to romantic fiction and fairy tales. The Southern general Robert E. Lee is a good example. The general's admirers insist that he was the perfect Southern gentleman, a refined, high-minded, polite, and respectable man. Perhaps he was, but he was also complicit in the slaughter of more American troops than Hitler, Kaiser Wilhelm, George III, Ho Chi Minh, and Kim Il-sung—combined.

Lee seemed to recognize his own contradictions: "It is well that war is so terrible, otherwise we should grow too fond of it." Lee was of two different minds, because he was arguably two different people.

We have considered that soldiers should be Machiavellian in battle and more conventional at home. We can add to those considerations the business textbooks that advocate Machiavelli's ideas for the workplace,[15] something few would advocate for the home or the community. Then we might also add certain moral considerations. Consider John le Carré's description of the ideal spy, someone who is "by instinct a befriender, a seducer, and a liar, in the sense of a gentleman who lies for the good of his country."[16] The Machiavellian general commits to slaughtering some in order to prevent the slaughter of even more. It is what we expect of the cold calculations of a Machiavellian: to ruthlessly choose the lesser of two evils.

In the first chapter we considered the similarities between the gangster and the conqueror-king. Machiavellianism gives us another tie among conquerors, kings, and mobsters. Consider Carlo Gambino, the Mafia boss who was a major model for Mario Puzo's *The Godfather*. Although flashy mobsters such as Al Capone dominate popular concepts of the mobster, the Mafia describes someone who is arrogant and ostentatious with the phrase, "He takes up too much space in the air." In contrast to Capone, Gambino was low-key, and he showed few overt signs of arrogance, narcissism, or sadism. Gambino was unemotional and calculating in his actions, conforming to the Machiavellian pronouncement in *The Godfather* movies, "Never hate your enemies. It affects your judgment."[17] This reflects a different model of the crime boss, a disciplined, professional, and hence, more effective, criminal.

Finally, consider the practice of medicine. It is interesting that a 'clinical demeanor' is an unemotional, cold, and analytical approach to medical problems. Then consider that physicians vivisect, dismember, poison, and violate our patients constantly, regardless of their complaints or suffering. We are so ruthless that we even drug them so that they cannot complain or resist as we do things to them that are as horrific as anything we discussed in the previous chapter.

These considerations present a possible irony. Is a Machiavellian necessarily the ruthless, vicious, and avaricious role models portrayed in *The Prince*? Or could a Machiavellian be Machiavelli himself, someone who may be ethical and moral in his personal conduct, but who unromantically recognizes the truth about how things get done in the larger world, who understands that conventional morality will not succeed in all situations, and who is willing to follow cold logic to its conclusion, however unappealing?

There appears to be a critical omission from the MACH IV, however. To be truly Machiavellian means more than a willingness to pursue manipulation and rule-breaking. It also means to do these while targeting a long-term strategy, for good or evil. Without that long-term strategy, the small-time grifter might score as high on the MACH IV as any Caracalla or Torquemada. For this reason, going forward we will assume that an essential aspect of the Machiavellian personality is the disciplined pursuit of long-term goals, with focus, patience, and often, subterfuge.

The Dark Triad

Violent criminals often fall under the classification of 'the dark triad,' a confluence of psychopathy, narcissism, and Machiavellianism. The three conditions definitely overlap in some people, but this presents a new problem: we should ensure that each of those three is conceptually distinct from the other two. If not, if they overlap but we cannot find a 'pure' example of each, then we cannot be sure we are not simply looking at varieties of cabbage: as distinct as they appear, cabbage, cauliflower, kale, Brussels sprouts, collard greens, and broccoli are all breeds of the same plant.

For instance, among the criteria we have considered for psychopathy, only Cleckley appears to contain no strong narcissistic elements. Adding narcissistic components to Cleckley's 'pure' psychopathy creates conceptual problems. For one, the psychopath generally has little empathy or long-term human commitment, but as we have noted, the narcissist appears to be protective and fond of those who are loyal to him. Second, the psychopath is disinterested in how others feel about their suffering, about him, or about anything else; the narcissist is similar, except that he is consumed with how others feel about *him*. Next, we have noted that a key, perhaps essential, aspect of the psychopath is his low arousal state and the general absence of emotions; in contrast, when ridiculed, insulted, or frustrated, the narcissist can respond with neurosis or rage. In addition, the psychopath is often poorly committed to his own safety and well-being and even seeks out risk and danger for the excitement of it. The narcissist is obsessed with his own safety and protection and often avoids personal risk. Finally, the psychopath is hyper-rational and perfectly aware of his lies and his reasons for lying. The narcissist, however, is hyper-*rationalizing*, ignoring the hypocrisy and contradictions in his thoughts, commitments, and actions. So combining those two presents conceptual and definitional challenges.

We have already considered Machiavellianism as a distinct entity and discussed how it may accompany several different personality profiles, some of them healthy. The vicious Caracalla was a Machiavellian, but so were respected American generals. And so perhaps was President Harry S. Truman, who made the decision to vaporize tens of thousands of people by dropping the atomic bomb and who nevertheless slept soundly that night.

Machiavellianism nevertheless presents problems when included with the pure narcissist or psychopath. First, it is important to note that Christie *et al.* stipulated that to be Machiavellian, the subject should lack any other marked psychopathology. The need for attention in the severe narcissist should interfere with working in the typically quiet and anonymous action-at-a-distance of the Machiavellian. Similarly, the self-absorption of the narcissist should interfere with the Machiavellian's requisite insight into the feelings and motivations of others. As for psychopathy, we have noted that the pure psychopath seems to lack interest in planning beyond the short term, obviating the Machiavellian aspect we added, 'the pursuit of long-term goals.'

These create problems for the dark triad, and it is not immediately clear how these conceptual tensions can be resolved. They do not, however, void the realities. The triad is a real phenomenon, as many criminals, and the atrox, prove. Rather, it is another example of difficulties inherent in mental health: these are problems that are important, but we simply cannot yet explain and reconcile them adequately.

Going forward with our considerations of the atrox, the most important factor may be, surprisingly enough, not psychopathy nor narcissism, but Machiavellianism. Without Machiavellianism, psychopaths and narcissists cannot easily rise to great power; if someone manages to achieve power but does not pursue Machiavellian ruthlessness, he will not hold on to it.

Machiavellianism is essential for conquest, defense, and societal control, all of which require a leader who is willing to sacrifice people—his own as well as the enemy—to establish and maintain control. But then, this is also true even for the most egalitarian and selfless military officers and elected officials. To be effective, they must be pragmatic, which means at times they must be ruthless. Just like the Prince.

Machiavellianism can succeed independent of the rest of the dark triad. The condition comes more naturally to psychopaths and narcissists, however. The low arousal state of the psychopath help him succeed in Machiavellian pursuits. The narcissist's desire for power and attention gives him the ambition for Machiavellian strategies. So it is not surprising the three behavioral traits often constitute a 'syndrome.'

THE DARK TETRAD

If we add sadism to the three components of the dark triad, it expands to 'the dark tetrad.' The diagnosis of sadistic personality disorder has proven controversial and is excluded from the DSM-5. The diagnosis of sexual sadism disorder is still included, however. We shall begin with the simplest definition of sadism, which is the enjoyment of inflicting or witnessing pain in others.

As with the preceding topics, sadism poses a number of diagnostic and conceptual mismatches. For our considerations, I will add one observation. Unlike the worst criminals, where sadism typically includes a sexual component, the atrox may derive other types of enjoyment from suffering.

The first and most common variation would be a sporting sadism derived from the excitement of warfare. The origins of Western athletic competition, the classical Greek games, were military competitions: running, jumping, wrestling, boxing, throwing the discus and the javelin, horseback and chariot racing, and the brutal *pankration*. American football is speculated to be an outgrowth of the military culture that influenced the country during and after the Civil War.[18] Conquerors such as Genghis Khan enjoyed conquest as something akin to sporting activity, and the polo played with victims' heads after the battle were, perhaps, a continuation of that sporting excitement. Also recall that Julius Caesar participated in the slaughter of his campaigns, and any number of other conquerors also mounted chariot or horse to participate in warfare. To those must be added the enjoyment that spectators derived from the carnage of the Roman games. Finally, recall the Robert E. Lee quote, "It is well that war is so terrible, otherwise we should grow too fond of it." There is excitement in grand carnage.

There also appears to be an intellectual sadism, a willingness to inflict pain on others out of ideology or simple curiosity. We will return to this problem, but consider Torquemada, Pol Pot, Shaka Zulu, Josef Mengele, and Jeffrey Dahmer, who inflicted pain on others and perhaps derived an enjoyment that was more intellectual or ideological rather than adrenal or androgenic.

Then there is the sadism of retribution, typically labeled as 'justice': consider Catiline's sadistic revenge on Gratidianus. With that, private and public torture was the standard response for dealing with those whom the crown or conqueror found offensive, including armed crimes such as rebellion; civil crimes of violence and theft; ideological crimes of heresy, or really, any violation of accepted orthodoxy; and *lèse majesté*, which covered affronts to the king's narcissism. As we noted, historical governments did not eliminate violence. They merely held the monopoly for it.

Finally, the atrox is often a conventional sadist, relishing human suffering as an excitement in and of itself, with or without a sexual component. Ashoka certainly enjoyed inflicting the tortures in his Hell, and Alexander was eager to try out sadistic punishments on his enemies. Roman sadism was, as we have discussed, a pervasive institutional trait and probably comprised all of the preceding variations.

These sadism variants may very well stem from different causes, and as such, may require different therapeutic approaches for the clinician. For our considerations here, however, the important aspect is that, regardless of the species of enjoyment, the eager pursuit of horror facilitates the brutal control of the atrox.

Malignant Narcissism

The preceding introduces an additional non-standard category, 'malignant narcissism.' Erich Fromm first proposed malignant narcissism in *The Heart of Man* as "the quintessence of evil."[19] The diagnosis roughly correlates with the dark tetrad and comprises the most notorious criminals, serial torturers-killers such as David Parker Ray, the sadist who introduced this chapter.

Fromm was a member of the Frankfurt School of refugees who escaped Nazi Germany and explored, among other things, the authoritarian and totalitarian dynamics they had witnessed and experienced under Hitler. Fromm's description of malignant narcissism did not include Machiavellianism, because it did not yet exist as a well-defined construct in the behavioral sciences. As we have noted, however, for the malignant narcissist to be successful in perpetrating and hiding the most heinous crimes, he must be strongly Machiavellian.

Clearly, if we admit the conqueror's lusty pursuit of war as sadism, then most conquerors will qualify as malignant narcissists. The title for this book probably should have been *Kings, Conquerors, Malignant Narcissists*, but snappiness sells books.

Fanaticism & Zealotry

There is a final aspect of the atrox that frequently appears, something we touched on under intellectual/ideological sadism. We need to consider the fanatic/zealot, someone whose motivation stems from passionate commitment to a belief, cause, or ideology.

Fanaticism is not currently considered a mental disorder, but it probably should be; it is definitely a thought disorder. The political or social fanatic is inflexible in thought, and he typically, perhaps necessarily, objectifies people as secondary concerns, or even as inconsequential concerns, in comparison to his fundamentalist ideology. When we look at ancient conquerors, their motivations were generally the bald narcissism of greed and glory. These dysfunctions continue into the modern world, and we have seen them in the Victorians, U.S. colonialism, and King Leopold. But the major civilian atrocities of the twentieth century were ideologically driven, primarily from Marxist, fascist, social Darwinist, and racist arguments, all of which attempt to dress themselves in scientific arguments. For the previous nineteen centuries, however, ideological zealotry was almost exclusively religious.

When zealotry appears in the atrox, there are historical reasons why it should be considered a mental disorder. The typical atrox wants the narcissism of *empire*, and once he has achieved complete political and economic control, he is satisfied. The zealot, however, wants more than control; he slaughters for ideological conformity and purity, even conformity and purity of appearance. As such, he will continue his terror in the civilian arena after warfare has concluded. The Khmer Rouge executed not only those with education, but also those who *appeared* to be educated, such as those who wore glasses. Paulus Catena and Torquemada tortured and executed not only non-Christians, but also Christians whose behavior or thoughts *appeared* to deviate from orthodoxy; the Pilgrims attempted to assassinate Roger Williams from a similar objection and executed any number of people as witches for any deviancy from some ideal. Mao and his successors deployed various purges of the ideologically impure, and Stalin sacrificed tens of millions to his hypocritical view of Marxism. As for Hitler, in his expansions of the Third Reich he attempted to purge from Germany and conquered nations anyone who *appeared* to be physically or genetically imperfect. Zealotry is the defining difference in these: objections to Hitler stem less from his wars and much more from his fanatical bigotry and the civilian purges which resulted. The same is true of Stalin, Mao, Pol Pot, and so many others.

I have offered the observation that military action often claims about 12 percent of the lives in a conquered population. If that number holds up, I predict we will find that ideological conquest claims much more than 12 percent; from the few examples we have considered here, ideology seems to aggregate around double that number, about 25 percent. So it intensifies the toxic effect of conquest and empire; it creates many additional deaths. Certainly within the civilian population, any thought processes that regularly result in murder would be considered psychiatric diseases. Zealotry is a thought disorder of large societies that results in large scale murder; so it is not clear why it should be excluded from psychiatric consideration.

Eric Hoffer argues that fanaticism is a Judeo-Christian invention.[20] Certainly the original zealots were Jewish agitators under Roman oppression. Or we assume the first zealots were Jewish; the word derives from the ancient Greek ζηλωτής, *zēlōtēs*, meaning 'emulator, zealous admirer, or follower.' The fact that the Greeks had such a word leads us to wonder if they had dealt with similar behaviors. Added to that, the cult of personality supporting the divinity of so many ancient kings would appear to require some aspect of zealotry.

There are, however, historical patterns that make Hoffer's observation intriguing. If we define zealotry and fanaticism as passions that are ideologically driven, and then note that ideology generally requires a fundamental, referential text, the Jews—the original 'people of the Book'—appear to be one of the earliest groups to promote general literacy and to build their ideology around a core of unchanging scripture. Christianity, of course, grows out of that Hebrew tradition and ideology.*

That motivating role of a central document ironically ties communism to U.S. Constitutional fundamentalism. The French Reign of Terror was partly driven by a fanaticism for republican ideals as described in a different revolutionary document, *The Declaration of the Rights of Man and of the Citizen*. As for Hitler, his influences certainly included the racism of Ernst Haeckle, but his fundamental text may have been his own work, *Mein Kampf*. Hitler's primary ideology, it would seem, was his own racism.

If these ideas have merit, then perhaps the growth of fanaticism is an unfortunate side effect of the outgrowth of increasing literacy over the past two millennia. As more people read, as they inherit texts from earlier times, perhaps written authority comes to rival, or even supplant, the father, deity, or other authority figure. The written word can take on a sacred significance

---

* It is worth considering that this focus on general literacy, particularly in the Protestant countries, may have assisted northern European nations in dominating so much of the globe.

that potentiates it and makes it dangerous. In fact, I suggest that the added toxicity of fanaticism may offer a new historical, psychiatric category: the dark pentad.

The Atrox & the Anempath

We have considered different sources of slaughter and suffering in the historical and modern worlds: psychopathy, narcissism, sadism, and zealotry. We have considered that if the king is to maintain empire, he must also reflect a strong Machiavellian tendency.

With these, we have looked at the duty-bound conqueror, the military leaders we admire when they are allies and revile when they are enemies. There are also confusing areas, such as the soldiers of the My Lai Massacre. The brutal photographs that blew open the scandal are often reprinted. But the text and the comments from the soldiers who perpetrated the massacre present a more complicated picture. After the slaughter, some soldiers sat down with the survivors and shared their K-rations. These men, in a matter of minutes, transformed from some of the worst of humanity into some of the best.

What connects these? I propose that the unifying characteristic is an inability to empathize with the suffering of others. I could find no satisfactory word for this and propose the term *anempathy*.*

There are various situations in which empathy simply fails. The pure psychopath does not experience empathy. The narcissist appears to be capable of some degree of empathy, but when he is absorbed in promoting and protecting himself, he becomes blind to the suffering of others.

Particularly, when the narcissist becomes enraged, he becomes anempathetic; but in that situation, he is much like the rest of us. When we are angry, our empathy drops, and it is only self-discipline and intellectual analysis that keep us from harming our family and friends. Anger suggests that we can all be temporary anempaths.

Another subcategory of temporary anempathy comprises the duty-bound soldier. These are not people who feel no empathy; rather, in the course of soldiering, in the heat of kill-or-be-killed, they lose compassion. With experience, they can apparently learn to switch empathy on and off quickly, as the soldiers of My Lai demonstrated. As I described, this ability would also include my experiences in the emergency room: in a dire situation, I quickly

---

* Instead of anempathy, I might have used alexithymia, an existing word describing someone who is largely without emotions. But it already has a definition that makes the application here difficult. That, and it's hard to pronounce.

objectify my patient and become anempathetic. What morality remains in this situation is an intellectual commitment, the morality of a James Fallon.

Anempathy is of importance in explaining the Victorians. For much of Victoria's reign, the English empire was largely a front for a multinational corporation that consumed the island nation. At its height, the British East India Company was responsible for half of the world's international trade, employed one-third of the English population, and maintained an army that was twice as large as the Crown's.[21] The Company was disbanded some years before the end of Victoria's rule, but the E.I.C.'s culture of wealth from plunder had great inertia, and conquest continued for some decades. Through it all, the English managed the delicate juggle of maintaining a strong free press while whitewashing the realities of conquest. For this reason, much of the Victorians' anempathy was one of ignorance; government, the public, and the English investors were kept blissfully ignorant about the realities of conquest.

And, of course, they preferred the fairy tales. They, like most conquering nations, believed that conquest was a brief, exciting, and generally painless operation, where the victims were overwhelmingly evil and/or unimportant people. They did not witness the horror and suffering, and so they could not empathize with them. They were anempathetic by virtue of ignorance.

This chapter lays out the psychiatric characteristics that define the atrox so that we might better recognize him when he appears. But we must also recognize the atrox within ourselves, which is not always easy. We are all of us ignorant anempathetics; we conspire with militaries and corporations who do our skulduggery for us, who provide us with safety, comfort—and of course, great wealth—while keeping us in the dark and carefully whitewashing the realities that occasionally emerge. If we are to change this, then we need to watch ourselves for the characteristics of the ignorant anempathetic, or worse, the willfully ignorant anempathetic.

Interlude:
Genetics, Eugenics, Genocide

Love and coughing are not concealed.
—Ovid

"How are you in regard to sex, Sophocles? Can you still make love to a woman?"
"Hush man," the poet replied.
"I am very glad to have escaped from this,
like a slave who has escaped from a mad and cruel master."
—Plato

Because of various social and military persecutions over the past two centuries, particularly with the Holocaust, as well as with the racial atrocities in the U.S. and other countries, political correctness tends to equate genetic human behavior with eugenics and genocide, and hold all three as anathema. They are distinct issues. Certainly the racist groups them as one concept and mindlessly slides among them. But that is a problem with racism, not genetics.

Human genetic behavior is ruts, not rails. Every moment of our lives, we are under genetic influences. Sometimes, they are powerful influences, but few of them are inescapable. The few that seem inescapable (breathing, for one) are often essential for short-term survival. The rest often play critical roles in decisions we make, although we are generally unaware of them.

Genetic behavior influences us in a myriad of ways. We nevertheless are confident that the conscious mind controls the body: I 'will' my finger to move, and it moves. That is true much of the time, but not always. I remember the point in my medical training when I became aware that sometimes our genes overrule our minds. I had a patient in advanced labor, and I told her not to 'push' yet because I was still getting everything ready.

It didn't work. In our basic science classes we were taught that, except for the uterus itself, most of the muscles for pushing out a baby are 'voluntary,' conscious muscles, as opposed to the 'involuntary,' genetically governed muscles of the heart, digestive tract, *etc*. And most of the time, those other muscles are voluntary.

But at some point in labor, the mother's genes just take over and tell the mind what's about to happen. It's a sobering experience. The mother screams,

"I gotta push!" and the midwife* had better be there or the baby will end up on the floor.

We have all experienced the same thing with sneezing, coughing, hiccuping, vomiting, or if we hold it too long, with urinating and defecating. Sometimes we can stifle these, but often we cannot. When we cannot, our genes dictate our behavior.

There are other genetic urges that are powerful but not so dramatic. In the United States, about one-third of adults are on a weight loss diet at any time. We attempt four to five diets a year and spend $20 billion on our efforts.[1]

It is quite easy to override our genetic drives and go on a diet, at least for a few days. Beyond that, we enter a struggle between our intellect and our genes. The genes almost always win: less than 5 percent of dieters will succeed and keep their weight down for a year. †

There are other genetic drives, including anger, sexuality, greed, and pride. As we noted, when these express themselves we often regret our actions later. That regret suggests that our actions were not logical, intentional choices. These very old animal drives kick in when we are tired, frustrated, or encounter strong stimuli.

Genetic behaviors can also escape when we take drugs. Alcohol is a popular drug, and it is the cause of many sexual indiscretions, inappropriate comments, fights, and other embarrassments that perpetrators are less likely to commit when sober. Alcohol depresses our intellects, which liberates our genetic behaviors.

As another example of genetic influences, I have very poor eyesight. Without my glasses, anything more than ten inches from my eyes becomes blurred. I remember as a child telling my ophthalmologist that I had ruined my eyes by reading so much. He explained that it was more likely the opposite: because I can't see what other kids are doing, I prefer to read. The genetics of poor eyes influenced my behavior in unexpected ways.

Subsequent research has revealed a surprising twist to that explanation, however. Children with bad eyes often start out with normal vision and may show an interest in doing things up close *before* their eyes worsen. This suggests a genetic interest in creative and intellectual activities that

---

* 'Midwife' does not refer to an attending woman, but to any person delivering the baby. It comes from the Old English *mid* ('with') + *wīf* ('wife/woman'). In the nineteenth century, obstetrics was referred to as midwifery.

† Scholars have begun to question those traditional numbers, but note that in this article, no new number is produced, only a speculation that the 5 percent number may be erroneous. Jane Fritsch, "95% Regain lost weight. Or do they?" *New York Times*, 1999.

is only later reinforced by poor eyesight. So the genes for bad eyes, and a genetic interest in close-up activities, may run together. This pairing suggests that in the past they carried a survival advantage. Which seems odd; without glasses, I would make a poor hunter, soldier, or farmer. But humans have succeeded more because of our intellectual advantages than our physical attributes.

Unfortunately, for many critics the topic of human genetic behavior is a lightning rod. The biologist E.O. Wilson won the Pulitzer for his book *Sociobiology*, which considered the parallels between human and animal behaviors.[2] Despite much praise and many awards, his ideas were vigorously attacked from academic quarters, and angry protests greeted talks on the topic at prestigious universities.

As noted, the source of some of this anger and resistance goes back to the Nazis and to African-American oppression in the U.S., and to racial abuse elsewhere. In many of these persecutions, genetic arguments supported the injustices by 'proving' that the victims were inferior, subhuman, and therefore inconsequential. Because of the problem of racial genetics, unfortunately, genetics has often been condemned along with the racism.

The problem isn't the tool; it's what we wish to do with it. A knife can be used to kill or cure. Likewise, examinations of our genetic drives can hobble or heal. To our topic here, if genes influence our behaviors, then we would do well not to ignore the ruts, but to fix them. So we have to learn to recognize the ruts and understand how we got in them. Then we can design strategies that will allow us to jump our genetic gantlets.

Fortunately, just as our intellectual abilities have empowered us to dominate the planet, they can also empower us in our personal lives. Specifically, they can empower us to escape the atrox. In the following chapters I will argue that part of our bondage under the king may be genetic; we obey because there has been intense survival pressure to do so.

Genetics, Eugenics, Genocide

We have noted that the tool which can free us of our genetic handicaps is the human intellect—the fourth leg of the stool. James Fallon illustrates our argument well: he seems to have the genes of the psychopath, but he does not fulfill the diagnosis because his intellect overrules his genes. His *attitude* rules his *aptitude*. Fallon becomes a model for what we must do to heal ourselves. We must train our intellects so that we may escape our genetic influences.

I will briefly jump ahead: the atrox snaps off the fourth leg. However, the insight of attitude vs. aptitude allows us to refine our understanding of what the fourth leg really is. The leg is not only an innate aptitude for intelligence, because—and this is an argument against the racist—all normal children are born with a strong *genetic* drive to learn and think. The part of the leg that the atrox has forbidden, and to which we submit, is our attitude of curiosity; without it, the aptitude for intelligence lies largely unused and atrophies. We have been conditioned to leave our brains underdeveloped and in particular not to question or challenge what we are taught. So the atrox has literally killed our curiosity, and without that, we cannot see the authoritarian leader's injustice and inefficiency (and I will later argue that injustice *is* an inefficiency). We remain trapped in our ruts.

After ten thousand years under the atrox, we now remove the fourth leg from our children even when there has been no atrox present for centuries. Blocking curiosity has become automatic in our parenting and our schooling. The full argument for that goes beyond our scope here, but I will simply make two observations.

First, the basic processes of schooling have not changed much since the Middle Ages. Memorize, don't analyze; listen, don't discuss. And above all, don't object, don't challenge or question the authorities, particularly not the school authorities.

Second, every healthy pre-schooler is intensely curious. After thirteen years of schooling, few high school seniors still are. It is telling to note, in fact, that those who are still curious are persecuted as 'nerds.' A nerd is simply a teenager who has retained her childlike wonder and curiosity through puberty and industrialized education. The fact that curious students are ostracized, ridiculed, and even bullied for behaviors that are not only natural, but are also essential to our success on the planet, reflects the continuing power of the atrox.[*]

Some of the reasons we remove the fourth leg are cultural. But to our topic here, some of them may be genetic as well. When we consider the authoritarian personality in an upcoming chapter, we will see a powerful resistance to thinking and analysis that appears to reflect some characteristics of innate, genetic behavior.

It is not critical either way, however; culture and genetics are both very powerful, and one way or the other, we will see that we have inherited an ugly anti-intellectual culture. Recall our comments on psychiatry, about how we ridicule the intellectual and how that creates problems for us. Our anti-cu-

---

[*] In the final chapters we explore this more fully, but as progress accelerates, this problem of curiosity-crippling education becomes logarithmically more pressing. Hence the joke, "In the old days, 'nerd' was a four-letter word. Today, it is a six-figure one."

riosity, anti-intellectual culture cripples us, and it cripples our children. And it is a double trap: the atrox trains and selects us to run in ruts. And then he trains and selects us to sabotage the tools that might free us from our ruts.

So it is important to recognize that genetic behavior is not determinism. Our genes are only one voice speaking to us, and we can choose to ignore their advice. This appears to be true even for some physiological functions. Yogis can dramatically lower their heart rate and body temperature.[3] With hypnosis, people can achieve feats of mental concentration and physical performance that they cannot duplicate without the hypnosis.* It would be interesting to know if the advanced yogi or the hypnotized patient could suppress uterine contractions, coughs, sneezes, and other 'involuntary' behaviors.

It takes effort and intellect to escape our genetic influences. And practice: the more we break from the ruts the more they wear down, and the easier it becomes to escape each time. Unfortunately, the reverse is also true. If we do not struggle against our ruts, we dig them deeper, and our genetic tendencies become more ingrained, unquestioned habits.

Sexual Orientation & Addiction

We noted the effects of alcohol; alcohol and drug addiction are behaviors with a strong genetic component. Some people can have one or two drinks and feel no need to have another. Other people can't stop themselves. Some of the addicts, however, manage to master their addiction, master their genetic drives, and get back to a healthy lifestyle.

Another example is sexual orientation. We are presented with the simplistic choice that sexual orientation is either genetic or it's a choice. When I consider the suffering and confusion among my friends and patients who have non-heterosexual orientations, it would be hard to defend sexual preference as pure choice: if it were that effortless, many would simply choose the easier path. As so many of them do not, it suggests a strong genetic drive.

At the same time, we still have our intellects, and so we still have choices. I have known men and women who decided that a traditional family were more important to them than their non-heterosexual orientation. Of course,

---

* And possibly change the course of history. There is an anecdote about Hitler, that the course of his life was changed when he was suffering with hysterical blindness after WWI. The doctor treating him, probably thinking that he was simply helping Hitler to calm down with his polemic rants and help him recover, hypnotized him and told him he would lead Germany back to greatness. The story is unsubstantiated but tantalizing; it would explain how he went from being an insignificant corporal to rebuilding Germany and creating exactly the sort of racist, vicious meat grinder that he had envisioned.

some argue they have not changed their orientation, only blocked it. But that makes my point here, that genetics is not determinism.

So both are true, it's genetics, and it's a choice: we run in ruts, we do not ride on rails. The real problem is that it's a simplistic dichotomy and that sexual activity among consenting adults is no one else's business. Which brings us to an irony: the racists, the homophobes, and the other critics are stuck in their own ruts; they defer to some authority, some atrox, who has dictated what is acceptable private behavior and what is not. The criticism is dishonest because it is based on obedience rather than objective analysis. The point that sexuality is a choice is simply a pretext for arguing that everyone must conform to some orthodoxy. So the same critics who insist that others have a choice are suppressing their own choices; they are refusing to think and choose independently. That is the point of this chapter. That is our bondage to the atrox in a nutshell.

...

The psychopath and the atrox may live in ruts of their own. Genetics is responsible for anywhere to 50–80 percent of anti-social behavior. But genes are an influence, not a determinant. As James Fallon demonstrates, even when genes appear to deal someone a pat hand, the hand does not have to be played. Genes do not have to win.

Finally, there is the temporary insanity of the good warrior, of the decent men who become evil in wartime. The ability to quickly slip from one set of moral and emotional clothes into another might reflect an intellectual choice based on the situation. But recall the film *Japanese Devils*. The soldiers' remorse, and the remorse of so many soldiers, suggests that their behaviors possibly resulted from genetic influences. The flip side is also illustrative: their critics' refusal to consider the possibility of Japanese war crimes, their rejection of their own analytical abilities, seems to reflect yet another genetic predilection.

A genetic component also seems to be reflected in the conformity and uniformity of the soldier: If everyone's thinking the same way, who's thinking? Consider Hugh Thompson and his actions at My Lai. Thompson was a warrior, and he had previously been complicit in the deaths of many men. But he was not a genetic automaton, and he was willing to stand against the crowd. When he saw a violation of basic human decency, he stood up and stood against. His intellect won. But where were the intellects and the moral compasses of the other men involved that day? Today, the evil of My Lai is obvious; why wasn't it obvious in 1968? In Task Force Barker, no one other than Thompson saw it, or if they did, they said nothing. An important clue is that when Thompson complained, the operation was quickly called off. It suggests that many of the officers and troops could also see the problem, but they ignored it and complied anyway; they praised the emperor for his new clothes. We apparently have a genetic urge to fight in war. On top of that, we apparently have a genetic urge to listen to the mob rather than our own intellects. But we still have an intellect. We just need to learn to listen to it.

Thompson was unique at My Lai. But if we can understand how one person managed to escape tradition and genetic influences, then perhaps the rest of us can learn to escape, too.

Another human rut is the willingness of the victim to accept unjust blame. We used the example of the rapist to show how the atrox blames his victim. This is an area where I have some professional experience. The ER physician typically performs the forensic rape exam, and I have done too many. Some years ago, it occurred to me that, of the several dozen exams I have performed, only one victim had physical injuries.

They all had psychological injuries, however. This is one of the more convincing illustrations of the power of genetics in our thinking and in our decisions. Every rape victim knows, intellectually, that she is innocent and did nothing wrong. And in the modern countries we not only agree that the victim is innocent, we provide her with social, legal, and emotional support. So there is no intellectual reason for her to believe that any of it was her fault.

But she is nevertheless filled with shame and guilt. Her life is irrevocably damaged by an injury inside of her mind. This is the same mind that we naïvely tell ourselves we completely control, the mind that we insist is purely logical and practical. The victim's self-blame makes no sense logically nor practically. Shame and resignation also appear to have genetic components.

It is another legacy of the atrox. For ten millennia, the conqueror assaulted us physically, mentally, intellectually, and sexually and blamed us for our suffering. We not only agreed, we not only submitted to the abuse, but we absolved him of responsibility for his crimes. We have come to agree that the conqueror is not a criminal, he is a great man; any fault, any blame, any suffering, are the result of our own flaws.

Our position is ridiculous; we are not in the wrong, he is. Once again, when we respond in ways that make no sense intellectually, when our logic fails in the face of our emotions and our actions, we must wonder if our genes are asserting themselves.

We began this chapter considering the dangers of racism. The desire to thwart the racist is a major motivation for rejecting the role of genetics in directing human behavior and to prevent racism from limiting human potential. I suspect that racism itself may be influenced by genetics.

Consider that a common response to anything that is untested, or which differs from our experiences, is to react with caution, even suspicion. This is true in animals as well as humans, suggesting there is a genetic drive at work. In the past, when survival forced humanity into a perennial 'us or them' mentality, prejudice was important for survival. One's extended family and tribe shared the same genes and culture, and recognizing the associated genetic and cultural clues was a quick way to separate kinsman from encroacher, friend from foe. So superficial aspects became important; we could glance at someone's hair, eyes, face, body type, clothing, and listen to him speak, and make a rough determination: Us, or them? It was the best available strategy. We would not be surprised to find that at least some of our mistrust of the outsider is a genetic, visceral reaction.

In the modern world, however, 'us or them' is an inferior strategy. In a complex, advanced economy, we realize that exotic appearances and culture say nothing about important things. Today, there are only two critical questions about other people: Do they do good work? Can we trust them? We do not have to search far to find people who were badly burned by placing their trust in family, friends, political allies, church members, or the members of their own race; but we can also easily find industries and communities that flourish by welcoming those who are trustworthy and competent, exclusive of their race, creed, color, or any other differentiator. Racism is the inferior social approach; it is an obsolete strategy inherited from the past. It is a biting irony: until the racist can escape his own genetic ruts, he is the genetic inferior of the very people he believes are inferior to him.

Racism is not that simple, however. The racist demonstrates the cryptic interplay among genes, culture, experience, and intellect. Consider that racists disagree about which races are inferior; recall Weber's quote about anti-Semitism and football. The malleability of racism can become quite confusing. I remember a patient who was Chinese-American, born in Hong Kong, who told me that he hated the mainland Chinese. A biracial child, raised in a family representing only one of her races, can struggle to understand the racism on both sides.[4] So our *potential* for racism, and the intellectual mechanisms that support racism, must have a genetic component. Whether or not racism emerges in an individual, and if it does appear, the targets of that racism, are almost definitely *not* genetic. The ability to be a racist appears to have a genetic component, but the expression of the racism would seem to be the result of the post-natal effects of education, personal experience, and intellectual analysis.

My anti-Semitic friend we noted earlier illustrates the complexity. Despite his culture, his friends, and his news sources, he has had positive experiences with Muslims, and so he has no objections there. His experience and his intellectual independence have helped him to escape his cultural cues. Perhaps more illustrative of how convoluted, complicated, contradictory, and inconsistent the situation is, however, is reflected in his reaction to blacks, Latinos, and others. He is engaging and affable with his minority coworkers and can be quite sympathetic and empathetic with many of his minority patients. He can become irritated with patients of all races whom he thinks are personally irresponsible or who appear to exploit public services. When these objectionable patients are minorities, it seems that the standard right-wing saws more often emerge—comments about entitlements, the welfare state, and wasted tax dollars. But even here the picture is unclear. I cannot tell whether he is really more critical of minorities, and whether his reactions truly differ depending on race; or whether minorities simply trigger those words and phrases that the alt-right media associate with those races. I could ask him, but that brings us back to the previously considered problem of self-assessments: I do not believe we are truly honest with ourselves.

The problem with racism and other dogma is much like the problem of temporary psychopathy. In response to different clues, it appears that the brain centers controlling empathy may be switched off for a time, only later to recover. The trigger mechanism itself must be a genetic construct, but the indicator pulling the trigger may be genetic (anger or fear), acquired (military or clinical conditioning), or intellectual (Robert E. Lee suggesting that it is good that war is terrible).

If the trigger works like that of a weapon, then it can be on or off, we can slip in and out of the condition; in temporary anempathy we can experience a transient emotional deafness. But in the case of racism and other ideology, the trigger can, instead, release a trapdoor. Once the mechanism trips, either from a genetic or non-genetic pull, the brain becomes locked against considering certain kinds of problems. Culture and conditioning may choose which trapdoors will shut; but the trapdoors themselves, and our historical *need* for traps against logic, must be selected, genetic traits. Humans are ostensibly the only living things capable of in-depth logical analysis, and so we need to ask what factors have created a selective pressure for our illogic since the beginning of humanity; or perhaps, since the beginning of civilization.

We will return to this, but we will see that someone who may be quite free and unorthodox in thinking about engineering or music may become quite rigid and intolerant about minorities or the visual arts. Or vice versa.

Ironically, an ideological response, the combination of a non-genetic trigger with a genetic trapdoor, can be worse than a purely genetic response. We may find that it is easier to master our heart rate and our fears than to overcome our prejudices. Hence the importance of zealotry and the dark pentad.

So the racial or ideological bigot may be under lockdown for only certain classes of the human experience but not others. Somewhere, of course, the bigot still has the key, but he is uninterested in finding it and using it; he does not wish to escape. So the problem becomes: How do we lead him out? How do we interest him in finding and using his keys?

That is the forté of the mental health worker and of the wise and nuanced mind. But as we have noted, we often ridicule such people. That is where we have shut our own trapdoors.

We will return repeatedly to this problem, the point being that when we encounter illogic, the choice of topic may result from cultural or other non-genetic influences. But the ability, even the propensity, for illogic in some areas of our lives but not in others, has an important genetic component. And the only thing that can free us is the fourth leg of the stool.

It is essential that we recognize how our genetic ruts, and even our genetic traps, often hobble us. In the modern parts of the world, we no longer struggle for survival. We are struggling for progress, which requires collaboration and diversity: diversity of experience, diversity of education, diversity of ideas. Our genetic influences, and the superficial thinking they often facilitate, simply hold us back. If we don't learn to recognize and resist those genetic influences, we will stumble back into our ruts, slide off the edge of recent human progress, and descend once again into horror, superstition, and intolerance.

Chapter IV:
The Breeding Programme[*]

There's been no biological change in humans in 40,000 or 50,000 years. Everything we call culture and civilization we've built with the same body and brain.
— Stephen J. Gould

I am the good shepherd. I know my sheep, and they know me.
— Jesus of Nazareth

Damn, what a gullible breed.
— Agent Kay, *Men in Black*

In Christian tradition, the members of a church are sheep, they constitute a flock, and the clergyman is a 'pastor,' a shepherd. This goes back to Jesus who claimed that he was 'the good shepherd.' But there are Biblical references preceding that, such as the Old Testament's 23rd psalm. It is even older than that, however, as various kings throughout Mesopotamia referred to themselves as shepherds and to their people as sheep.

It is no great compliment. Sheep are dim-witted, clumsy, brutish beasts. They have to be constantly retrieved from entanglements in vegetation and rough terrain. This is the reason for the humble shepherd's crook, to pull them out. Sheep allow themselves to be fleeced, they meekly allow their lambs to be taken to slaughter, and eventually, they follow quietly when their time comes. This is the reason we refer to someone who appears humbled as 'sheepish' and to unthinking people as 'sheeple.'

When kings use the metaphor, the implication is that we are too simple to make decisions for ourselves. The king is the only one smart enough to help us, he must make our decisions for us, even as to who among us lives, who breeds, and who is sent to slaughter.

---

[*] The word 'program' comes from Greek and refers to something that is 'written before.' In American English it typically refers to something that is carefully scripted. In British English, however, 'programme' appears to take on additional nuance and may indicate a system or pattern that is not so carefully controlled or predictable. For instance, in biology the 'adaptationist programme' refers to a general approach for analyzing evolution. Stephen Jay Gould and Richard C. Lewontin, "The Spandrels of San Marco and the Panglossian Paradigm: A Critique of the Adaptationist Programme," *Proceedings of the Royal Society of London* B 205 (1979): 581-98.

All of this is striking because wild sheep differ on all of these points. The feral animals from which our domestic breeds derive are wily, belligerent, and very dangerous. The wild ram, in fact, was a celebrated symbol of virility and bellicosity in the ancient world.* Ram's horns were a symbol of Alexander, and in the Qu'ran, "the two-horned one" is often interpreted to be Alexander. The ram-headed sphinx was the symbol of the Egyptian god Amun-Min, the god of virility. One of the Celtic gods of war, Camulus, is also symbolized by a ram, and he is often associated with Mars, the Roman god of war. The point is, domestic sheep are docile and submissive, while wild sheep are so fierce and independent that they were chosen as symbols to represent some of the most vicious people of history.

The same is true for many domesticated animals. The much-feared wolf is the symbol of Mars, and the she-wolf nursing Romulus and Remus is still the symbol of Rome. Today our domesticated wolf, the dog, may protect us fiercely from strangers, but within the house he is completely submissive. The now-extinct auroch, the ancestor of modern cattle, was so feared by the ancients that it inspired the legend of the Minotaur. In contrast, today the word 'bovine' refers to someone who is dim-witted and lethargic. The wild boar is one of the most dangerous animals in the forest, but the modern farm pig is invoked as a model of sloth and filth. Wild turkeys are prized as game animals because they are so wily, but the domesticated turkey is so dumb that he will drown staring up into the rain. Wild horses are nothing to tangle with, as they can easily kill a man with their hooves or by rolling over him. The domesticated horse, however, quietly submits to direction and discipline from humans who may be one-tenth of his weight. The domesticated cousins, the camel, the llama, and the vicuña, can all be dangerous when wild, but once domesticated, submit as pack animals. Finally, there is the elephant, the largest land mammal at up to six tons, so large that even large predators avoid it. The Indian elephant, however, has been domesticated, and like the rest of these, takes direction from a human that it could easily crush.

So who tamed the ram, the wolf, the boar, and the auroch? Doubtless some domestication began with capturing the young of these species and keeping them tied or penned until they were old enough to slaughter. But at some point, there were people brave enough—or, as we have seen with the psychopath, fearless enough, or risk-seeking enough—to attempt to domi-

---

* The Latin word for 'war' is *bellum*, hence 'bellicose' and 'belligerent.' The French word for 'ram' is *bélier*. The two are not related; apparently, *bélier* is related to the English 'bellwether,' because the lead ram wears a bell. In an interesting parallel, the Zodiac sign *Aries* gets its name from the Latin word for 'ram'; but *Ares*, the Greek god of war, is unrelated and related to the English 'ire.'

The Breeding Programme

nate the mature animals. We see a bit of that recklessness preserved in modern rodeo, where men ride horses and bulls that behave like their wild ancestors. The human-animal struggle makes rodeo one of the most dangerous of all spectator activities.[1]

In his Pulitzer winning *Guns, Germs, and Steel*, Jared Diamond points out that only a handful of animals have been truly domesticated.[2] For the large animals, almost all of them derive from wild herd or pack animals with a strong hierarchical aspect, typically dominated by an alpha male, often with a strict social structure below him. For instance, the horse, *Equus feris caballa*, comes from one such wild group structure, and the horse may have been domesticated more than once. In contrast, the zebra, *Equus quagga*, although closely related, lives in a large and loosely associated herd structure without a clear alpha male. It has never been domesticated despite several modern efforts and probably many ancient attempts.

These insights also apply to humans. We come out of an alpha-male pack structure. And the same sort of reckless man who subjugated animals for the farm, subjugated humanity for the kingdom. Early in civilization the atrox broke us, much as some brutal man broke the first horse.

• • •

My family and I live in a home perched on a slope over a quiet lake. A few weeks each year, white herons roost in a nearby tree. There's an osprey that appears intermittently, there are hawks and owls, and hummingbirds and dragonflies zoom around. Raccoon families forage around the lake, and from time to time coyotes pass through. Squirrels chase each other through the trees while songbirds fill the air with melody. We occasionally see young animals in nests or shyly foraging with their families. The lake is full of fish and turtles, and once in a while a community notice goes out that a small alligator has gotten in from the bordering bayou. There are fascinating insects and other small animals everywhere. Wildflowers, large and small, bloom around us. There is beauty and fascination from the tiniest bug to the tallest tree.

As a biologist, I'm aware that it's all illusion. The songbirds' melodies are actually avian challenges and warnings to potential competitors. The squirrels' games are struggles over territory, where the loser has a good chance of starving slowly (if he is unlucky) or being a quick meal for a predator (if he is less unlucky). The birds of prey we see are hunting the songbirds and the squirrels, and the raptors are stalked by yet other predators, from microbes to humans.

The large trees probably have it made—for the moment—but tree seedlings are chopped beneath the lawnmower or pulled up by the squirrels who chew on what's left of the seeds, and the saplings struggle against overcrowding in the untended woods and border scrub. All of them are exposed to the elements and face countless diseases. Each animal is one broken bone or infection from an almost certain death. As for the nestlings, cubs, and other cute young animals, the odds for them surviving to adulthood are very poor. If they are fortunate enough to make it that far, their probability of establishing and defending a territory and raising their own brood is also low. All wild animals constantly live on the edge of starvation. A few days of poor foraging or the loss of a territory spells almost certain death. Every waking minute is a struggle against the odds.

As we putter around in our loveliness, we almost never see any of this. Predators strike quickly and stealthily. Diseased, famished, or injured animals are killed and eaten quickly or are driven off to isolated deaths. Parent animals have little time to worry over the loss of careless or unlucky offspring. And the corpses that might serve as testament to an animal's passing do not last long. There are too many starving organisms, from bacteria to bugs to buzzards, to leave even rotten meat uneaten.

The essential insight for nature is that for every breeding organism we see, on average only two of its offspring, over its entire lifetime, will survive to also leave offspring. Large oak trees produce tens of thousands of acorns, every year, for centuries. Fruit flies lay perhaps five hundred eggs in a six-week lifespan. The common toad secrets away three thousand spawn annually, in a ten-year effort. And the rare songbird that manages to live five years might produce twenty chicks in her career.

It doesn't matter how many offspring are produced. On average, all mature organisms raise just two offspring to adulthood. If the environment improves to support more living things, then that number will briefly increase, then stabilize again at two offspring. If the environment decays from drought, freeze, over-browsing—or often, from human encroachment or pollutants—the numbers will decline for a while and then return to a steady state of two offspring. It doesn't matter. Beyond an average of two successes in each generation, all of the other offspring must die.

Peaceful, romantic nature is an illusion. Nature is a scene of struggle, suffering, and slaughter. No matter how much loveliness we see, just beneath the surface is a deathscape where few survive; and except for the occasional tree, almost none die quietly of old age.

When we study 'survival of the fittest' and natural breeding programmes in the wild, we focus on the improvements and the successes. We overlook the reality of the struggle for survival, that for every success there are a multitude of deaths. It is true in all of nature.

And until quite recently, and with the exception of only a few advanced economies, it is also true for humanity.

⋯

Both sides of the equation, fecundity and death, are critical for understanding the human condition. To our thesis here, it explains the breeding programme that the atrox imposed on humanity. Consider Tamerlane, who slew seventeen million people; that represented about 5 percent of the Earth's human population in the fourteenth century.[3] Likewise, we noted that the slaughter of Genghis Khan was probably in excess of sixty million people, which comprised over 15 percent of the world's population.

The other side of the equation is the reproductive impact of the conqueror, and Genghis provides a unique perspective. The great Khan carried a unique Y chromosome gene that can be identified in his modern male descendants. By tracking that gene, we can show that about 8 percent of the people in modern China, about .5 percent of everyone alive today—around thirty-five million people—are direct descendants of Genghis Khan.*

Every generation has spawned hundreds of lesser Khans, each of whom attracted and promoted large gangs to share the conqueror's bloodlust and loin-lust. Humanity has suffered constant predation and forced paternity from men who may not have equaled the extent of Khan's conquests, but who were easily his equals in perverse dysfunction.

The atrox has ensured that his genes have spread throughout humanity, while the genes of anyone who stood in his way have dwindled. It is inescapable that we are all descended from many atroces and their troops. But we are also descended from their victims.

In *The Times Atlas of World History*,[4] humanity is represented by seemingly innocuous arrows crisscrossing the continents and spanning the millennia. Each arrow, however, describes the movements of large populations, either invading in conquest or fleeing crowding, famine, and/or yet other conquerors. The refugees migrated thousands of hostile and hungry miles and then invaded and displaced, or even annihilated, yet other masses of humanity. We must assume that most populations—those who did not escape *en masse*, those who did not survive migration, and those who did not follow a bloodthirsty conqueror of their own to lead them in relocation—were eradicated or enslaved, and probably left no record at all. There are some six hundred maps in the book, and each map presents numerous such arrows. What

---

* Note that this is still far fewer than the number of people he killed.

percentage of humanity do they represent? What percentage of humanity do they omit? How many of the conqueror's victims are completely missing from the historical record, anywhere?

Second, and resulting from the constant problem of whitewashing we previously considered, what historical records survive are clinical, sanitized, even Bowdlerized: the troops moved like this; the battle was a rout; the city was razed. So while the successful conqueror might wish to exaggerate the number of enemy combatants slain,* until the Romantic period, there was little interest in the plight of the peasants. The suffering of commoners was of marginally more importance than the misery of livestock, and chroniclers only rarely considered them. So to begin to understand warfare and the scope of historical atrocity, we must extrapolate from the few examples here to consider the scope of slaughter.

However, we must go even further, because as we have noted previously, what records we have focus almost exclusively on large wars. We have little knowledge of the constant smaller horrors, the lesser battles and skirmishes, the raids of nobles upon neighboring states, or even the king's raids upon his own subjects. In the Middle Ages, for instance, it has been proposed that more death and destruction came from raiding than from direct warfare.[5] There is no reason to believe that this was unique or even rare in history.

In addition to raiding from the nobility, there has also been the problem of unattached soldiers. Once a war is finished, many of the troops are discharged; expendable in war, they are certainly expendable in peace. But many either have no home or trade to which to return, or they have decided that they prefer the excitement and profitability of human bloodsport. A warring army is no small thing, and the numbers of discharged troops after recurrent, endless campaigns would have been considerable.

We have scattered records of freelancers, freebooters, unattached mercenaries, rogue knights, *routiers*, Japanese *rōnin*, and many others who prowled the countrysides of the world, preying upon the locals and—much as we saw with David in the Old Testament—perhaps slaying everyone for expediency. Possibly the kindest fate for the victims was quick murder. We can only imagine the sadism of professional killers when they were isolated and bored, and able to leisurely torture the occupants of some remote farm or village. Odysseus's treatment of Melanthius and

---

* For instance, some historians have begun to doubt the large troop mismatches that Henry V reported at Agincourt, *e.g.*, A. Curry, *Agincourt 1415: A New History* (The History Press, 2015).

Catiline's torture of Gratidianus suggest what the professional solider is capable of doing. That danger still exists today: for all of their cultural differences, their superior training and discipline, American troops will occasionally kill for no reason. Witness the sadism of American troops killing Afghan civilians, including a fifteen-year-old boy, for no reason other than boredom; and note the officers' willingness to allow such things to happen.* How much more common were these activities when there was no free press to report such things nor democratic citizens to complain?

I will add to these the history of Jewish persecution. The first book of the Old Testament is *Genesis*, describing the origins of Judaism. But the very next book, *Exodus*, is the first chapter in a chronology of repeated Jewish persecution. *Wikipedia* lists several hundred incidences of Jewish persecution over almost three millennia.† The comedian Alan King quipped, "A summary of every Jewish holiday: They tried to kill us, we won, let's eat!"

We noted that Jews are 'the people of the Book.' It must be remembered that a major distinguishing tradition of the Jews is that, first, they created their own records of their history, including the accounts of their persecutions; the rest of us are forced to largely rely on the whitewashed chronicles of the conqueror. Second, unlike our other ancestors (we are all more closely related than we realize), the Jews survived their persecutions while maintaining their cultural identity and preserving their records as they fled.

But all of our ancestors faced constant attacks, persecutions, and atrocities. Our considerations here suggest that, unlike the Jews, the overwhelming majority of historical cultures either did not survive, were dispersed and/or absorbed, and/or left no records of their persecutions. We would do well to study the Jewish histories, and rather than viewing them as records of 'the other,' find ourselves reflected in them. Again, identifying the universal in the suffering of all people is our best chance for mapping out a better future.

---

* In 2011, members of the 5th Stryker Brigade stationed near Kandahar intentionally started killing innocent civilians. At one point they selected a fifteen-year-old boy and simply killed him. They showed no remorse, not even when the elder brought over to identify the child turned out to be his father. To the contrary: they proudly took pictures of their victims and amputated fingers as trophies. The event was hardly a secret, and in fact senior leadership dismissed the complaints of the boy's father after a brief investigation. "The Kill Team Photos: More war crime images the Pentagon doesn't want you to see," *Rolling Stone*, March 27, 2011.

† Interestingly enough, the timeline omits Exodus. *https://en.wikipedia.org/wiki/Timeline_of_antisemitism*, 08:08 CST, 2018.02.25.

•••

Physicists postulate that about 95 percent of the universe is dark matter and dark energy: we can't see it, so we can't know much about it. Quite likely we are missing much more than 95 percent of the grinding, suffering, and horror of our ancestors. It is possible that what histories we have are not the tip of an iceberg, but more like an occasional ice floe, orphaned from some distant glacier.

As a physician and biologist, I will offer a few observations. First, humans can jog for days without sleeping. A reasonably fit man or woman can run a horse or hare to exhaustion; Louis Leakey once ran a wild antelope to collapse.[6] No other land animal can match our endurance. Birds and butterflies match us by flying nonstop while migrating over ocean, and some swifts apparently live their lives in flight, almost never alighting nor even sleeping.[7] But these behaviors are the result of strong survival pressures. What possible selective pressure could produce this migration endurance in humans? Because if no other animal can match our stamina, then what possible predator or prey would require us to evolve such a capacity?

Second, there is the childhood game of hide and seek. Child's play often rehearses behaviors that may later be needed for survival, and hide and seek seems a likely skill for learning to escape predators. But the large predators we might wish to escape—wolves, big cats, the occasional bear—all have keen senses of smell. And until recently, humans did not often bathe, so our odors were strong and distinctive, particularly with the unique human smell of smoke.* So hiding from wild predators wouldn't be of much use in survival.

Hiding would be useful only when avoiding a predator who is a sight hunter with a poor sense of smell. In addition, the presence of hide and seek in all cultures suggests a predator with worldwide distribution.

Then consider that tiny children, who can be quite noisy while awake, quickly fall asleep when swaddled, rocked, and exposed to soft or muffled noises. For other animals, sleeping would seem more likely under peaceful and unrestrained conditions and less likely when the subject is constrained and jostled.* In fact, the latter situation suggests that the animal has been trapped and is headed for the picket or the pot.

---

* I became aware of smoke as a human odor during a clerkship in rural Jamaica in my senior year of medical school. I wondered why so many of the clinic patients smelled of smoke. One day, I accompanied a local nurse on her home visits and realized that the poor cooked their meals over open fires in front of their huts.

The Breeding Programme

These behaviors and capabilities suggest creatures who must be able to hide and then to quickly and silently flee for days, while maintaining a quiet, rapid pace and continuing nonstop through several nights. We are left with a disturbing conclusion. It is possible that historically, escaping other human predators was a strong selection pressure, a chronic and recurring challenge to our survival. Recall, we considered only the first half of 'hide and seek'; the second half of the game is 'find the victim.' Our children train to be both victim and victimizer.

There is a tantalizing jot of evidence in early civilization to support this idea: the thirty-four victims of the Talheim Death Pit, murdered around 5000 BCE, were chiefly attacked from the rear. The arrangement of their injuries do not reflect a battle, which has led anthropologists to suggest they were trying to flee.[8] That, chillingly, suggests that others were stalking them.

So perhaps escaping and avoiding raiders has been a regular problem throughout civilization, perhaps even before. Apparently humanity has been constantly subjected to intense survival pressure to either conform or flee.

• • •

History focuses on the tremendous spoils of the victor and the luxurious cities he creates with his resultant wealth. To understand our erroneous ideas about the conqueror, however, we need to consider the conquered, who lose everything. The disasters served upon the vanquished extend far beyond the battlefield, as invading armies force large populations into starvation by raiding their food and possessions, or worse, through wholesale sabotage for strategic advantage.

After an invader wins, there follows the transition to the rule of a new monarch, brutally implemented, typically incompetent, and arbitrarily indifferent. Regime change may kill more people than conquest. Either way, throughout history there has been massive, deadly pressure to enthusiastically join and support the conqueror, in war and in peace, on and off the battlefield.

---

* One counter-thesis would be that swaddling, movement, and muffled sounds recreate the environment of the womb. But only the swaddling reproduces a constant condition of the womb. Movement and muffled noises within the uterus are inconstant, and yet they are very effective in inducing sleep. In addition, there is no obvious reason that these responses should persist after birth without some other selective pressure. Finally, it would be interesting to know if this response is observed in other mammals.

Even for those who conform, however, the survival pressures do not stop in peacetime. We have noted the dangers from freelancing knights and the raiding by one nobleman upon the lands of another. We must add peacetime justice to those considerations.

In a brief example, the Tyburn 'triple tree' (pg. 6), also known as 'the nevergreen,' was a gallows that allowed for triple hangings. That is an insight in itself: a single gallows could not handle the necessary executions. It is estimated that over fifty thousand children, women, and men were hung there for crimes as small as stealing a candle. Granted, those executions took place over several centuries, but for much of that time, London itself was smaller than fifty thousand. Then consider that Tyburn hosted the execution of only the criminals from the London area. Every city in every kingdom in the world held its own, regular executions, many of them for minor crimes; the atrox was not given to gentleness or forgiveness.

Hunting in the king's forest was a major offense, even though it was the only place to hunt. Cutting firewood in the forest was also forbidden, but wood could be collected from the commons; sometimes it was loosened from the trees 'by hook or by crook.'

Restrictions such as these meant that even in peacetime, many died from want, and many others were executed for trying to address that want. We must remember that the historical record almost exclusively reports the histories of the powerful, the wealthy, and the comfortable. But throughout most of civilization, there were very few such people, and the great bulk of humanity was poor and living on the edge, facing the constant threat of starvation, exposure, and disease: a person came down with a fever one day, was bedridden the next, and was dead the day after.

Through most of history, and even in the developing world before the arrival of birth control, the lifetime birthrate for the average couple was about six offspring; clearly, four of those must die from disease, starvation, injury, war, or execution. Life for the great bulk of civilization, as for the animals who struggle near my home, was a daily, deadly game to which they often succumbed.

And they generally succumbed quietly and stoically. As with other victims, they accepted their fate and agreed with their exploiters that their suffering was a result of their own flaws, perhaps for being weak, for being poor, or even as God's punishment for their sins. It was never the result of noble exploitation, abuse, or neglect.

There are a few examples of the have-nots refusing to accept their lot and rising up against the haves. Spartacus and Boudica are often celebrated for their temporary successes, and we will later come to Arminius, who permanently defeated his Roman masters. In the spring of 1196, William 'Longbeard' Fitz Osbert led one such uprising against the English crown and was unsuccessful. He was one of the earliest people known to be hanged at Tyburn. Or rather, he was hanged after he was "drawn asunder by horses." Rebellion almost always failed, and unsuccessful rebels were often tortured to death.

Which is why rebellion was infrequent. We can imagine that at the earliest stirrings of civilization, when the first atroces captured a people, the victims might not have accepted their fate and perhaps rose up against their rulers in attempt to escape or simply in an attempt to feed themselves. This behavior is reflected in the responses of Native Americans to the Pilgrims' abuses.

The king responded to uprisings in the same way as the conquerors we have already considered: he crushed resistance with broad reprisals that extended far beyond the offenders, in order to 'teach the people a lesson.' With time, subjects learned to suffer in silence, to go to their deaths quietly, and to encourage others, their children included, to do the same. So even as the upper classes might rejoice that peace and prosperity were upon the land, in war or peace the peasants died all around them, some in their private hovels, but many in the public streets.

They went to their deaths like sheep. Go back and reconsider the descriptions of those slaughtered on the beach at Jaffa. As they were bayoneted to death with their children, "They did not cry, they did not shout, they were resigned."

There is little record for any of this, but records are not always necessary in order to arrive at conclusions. We know that soldiers ran amok in warfare, because they still do it today. We know that despotic governments carried out unrecorded summary executions, because it still happens today. We know that the poor had too many babies to feed, because in many starving countries they still do today. We know that most of the children died quietly of starvation, disease, exposure, and war, because it still happens today. We therefore must assume, just as we must assume about the constant demise of the animals and plants around my home, that death was a frequent, daily occurrence. It is scientifically inescapable. The histories record almost none of it, but it does not mean it was not a constant occurrence.

• • •

Today we speak of terrorism as if it were something new, but civilization was constant terror. You woke up in the morning, set about your work, and an army, or marauders, or your own nobleman came through, trampled your fields, raped your women, poached your livestock, and confiscated your meager possessions. If they did not kill or enslave you, and if they left you anything at all, it might not be enough for you and your family to survive.* That began changing in the U.S. only a quarter-millennium ago. Or at least it changed for the European descendants; the Europeans perpetrated the same fate upon the natives, and African slaves were captured and brought here under the same abuses. Such things still occur in much of the world.

The pressure to survive, and the unlikelihood of that happening, have been intense since the dawn of life. With the onset of civilization, however, a new style of lethal pressure arrived, one that produced different cultural and genetic selections. Starting about ten thousand years ago, an essential part of survival included obeying whatever the atrox dictated. We were required to conform not only in body, but as we will see, in our thoughts and beliefs as well.

Psychopathy contains a strong—but again, not a determining—genetic component. There is a modern scholar who claims that perhaps one out of every seven people is a sociopath/psychopath.[9] That number seems high, but considering the millennia of conquest and raiding, constantly attended by rape, we might wonder why we are not all psychopaths. The answer is probably another consideration of biological competition: a group of nothing but psychopaths, particularly narcissistic psychopaths, would not be very successful; all chiefs and not a follower among them. A group with a few psychopaths and a lot of followers would make for a stronger, more competitive organization. With the limited theoretical tools available to us today, biologists have at times struggled to explain the biological basis of cohesion, cooperation, and self-sacrifice in groups. Regardless, these behaviors exist, they make their groups stronger, and groups are selected by precisely the same Darwinian principles that individuals are.

The genetic legacy of the atrox will return in upcoming chapters, but I will offer a problematic bit of research that has traditionally been cited in racist screed and turn it around in a reconsideration of the atrox and the horrors of conquest.

Some years ago, several papers appeared suggesting that Asian children are the most compliant and docile, Caucasian children are intermediate, and African children are the most boisterous and independent.[10] This research is often cited as evidence of the superiority of the white race, although white

---

* It occurs to me that a bit of this abuse has been preserved in fox hunting, where hunters ride their horses through the fields, farms, and other holdings of the commoners, without concern for loss or damage.

racists conveniently ignore the implications that under this distinction, whites would be inferior to Asians.

If this research accurately reflects reality, and if that reality is based upon genetic differences, then there is a much darker interpretation, one based on our observations in this chapter. First, we can imagine that pre-civilized children, raised in open areas with room to explore and play, were all boisterous and independent; that was likely our natural state. Second, consider the unimportance of children under the absolutism of the atrox: the Spartans cast undesirable children in a pit to die; Alexander's father attempted to kill him; after conquest, ancient cultures enslaved children, executed them, or abandoned them to die; under Roman law, the father owned his children much as he did livestock, and he could have them sold, abandoned, or executed; and even today in some cultures, fathers are not only permitted, but expected to commit honor killings against their children who have violated some social code. With these, recall the implications of hide and seek we considered.

Then recall that Kim Jong-il jailed families for the misbehavior of a single child. The atrox pursued punishment and casual slaughter in both war and peace. We cannot imagine that he or his henchmen would show much patience to unruly children who offended the dignity of the royal presence.

The atrox domesticated us by means of lethal force. We must assume the same lethality was applied to children. So if it were indeed true that Eurasian children are more docile than African children, rather than impugn African culture and genes, we need to instead ask what horrors were perpetrated against children across ancient Eurasia in order to breed the quieter children we see today.

As I noted, we will return to the legacy of the atrox in a few chapters. The objective here, as with the previous chapter, is to introduce a critical possibility: there is almost definitely a strong genetic aspect to our modern problems, and those problematic genetic drives are the result of ten thousand years of bondage to the atrox. Some part of our genetic baggage is our drive to behave like the atrox and to exploit others. The other part is our drive to behave like sheep and to submit to the atrox and his henchmen.

Chapter V:
The Noble Classes

We hang petty thieves and appoint the great ones to public office.
— Aesop (attributed)

We did everything adults would do. What went wrong?
— Piggy, *Lord of the Flies*[1]

When a conqueror won new territories, he installed his army officers as his new government, in a similar chain of command. They administered his possessions and shared in his protection racket. They are his *lieutenants*, a French word literally meaning 'placeholders.'

These 'nobles' implemented the same brutal hierarchy among the commoners that existed in the army. Discipline was harsh for those within the chain of command and even worse for those outside of it. For the commoners in a feudal society, particularly the peasants, there were few rights or protections; conditions might remain as bleak as they were in warfare. There is peace, but as we have seen, in the peasants' lives any improvements were small. The peasants simply weren't important.

• • •

A few years back, friends of mine were working to create a children's educational center. They approached another nonprofit for help and support, one whose mission is the general improvement of the community. The second group's representative met with my friends, and after going through their documents, the visitor pointed out that they needed a board.

"Oh, we have a board," they responded. "All of our organizational and legal structures are in place."

"No," the woman responded, "you need a *board*." My friends explained, again, that they had a board. The conversation then went through a couple more iterations of the same.

Growing impatient, one of my friends said, "Look, *we* are the board."

The woman stared at them blankly for a few moments and responded, "But you aren't anybody."

There was an icy silence. Finally, one of my friends replied, "That's funny. I always *thought* I was somebody." The meeting quickly concluded.*

The word 'noble' means 'someone who is *known*.' Reality TV has popularized the phrase 'famous for being famous,' but the concept is hardly new. A coterie of people surrounded the king, many selected for their ability to help him subjugate and exploit his subjects, but quite a few for their personal connection to him: relatives, friends, gaming companions, concubines, and other entertainers and flatterers. The first group were known because they were feared; the second were known for being known. Both groups actively supported the king's narcissism and fostered his cult of personality. They were the nobles, the 'important' people; implying, of course, that everyone else is unimportant.

To the narcissist, only some people matter, and the rest are expendable. This culture continues into the modern world; we believe that there are 'important' people in a society. And if you are not someone important, then the implication is that you are no one at all.

Again, it is a reflection of how the atrox sees us. His narcissism leads him to associate, on the one hand, with other 'important' and famous people; and on the other, those who are loyal to him. The rest are inconsequential and disposable. As noted, historically the peasants were no more important than the wild animals in the king's forest; killing a deer or killing a person both carried the death penalty. But then, even stealing a candle carried the same penalty. Much as the quarry in a fox hunt, the *hoi polloi* were inconsequential clay pigeons, bodies to be slaughtered in the sporting hunt of war, game pieces to be sacrificed to provide the king with entertainment, and points on the way to the trophies of captured cities.

A strong class consciousness emerged from earliest civilization, and the safest route to survival was to become a member of the highest possible class. That required aping the narcissism and superficial materialism of the nobility: larger homes, lavish gardens, vast estates, rich furniture and conveyances, refined clothing, and expensive jewelry. Part of that prestige, and essential to it, was the number of people one controlled: the malignant narcissist needs to control people. Brief reflection shows, in fact, that the importance of ostentatious possessions and ruinous fashions first serve to exclude the unimportant people; and second, to demonstrate one's power, wealth, and social

---

* The larger organization annually canvassed their members as to what local project or organization they should focus on for the upcoming year. My friends' educational initiative came back overwhelmingly as the first choice. There was much scrambling as the officers of the larger group struggled to make amends.

The Noble Classes

standing, which is code for how many people one controls. The Earl controls more people than the Baron, the Duke controls more than the Earl, and the king controls them all.* Wealth and status reflect how many people that one controls, completely or partially: slaves, serfs, servants, servicers, sycophants, and supporters.

⋯

The atrox and his nobles create laws and rules for self-promotion and for the subjugation of others. Throughout history there have been sumptuary laws, prohibiting the common classes from purchasing and owning certainly luxuries. These laws often dictated clothing, jewelry, furniture, conveyances, and even food. In sixteenth-century France, beef and lamb were outlawed for commoners, and at about the same time, Milan outlawed peacocks, pheasants, and roe deer for the inferior classes.[2] These laws served several goals: they distinguished the nobles from the commoners; they reinforced the power of the nobility as they reinforced the commoners' subjugation; and they artificially depressed the price of key luxuries.

All of these supported the narcissism of the king and his nobles, and fostered a preoccupation with superficial appearance, up and down the hierarchy. From there, those priorities spread out into the common classes, who also became preoccupied with social standing and social climbing.

Everyone was constrained. Even the senior nobility were constricted by tight rules and customs that dictated how they must behave, how they must dress, and how they must spend their day, in manual labor, in a trade, or in whatever diversions were acceptable in the leisure classes. It would seem that the king alone could escape these rules, but he was caught in his own game. To reinforce his power, he had to exceed the ostentation of his nobility; his homes, clothes, and provisions must exceed those of everyone else.

The hierarchy lived in a 'pecking order.' This is a real phenomenon among chickens and other animals. The top rooster pecks all of the others in the flock. Below him is another chicken, who abuses all the birds except the alpha rooster. The abuse continues down the line until one poor hen is abused by everyone and ashamedly awaits the arrival of someone newer, younger, or weaker.

---

* The belief in an absolute monarch is part of the fairy tale. Absolute power may exist for the first king of a lineage, *i.e.* for the new conqueror who installs his own hierarchy. With each successive atrox in a dynasty, however, it is not unusual to see the hierarchy increasingly jostle and jockey for more power and elevated status. That lust for appearances, we will see, is one of the dysfunctions of the nobles.

This was the king's hierarchy. Each level was required to defer to superior levels and quietly accept any abuse they might impose. In turn, one expressed one's position in the nobility by abusing everyone below him or her. The French called it *une cascade de mépris*, 'a cascade of contempt.'³

This hierarchy has been somewhat blunted in the United States, but it is still visible in any variety of situations where individuals hold power, sometimes only a little power. Many exposés are published every year, with hackneyed but still salacious details of how the powerful abuse their inferiors, socially, sexually, mentally, and economically.* Outside of America, there is a range of balance points between rigid hierarchy and equality. The hierarchy can be particularly strong in poorer countries, but it is also visible in many advanced countries, such as the upper levels of British society and in their elite boarding schools, where often remains a strong sense of class consciousness.

Supporting the cascade, commoners are required to bow, or even kowtow, in the presence of a superior. They may be prohibited from making eye contact or from speaking until spoken to. When permitted to speak, their words and manner must be meek. They will be required to use titles that emphasize the narcissism of the dignitary, 'Your Majesty,' 'Your Highness,' 'Your Lordship,' 'Your Worship,' or similar. The inferior classes must constantly show 'humility'; they must be 'humble' in speech and behavior. Both of these words derive from the Latin word for 'dirt,' related to the modern 'humus' and 'exhume.' Commoners were dirt.

• • •

It is interesting that the following words begin with 'p': plebeian, parochial, provincial, pedestrian, proletarian, *hoi polloi*, peasant, plain, prosaic, pawn, and peon.† Beyond their initial letter, they all have two additional things in common. First, they represent the working classes. Second, they imply insult. In fact, when these words are insulting, it is *because* they represent the working

---

* One of the more popular (and tamer) tellings of these sort of abuses was the best seller *The Devil Wears Prada*, supposedly describing Anna Wintour, notorious fashion diva and longtime editor of *Vogue*. Wintour publicly expressed modest support for the book and even attended the movie première (wearing Prada, no less), but a curious detail emerged that none of the Condé Nast publications ever reviewed or so much as mentioned the book even though *Vogue* is one of its properties. Lauren Weisberger, *The Devil Wears Prada* (Anchor, 2003).

† 'Pawn,' 'peon,' and 'pioneer' are all descendants of the Latin *pes/pedis*, 'foot,' and refer to those who go before the main body and clear the way. That also links them to 'pedestrian.' The important people ride horses, litters, or carriages; only expendable people travel by foot.

classes. In their origins, there was nothing inherently negative about any of them. They simply represented those who were not part of the noble, upper classes. And so they came to represent people who were undesirable.

There are other words that denote class contempt. Originally, these words simply referred to a commoner: idiot, knave, churlish, vulgar, mean, ordinary. There are also terms for someone of questionable birth: base, lowly, low-born, bastard. We have names for those who come from outside of city and civilized culture, or even from outside of the nation: yokel, villain, vile, uncouth, barbarian. There are names for those who do not conform to acceptable behavior, particularly to those who don't 'know their place': bad, sinister, bounder, brazen, freak, bawdy, rogue, rabble. Then there are men who work outdoors and whose hands and clothes might be dirty: obscene, filthy, ruddy, rude, rough, crude, cruel, sordid, and of course, 'dirty' itself.*

Some of the ugliest pejoratives derive from working-class women, particularly those who did not have the time or the means to always appear in neat, refined clothing: hussy, slut, tart, wench, drab, slattern, and of course, the phrase 'working girl' itself. Even the term 'commoner' was formerly a euphemism for a sexually promiscuous woman.

These are instructive for what they are not. They sit in contrast to terms for the upper classes: pure, white, fair, refined, and blue-blood.†

These represent the tension between *nobility* and *mobility*. The Latin *mobile vulgus* means 'the fickle crowd.' At a point in English history it was shortened to 'mobile,' *i.e.*, 'the fickle'; and then, once again, to distinguish the important people from the unimportant lower classes, it became 'mobility' as an opposite of 'nobility.' From there it was shortened to 'mob.' This brings us back to the first chapter: the leader of the lower class undesirables was a mobster.

As we observed in our discussion of magical horses, our words often trace the evolution of our thinking. The preceding terms reveal much about how we viewed one another in the past and how those attitudes color our thinking in the modern world.

---

* For a number of these words, the etymologies are unclear. When there is more than one proposed origin, I have eliminated extra meanings for brevity and clarity, which admittedly does not necessarily produce the best scholarship.

† 'Blue blood' refers to those whose skin is so white that the veins can be seen. Occasionally in portraits from early centuries, the painter artlessly, even 'vulgarly,' emphasized the veins of the temple. This distinction of extreme whiteness is racist as well as 'classist': it excludes not only those lower classes who work in the sun, but also everyone who is not descended from northern Europeans. It also explains the broad-brimmed hats, long sleeves, and gloves that upper classes women wore when outdoors, particularly in the heat of summer.

To my mind, there is one word that sums them all and best explains the history of these: ignoble. In effect, to be recognized as *not* being a member of the nobility was an insult. Spanish has a surname that prevents such an insult. The name *Hidalgo* is a contraction of *hijo de algo*: 'son of someone.' Granted, it suggests someone low on the totem pole, but it was better than joining the great unwashed and unvalued masses.

Aggressive exclusion is key to the hierarchy. I suspect that this reflects the impossibility of the fairy tale, and from that, an inherent hypocrisy in the upper classes. The nobility needed to prove that they were clearly superior and that they had a right to rule others. But they were not superior. So they described those below them in terms to show what they, themselves, were not. Hitler and the Nazis provide an illustration; to define the proper Aryan, they took facial and body metrics of Jews and other 'undesirables.' They then used those metrics to define the master race, not by any positive attributes, but by what they were *not*.

In addition to the term 'noble,' there is another opposite to the 'p' words. Consider how many historical figures carry the designation 'great': Alexander the Great, Catherine the Great, The Great Genghis Khan, Cyrus the Great, Louis *le grand*, Suleyman the 'Magnificent' (literally, 'greatly made')—Wikipedia has an entire page devoted to people bearing the sobriquet 'the Great,' with over 130 people listed. Not one of them is a philosopher, artist, or scientist; excepting a few pious men, they are all kings and conquerors. Of course, some of the conquerors are also listed as pious men, but as we have seen, it would appear that one job description or the other is unlikely. All of these words simply mean 'large,' which refers to the advantage of being the larger bully, but also to being 'larger than life,' a concept that feeds the king's cult of personality.

• • •

Dr. Wilfred Grenfell was a celebrated medical missionary of the early twentieth century, providing care to remote areas of northeast Canada. At one point he and his dog team were trapped on an ice floe, and Grenfell was wet and freezing. To save his life, he decided to kill three of his dogs and skin them for their fur. He tried to kill them quickly and humanely, but nevertheless two of the dogs bit him before they died.

His other dogs, however, seemed to take no notice. In fact, even after he had killed and skinned the three, when he called one of them over to him to huddle with him under the skins for warmth, the dog came without hesitation.[4]

We have considered humans as sheep and how the atrox domesticated us just as he domesticated other animals. Grenfell's grisly tale also has a parallel with humanity under the atrox. As we have seen, the atrox views his family and closest supporters in much the same way as Grenfell viewed his dogs. Alexander slew his close friend Cleitus the Black in a drunken rage. He and his mother may have engineered the assassination of Alexander's father. Constantine killed numerous family members, including his own son. Sulla ordered the assassination of any number of people who had formerly been allies. Nero had his mother killed and ordered his childhood tutor, Seneca, to commit suicide. These victims had been useful at one point, but when the need or even the desire arose, they were expendable.

As these killings are ongoing, those who survive nevertheless remain loyal. Stalin's inner circle was devoted to him. He jailed Vyacheslav Molotov's wife, Polina Zhemchuzhina, and she was held in a labor camp until after Stalin died. If he had not died, she probably would have been executed; her crime appears to have been her Jewishness. Despite all of this, when she was released her first comment was, "How is Stalin?" When told that he had died, she fainted. She and Molotov remained staunch Stalinists for the rest of their lives.

Then there was Kira Kulik-Simonich, the prettiest woman in Stalin's circle, and the wife of trusted aide Grigory Kulik. She was whisked off a public street and then executed by the notorious Lavrentiy Beria. The inner circle knew that only Stalin could have ordered her death, but they remained loyal to him nevertheless, including Kulik. For his loyalty, two days after his wife's disappearance, Kulik was named 'Marshall of the Soviet Union.' There are different theories about what her offense against Stalin might have been. One plausible explanation is that she rebuffed his advances. This theory is perhaps supported by an odd detail—we have no idea how pretty Kira was. All photographs of her subsequently disappeared. It seems that Stalin ordered a *damnatio memoriae* against the hapless woman.[5]

This is a facet of the cult of personality. In his narcissism, the atrox tells us that he is superior to us in every way and that he and his concerns for the whole flock are more important than our lives. And we believe him.

We touched on this with Kim Jong-il and the bizarre way in which he was perceived by the North Korean press and his much-abused people. There are many aspects to the atrox's narcissism, but perhaps the most striking is not that the leader demands that his subjects should believe extraordinary things about him. It is that we believe them. After death, important Greeks and Romans could be declared gods. It would be hard to aim higher than that, but people unquestioningly accepted it.

There are many books that examine the cult of personality, but it is curious that the term was originated to describe Stalin. Nikita Krushchev pointed out how the cult interfered with communist ideals and ideology. His criticism also implicated Mao Zedong. Ironically, it also indicted Kim Il-song, the father of Kim Jong-il.

The atrox wants to be worshiped as an all-powerful deity. He controls us, and our devotion to him must be automatic, absolute, and unwavering. Stalin even tried to purge the thoughts of his people so that they were uniform and uniformed, even within their heads.[6] The extraordinary thing is that, as Kulik and the Molotovs demonstrate, Stalin frequently succeeded.

This brings us back to our first chapter. Here fairy tales begin; here the emperor dons his fictional new clothes. We are taught—under pain of death—to agree that the king, his family, and his nobles are not crazy or sadistic; they are simply better than the rest of us, even perfect. After ten thousand years of cultural and genetic selection, the king's narcissism prevails, and we truly believe that the nastiest, most vicious people who ever lived are in reality paragons of grace, elegance, wisdom, and gentleness. We will scramble our whole lives for one opportunity to bow and scrape to despicable people and their heirs. Like Grenfell's dogs, we obey their every whim out of love and respect, never realizing that our behavior has been selected through centuries of fear, death, and horror.

Chapter VI:
Privilege & the Double Standard

> *What thou meanest by seizing the whole earth;*
> *but because I do it with a petty ship, I am called a robber,*
> *whilst thou who dost it with a great fleet art styled emperor?*
>
> – A pirate brought before Alexander
> Augustine of Hippo, *City of God*

> *Immorality: the morality of those who are having a better time.*
> – H. L. Mencken

In addition to the flattering terms we use for the nobility, two others are highly prized by the upper classes: honor and virtue. We have compared mobsters to kings; we noted, however, that kings can be worse than gangsters. On the points of honor and virtue, there may be honor among thieves, but there is little among kings. And second, as we have seen throughout the book, there is certainly very little honor between the king and his men or the king and his other subjects.

Duplicity and treachery are constants among the noble classes. In the nobility, there are no permanent friends and no permanent enemies. We have seen that atroces will kill their own family members, often from paranoia. The paranoia may be justified, however, because we have also seen that the family members are often trying to kill the atrox. In the upper classes, no one is to be completely trusted; everyone will be duplicitous at times. The noble hierarchy is much like a reality show, but one where the eliminated contestants lose their heads.

So in contrast to honor and virtue, the king and the noble live lives of *duplicity*. The word means 'double,' as in 'double-dealing' or 'two-faced.' Kings and conquerors are completely Machiavellian; go back through the MACH-IV, and look at how many of the 'wrong' answers are duplicitous responses.

The king and nobles codify duplicity and dishonesty with the 'double standard.' The codification of the double standard was handed down to us as *privilege*, from the Latin *prīvilēgium*, 'private law.' There is a public law for commoners and a different, private law—or no law at all—for the king and his circle. Privilege legalizes the double standard.

Constantine is a good example, a man who encouraged Christianity for his subjects while pursuing fiendish, anti-Christian activities in his own life. In fact, critics have suggested that Constantine's real interest in Christianity, besides the fact that *chi+rho* seemed to bring him luck in conquest, was that it provided him a docile, industrious workforce—Christian sheep, if you will—to build his empire while requiring minimal governmental support or attention.* Christians gave Constantine a workforce with a middle class morality, which constrained them but not him. Constantine's Christianity was simply a sharper picture of the double standard that the narcissist desires.

The phrase 'middle class morality,' however, requires a reconsideration of terms. The meaning of 'upper class' is clear, but in traditional scholarship, the 'middle class' were the professionals and businessmen above the wage-earning 'lower class' or 'laboring class.' Today we distinguish these two groups of workers as 'white collar' and 'blue collar.'

That presents a couple of problems. First, there is another 'lower class' beneath the working class, comprising the unemployed poor and criminal elements. But that gives us four classes, and the 'middle' class isn't in the middle any more. More important to our discussion, however, is that the two central classes both operate within the same middle class morality, and as we are discovering, the peripheral classes do not.

The term 'middle class' apparently goes back to the eighteenth century but became formalized in the early twentieth. I suspect the categories of 'middle class' and 'laboring class' were designed to reinforce the hierarchy, to distance the professionals (who, by the way, created the categories) from their working class inferiors. It is another superficial expression of the cascade: you are poorly educated, while we are better-educated; you earn a poor living, while we earn a better one. And, you are rough, we are refined; it returns us to the previous chapter and the pejoratives applied to the laboring class.

I suggest that the critical consideration for the two inner classes is not the kind of work they do but that they *do* work: they go to work regularly and work conscientiously. This work ethic is not a requirement of the outer classes, and in fact, there is often a decidedly anti-work ethic in both the upper and lower leisure classes. This is the significance of the adjective 'leisure': the outer classes are identified by their lack of work. For our considerations

---

* The situation is mildly reminiscent of the modern gambling industry, where Mormons are often sought after as employees. In an industry that is plagued with corruption and vice, Mormons tend to be hardworking and honest, and their religion prohibits them from gambling or drinking.

here, economics and education are not the critical distinction among the various classes. Values are.*

That insight is important for understanding noble privilege. We do not simply refer to 'morality,' with one set of rules for everyone. 'Middle class morality' strongly suggests that there are other moralities. These, I contend, are the outer class morality of nobles and of gangsters.

Middle class morality is about productivity and personal accountability. If the peripheral classes are identified by the amount of leisure, then someone must produce wealth for the outer classes. Given that insight, the inherent principle of the outer classes is sponging off of the productivity of the middle class: the outer classes view the conscientious middle class as suckers to be exploited.

So we have four traditional social classes, upper/middle/laboring/unemployed, which are perhaps better understood as three classes, upper-leisure/middle-working/lower-leisure. Their value systems, however, collapse them into two classes, middle class/normal morality; and outer class/abnormal morality.† What really separates the upper and lower leisure classes is how far they have succeeded in their crimes and other exploitations. Minor criminals are lower class, but with great financial success they move into the upper class. As we will see in future chapters, however, it runs both ways. Legitimate industry constantly crosses over into unethical or criminal activity when the profits are sufficiently attractive.

The two faces of the dual moral system, obviously, are diametrically opposed. We opened this book with a quote about *The Iliad* by the late Eugen Weber. It comes from a paper he gave in which he pointed out that the concept of honor has changed. In its origins, Weber noted that virtue is manly honor, which goes back to the Greek concept of *arete*, 'the best.'[1]

Weber pointed out that the Greeks' concept of virtue had two conflicting meanings. It began with the Greek gods, whose concept of honor is very much like that of the gangster: it is the advantage gained by cunning, deception, and brute force. Those advantages, in turn, served the gods' vanity,

---

* The sociology student will see some correspondence between this scheme and the proposed class structure of Karl Marx. Marx proposed a class level below the proletariat, the Lumpenproletariat, which corresponds to the lower leisure class described here. Marx's 'petite bourgeoisie' might either fall into the middle class or upper class, depending on their values about work and social obligations. As we will see in the last chapters, there is more correspondence between the ancient noble classes, and Marx's capitalists, than might be apparent at first glance. Thanks to George Wooddell for his helping me think through these considerations.

† I am using the terms 'normal' and 'abnormal' in both the common and statistical senses of the words. The middle class is normal/healthy (or at least healthier), and they are also the normal/middle of the curve in several valuations: income, education, other social metrics, as well as in sheer numbers. So the upper and lower classes represent the 'abnormal' tails of the bell curve.

power, and sexual appetites. The later concept of *arete*/virtue emerges, however, as a cornerstone of progressive, pragmatic Athenian culture, in no small part from the philosophical troika of Socrates, Plato, and Aristotle.*

Weber then looked at Achilles, Roland, el Cid, and other ancient 'heroes,' noting that there was not much heroic, virtuous, nor honorable about any of them. They were hotheaded, vindictive, rapacious, perfidious, vain men who could not get enough loot, slaughter, or sex. In order to have the smallest thing they desired, they eagerly preyed upon weaker people and willingly sacrificed their friends and followers in the process. Weber concluded that the concepts of honor and virtue had changed greatly from earlier times.

The next evening at a small dinner party, I politely buttonholed Weber and pointed out that the concept of honor could not have changed, simply because commerce, and therefore civilization, are impossible without the 'modern' concepts of honor and virtue. I also noted that the thuggish concept of honor is still very much alive, well, and all-too-malignant in the machinations of government, business, and even religion. It would seem that humanity has maintained two different concepts of honor throughout civilization, and that we have lived under a chronic double standard.†

So what are the characteristics defining middle class and outer class morality? For the middle class, the *arete* of the philosophers that Weber mentioned heavily influenced Christianity. But the concepts are clearly older than the Athenian philosophers, though, as the great religions largely agree on the central concepts of morality. Given that, Christianity is both a reasonable and convenient place to start. Consider the Seven Heavenly Virtues of Christianity: humility; chastity; temperance; charity; kindness; diligence; and patience. These certainly describe many things that the middle class value, although they do not specifically include the critical virtues of honesty and personal accountability.

None of these, however, would seem to be in line with what we have learned of the atrox. Consider humility. Even in the modern military, we like our warriors brash and cocky. The modern militaries lost some of this bravado

---

* I wish I could say that the philosophers' revisions of *arete* were a defense of democracy, but these three were no fans of popular rule. I do contend, however, that their arguments for aristocracy, with their newer concepts of virtue and honor, were heavily informed by an Athenian culture of democracy and equality, whether they realized it or not.

† Eugen listened thoughtfully to my comments and then engaged me in a lively discussion. He behaved as the scholar is supposed to behave: open, collegial, and curious. That discussion was pivotal to this book, and it is a great sadness to me that Eugen is not here to critique my work and challenge my ideas in return.

after WWII, a conflict that featured the swaggers of Douglas MacArthur, George Patton, Bernard Montgomery, and Charles de Gaulle. These are in marked contrast to the buttoned-down WWII generals such as Dwight Eisenhower, George C. Marshall, and Omar Bradley or to many of the modern Joint Chiefs of Staff. It would appear that the warrior has begun conforming to our modern priorities.*

After humility, we have chastity. We fully expect the king, the great warrior, and really, all of our celebrities, to have larger-than-life sexual appetites and to enjoy as many conquests in the recumbent sack as they do in the plundering sack. Even today when we see improper sexual behavior among powerful people in the U.S. and abroad, we are only mildly scandalized.

As for temperance, charity, and kindness, a review of the second chapter shows that these are also recent concepts for the warrior. They are not useful qualities in a firefight, less so in sword fight. War requires soldiers who aggressively avenge any attack or injury.

The last two Christian virtues are diligence and patience. These we certainly understand in the modern military as essential to strategy and leadership, and the most successful conquerors have always expressed these at least some of the time. But first, consider that these are also aspects of Machiavellianism. Second, these traits are variable in the conqueror. Weber noted how hotheaded early warriors were (Odysseus was an obvious exception). And even today, many people want successful imprudence; we admire the competitor who strikes back quickly and even rashly, as long as he prevails. As I noted, we like our warriors cocky.

So, if the conquering king does not exhibit traditional morals, how might we characterize him? Consider the Christian opposite of the Heavenly Virtues, *i.e.*, the Seven Deadly Sins: anger, greed, sloth, pride, lust, envy, and gluttony. These characterize many criminals. They characterize the Greek gods. And of course, they characterize kings, conquerors, and their nobles.

These sinful seven are also the ethos of animals, particularly predators. For example, they describe lions. It is interesting that we speak of kings and conquerors in leonine terms: there is Richard Lionheart; the lions of England, Bel-

---

* WWII doubtless played a role in our changing concepts of leadership in two ways. First, there was the international awareness that WWII was an outgrowth of the Versailles Treaty at the end of WWI and its vindictiveness toward the Germans; it was a hard lesson. Second, the general who emerged during WWII as the senior officer to all of these swashbucklers, and who emerged after the war as the leader of the free world, was Ike Eisenhower. It seems inevitable that he heavily influenced our modern concept of the flag officer.

The lion-headed column of Ashoka

gium, Ethiopia, Iran, and quite a few others; the lion-headed column of Ashoka; and the Christian fairy tale *The Lion, The Witch, and The Wardrobe*.

There is also the modern animation we considered earlier, *The Lion King*, which conflates king and predator. As we noted, there is little admirable about the king of the jungle. Real lions exhibit none of the virtues described by the Disney animators. But they definitely exhibit the dysfunctions of the predatory outer classes.

But really, to survive all successful animals behave the same way in the deathscape. Even the gentle, vegetarian rabbit fights vicious battles for dominance, and like the lion, kills the young of a displaced loser. We speak of the law of the jungle and apply it to business, government, and sports. These are not simple metaphors, they are ontological cousins, they are pups of the same merciless bitch. The conqueror is the vicious predator who walks on two legs.

Actually, he is worse. The atrox is not simply evil, he is the fullest expression of evil. Remember, Erich Fromm described malignant narcissism as "the quintessence of evil," and we argued that the conqueror is a malignant narcissist, writ across the continents.

Consider that the lion kills us to survive. The conqueror hasn't even that justification. He kills us for his ambition, his wealth, and his entertainment. The lion dines on our corpses; the conqueror leaves our bodies to rot.

The atrox is the evil lurking in our darkest nightmares and our scariest novels: he is the thing that tortures and kills us, and those we hold most dear, for nothing beyond self-service and amusement. And that cold immorality of the conqueror is the foundation for civilization.

Chapter VII:
The Authoritarian Personality

...if a system of death camps were set up in the United States of the sort we had seen in Nazi Germany, one would be able to find sufficient personnel for those camps in any medium-sized American town.

– Stanley Milgram

*We are all born mad.
Some remain so.*

– Samuel Beckett

In 1961, psychologist Stanley Milgram conducted experiments to explore the power of Hitler, the Nazis, and all authoritarians.* Men were recruited from the New Haven, Connecticut, area for an experiment in 'learning.' They were told that the experiments involved a 'teacher' and a 'learner,' both of whom were directed by a man in a white lab coat, posing as a research scientist. The men drew slips of paper ostensibly designating one of them as 'the teacher' and the other as 'the learner,' but both slips read "teacher"; one of the two men was a confederate. There was really only one subject of the experiment, the teacher.

As the experiment was described to the two men, the learner was to memorize word pairs and to recall them. They were then shown a room with an electric shock chair. The learner was to be strapped into it, and he was to be shocked for failing to recall the matching word. The teacher was placed in an adjacent room where he could hear but could not see the learner. In front of the teacher was a fake electrical switchboard, with shocks running from 20V up to 450V. Before they started, the confederate learner claimed that he had a heart condition, but the 'scientist' assured him that the experiment would not hurt him.

The responses from the learner were tape recorded so that the experiences for each teacher would be as similar as possible. At one point in the experiment, the recorded learner demanded that the experiment be stopped, but

---

* The video 'Obedience' examines the experiments and is available on various Internet video websites. Most of the edited presentations are less than ten minutes long and worth the time to watch.

the scientist insisted that the teacher continue. If the teacher continued, a bit later on the learner would stop responding, presumably from a loss of consciousness. The scientist would instruct the teacher to continue.

Even though the learner was a supposed heart patient who had lost consciousness, about two-thirds of the subjects continued the experiment all the way up to 450V. In addition, not one of the teachers ever checked on the condition of the learner, even those teachers who refused to continue. Most concerning, not one of the teachers complained that the experiments were unethical nor insisted that they be discontinued.

Ten years after Milgram's study, Philip Zimbardo performed a related experiment. In his study, volunteers were randomly assigned as inmates or guards. The inmates were suddenly 'arrested' one morning, strip-searched, shaved, and deloused. The guards were given few instructions except that they were to maintain order and that they could not use physical punishment.

The study was scheduled to last two weeks. It was canceled after only six days, in part because of concerns about the psychological harm to the prisoners; they were withdrawn, depressed, and submissive.

The other part of the researchers' concerns, however, was over the guards. Even though the guards were aware that they were part of an experiment, they became oppressive, unfeeling, and even sadistic toward the inmates. After three of the prisoners barricaded themselves in their cell, the guards began engaging in psychological abuse, depriving inmates of basic comforts such as mattresses and even clothing.

Most disturbing of all, a majority of the guards expressed disappointment when the experiment was prematurely terminated.

Two years after Zimbardo's researchers were entrapped by their own experiment, Jan-Erik Olsson carried a machine gun into the Kreditbanken in Stockholm, Sweden, and attempted to rob it. He ended up taking four hostages, and by demand, added an accomplice he had met in jail, Clark Olofsson. Over six days—the same number of days that it took for the Zimbardo experiment to implode—the criminals were holed up in the bank vault with their hostages.

When the hostages were freed, they were noted to be warm toward their captors but hostile toward the police. They subsequently explained that they had been more afraid of the police than the criminals. All of them refused to testify against the hostage-takers, and one started a defense fund for her imprisoners. This codependency between captives and captors has become known as 'The Stockholm Syndrome.'[1]

The next year, heiress Patty Hearst was taken hostage by the Symbionese Liberation Army, and she also came to strongly identify with her captors. The phenomenon has subsequently been observed with other kidnap victims and has been extended to a broad variety of abusive and exploitive situations, including the defense of abusers by their victims, often by their spouses and children.

Stanley Milgram began his experiments three months after the start of Adolph Eichmann's trial in Jerusalem for Nazi war crimes. Eichmann's argument was a continuation of the Nuremberg Defense, *"Befehl ist Befehl"*: "An order is an order." This explanation has seemed an insufficient explanation to the many scholars who have studied the Holocaust, including Milgram. So Milgram opened his considerations with the question, "When I learn of incidents such as the massacre of millions of men, women, and children perpetrated by the Nazis in World War II, how is it possible, I ask myself, that ordinary people, both courteous and decent in everyday life, can act callously, inhumanely, without any limitations of conscience?" This book adds a new consideration for the compliant behavior of the Nazis. The best path to survival under the king was to conform to whatever he demanded.

In the previous chapter, we considered the control that the atrox exerts over his lieutenants. In this chapter, we will consider how the culture of the atrox and his hierarchy influences the commoners—which means the rest of us. We have seen evidence for this impact in the chapters leading up to this one.

What follows is a list of human problems, contradictions, and hypocrisies. Delving into any of them could consume an academic career, and some of them have consumed many careers. I aim only to add to previous work the historical perspectives we have covered here. Of course, many of the following behaviors are part of our biology and precede the atrox. Nevertheless, it seems reasonable that the cruel men who shaped civilization influenced and expanded pre-existing dysfunctions to outsized proportions.

CODEPENDENCY

In recent decades, the concept of 'codependency' has emerged, a recognition of a dysfunctional dynamic that appears between an abuser and one or more victims who often seek to ally themselves with a stronger, more assertive personality, despite the suffering of the codependent in the relationship. Throughout civilization, the atrox has been the strongest and most assertive personality available. The Stockholm Syndrome is one example of this codependency, but so are other behaviors we have considered throughout the book. In a way, even the rape victim becomes codependent: as we have seen, the rapist treats her as someone of no importance, and she will spend years struggling to break free of his assessment.

Codependency derives from the formal psychiatric diagnosis of Dependent Personality Disorder (DPD), an illness in which the patient craves the approval of others. This insight presents a disturbing reflection between the atrox and his subjects. The narcissistic atrox craves the approval of the masses, and to survive, the masses come to crave the approval of the atrox. Research shows that over half of the propensity for DPD is genetic.[2] A codependency with the atrox is historically pervasive and influences all of us to some extent—delusion as survival.

So throughout civilization, our choices were to agree with the king or die. But only pretending to agree with the king, simply stating that we agree when we really don't, or complying with his commands reluctantly, is a dangerous game. One incautious comment, the expression of an independent thought, a brief pause before obeying a command or the smallest criticism, could spell ruin or death. Recall that Catiline executed a soldier for merely fainting as Gratidianus was tortured and that Shaka Zulu's followers were killed for even a moment's hesitation.

In addition, we need to remember that the great unwashed who were not part of the atrox's hierarchy were in constant peril from starvation, exposure, warfare, and raiding. As we noted, the higher one climbed the social ladder, the greater the chance of survival.

Given these, the tactic with the highest probability of survival would be to sincerely *believe* whatever the king says, no matter how illogical, no matter how large the gap between his claims and the tangible evidence. Enthusiastic adoption of the king's narcissistic distortions and his cult of personality, to the point of boosterism, increased one's chances of surviving, particularly when it helped one ascend to the safer strata of society.

We have noted that when we behave in illogical ways, then it suggests that we have abandoned the *tabula rasa* and have succumbed to our genetic traps, possibly guided by cultural conditioning; if our thinking were only the product of learning and dispassionate, logical analysis, then we should not see illogic. Our considerations of genetic behavior were made in preparation for this chapter. It would appear that our illogic, our delusions, and our fairy tales are evidence of both our cultural and genetic legacy of bondage under the atrox.

Authoritarian Personality

The devastation of Adolf Hitler and the Nazis was considered in the moral and philosophical question that Milgram pondered above: How did seemingly normal and moral people behave so horrifically? Addressing the question, Theodor Adorno and other exiles from the Frankfurt School published *The Authoritarian Personality*.[3] Their work was based on earlier ideas from Erich Fromm, the same man who gave us the concept of the malignant narcissist.

The Frankfurters probed various aspects of prejudice and anti-democratic tendencies, and from there, they explored the fascist's attitudes and personality characteristics. From their researches they developed the Fascist Scale, or 'F-Scale' for short. There are nine aspects of the Scale:

- conventionalism;
- authoritarian submission;
- authoritarian aggression;
- anti-intellectualism;
- anti-intraception (*i.e.*, an opposition to self-analysis, imagination, and tender-mindedness);
- superstition and stereotypy;
- power and "toughness";
- destructiveness;
- cynicism;
- projectivity (a tendency to project one's own unconscious impulses onto others); and,
- exaggerated concerns over sex.

There has been controversy over the F-Scale.[4] Many of the objections focus on the Freudian interpretations the Adorno group proposed for understanding the fascist mindset. In one of the more puzzling challenges, however, Zillner and colleagues report that when the F-Scale test was given to several convicted Nazi war criminals, only three of the nine traits proved applicable: anti-intraception; superstition and stereotypy; and projectivity.[5] This certainly presents a problem, but not necessarily for the F-Scale. Adorno and his colleagues were describing what they and the whole world had seen and experienced from the Nazis, and they developed their list to identify people and situations where Nazi-like activity might occur again.

Given this, Zillner's research seems to suggest that Nazis were not Nazis. Consider the six of the authoritarian personality characteristics that Zillner could not verify. Would we argue that the Nazis were not destructive, not given to authoritarian submission and aggression, did not support Hitler's power and 'toughness,' and that these behaviors did not reflect a strong conventionalism? The problem with Zillner's work may be similar to those we considered for the MACH IV.

First, diagnoses based on subjects' responses, are, well, subjective. They have the same vulnerability as any self-assessment: they do not necessarily tell us who we are but who we think we are. For instance, subjects may lie to themselves or ignore negative facts. Consider that prejudice and racism are constants throughout history, and our choices and behaviors show that they continue today. Nevertheless, almost everyone denies being prejudiced or a racist. Add to those the whitewashing of history we have repeatedly seen; A.C. Doyle maligning the mother of a starving child, critics of *Japanese Devils* rejecting firsthand accounts because they did not fit their preferred vision of the world.

Second, and as the Zimbardo experiment showed, we behave differently, and therefore think differently, in conflict: if Zimbardo's 'guards' had been tested before the experiment, it seems dubious they would have met many criteria for the F-Scale. During the experiment, however, their scores might have risen dramatically. With that, remember the anger/temporary psychopathy of my friend who survived an IED explosion in Iraq; his thinking and his desires changed dramatically when he was surprised and endangered.

So giving the F-Scale test to someone who has been separated from the Nazi regime might give a different response than giving it to the same person in the middle of fascist fervor. Finally, fascism may work much like the attitudes of the soldier in warfare: it does not matter if the individual is personally fascist; the system in which he operates is fascist, and he will often comply; that was what Milgram's and Zimbardo's experiments showed. Zillner's work is intriguing and warrants further exploration, but it contains a disconnect with the facts, even the defining facts.

Robert Altmeyer took the work of the Adorno group, and tightened it in the consideration of right-wing authoritarians.[6] Altmeyer's research produced three key indicators for this group: conventionalism; authoritarian submission; and authoritarian aggression. It should be noted that some argue that there are also left-wing authoritarians, particularly in the Marxist regimes of Stalin, Mao, and the Khmer Rouge. It depends on the definitions; this will be addressed in a later chapter.

There would seem to be a conflict between authoritarian submission and authoritarian aggression. Within the atrox's hierarchy, however, we see no contradiction: we are submissive toward those above us and aggressive toward those below, as well as toward any who oppose the supremacy of the hierarchy. It is more evidence of our domestication and reminiscent of our dogs. The family dog is submissive to the family, aggressive toward subordinate animals, and vicious toward an intruder. It is interesting that aggression and submission have little to do with relative size, as a Mastiff may cower before a dominant chihuahua. There is apparently no limit to this absurdity—Napoléon was the chihuahua who dominated Europe.

The authoritarian personality is loyal, obedient, and unquestioning toward his master. The unquestioning aspect is essential. We assume that the dog has no logical structures either supporting or undermining his loyalty to us. But human beings constantly rely on logical analysis for making decisions. So it is not enough for the authoritarian personality to submit bodily; as we noted, he must also submit intellectually. In order to be completely loyal, the authoritarian personality must spring the trapdoor and ignore the appeal of internal and external logic, even though logic is essential for human survival, and even for day-to-day activities.

The good soldier is the ultimate authoritarian personality. When commanded, he will commit murder and other atrocities as directed or as permitted by the atrox. When the atrox commands him, he will also submit to severe, even lethal punishment. We saw this in Shaka's followers who accepted his sentencing; Nero ordered Seneca to commit suicide; Stalin's lieutenants quietly accepted their sentences; and every king sends men to die in battle. One interesting example to add to these is the Roman *decimation*, 'a reduction by a tenth.' For particularly egregious offenses, such as rebellion or desertion, members of a convicted Roman military cohort would draw lots; every tenth soldier would then be stoned or clubbed to death by non-implicated cohorts.[7] This demonstrates the extremes of the atrox's power: the murderous soldier kills his comrade, and the condemned submits to his fate.

Many of the following behaviors did not originate with the atrox, as they have also been documented in modern neolithic peoples. Some of these also fit the patterns we noted in groups of social animals with a dominant alpha. The atrox, however, intensifies these behaviors.

Both humans and dogs tend toward codependency; the difference is that humans have the ability to escape. Almost all of the following are undesirable within an egalitarian group. Which is what the modern world seeks to achieve, increasing equality. If we are to disabuse ourselves of our codependency, we must recognize these influences in ourselves, in our children, and in our fellow citizens and work to rectify our thinking.

Authoritarian Submission

We have noted authoritarian submission in a number of contexts, particularly the obedience of both the soldier and senior officer. There are other aspects to the problem.

We examined the cult of personality around the atrox, but hero worship can extend to everyone in the noble classes. In the modern world, these include the powerful, famous, or rich. Here we touch again on fairy tales, as we often imagine these people to be heroic, larger than life, and everything we would like to be. Their influence can be seen in the commercial advertisements in which celebrities advocate various products. Even though the advertised product may be completely outside of the celebrity's area of knowledge or success, we nevertheless ape his style and bend to his recommendations; if we did not, the advertisements would cease. The celebrity pitch is so effective, and from that effectiveness so lucrative for the pitch man, that endorsing products can generate more wealth for some celebrities than their primary occupation. Even someone who merely looks like they might be a celebrity can be effective. Physically attractive models can support themselves comfortably by appearing in print and media advertisements.

When confronted with evidence that celebrities are flawed or even reprehensible, we may deny it; or worse, we may excuse it. If our neighbor is abusive, a womanizer, or a drug abuser, that is offensive. In celebrities, these behaviors are acceptable.

This is one of the most important dysfunctions we will encounter, and it will emerge as a critical insight later. We bow and scrape to the famous and powerful, sing their praises, and ignore their dysfunctions, even as they abuse and exploit us.

We may also submit to them sexually. One cliché is that women make themselves sexually available to the powerful, but it is also true for men. Consider the descriptions of Mao's advances on the young soldiers who massaged him or the enforced homosexuality of the Spartans. Particularly among the Greeks and Romans, homosexual submission by young men was not unusual. In both sexes, the attraction and the ensuing submission are understandable: for an appealing young boy or girl, attracting the sexual interest of a powerful man could mean food, shelter, protection, and salvation from the plight of the poorer classes and perhaps an opportunity to move into the safety of the hierarchy.*

---

* Marguerite Yourcenar explores this phenomenon in the relationship between Hadrian and his young lover Antinous, whom the emperor apparently chose from an undistinguished family. Marguerite Yourcenar, *Memoirs of Hadrian*, transl., Grace Frick (Macmillan, 2005).

We can see echoes of hero worship and celebrity deference even in the halls of academia, as witnessed with *House* and Houseman. In the television series *House*, Hugh Laurie's Dr. Gregory House treats his patients and his colleagues with as much contempt as he does his students and residents. Similarly, in the book and movie *The Paper Chase*, the students—of hallowed Harvard, supposedly the brightest in the country—meekly submit to John Houseman's character of Charles W. Kingsfield Jr., as he verbally abuses and publicly humiliates them.[8] The central point is not the abuse, but that we all, including the brightest among us, accept the abuse and even expect it.

The book *Fifty Shades of Grey* describes a rich, handsome, powerful young man who dominates women and subjects them to mild sadism.[9] The book was a bestseller, proving the broad interest in such a dysfunctional relationship. The illogicality of it is neatly summed in a popular Internet meme, showing a run-down mobile home on an overgrown lot, with the caption pointing out that the book is romantic only because the protagonist is a billionaire. If he were instead living in a trailer, the story would become an episode in a criminal television series.

Our attraction to power extends all through the hierarchy into the lower military ranks. Both women and men are attracted to men in uniform. That does not make much sense in the modern democracy where military enlistment may not be particularly exclusive, and the uniformed public service jobs are not always paid particularly well. In the past, however, a soldier's official position within the hierarchy provided some protection for his family; and the pay, though meager, was steady.

HERD MENTALITY

The 'herd mentality' is a human behavior that precedes civilization.[10] Prehistoric tribes became overcome with passions and lost themselves to the larger group in dance, mystic rituals, and warfare. We considered an extreme example after the death of Shaka Zulu's mother, and we will see other examples below. This behavior still exists today whenever we get swept up in crowds and conform to the herd.

We not only conform, we may also agree even when we might not have agreed if we had considered the issue away from the group. Years ago, I met a physician from a prominent Latin American family who had been trained in counter-revolutionary tactics. He explained how a handful of people could control thousands. In an auditorium, one person is positioned at each corner of the crowd and at the exits. When the speaker arrives at pre-arranged points in her speech, the conspirators begin applauding. Many in the crowd will follow suit; by the end of the speech, almost the entire crowd will not only applaud, they will also agree with the speaker.

Return to the photo of the Nuremberg rallies. Hitler and his inner circle understood the power of the herd mentality: assemble a large number of people, present them with a grand spectacle, and give them a stirring speech peppered with obvious applause points. They will yield their autonomy, conform, and submit.

Sacrifice

When so commanded in warfare, we have seen that the soldier will throw his life away, often in clearly hopeless initiatives. Such actions are common in warfare, but two historical examples are striking. One is the trench warfare of WWI, where tens of thousands of men died in order to move the battlefront a few yards one way or the other. Early in the war, in the First Battle of the Marne, the Germans, French, and English suffered over five hundred thousand casualties in four days of fighting. Throughout the slaughter, the men continued to charge into the battle undeterred.

The second example was the Bloody Angle in the U.S. Civil War Battle of Spotsylvania. In one of the deadliest days of the war, wave after wave of men destroyed each other in close hand-to-hand combat. As the day wore on, they were forced to clamber over the corpses of the hundreds of men who had already died. As they charged in, all around them was proof that they were almost definitely going to die themselves. And still, they charged.

The word 'sacrifice' means 'holy act/deed', and in the service of the atrox, the soldier often gives his life with something akin to religious faith and fervor. Prehistoric peoples certainly fought to the death as well, but the scope of the bloodshed and death under the atrox has grown far beyond the gang warfare of our pre-civilization ancestors.

Happy Slaves

Frequently in the United States, racists and Neo-Confederates will make the statement that "many blacks were happy to be slaves." It is a repulsive attempt to justify racism and bigotry.

But slavery is as old as civilization, and we all have slaves among our ancestors. Everyone in early civilization was in some sort of bondage to the atrox; we must speculate that the first conquerors treated their first captives in much the same way that Columbus and the early European explorers did:

viciously, and enslaving many of them. This returns us to the terms serf, servant, service, servitude—and in the military, sergeant—which, as noted, are all descendants of the Latin *servus*, 'slave.'

All Soviet citizens were basically Stalin's possessions to do with as he pleased, to kill when he desired. For all practical purposes, they were in bondage to Stalin, often treated as little more than slaves.* We have seen that this *de facto* subjugation applied to his inner circle, who remained proudly loyal in their servitude. We would expect to find the same within any cult of personality: people who accept their status as unimportant inferiors to the authoritarian leader; loyalists who are content with their exploited lives.

When we consider the examples of our submission to authoritarians throughout this book, we see that the slave is the extreme situation for all of our ancestors: they either adapted to their situation or died from punishment or despair. Simply accepting and adapting did not provide as much protection as embracing the master's dysfunctions with enthusiasm and happiness. The best course was to rationalize servitude as a good thing: the king is our shepherd; he is a god; he loves us; and he has only our best interests at heart. If our dogs and our sheep could speak, they would voice the same thoughts. It is further evidence of our domestication.

So yes, some slaves and others in subjugation might be happy. But that is a testament to the slave's determination to survive, not a justification for the exploitation and injustice of slavery.

FATALISM

We see our servility reflected in our fatalism. In Flannery O'Connor's darkly humorous short story "A Good Man is Hard to Find," she mockingly describes a family who live such a shallow existence that they go to their deaths with only some whining. When compared to the civilians of Jaffa, who submitted meekly to death along with their children, O'Connor's story loses much of its charm.

Then recall the recurrent, consistent behavior of the untold millions who have starved to death while their overlords had access to sufficient food to save them: the Madras Famine, the modern North Korean starvations, the Irish Potato Famine, Stalin's *Holodomor* in Ukraine. Descriptions of these persecutions relate that most of the victims accepted their situation, and quietly died along with their children.

---

* There is an unfunny pun that should be mentioned here. 'Slave' is a derivative of 'Slav,' because the Slavs were regularly conquered and sold into slavery. So the Slavs were Stalin's slaves.

There is some evidence of our fatalistic heritage in our children today. At one point I was visiting a swamp containing alligators and teased a little girl that I would throw her to them. Later she asked me, very concerned, if I would really do such a thing to her. I was horrified. It was concerning enough that she took me at my word; but it was much more disturbing that she accepted that I had the right to do such a thing.

Likewise, even healthy children will occasionally express fear that their parents do not love them or that the parents might abandon or betray them; this includes children who are constantly told and shown that they are loved and treasured. Their mistrust in the face of contradicting evidence, again, is only part of the story. The more disturbing part is that children accept, as a matter of course, that we have the right to do such things. Because the truth is, in the past, parents did have those rights, they were free to sell, abandon, or kill their children. And the greater horror is that, in the past, parents exercised these rights.

Pedigree

We are fascinated with ancestry, pedigree, and antiques and heirlooms. We have considered the name 'Hidalgo', 'the son of someone [important].' We may follow celebrities' children as avidly as we follow the celebrities themselves, even when it is apparent that the children exhibit no extraordinary talents or other attributes. We speak with great pride of our notable ancestors, and others are often impressed when we do. In the United States, we also have groups such as the descendants of the original Pilgrims—we touched on some of their markedly un-Christian activities previously—and the Sons and Daughters of the American Revolution.*

---

* There are Cajuns who participated in the American Revolution even though the Revolution took place years before the Louisiana Purchase. I am told that some of the stuffier members of the SAR and DAR have been scandalized by the arrival at important meetings of the affable and egalitarian Cajuns, with their dark skin and pronounced accents. In addition, the first ancestors of the Cajuns and Creoles arrived in the New World sixteen years before the Mayflower sailed. So far, these French descendants have shown little interest in forming their own exclusive clique to celebrate their earlier arrival and to show up the Mayflower descendants as *parvenus*. (Of course, the Spanish arrived much earlier than either, and the Cajuns and Creoles also have Spanish blood. But then, the Italian Columbus arrived first; well, except for the Vikings; well, except for the Native Americans; well, except that they were preceded by even earlier Native Americans; *etc.*) Yale Historian John Mack Faragher once speculated that the Cajuns may have been the first New World republicans. There are a number of other cultural and historical oddities about the Cajuns and Creoles of south Louisiana. My reflections on how they differ from the rest of the South, and really, from the rest of the world, were a starting point for several of the topics in this book.

That last one is jarring. One of the reasons for founding the United States was to escape the hereditary distinctions of the Old World in favor of a New World meritocracy. Nevertheless, we continue to place great importance on someone's ancestors, irrespective of the character or contribution of the current descendant.

Authoritarian Aggression

Authoritarian aggression, destructiveness, and power/toughness are all interrelated. The full expression of aggression results in harm and destruction. A macho culture of power and toughness is essential to both.

Culture of Coercion

The conqueror seizes power by cruel force, the king holds it by cruel force, and cruel force supports the hierarchy. Not surprising, cruel force becomes the fundamental concept of justice and civil order for many people. In some countries today, theft is still punished by the loss of a hand; flogging is the punishment for kissing in public; and children can be sentenced to jail with their parents and grandparents. We find such things reprehensible, but those objections are cultural and recent. People of the past accepted Ashoka's Hell, Alexander's tortures, the Romans' viciousness, the Inquisition, the Tyburn Tree, and the many other cruelties we have considered here. Kings employed horrific tortures to maintain order, and at times these tortures were presented in public spectacles that our ancestors gleefully attended. When we were entrained in the atrox's civilization, we believed such things to be fair justice. Only today are they objectionable and noticeable as anachronisms.

In earlier England, stealing a loaf of bread, even in a famine, resulted in hanging. Insulting the king, or failing to show sufficient deference to the noble born, could also result in death or lesser but gruesome punishments. A man could be flogged for not working hard enough. Gossiping was punished with the scold's bridle, a metal cage for the head with a bar that went in the mouth; the bar might be sharpened or spiked to slice the tongue, preventing the offender from talking, eating, or easily drinking, and there was no standard time for how long the convicted wore it.

Then there were punishments for children. There were beatings and canings. The Aztecs, who sacrificed their children in ritual, also punished them by forcing them to breathe smoke from burning peppers or by stabbing agave or cactus spikes into their skin.[11] We noted that historical cultures permitted the selling, abandonment, or execution of children. We have also noted honor killings, where a family member—almost always a man—will kill his wife or his child for embarrassing the family. This is perhaps the most egregious legacy of the atrox—that we will torture and kill our own family in submission to some authority.

Culture of Impatience

A culture of coercion becomes a culture of impatience. Time is not taken to study problems or people, to understand them, and to pragmatically consider various options and outcomes. This is reflected in our considerations of mental health in Chapter III; we will not take time to understand the problem, and so we do not solve the problem. Then in our frustration, even those who have learned the importance of patience and self-control are often tempted by instinct and emotion to respond with immediate, summary force: a law should be written, a stiff punishment should be meted out, the person in question should be forced to comply. Impatience is a temporal intolerance.

This problem starts early in life with our punishment of children. We can consider the preceding and add to them that traditionally, children were frequently humiliated, whipped, or otherwise punished for failing to learn on a pre-determined schedule. This remains our fundamental concept of education, as we still humiliate children for failing to learn on demand.

Educational impatience results in two regrettable outcomes. First, as we saw in our discussion of the nerd, for most children it undermines curiosity and creates an avoidance of learning. Second, it perpetuates the culture of coercion and impatience, it increases the likelihood that as children grow, they will respond to their own families, coworkers, and communities with the same impatient intolerance. So rather than patiently engage people to excel, we coerce them to be minimally competent. When it comes to curiosity, learning, and critical thinking, as with almost everything else, destruction is easy, but building and fostering are very hard. In a coercive culture, robust and nurturing education become difficult, and the culture of impatience grows.

These approaches support the anti-intellectualism of the authoritarian personality. In the atrox's culture of conformity and blind obedience, there is no need for wisdom, subtlety, or faith in others; there is no room for doubt or introspection. The loss of those human capacities, in turn, fits the atrox's agenda. We do not teach children to learn and think for themselves; we teach them to comply unquestioningly. Without independent analysis there can be no innovation, and so in fashioning obsessive-compulsive clerks, the casual-

The Authoritarian Personality 169

ties include exploration, experimentation, and progress. There is a tension between discipline and innovation: people can do it the way they have been taught, or they can be allowed to do it in a new way.

One modern problem that reflects this culture appears in democratic elections. Impatience with the slow pace of democracy leads frustrated voters to prefer candidates who are political innocents but who promise to 'shake things up.' We would never trust our lives or finances to a surgeon, engineer, or CEO who had little experience and who wished to apply untested ideas, particularly coercive and destructive ideas. But when mapping out the course for our mutual security and growth, voters will recklessly put everyone at risk by selecting exactly the sort of person who created our culture of impatience in the first place. Adolf Hitler was an untested political novice who manipulated and even fomented popular frustration, and who then promised to fix it by shaking things up; he was then democratically elected as chancellor. Impatient electorates around the globe frequently select candidates who, at best, prove incompetent and destructive. At worst, they arrogate power for themselves and eliminate free elections altogether.

An attitude of impatience and coercion tears at the fabric of government and society. If improvement emerges, it may be much like the aftermath of the French Revolution or the Nazi ascendancy: progress will appear only after a reactionary explosion of oppression, chaos, and horror. With time, after seeing where popular impatience leads, voters and later leaders may come to understand that some basic competency, and a respect for the rules of politics and governance, are inescapable; and that patience and prudence are critical for any real stability.

Sabotage: The Football Mentality

In the U.S., and particularly in the Deep South, American football approaches religiosity. In most states, the highest paid public employee is a football coach; in one extremely fanatical state, the football coach's salary approaches one hundred times that of the governor. Many Americans regard the quality of an institution of higher learning, not by teaching or research, but by the success of the football team.

Metaphors in football and other sports are common in business and government: 'punt' (send the problem elsewhere); 'take a knee' (admit that the game is over); 'smash-mouth football' (a situation that calls for dispensing with politeness, mutual respect, and perhaps the rules); 'spike the ball' (either celebrate over a score or sacrifice a play in order to buy time); and others.

A particularly toxic football saw is 'Defense wins championships.' When carried into politics and business, this translates into an unfortunate strategy: 'If I can stop you, I don't need to produce much progress.' In a way, this is what the atrox does with our education and our intellectual progress: as long as he can control us, *i.e.* as long as he can stop us from growing in intellectual, economic, or other power, he doesn't have to do much to maintain his power. And so little progress emerges.

It is the trap of the stagnant hierarchy. The critical consideration in the hierarchy is narcissism: status must be maintained. As we have seen in history, *e.g.*, the Madras Famine, as long as the comfortable can maintain their every status symbol, it is unimportant what horror befalls others. The luxury and privilege of the hierarchy are worth more to the upper classes than our lives. It is the culture we have inherited: the atrox tortured and sacrificed large numbers of our ancestors for nothing more than fame, power, and riches. He not only blocked their progress, he destroyed them and became fabulously wealthy from the conquest. Sabotage is the ultimate defense.

People with new ideas and practices threaten the status quo. They create competition and push the system toward a fluid meritocracy, which is a threat to sclerotic privilege. The intense conservatism of the hierarchy creates a culture of self-protection that aggressively stifles progress. So the powerful sabotage progress itself.

Games such as football are 'zero sum'; nothing within the game is created or destroyed. At the end of every season, the number of wins exactly equals the number of losses. In zero-sum games, defense and sabotage destroy nothing because within the game, there is no advancement.

But progress and the human condition are *non*-zero-sum games. Resources can be added or lost; the Roman Empire rose, and then it fell. With an increase in efficiency and total resources under Roman rule, the population grew; when Rome fell, Western civilization regressed and was plunged into the feudalism of the Dark Ages, and the population dropped. It is telling that, although we mark the fall of Rome by the invasions of the Goths, those assaults were largely successful because the Romans were preoccupied with civil wars and other internal struggles for dominance. In an illustration of the thesis here, as the Roman leadership sabotaged one another for personal advancement in a stagnating system, security and stability declined. Meanwhile, the Germanic tribes were working the other side of the non-zero sum game: they were growing in size and military effectiveness.

So in non-zero-sum games, defense and sabotage cripple everyone, allowing other societies and other regimes, those that are slightly less repressive and slightly more cohesive, to advance, to become more innovative and more progressive, and to win the competition. There is slow pressure away from repression, exclusion, and stagnation, toward tolerance, inclusion, and growth. Progress eventually prevails, but the hierarchy constantly sabotages it.

Blame the Victim

We have considered the exploiter's defense, "Now see what you've made me do?!" We have seen it with the 'smaller' malignant narcissist, such as David Parker Ray, who tortured a woman to death because she gave him gonorrhea. We have seen it in the 'full' malignant narcissist: Ashoka, David, Alexander, Caracalla, and really, all conquerors. They all find reasons for blaming the people they torture and kill.

As such, blaming the victim becomes part of our traditions. In many cultures, the rape victim is still blamed, and as we noted, she blames herself as well. In modern countries we boast that we have progressed beyond this, but in reality, not by much. In the court of law and the court of public opinion, the standard technique for refuting a rape accuser is to attack her and blame her: she is a liar; she wanted the sexual encounter; she is sexually indiscriminate; she is pursuing only money, attention, or retribution.

The same approach can be seen in many political and social policies. We blame the poor for their poverty as we deny them access to quality education and trap them in unstable social environments, ensuring that they remain poor. Our legal system perpetuates racial inequalities by disproportionately pursuing and convicting minority defendants, and giving them harsher sentences. We blame the minor criminal for the dysfunctions in his family, community, and education and then saddle him with probation restrictions that make it likely he will return to prison, where there is a good chance he will morph into a major criminal; we will then blame him yet again.[12] Social programs that are designed to help these groups escape their traps sustain constant attacks from self-proclaimed 'watchdogs' as wastes of resources. Of course, those same watchdogs ignore much larger waste from programs that fit their ideology, which enrich their major donors, or that personally benefit them or their constituents. Clearly they do not object to waste. They only rationalize to prevent the victim from escaping, from rising up, and threatening privilege and the hierarchy.

Blaming the victim begins when we are young: children cruelly tease and bully those who are not attractive, not socially confident, not economically advantaged, not smart enough, or even too smart. This continues into adulthood, where executives, political leaders, and the public often privately, or occasionally publicly, ridicule and reject others over similar criteria.

Again, it is an expression of the malignant narcissist and the hierarchy of the atrox. They seek to bind us in helplessness and then to humiliate, dehumanize, and abuse us precisely for our helplessness.

Anti-Intellectualism

Five of the F-Scale measurements are all aspects of the same general problem, a lack or limitation of certain intellectual capabilities. These five are anti-intellectualism; anti-intraception; superstition and stereotypy; cynicism; and conventionalism.

It must be noted, however, that authoritarian personalities may be limited in certain intellectual domains but not in others. The engineer, the writer, the doctor, or the artist may be creative and analytical within their fields, and they might remain intellectually quite daring within acceptable parameters. Outside of those areas, however, they can become rigid, intolerant, and reactionary. Hitler and his inner circle were evil, but no one argues that they lacked intelligence or even flashes of brilliance. Fascists are certainly capable of technical excellence: WWII Germany comprised some of the foremost scientists and engineers of the day, many of whom nevertheless embraced a mindless Nazi ideology of racism, conquest, and world domination.* The same patterns can be seen in ancient Athens, imperial Rome, Stalinist Russia, Maoist China, and many others.

Thinkers who excel intellectually in one area may nevertheless be bigoted and narrow-minded in others. Clearly, there is nothing wrong with the analytical capabilities of the thinker; rather, that analysis is simply switched off for some topics. This is a continuation of the problem, 'delusion as survival,' and the earlier discussion of breaking off the fourth leg of the stool. The brain turns off certain functions, typically in response to either self-service or authoritarian instruction. It's as if a person could lift thirty kilograms of potatoes but not thirty kilograms of books. Clearly the aptitude is there, but the attitude responds to other cues. The unevenness of our analytical activities, our ability and willingness to fully consider some topics but not others, again suggests a genetic mechanism at work in our intellectual preferences.

---

* And even artists and philosophers. Filmmaker Leni Riefenstahl and philosopher Martin Heidegger both come to mind as brilliant Nazi sympathizers, although apologists question the sincerity of the commitment of either to Nazi ideals. On the other hand, architect Albert Speer belatedly recognized his contribution to the horrors of the Nazis and spent the rest of his life trying to make amends. Speer's very public, post-war renunciations serve as a striking foil to the muted responses of Riefenstahl and Heidegger. Why did they never atone? Why did they never forcefully renounce the regime?

Anti-Intraception

We noted that the fascist does not need to be completely anti-intraceptive, but only within defined areas. He may think deeply about the nature of the world around him; certainly, Hitler and his lieutenants thought deeply, and often incisively, about human motivations. Nor were they completely devoid of compassion, but their compassion was limited to their own group, and extended only to the people who resembled them and their ideal. So most Nazis cared about people, but only some people; they could examine and analyze many things, but not their prejudices and hypocrisies. In particular, they would not examine the self-service and inflexible dogmatism inherent in their attitudes.

Anti-intraception has a bizarre aspect. Notice that superstition is also a characteristic of the authoritarian personality, which would seem to be an opposite of anti-intraception. The Nazi might scoff at fairies but seriously discuss werewolves.[13] They might sneer at the masterful *mazurka* from a Polish peasant's fiddle but turn rapturous at the dissonance of Wagner's orchestrations. They could be tenderhearted toward blond, blue-eyed children playing fanciful games but turn murderous toward brunette, brown-eyed children playing exactly the same games, or worse, playing those games *with* the blond children. It is much like the dog nursing her pups and suddenly killing and eating the one with a defect. Subtle clues, perhaps otherwise meaningless clues, can quickly render the sacred obscene and transform the brilliant into the horrific. This again suggests a genetic mechanism, with or without a cultural ignition: some cue flips us from sentimental to sadistic.

So the authoritarian personality need not completely lack compassion or analytical imagination. The right-wing militant simply will not challenge his prejudices. Unfortunately, in the modern world the extreme liberal often responds to the far right with the same militancy and the same culture of coercion, impatience, sabotage, and victim-blaming as the right. Liberals can be very tenderhearted to the impoverished and marginalized crook but may have no compassion for the rich crook. Perhaps all political approaches are susceptible to these cultural and genetic influences.

This compartmentalized anti-intraception also brings us back to our romances and fairy tales. Armies of historians and historians of armies study military conflicts all over the world, in depth and in detail. And as we saw from our investigations of various conquerors, some of them overlook the essential gore. War is horrific; it is people reducing one another to shreds of bloody meat.

Anti-Intellectualism

The herd mentality precludes independent and analytic thought, and the soldier will, against all logic, give his own life when ordered by authority.

Anti-intellectualism, however, extends beyond the battlefield and even into the halls of academia. Our traditions say that our universities are centers of impartial, open-minded investigation and analysis. It is simply untrue.

In the introduction, I cited the work of Thomas Kuhn and Bernard Barber and the tendency of scientists to reject experimental data and new analyses that threaten accepted authorities and their own research. The sciences are basically the only aspect of human activity where a robust proof is possible; in fact, if a universal proof is not possible, the problem becomes the purview of other disciplines.* So if scientists are resistant to contrary data, arguments, and proofs, then we should hardly be surprised that scholars in the rest of human intellectual activity, where definitive proofs are not possible, might be even more recalcitrant.† And as we have argued, illogic suggests that a genetic mechanism is involved; genes may or may not choose what topics are forbidden to logic, but genes would seem to be involved in blocking our logical capabilities.‡

At least in academia, however, few would argue that the heretic should be denied the right to speak and publish. In contrast, resistance to new infor-

---

* Problems that resist clear proof will migrate into philosophy, business, political science, or others. The scholars can move as well; physics has begun dealing with ideas that are not universally verifiable, particularly when dealing with various aspects of uncertainty. As they do, they find philosophers encroaching upon those problems.

† Ironically, it is often within the 'applied' technologies—which the scientist often derides—that we find a lowered level of dogmatism and a healthy pragmatism. Once the engineer or the businesser shows his colleagues that some new approach is effective, there is little debate about theory, and resistance dissipates. Medicine is more dogmatic than engineering, and education seems to fit somewhere between medicine and engineering in flexibility of outlook.

‡ Thomas Kuhn makes the curious observation that sometimes those who produced new ideas entered a discipline later in life. We are certainly more susceptible to authoritarian ideas when we are young, particularly when we are children: our religious, social, political, and racial ideas can become ossified if taught to us when we are small. We become less gullible with age, but some intellectual submission typically continues. It seemed to me that from my undergraduate days, to medical school, to residency, my classmates became increasingly more skeptical of the books, our professors, and the latest research. Supporting this, recall the prologue and my difficulties in introducing a new theory to my field. Those outside of the field immediately saw value in the new idea. Those within the field—virtually all of whom, I assume, acquired their authorities in young adulthood, and whom, I also assume, never subsequently questioned them—insisted that the idea was invalid, although curiously without rebuttal.

mation within stronger authoritarian cultures becomes codified. Historically, there have been secular and ecclesiastical laws that declared dissent and new ideas to be heresy and that required proponents of such unorthodoxy to be punished with torture and possibly death. Even in the modern, supposedly advanced countries, we frequently see the demagogue arguing for laws to limit freedom of expression, shutter the free press, and muzzle dissenting opinions; and the authoritarian personality supports him in these things. The authoritarian and his followers attack and vilify the dissenter and often encourage ostracism or even retribution from the larger public. It becomes difficult for the dogmatic to escape their dogma.

Campaigns, Inc., was the first political consultancy firm in the world. They noted, "The average American doesn't want to be educated; he doesn't want to improve his mind; he doesn't even want to work, consciously, at being a good citizen. [But] most every American likes to be entertained. He likes the movies; he likes the mysteries; he likes the fireworks and parades... so if you can't fight, put on a show."[14] These and other insights from American advertising and public relations, ironically, were carefully studied by Joseph Goebbels and the Nazis, who used them to great effect. The Nazis even hired a New York public relations firm to help them improve their image in the United States, just as antagonistic foreign governments today invest heavily in media and lobbying to convince our citizens and government that the truth is untrue and vice versa.[15]

Today, talk radio and extremist cable news use a stream of anger to broadcast an authoritarian and anti-intellectual message. By riling the emotions, genetic responses emerge, trapdoors begin snapping shut, logical analysis is suppressed, and the misleading message penetrates uncritically. From there, the information often becomes dogmatic. For many people, anger media becomes an intellectual black hole from which they cannot escape.

Illogic

We have repeatedly noted that our brains have a great capacity for logic, but we often ignore logical argument when it disagrees with our dogma or our desire for self-service. This is reflected in the admonition to avoid discussions of religion or politics, areas where we tend to become authoritarian. Those two are common trapdoors. When either come up in conversation, we often shut down our logic centers and permit no objective discussion. This is curious, because we can easily see the problems in the dogmatism of those who disagree with us; they are blind to the obvious flaws in their religion, their politics, or their other preferred authorities. As we criticize them, however, we often insist that our *own* religion, political views, or authorities are above criticism. It never occurs to us that we are as blind as they are.

We have also seen that when our emotions overtake us, we can make decisions for which we are later remorseful; that remorse suggests a lapse in logic, for which genetic mechanisms have been engaged. Our illogical dogma can be similar. If we search for the keys and open the trapdoors, however, if we manage to recover from years of bondage to some ideology, then we look back and are puzzled that we so strongly believed something that even brief consideration would have exposed as obviously untrue. This happens when we begin questioning our politics or religion. But it also happens when we question Santa Claus.

In addition to the examples provided by Kuhn and Barber, I will offer a few historical anecdotes and one or two modern ones. Human cadaver dissection had been sanctioned in Europe from at least the thirteenth century, but the continent was crippled by strict scholasticism: the medieval scholar embraced the idea that previous authorities, the ancients of Jerusalem, Athens, and Rome, had already produced all of the knowledge that the world required. There was no need, nor was there really the possibility, for anything new. Humanity would never rival the ancients.

The accepted authority on human anatomy was the Roman physician Galen, who had not dissected human cadavers, but Barbary apes. Nevertheless, his texts served as the anatomy guides for the medieval medical student. Every scholar who worked from Galen for any length of time could see for himself that Galen's descriptions did not always match the human cadavers. But no one complained until the mid-sixteenth century, when Vesalius published a criticism of Galen's work. Despite the fact that Vesalius was pointing out what every anatomist could see for himself, Vesalius's observations were savaged by the academic community.

Not long after Vesalius published his observations, Sir William Harvey published his conclusions that the heart pumped blood through the body. This was also roundly attacked. The problem was that Galen, once again, had argued that the heart produced 'vivifying' humors that kept the body alive but that the arterial and venous sides of the circulatory system did not connect.* Harvey's solutions were not so obvious as the modern student might

---

* In Galen's defense, the connection between the two limbs of the circulatory system is microscopic. Ironically, Galen proposed invisible 'pores' in the heart through which the blood might slightly mingle. If he could have known that the 'pores' were everywhere in the body, he might have solved the problem.

assume; it took him some years to work out his demonstrations. The point that is critical to our considerations here, however, is that some contemporary anatomists announced that they would "rather err with Galen than proclaim the truth with Harvey."[16] The anti-intellectualism and authoritarian submission reflected in these responses are reminiscent of Groucho Marx's challenge, "Well who you gonna believe?! Me, or your own eyes?"[17]

When I mention these problems as continuing into the present, my colleagues object. They insist that we have changed so much since then. In my less collegial moments I sometimes respond, "Where? What in our educational practices has changed?" Seventeen-plus years of memorization do not a thinker make. We still teach students to memorize rather than challenge and analyze; and what we teach them to memorize is too often presented as facts and absolutes even as research, within science and without, makes it clear that knowledge is becoming increasingly elusive. One of Kuhn's arguments in *Structure* is that students of science eventually become very good at history and philosophy of science, but only *after* they disabuse themselves of the scientists' belief in absolute truth.

I have already introduced my own puzzling research experiences in the prologue, and Kuhn and Barber document that my experience is hardly new. To those I will add the Solutrean hypothesis, the idea that Europeans crossed the ice bridges into North America many centuries before we had previously hypothesized.[18] The theory has proven highly controversial: when it was first proposed in 2004, the reaction included adamant rejections from the academic community. That reaction was likewise puzzling. No one denied that the ice bridges existed; no one denied that human beings, like all living things, were under constant pressure to move into new territory. Putting the two observations together makes the Solutrean hypothesis not only possible, but also probably imperative. The only apparent explanation for the objections was that they challenged the existing dogma. All of these examples suggest that we have not become much more open-minded than the scholastics of the Middle Ages and that our basic educational paradigm is also, quite literally, medieval: submit, do not question; memorize, do not analyze.*

I will finish with another contemporary, non-academic example. In one of the recent national political campaigns, reporters discovered an odd trend, reflected in the title of the article, "GOP Delegates Say the Economy Is Ter-

---

* I must note, however, that as I consider friends and colleagues who have attended better schools, those where analysis and disputation were encouraged, that those graduates can still be quite pedantic on selected topics. Often their training has simply armed them with more effective debating skills that allow them to carry the day.

rible—Except Where They Live."[19] Analysts, government agencies, and most news media reported that the economy was strengthening. The delegates could see this activity in their own neighborhoods and states. But for years they had heard from anger-mongering media that the economy was terrible. Caught in the black hole of ideology, they rejected the official reports and even their own experience. They ignored any evidence that the economy was improving and listened only to the authorities they trusted.

"Well who you gonna believe?! Me, or your own eyes?"

Fundamentalism

We have considered the cult of personality and the idea that in some cultures, 'great' men can become gods when they are dead. It is a 'sustained Stockholm syndrome': the dominator need not be present, nor even alive, for the codependency to continue.

The word 'authoritarian' derives from 'author.' Today, 'author' primarily refers to someone who writes articles and books.* Fundamentalism is often the adherence to, even the adulation of, a writer who is long dead; or more accurately, to his writings. The writings of an authority can take on sanctified, godly aspects; this is particularly true when followers insist that a text was written by God Himself. We have remarked on fundamentalism in religion, government, economics, and many aspects of academia, including science. If someone 'important' wrote it—again, implying that those of us who simply read it are unimportant—the fundamentalist will insist it is true and unquestionable.

Scientific fundamentalists are, again, illustrative. Scientists teach their freshman classes that they are willing to discard their ideas when presented with even one contradicting experiment or even a single fact. We saw in the previous section, however, that scientists adhere to their fundamental documents in much the same way that the pious do.

The fundamentalist tradition of scholasticism dominated the medieval university. The great thinker of the medieval world, Thomas Aquinas, sought

---

* We tend to conflate the words 'author' and 'writer.' I suggest we begin separating the two. Writing is the transcribing of concepts, but authoring is assembling those concepts: reading, researching, analyzing, synthesizing, defending, and logically organizing all of it into an easy-to-read and coherent narrative. In essence, authoring is getting to the detailed outline; writing is hanging the meat on the bones of the outline. It's an important distinction, because once we are clear about where the narrative needs to go, writing and rewriting can be extremely easy and enjoyable. Doing all of the essential things that are preliminary to writing, doing the 'authoring,' however, is often intimidating, confusing, frustrating, and exhausting.

to reconcile Athens with Jerusalem because neither set of authorities were questionable. That is telling: although he would never have admitted it, at some level Aquinas obviously viewed the classics as rivals to the word of God. It is further evidence of the blind illogic of fundamentalism. For Aquinas, the Bible was unquestionable, and the classics were unquestionable. Unquestionability is the problem with fundamentalism.

Fundamentalism is an extension of fairy tales. At some point, someone may finally tell us that a fairy tale is not true, that Santa Claus does not exist. But they may not free us from other fairy tales, they may not tell us that the emperor is naked. Frequently, it is because no one with sufficient authority ever told *them* he was naked, and so they believe the same fairy tales everyone else does, and then we believe it, too. We are prone to believe things that are false, pass them on to our children, and just as in hundreds of preceding generations, our children are prone to accept them unquestioningly. The spin cycle never stops.

Science gives us another perspective on the problem. The history of science shows that many things we believe today will doubtless be considered false in the future; and many things we believe impossible now should be ordinary in the future. But as we have seen, scientists are generally quite sure that what they believe today is the final word. Indeed, as one prominent scientist boasts, "The good thing about Science [*sic*] is that it's true whether or not you believe in it."[20] To see the fundamentalist nature of this comment, substitute "the Bible" for "Science." Then consider the hidden fundamentalism in his underlying message: "You may not question my authorities"; which strongly suggests that he has not questioned them, nor is he going to. Finally, as is also true with statements from the religious fundamentalist, the quote only appears to be a clever riposte. Science, particularly with a capital 'S', is a branch of investigation comprising certain processes. Those processes are based upon *assumptions*, which we conveniently forget. Science *per se* can be neither true nor false.

Our problem is that we won't question our fundamentalist ideas either way. That's what fundamentalism is, a blinkered, unquestioned opinion of ultimate truth. We blindly believe the authorities we have read, or heard, or have been taught about, and whom we have never doubted. Again, that is the central problem: fundamentalism is believing things that we have never doubted or challenged, often because we have been forbidden to question them. The doors have been locked.

Simplisticism

To maintain a belief in unquestionable things, the fundamentalist requires simple, clear concepts, which means an absence of nuance. Nuance comprises areas of interpretation or disagreement. That, in turn, strongly suggests something that is not universally applicable, something that may not always be true. As a monumental truth must always be true, it cannot tolerate the reality of messy details.

So fundamentalism leads the believer to a simplistic view of his world and to believe that simplistic solutions will work. One simplistic solution is the previously considered culture of coercion, the idea that simply forcing people to do what the fundamentalist and the authoritarian desire will solve all problems. From these initial simplistic approaches, darker simplistic beliefs arise: religious purity, ideological purity, racial purity.

'Simplistic' is an adjective describing a concept that omits important details. 'Simplisticism' is an extension of that, it is a chronic and even global condition, one where the authoritarian personality insists that simplistic solutions will work in many, perhaps all, situations. Prayer, religion, free markets, democracy, coercion, swift retribution, or some other approach will solve all of our problems.

Unification Delusion

The lack of nuance inherent in simplisticism leads to the unification delusion, the belief that the fundamentalist's various simplistic ideas are all facets of the same thing and that there are no contradictions among them.

A common example is the Biblical fundamentalist who sees no contradictions among the Old Testament, the Gospels, and the Epistles. We specifically discussed how the Old Testament and Paul disagree with Jesus's teachings, partly in anticipation of this point. Even within the four Gospels, however, Biblical scholars analyze variations, nuance, and even apparent contradictions, sometimes within the same Gospel.

From that starting point, the unification delusion extends beyond scripture. In the United States, for instance, there are those who think that Thomas Paine, Adam Smith, the Bible, free markets, the Second Amendment, military power, and the believer's political party all agree, and in fact, all basically say the same thing. For many Southerners before the Civil War, slavery was lumped in with those as well. The fundamentalist will likewise pile together all doctrines that he opposes, such as atheism, Marxism, the validity of other denominations and religions, and perhaps racial equality, and consider them as one monumental evil. Our team is not only perfectly good and true, it is also entirely consistent; their team is perfectly evil and false, it is a monolith of perfidy. Nothing on our side can be questioned, nothing on their side can be allowed. When confronted with any contradictions among these, even obvious contradictions, the fundamentalist prevaricates, pivots, or quotes preferred authorities.* Or frequently, he simply discontinues the discussion.

The unification delusion then extends to people. Fundamentalists tend to believe that those who agree with them, agree with them perfectly, that there is no disagreement among adherents. This is not only a problem in religion and politics, it is also seen in science. Thomas Kuhn explains that prior to the paradigm shift, a field of study often undergoes a paradigmatic crisis marked by a proliferation of theories that eventually result in a situation where most scholars in the field can no longer agree what the field even is. *But they nevertheless continue to believe that they agree.* The field of study has come to comprise competing and conflicting theories that cannot all be true and some of which may violate the starting assumptions and conditions. But when confronted with these problems, the practitioners often insist that there are no substantial conflicts, only details to be worked out.†

---

* In fact, it seems that quoting authorities is more common in fundamentalist writing and speaking than elsewhere. Relying heavily on quotes from 'important' people, particularly when presented as fiat, suggests a fundamentalist personality.

† I have personal experience with this phenomenon, which influenced my thinking. In the prologue, I mentioned my work in sexual selection, the puzzles I encountered in the reactions from my colleagues, and how those puzzles motivated me to abandon unfinished papers and begin writing this book. One of those papers was to be a write-up of a talk I gave at a conference in Münster, Germany, in 2002, arguing that the field of sexual selection was in just such a paradigmatic crisis. In the talk I showed that the field had generated a proliferation of inconsistent theories, some of which violated the formative assumptions. (In fact, I suggested that Darwin himself had presented three partially incompatible versions of his own theory within his foundational volume and so the field may have begun in paradigmatic crisis.) The paper fell flat, which would be expected if I were completely wrong; but from our considerations here, and in a circular irony, it should also fall flat if it were completely right. One of the most intriguing and startling responses, however, was that one scholar roughly interrupted me in the middle of my talk; she did not simply object to my thesis, her objections were accompanied with scorn and sarcasm. Suggesting to scholars that their field is in a paradigmatic crisis would certainly offend their unification delusion. A diagram showing the proliferation of theories is shown on page xx, and a copy of the slide show and the outline of the talk are available at www.researchgate.net/profile/Joseph_Abraham4/.

As noted, this problem works in the negative as well: the fundamentalist tends to unify all of those who disagree with him, and believes that they all represent the same set of beliefs, and that they disagree with him on every point. All of this, in turn, leads to a problem in statesmanship and negotiating; there is no middle ground, so there is no room for compromise.

We can see the unification delusion in personal conversations and online discussions, where simplistic thinkers quickly glide over catchwords: liberals, mainstream media, activist judges, term limits, shake things up, Christianity, military funding, guns, law, and order. Each of these is a legitimate topic for consideration and discussion, but it is telling that there is no serious consideration nor discussion. These concepts cannot be examined because they cannot be questioned nor even separated. And so there is no contradiction between Christianity and capitalism on the one hand or gun reform and socialism on the other.

Again, the larger problem isn't that the fundamentalist could not see the disagreements among these. It's that the trapdoor has sprung, and he refuses to consider the possibility that any disagreement exists. He believes what he has been taught is true, absolute, and perfect. It is another idealized fairy tale and another legacy of the atrox's dysfunctions.

TUNNEL VISION

Some patients suffer from a constricting blindness: their vision begins to decay at the periphery and slowly spreads inward. It's tunnel vision. To our point here, the patient is often unaware that he has lost anything; he still thinks his vision is complete.

As a part of the preceding points, the authoritarian personality sees various spots of reality that he understands and fails to see how they connect or even contradict. And he cannot see his blindness. He thinks that his few spots of understanding give him complete, even global vision. He believes he can see everything.

And so again, he believes that because the free market is effective where he works, it is clearly effective everywhere. Because guns make him feel safe within his home, more guns will provide safety and security for everyone. And in religion, the problem can be compounded by even smaller spots: he believes a few things and assumes he believes it all. He does not see the contradictions among different parts of his scripture; he does not see that he picks and chooses what scripture he likes; and then he rationalizes even more by focusing on the spots within his own life where he complies while ignoring the many areas where he is in hypocritical violation.

Rationalizing

Before lawsuits and governmental actions forced R.J. Reynolds to admit the dangers of tobacco, employees were encouraged to smoke. At important meetings, cigarettes, matches, and ash trays were available at every seat. Presumably, RJR employees also smoked at home, endangering their families with secondhand smoke and fostering a culture of smoking in their children.* The tobacco industry knew about the injuries and deaths from smoking for decades, but the corporate culture rejected it, ignored it, and rationalized it away.

The sugar industry pursued the same strategy. Farmers, processors, and distributors pushed sugar on the public and manufactured data that suggested that the real cause of heart and blood vessel disease was dietary fat.[21] The shift to refined carbohydrates, particularly sugar, has created an American epidemic of obesity and diabetes. The sugar industry poisoned themselves and their children and rationalized away the dangers.

Today, we see the same thing with multiple environmental threats, particularly global warming. The fossil fuel industry and other corporations spend aggressively to support research that rejects fossil fuels as a possible contributor to global warming. For their profits, they are risking the future of the earth and their children with it. The larger problem isn't a difference of opinion, it is an unwillingness to *consider* other opinions and the unwillingness to consider the magnitude of the impact if their critics were correct. So fossil fuel supporters rationalize away open-mindedness along with the danger.

These are the large corporate rationalizations, but they become part of our culture. We rationalize away the dangers of our political beliefs, our religious beliefs, our business beliefs, and even research data if they do not fit our self-service and our authoritarian sources. One group of partisans frequently attacks the other group for this illogic, but no one is exempt. At times we all rationalize, only on different topics and opinions.†

---

* It can backfire. My father smoked cigars, my mother, cigarettes. On long summer trips, both of my parents would be smoking with the car windows rolled up and the air conditioner blasting. My siblings and I detest smoking.

† Having written that, and reflecting on previous discussions here, it occurs to that the profoundly autistic and the pure psychopath perhaps do not rationalize. The autistic cannot stand it and cannot understand people who do; and the psychopath is perfectly aware that he is lying.

Hypocrisy and Lying

By design, civilization is riddled with lies and therefore hypocrisy. The atrox lies. The nobles lie. The double standard is a lie. The conduct of the upper classes generates more lies in pretending that they are middle class in their morals when they are not, in pretending they care about the well-being of their subjects when they do not, and in pretending that they are refined and knowledgeable when they are neither. The emperor goes naked everywhere. It is not surprising that lying has become systemic.

The problems noted in this section on anti-intellectualism create yet more needs to lie, to reconcile the grating dissonance between our capacity for logic and our chronic rejection of it. We must lie to justify our blind allegiance to the atrox and his lies. To defend our indefensible intellectual and social positions, we tell lies of commission; and we tell lies of omission, the lies of ignorance. We insist the truth of things which we have never questioned. And when cornered, we fabricate even more lies in an attempt to hold it all together.

Politeness & Stoicism

A major problem of our codependency is the constant dishonesty of 'politeness.' It is considered rude to speak the truth, and we are taught to be deliberately dishonest. Some of this comprises 'white lies,' when we compliment what we do not like. Much politeness, however, allows the powerful to more effectively exploit us: we remain quiet when we are swindled or otherwise abused. All around us we can see people who refuse to speak up when they have been lied to, cheated, or deprived of rightful benefits.

On the other hand, those who do choose to speak up about corruption, exploitation, and incompetence often face retribution. Employees who expose criminal activities in the workplace face ostracism and persecution from management. In demonstrating the extent of our dissimulation and codependency, the whistle-blower may also face harassment from coworkers and neighbors even though they may be suffering the same abuse. And as we have seen, women and men who are sexually harassed and assaulted find themselves accused of promiscuity and dishonesty when they stand up for themselves. It is true for other types of abuse and exploitation.

When the exploiter is a member of the upper echelons of business and government, we often find that powerful peers close ranks around the offender and collude, often successfully, to end the career of the honest whistle-blower. This is the narcissism of the atrox, attacking those who criticize or expose his duplicity. It is also an aspect of blaming the victim and of the herd mentality.

This encourages stoicism. The Athenians who developed stoic philosophy argued that we should live life with quiet dignity, absorbed in the moment and separated from either the fear of pain or the desire for pleasure. The Romans continued and expanded that tradition, and Christians brought it into the modern day. Similar virtues are expressed in Buddhist, Shinto, Hindu, and other traditions.

For many misfortunes, gratitude for what is good, and a minimization of what is bad, is our best strategy. But it is also the legacy of the atrox: accept whatever horror he sends your way, do not complain, and do not fight back. If you do, you will be punished. Indeed, stoicism emerged in ancient Athens in part as a reaction to the horrors and abuses of Alexander. Stoicism becomes a codification of submissive fatalism and a protection for the powerful.

Politeness and stoicism, however, appear to be reserved for the middle class. The upper classes complain freely and unreservedly abuse their inferiors over minor inconveniences. They complain constantly about the least sacrifice; consider the Madras Famine and the insistence that it was more important that millions starve than the wealthy pay even a small tax increase. Like taxes themselves, politeness and stoicism are for the 'little people.' This is another example of the double standard and hypocrisy.

THE CULT OF PERSONALITY

In the preceding set of dysfunctions, we can see the foundations for the cult of personality: the ability for illogic, the tunnel vision of seeing only what one wishes to see, the rationalizations necessary to defend the atrox, and the simplisticism of believing that some 'beloved leader' is perfect. Perhaps the most important of these is the unification delusion: if someone is rich, beautiful, talented, or famous, then they are all of them, and they can do everything. They are honest, generous, trustworthy, and smarter than everyone else.

Together, these distortions synergize to create the illusion and the fairy tale that the demagogue is everything we need him to be, everything we wish him to be, and that he is the fulfillment of our wildest dreams.

Superficial Culture & Vapidity

The narcissistic hierarchy leads to a static lifestyle, one where important people are recognized by their positions and their possessions rather than their principles and their productivity. Who we are is how we appear: the famous are famous for being famous. Hierarchical standing is very much a niche, a station on a societal ladder that is often disassociated from anything essential about the occupant.

So we inherit a culture that focuses on superficial appearance and ignores essential activity. We encountered this attitude when we considered psychiatrists, and our tendency to ridicule those who attempt complex topics.

Our problems are undergirded by a certain vapidity, an avoidance of anything deep; not just deep ideas, but deep emotions, deep passions. It seems that the more authoritarian the culture, the more attenuated the breadth of feelings; there is little emotional range beyond fervent zealotry and searing hatred for the enemy. Emotions such as joy and sadness seem to be crushed down to the saccharine, the maudlin, and the sentimental. In authoritarian cultures, even engagement with one's children is often muted, blunted, and shallow. Everything is a militaristic, 'stiff upper lip' approach to the human condition; beyond the rage in conflict, we tend to be emotional automata. Our emotional atrophy further supports our stoicism and vice versa.

Narcissism / Materialism

We spend much of our money, and our lives, in physical appearances, in playing the same game of superficial appearance that the hierarchy plays. We wish to keep up with Henry VIII. Of all of the problems that we inherit from the atrox, this is one of the most damaging. If we could divert the money that we spend in appearances toward progress and real benefits, our world would be dramatically different and better. It would be much more peaceful, cooperative, efficient, productive, and inclusive than it is today.

Form over Function

The word 'luxury' stems from the Latin word *luxus*, excess. It is often synonymous with comfort, but if we look at the truly wealthy, we see that only a small portion of their luxury is comfort, while the great bulk of it is wasted on opulence. Luxury reflects the old artistic problem of form vs. function: Does good design mean that a chair works well and is comfortable? Or does

The Authoritarian Personality

it mean that the chair is visually attractive and that it serves the narcissism of the person who owns it or sits in it?

When most of us come into sudden wealth, our first thought is to spend it on opulent luxury, to impress others, to socially crush the Joneses. We don't think of it in those terms, of course; we have simply inherited a culture where that has been the goal. Wealth is a statement of one's rank in the hierarchy, and power is to be wielded for subjugating the *hoi polloi*; it is not to be used for mutual progress. So we have little concept of wealth beyond ostentation. Most of us would be bewildered if forced to spend our excess money on anything other than acquiring status and impressing others.

And so the wealthy live in absurdly large and lavish homes, ride in ridiculously expensive cars, and dress themselves in the latest Lucullan fashions. Ostentation even extends to their bodies as they diet, exercise, and undergo repeated surgeries to match fashion. These superficialities simultaneously announce both the superiority of the upper classes and reinforce our inferiority.

The rest of us are following the lead of our 'betters.' We never consider that opulence costs us more than money; it robs us of our time, our lives, and our enjoyment. Expensive things need to be cleaned, insured, repaired, carefully maintained, and protected—and then, after a few years, much of it must be replaced and updated. All of this distracts us from the substantial, from the function of life. We have less time with our family and friends, less time for substantial goals, and less time in pursuing life. The sixteenth-century Spanish playwright Fernando de Rojas put it well: "Riches do not make one rich, but busy; they do not create a master, but a steward. Rather than possess riches, men are possessed by them. Wealth has brought death to many and stolen pleasure from all…"[22]

Sports vs. Politics

A preoccupation with sports and outdoor activities is a prominent legacy of the atrox; sports are an extension of militaristic culture. They also reflect the culture of coercion, where others are to be defeated, beaten, and cast down. It likewise reflects the noble classes, as everyone is ranked in a clear, immediate hierarchy. Even the mascots of the best universities bow to the culture of the atrox: they typically portray dangerous, powerful predators, entities to be feared for their deadliness, not admired for their intelligence, kindness, or other human and humane virtues.

Noam Chomsky is one of many scholars who has asked why we are so interested in sports but not current affairs.[23] It appears to be another inheritance from the atrox. The serious examination of current affairs is a threat to the power and hypocrisy of the king. Consider how the medieval church discouraged the flock from reading the Bible and kept it in Latin to ensure that commoners could not understand it. With good reason: the appearance of Bibles in the vernacular led to a revolution against the authority of Rome. (That in turn quite probably contributed to other reactions against authority.) Also recall that the Puritan leadership of Massachusetts hid the colony charter from the other citizens. The atrox will struggle to maintain privilege in the face of a well-informed and intellectually engaged public. And so criticism of government and social policy under the atrox resulted in punishment or death. From that genetic and cultural selection, we avoid the topic of politics, and when we consider government, it is a shallow, perfunctory, and dogmatic consideration.

Participation in physical activities, however, trained soldiers for the atrox's army. It also served as a non-threatening distraction for the public. Remember the Spartans and their repeated attacks on the Thebans: distracting citizens can cover for the rulers' shortcomings. Sports can accomplish the same objective. Bread keeps the citizens full, circuses distract them from considering the obvious injustice all around them.

NOSTALGIA AND THE ROMANTIC PAST

The 1970s American television show *All in the Family* was built around the authoritarian personality of Archie Bunker, played by Carroll O'Connor. The show lampooned Bunker's hypocrisies in trying to resist a world that was leaving him behind. The theme song, "Those Were the Days," captured much of the nostalgia of authoritarian tropes; life was better when everyone conformed, when people agreed that everything was great, and suffered quietly. Two stanzas are illustrative:

> And you knew who you were then,
> Gals were gals and men were men.
> Mister we could use a man
> Like Herbert Hoover again.
>
> Didn't need no welfare state,
> Everybody pulled his weight.
> Gee, our old LaSalle ran great.
> Those were the days.[24]

Notice the reference to gender roles and sexual orientation, which were just starting to be challenged in the 1970s. Also note, the implication isn't that people were happy with their gender assignments in the past. They simply didn't question them.

But the two surprising references are to President Hoover and the LaSalle. The song is jarringly nostalgic about the Great Depression, when life was hard for almost everyone. During the Depression, only the wealthiest, together with the staunchest authoritarian personalities, thought well of Hoover. The nostalgia also ignores the fact that Hoover, despite his economic conservatism, was progressive on race relations, something that bigots such as Bunker conveniently ignored in his unification delusion. As for the LaSalle, it was one of the great luxury cars of the day. The only people who could afford one were the rich.

The song reflects Bunker's nostalgia, which is telling. His family was extremely poor and barely survived the Depression; they probably had no automobile at all. In a powerful episode, Archie and his liberal son-in-law are accidentally locked in a liquor storeroom overnight. As they drink, Archie begins to talk about his childhood. At one point during the Depression, Bunker's father lost his job, and Archie was humiliated by having only one shoe and one boot to wear to school. He then describes how his father spanked him and possibly beat him. He notes that once he even locked Archie in a closet for seven hours. He then explains that he learned his racial views by listening to his father.

Archie remembers it all with fondness and pride. In a drunken haze he fiercely defends his father, much as the hierarchy and the authoritarian personality defend the atrox: everything his father did, he did for Archie's benefit. Archie insists that his father was "...never wrong about nothin'." And then he adds, "How can any man who loves you, tell you anything that's wrong?!"[25]

Only children can believe that a world in frantic desperation is ordered. For Bunker's father, life was struggle, failure, and fear; Archie remembers it as security and protection. It is a metaphor for our fairy tales about life under the atrox. Much of our nostalgia comprises inaccurate memories of civilization's childhood, when we accepted what we were told, when we accepted all but the worst abuses as simple order, and when we believed that the abuse was actually security. These are the compromises we made to survive. When someone abuses a child and screams, "See what you've made me do?!" the child tearfully nods. It is the victim's fault.

Civilization spent its childhood believing the atrox was simply a loving father and a good shepherd. Our nostalgia is passed down through the generations, and it becomes the romance of civilization. We read the histories, and even when they have not been bowdlerized, and even when the carnage is described, we ignore the obvious facts and the necessary realities. It does not take much imagination to recognize how harsh life has been until quite recently.

Yet we do not analyze. This section is an attempt to explain why. We prefer to believe the past was different, better, partly because of nostalgia, partly because of tradition, and partly because survival depended upon believing that our past under the atrox was orderly, just, and beneficial.

Over the past few decades, novels of 'alternative histories' have become popular: the Nazis defeated the Soviet Union,[26] the South won the Civil War,[27] Germany and Japan defeated the U.S. and split the country.[28] These are disorienting because we cannot imagine them. But if they had happened, and if we now lived under authoritarian and/or slaving regimes, most of us would be grateful that 'our' side won; we would believe that the regime under which we were now living was infinitely better than the one that was defeated. In such a case, we might read fictions of freer societies with fear and loathing, in much the same way as the pre-WWII Germans and Japanese thought that Americans were deluded licentious libertines. Indeed, in the novel *The Man in the High Castle*, an alternative-alternative history appears, *The Grasshopper Lies Heavy*. In that fiction-within-fiction, the Allies won WWII. The book is banned by the ruling Nazis, and only fringe elements read it at great risk.

The point is, the authoritarian personality would have romanticized any outcome; he would have accepted any regime as superior and just, in the same way as too many of us romanticize the horrors of the past. Even if, as so many soldiers and Molotov's wife demonstrated, we might be required to sacrifice our lives to the atrox.

Humorlessness

The word 'humor' is related to the word 'humidity,' both of which relate to fluids. The classical view of human physiology was that our moods and natures were governed by four fluids, or 'humors': yellow bile, black bile, blood, and mucus. From the Latin versions of those terms we get, in order, the adjectives *choleric*, or angry; *melancholic*, or sad; *sanguine*, or enthusiastic; and *phlegmatic*, or tired. When we are healthy, the four are in balance, and the ancients believed that caused us to be 'in good humor.' Much medieval and Renaissance medicine was based on this theory.

'Humor' has come to mean laughter and gaiety, and in its modern meaning it still reflects personal health, as well as social and psychological health.

The laughter of healthy humor means that we laugh at ourselves as we laugh at our friends. It suggests that we are engaging with others in an informal, egalitarian, and communal way.

We have noted that humorlessness seems to be a diagnostic trait for narcissism. Of course, the narcissist often ridicules others, but ridicule is not humor. It is not healthy, and it is certainly not egalitarian: the hierarchy ridicules subordinates to keep them in their place. The noble classes also deride peers to lower them and thereby elevate themselves. Ridicule is a form of sabotage, and it supports the zero-sum game: if you fall, I rise; if you lose, I win.

The hierarchy may also ridicule superiors, but only in private settings and at some peril because the atrox and the hierarchy tolerate no laughter from inferiors. The narcissist does not forget slights and embarrassments and will dedicate years, even a lifetime, to revenge. Caracalla's slaughter of the Alexandrians is a prime example. Alexander claimed that he spent much of his career seeking revenge for the Persians' attacks on Greece even though the Persian Wars concluded a century before Alexander's birth. Caesar revenged himself upon the Tencteri and Usipetes tribes by exterminating every child, woman, and man among them. Even today, we can see despots assassinating those who criticize or otherwise embarrass them, even running afoul of other nations by assassinating them abroad.

We have also considered *lèse majesté*, laws that forbid criticizing or mocking the king. Narcissism tolerates no affront; not the egalitarian laughter of humor and certainly not the sabotaging laughter of ridicule.

A lack of humor is a characteristic of the hierarchy. Those who are humorless often reflect the mindset of the narcissist, the psychopath, and/or the authoritarian personality. Of course, we all lapse into humorlessness when we express an inflexible point of view, particularly on the topics of religion, politics—or our favorite football teams. Tandem with that, we are humorless when we are angry or otherwise succumb to our genetic impulses. Culture may choose where we are humorless, but our genes make it happen.

Humorlessness is striking in fundamentalists, particularly religious fundamentalists. Jesus was skilled in the ready Hebrew wit. When hecklers attempted to lure him into Judea's conflicts with Rome by asking Jesus if Jews should pay taxes, he asked whose face was on the coins. One can imagine the roar of laughter when he deftly pivoted with the famous line, "Render unto Caesar that which belongs to Caesar." He teased Simon Peter by saying, "Upon this rock [*petros*] I will build my church"; Peter had been no rock of faith. Jesus also speaks of straining water to remove gnats but swallowing camels whole. It is a quasi-pun, as the words in Aramaic sound similar, *gamla*, camel; and *galma*, gnat.²⁹ Despite these accounts, fundamentalists portray the Bible, particularly the Gospels, as deadly dry and serious; laughing at them is apostasy. The same reaction can be seen with any fundamentalist mindset. There are people who are offended by suggestions of humor about, or even from, the U.S. Founders, Adam Smith, Charles Darwin, or any authority they support.

Humor, however, can also be a therapeutic. The king's fool touched on problems that no one else could mention. The satirist and the allegoricist are often effective at introducing contradictions and hypocrisies from oblique, even tangential directions. Humor is likewise healing in everyday situations: getting people to laugh in a tense disagreement breaks down the hierarchical, authoritarian posturing; it seems to switch on and off those parts of our brains that deal with psychopathy vs. compassion, exclusion vs. inclusion, and arrogance vs. equality. As such, among normal people humor can often provide an opening to compromise and resolution.

Humor is also a great aid to learning and growth. When our children make mistakes, they laugh, suggesting their attitude is, 'No harm done, let's try it again.' And the humorlessness of the atrox reflects the opposite attitude, a sclerotic, inflexible, and intransigent culture that cannot reflect and therefore cannot change and adapt.

Self-Defeat / Lose-Lose

Years ago, *Sports Illustrated* published an article about the emerging popularity of paintball games. The magazine related a competition among men with experience in combat, hunting, athletics, and other masculine skills. Prior to the competition, the contestants jawed about who would win and who would slay whom.³⁰

Surprisingly, the winner was a quiet-spoken forest ranger. One advantage he held was that he was skilled with topical maps, which helped him locate the flags to be captured in the game. But his real advantage was his strategy. Rather than trying to run with the wolves, he browsed with the deer. During the competition he imitated the behavior of deer by taking a few steps, stopping and listening, and then taking a few more. Several times he saw other competitors walk within shooting range, but he stayed quiet, out of sight, and let them pass. He witnessed, and avoided, shoot-outs among other contestants. Despite the delay from his constant pauses, despite his detours to avoid other competitors, the ungulate strategy won the game. While the wolves were focused on defeating and humiliating one another, the deer was focused on the goal. The prey beat the predators.

Those macho wolves illustrate what happens in the self-serving hierarchy. As we have seen, competitions among the noble classes are zero-sum. Except for periods of successful conquest, the hierarchy is largely a closed system, and as we will see in an upcoming chapter, progress within it is slow and often serendipitous.

If the park ranger had not been competing in the paintball game, the players who were seeking dominance would have been playing a zero-sum game. But the park ranger created a new environment; the overall game was still zero-sum, but by introducing a more intelligent strategy, he trapped the more macho players in a lose-lose strategy. Go back and consider the description: the park ranger didn't defeat a single opponent. They defeated each other, and in so doing they also defeated themselves. The park ranger merely needed to avoid their narcissistic distractions and to focus on collecting his resources.

This happens inside corporations. Businesses that are focused on employees and customers, rather than the hierarchy or even rather than the product and profits, generate superior products and superior profits. As we will see, the importance of management is highly exaggerated. The point is, companies focused on people out-compete corporations where the wolves stalk each other for hierarchical and economic dominance.[31]

Political units, like corporations, must also must vie against one another; each city, region, and nation is in competition with others. Governments that are too distracted with ideology and self-service have a reduced capacity to change and grow. They will tend toward zero-sum and win-lose within their boundaries only to discover that when they attempt to compete outside of their borders, they are caught in a negative-sum game and a lose-lose situation. Any number of modern regimes illustrate this, perhaps none so dramatically as North Korea. Trapped under an intolerant military hierarchy, the country cannot feed itself and lives in medieval squalor.

As progress accelerates, the atrox's culture of exclusion and sabotage eventually excludes and sabotages everyone within it.

Human Aesthetic

We have considered the homosadism of some conquerors and the chronic desire to have soldiers who match a classical/metaphysical ideal: tall, square-jawed, with a polished physique. The ideal concept of masculine beauty goes beyond the physical, however; we are also attracted to the emotionless (*i.e.*, stoic) personality of the psychopath. We want the man who is never afraid, who does not blink at danger, and who always knows what to do. Of course, no one always knows what to do, and no healthy person is never afraid; but we believe that those who act like they know what to do really know what to do. And so ruthless and unfeeling narcissists and psychopaths attract our respect, while those who approach problems with doubt and a grasp of the complexity inherent in most problems are out.

The problem is right there in the word 'cool': we are attracted to people who portray the coolness of the predator and the rocky visage of the reptile. The classical ideal, the statues of Apollo and the Discobolus, present unintended metaphors: they are the contrived, rigid, and superficial images of the psychopath and the hierarchy. They are chiseled beauty, but they are nevertheless the cold and unfeeling marble avatars of the atrox's fantasies.

We find that we are often attracted to people who are not attracted to us, another part of the atrox's legacy. Somerset Maugham relates his personal suffering in pursuing someone who ignored and abused him in *Of Human Bondage*. Then there is Grace Kelley, one of the beauties of her age. Grace had a secret advantage—one that returns us to a previous consideration—in that she was extremely near-sighted. She became a movie idol in the days before contact lenses and corneal reshaping were available and before glasses were fashionable. And so as she sat terrified in social situations because she could not see the people around her, she appeared poised, cool, and aloof to others. That added dimension helped her net a prince.

Sloth

We noted that sloth is one of the Deadly Sins; it is also a celebrated and envied aspect of the atrox and other nobles. More than one modern student reading Jane Austen or the Brontë sisters has wondered, "When do these people work?" Within the modern democratic ethic, all capable adults are expected to work. Throughout history, however, the upper classes did not work, or certainly they did nothing that looked like work. We have the sultan in his seraglio, the king on the stag hunt, the emperor at the gladiatorial games, the raj playing chess, the khan falconing, and all of them attending sumptuous dinners and parties and being entertained with music and plays. And for the atrox, of course, murder and theft in conquest was yet another entertainment, a highly lucrative hobby; hunting people is much more exciting than hunting a fox or a stag. For all of these, the 'working classes' were the inconsequential people far below them.

The upper classes might, however, apply themselves passionately to their hobbies: much of the beginnings of science, technology, poetry, and literature originated from the idle upper classes. Thomas Dewey generated a defense of pragmatism and a criticism of traditional philosophy by pointing out that the early Athenians supported a wealthy leisure class who focused on philosophical problems while ignoring more practical ones.*

The upper classes have historically despised real work, and the workers, as we have seen in the many offensive words that describe them, were the blamed victims. The hierarchy required that the nobles loathe the classes below them, particularly the working class commoners. Or more tellingly, the working slaves: after visiting the post-Revolutionary U.S. South and observing the slave-owning aristocracy there, Alexis de Tocqueville noted, "Slavery dishonors labor."[32]

This unfortunate attitude can still be seen in some of the older southern universities, where the anti-work culture colludes with the anti-intellectual culture; because, of course, the work of the university is intellectual. Within some of these universities, there is a culture of privilege and a resistance to effort. The students coming from the fading remnants of the Southern leisure class are expected to earn no more than 'gentleman's Cs' in their courses. Of course, strong grades are tolerated from students wishing to enter selective professional schools, particularly medical or law school, but even here a certain anti-intellectualism remains. Superior students are expected to make their grades as a *de facto* product of their genetic superiority, but they should not appear to work too hard at their studies, and they certainly should not be curious in their classes. Nor should they demonstrate nuance in their understanding of the course work: an encyclopedic memory is fine, but one should not delve deeply into conflict and contradiction. A good student should be able to define communism, but he must never seriously consider it.

---

* The major flaw in that argument is that the most important Athenian thinker, Socrates, was a humble stonecutter. Manual labor can free mental time for pursuing philosophy. Jesus was a carpenter, Samuel Gompers was a cigar roller, Eric Hoffer was a longshoreman. In the Navy, I very much enjoyed the most repetitive job in the carpentry shop—the one that everyone else hated precisely for its repetitiveness—because it left me time to think. And at one point in my life I waited tables and was surprised to hear the dishwasher listening to NPR; he was actually from a wealthy family and had a degree in liberal arts. But he had read Orwell's *Down and Out in Paris and London* and wanted to try washing dishes. Finally, one of the reasons I do not enjoy medicine is because, to pull down that level of income, people actually expect me to think about them and their problems. (Imagine! And my family treats me the same.) Anyway, I suspect the reason more manual laborers aren't thinkers is because the low pay limits the work to the least educated.

On one occasion I was the dinner guest of an old Southern sorority at one of these colleges. Each night, a different sorority member was assigned to be the hostess. It was her job to supervise and to ensure that everyone had enough food and drink. It was also her responsibility to keep the conversation going while redirecting it from unsuitable topics. Although we were on the campus of a university, there apparently was to be no talk of anything weighty or intellectual and certainly nothing that might lead to a disagreement. The cooking was done by a hired staff, mostly African American, and the young women were waited upon by hired male students, who were all white. It slowly dawned on me that the young women were in training to serve as society matrons, to perpetuate a shallow culture of anti-intellectual leisure.

There is an additional intriguing aspect of the evening. The event was billed as 'Apple-Polishing Night,' in which each sorority member was encouraged to invite the faculty member from a class in which her grade was in doubt. The young woman who invited me had a strong 'A', and so I assumed she invited me because she liked me. Other students later informed me that she despised me. Entertaining powerful people whom one dislikes is another useful skill in the hierarchy.

Historiography

In 1796, Napoléon re-took the town of Pavia. The inhabitants had not harmed the men of his garrison and had even fed them a nice meal when they surrendered. But the citizens had nevertheless revolted, and for this, Napoléon gave the city to pillage. 'Only' seventy to eighty people were killed.[33]

Stendhal, in his *Life of Napoléon*, defended the general, "It was a duty of which it seems cruel even to speak. A top general was obliged to shoot three men to save the lives of four; what is more, he had to shoot four enemies to save the life of one of his soldiers... To have shown mercy in Pavia would have been a crime against the entire army. It would have been preparation for a new 'Sicilian vespers' [a massacre]..."[34] But Stendahl, as with some other historians, leaves out the critical details: Napoléon seized Pavia without justification; Napoléon invaded Lombardy without provocation; Napoléon started a continental war for nothing beyond greed and narcissism.

Stendhal is defending the victimizer and blaming the victim. Again, the contemporary historians often defended and rationalized the horrors of the atrox. To be fair, history is a cumulative discipline, and when the historian studies the past, she is primarily studying past historians and other chroniclers. They, like all of the king's subjects, had few options: to survive they were required to praise and exault the atrox.

Chapter VIII:
The Atrocino

> *Serial killers ruin families.*
> *Corporate and political and religious psychopaths ruin economies.*
> *They ruin societies.*
> —Bob Hare, *The Psychopath Test*

> *What's picking a lock compared to buying shares?*
> *What's breaking into a bank compared to founding one?*
> *What's murdering a man compared to employing one?*
> —Elisabeth Hauptmann and Bertolt Brecht, *The Three Penny Opera*

> *And you, still a pile of squirmy crap in a different wrapper.*
> —Zed to Serleena, *Men in Black 2*

In 1973, a General Motors engineer wrote a memo detailing a cost-benefit analysis for preventing deaths from fuel fires in the company's automobiles. The cost, per vehicle, for paying out lawsuits for the loss of human life was $2.20. The cost, per vehicle, of preventing those deaths was slightly more expensive, at $2.40. The engineer made no recommendations and readily admitted that "human fatality is really beyond value."

The memo became important years later. In 1991, the McGees, a family of four, were traveling in a GM automobile when they were struck from behind by a runaway trailer. Although the collision itself was minor, the trailer punctured the fuel tank and ignited it. The family's thirteen-year-old son was the last to emerge, and he was unrecognizable, burning and bleeding as his incapacitated family could only watch; he died soon after. The other three required skin grafts, and the mother required even more extensive plastic surgery.

Various plaintiffs had tried to get the 1973 memo admitted into evidence for years, but GM blocked them by arguing that the document was simply an academic exercise. The judge in the McGee case, however, sided with the plaintiffs and allowed the memo to be presented at trial. During the litigation it got worse for GM: it emerged that the car manufacturer had been withholding other evidence that suggested that the memo was more than an academic exercise.[1]

In addition, other evidence introduced in the trial showed that GM knew their fuel tanks had other vulnerabilities. A GM engineer testified that he had been looking into the problem and had suggested inexpensive remedies to reduce the danger. His suggestions were rejected, and he testified that "Roger Smith, the chairman of the board, told GM engineers not to spend 'one penny more' on safety than needed to meet the minimum federal standards." The jury awarded the McGees damages of $33 million from GM and $27 million from the driver of the trailer.[2]

At the time, GM's annual revenues were over $150 billion per year; not surprisingly, that penalty left the company undeterred. Soon after the McGee trial concluded, GM technicians became aware that some of their ignition switches could easily be jostled into the 'off' position, shutting down both the engine and the airbags. In 2005, sixteen-year-old Amber Marie Rose was killed when her car's ignition turned off and her airbag failed to discharge as she hit a tree. Despite her death, for the next eight years—most of it under the leadership of CEO Richard Wagoner—internal reports and external complaints about the ignition switch continued to surface, and another dozen people died because of the problem. Repeatedly, however, the GM leadership decided the problem was too costly to fix. Not until 2013 did GM begin addressing the problem.

In a situation paralleling the McGee lawsuit, Ford lost a series of suits over the design of its fuel tanks in the Pinto, even though dramatic improvement in car safety could have been added for less than twenty dollars per car. One former Ford executive testified that the "highest level of Ford's management made the decision to go forward with the production of the Pinto, knowing that the gas tank was vulnerable to puncture and rupture."[3] The period in question straddled the presidencies of Semon Knudsen and Lee Iacocca; Iacocca had been the driving force behind the Pinto.

Economic & Political Conquest

We have considered the atrox through civilization, but in the past quarter millennium, he has found his opportunity for conquest increasingly constrained geographically, politically, and culturally. In recent years, opportunities for wealth through widespread horror have largely been contained within the developing countries.

As a result, in the modern world economic and political conquest have gradually replaced the military expedition, and the atrox has adapted. His opportunities for physical sadism are diminished, while his eagerness for dominance and status remains; and he continues to recruit followers by employing shallow and emotional, but effective, rationalizations.

Today's conqueror seeks power and wealth in the opportunities afforded by the corporation, government, and bureaucracy. The narcissistic drive for riches, dominance, and notoriety—carefully refashioned as 'the bottom line,' 'executive leadership,' and 'media presence'—still dominate his priorities. Just as throughout history, those priorities minimize people, human suffering, and any progress that does not further distinguish the narcissist from the rest of us. As we have seen with GM and Ford, and as we will see in ensuing examples, the modern conqueror is still more than willing to trade human life for his power, personal prestige, and luxury.

Corporate Psychopaths

We previously considered corporate psychopaths, particularly as discussed in Babiak's & Hare's *Snakes in Suits*. Examples are plentiful. Bernie Madoff's investment firm ran the largest Ponzi scheme in U.S. history, and he defrauded investors of $65 billion. Jeffrey Skilling and Andrew Fastow oversaw systematic and systemic fraud at energy trader Enron, which cost investors perhaps $60 billion. Bernie Ebbers built WorldCom into a major telecommunications company but was convicted of accounting fraud of $11 billion, which razed the company and cost investors over $175 billion.[4]

In his highly entertaining and informative book *The Psychopath Test*, Jon Ronson searches for corporate psychopaths and finds a likely list in the magazine *Fast Company*.[5] Unfortunately, Ronson discovers that all of his potential candidates are dead or in jail except for Al 'Chainsaw' Dunlap, the hard-charging former CEO of Sunbeam. As Ronson visited with him, Dunlap's explanations of who he is, and of his management philosophy, seemed reasonable. The only problem was Dunlap omitted the fact that many of his supposed 'business turnarounds' were shams, that he was found guilty of fraudulent accounting and management practices by the Securities and Exchange Commission, and that the SEC has barred him from serving on corporate boards for life.

Among the most shameless corporate psychopaths were the bankers and other housing lenders responsible for the 2007–2009 sub-prime mortgage crisis, which precipitated the economic pandemic that ensued. For years leading up to the crisis, the bankers aggressively pursued risky investments, which resulted in a steep worldwide recession. But they were not punished, and indeed, they gave themselves almost twenty billion dollars in bonuses as they enjoyed bailouts from the government.[6] This is the psychopath/narcissist at his smoothest.

It may seem that the crimes here are simply aggravating white collar crimes, similar to stealing a loaf of bread, albeit many millions of loaves. But many of the victims of these financial schemes were bankrupted or reduced to poverty. There were large populations of aging workers who found that their retirement accounts were demolished and they would have to continue working a decade or more beyond retirement age. Some of the victims were retirees who physically could not return to the workforce and who were forced into public assistance. Many families who had done nothing wrong were summarily evicted from their rental homes when their landlords could no longer meet the mortgage payments. The victims also included many small businesses that had been run legally and ethically, but because they did business with the banks, were forced to shutter their operations and terminate their employees. These problems created yet larger ripples through the economy. The loss in the U.S. and European financial sectors was over two trillion dollars; homeowners lost over three trillion in equity; the U.S. stock market lost seven trillion; and the total impact on all markets worldwide is incalculable. White color crime is not clean. It is not victimless.

The corporate environment often attracts, and then promotes, those with poor priorities. Success in the corporation requires a particular set of skills: meeting stated objectives; making hard/profitable decisions; navigating and succeeding in workplace politics; and the willingness to work long hours on details and new initiatives that may or may not advance the company. This facilitates the emergence of a certain type of personality, someone motivated by money, power, and fame, someone willing to cut corners, to shove family, friends, and community aside, to exploit others, and to be ruthless with subordinates. It is fertile ground for the narcissist.

THE ATROCINO

Corporate psychopaths, as Babiak and Hare note, are not necessarily full-blown psychopaths; they may not meet the full diagnostic criteria. We have also seen that the full psychopathic diagnosis may not apply to military 'criminals,' *i.e.*, those who are heroes to the nation they represent but criminals to the nation they attack or oppose. Similarly, political, governmental, and bureaucratic psychopaths may not fit the full criteria, either. Nevertheless, the actions of all of these are sufficiently similar to those of the psychopath that the connection is unmistakable. They present an ontogeny and a kinship: the military, corporate, political, and bureaucratic psychopaths are the descendants of the conquerors of old.

Of course, the modern psychopath is more refined than the atrox. He is less inhuman and less deadly than his cultural and genetic ancestors. For this reason, I label the modern exploiter the *atrocino*, or 'little atrox.'

We do not need to consider the atrocino to the extent that we examined the conqueror, because evidence of him is in every newspaper, current events magazine, and news website. We can see big pharma, with Martin Shkreli as their poster child, pursuing public extortion: pay us everything you have or die. We can see the executives controlling the National Rifle Association, ignoring the desires of the democracy and even of the NRA membership, as they coldly sell out our democracy and watch our children murdered along with hundreds of thousands of others—fifteen thousand in 2016, including over 380 mass shootings—because it richly feeds their bank accounts. The tobacco companies kill seven million people a year, after insisting for decades that their products were perfectly safe, even healthy. And now we watch the fossil fuel industry risk the entire planet to maintain their wealth and privilege. Profit from murder and theft are still with us.

Nazi Collusion

The impact of the atrocino is everywhere, but there are few places where it is more jarring than when American corporations betray us to our enemies, even while we are at war with those enemies. Before WWII, Henry Ford was an outspoken anti-Semite and an admirer of Adolf Hitler. A few years back, internal Nazi documents emerged that for Hitler's fiftieth birthday, Ford presented *der Führer* with 35,000 *Reichsmarks*, about a quarter of a million dollars in 2018 money. Although Ford and the rest of the pro-Nazi 'America First' party fell silent after the bombing of Pearl Harbor, throughout the war Ford sold cars in both the U.S. and Germany, to American and Nazi militaries alike. Both Ford and GM converted their domestic and international factories to producing war matériel for both sides, and there is evidence that the American offices of the two corporations were complicit in the duplicity.[7]

In the thick of WWII, the Truman Defense Committee, headed by then-Senator Harry Truman, pilloried Standard Oil for collaborating with the Nazis. Not only had Standard sold tetraethyl lead to the Nazis from their facilities in England—without which the *Luftwaffe* could not fly their planes back to England for bombing raids—but Standard was providing the Nazis with technology for synthetic rubber *and withholding that same technology from the Allies.*[8] Despite the public outrage, little changed. Standard continued supporting the Nazi war machine until the end of the war, even as their efforts killed our own troops and assisted the Nazis in terrorizing the world.

There are countless others, many of which may never be known. Chase Bank collaborated with the Nazis and froze Jewish accounts.[9] IBM Hollerith tabulators were used to track war matériel, to schedule trains, and to process Jews for the concentration camps. Siemens helped build the gas ovens. Coca-Cola made great war profits behind both lines; when Coca-Cola syrup became unavailable in the Axis countries, the German subsidiary used processed fruit leftovers to create Fanta.*

Peacetime did not stop corporate treachery. Soon after the end of the war, Rolls Royce sold the Nene jet engine to the Russians—with the understanding, of course, that it was not to be used for military applications.

It continues today. In 2012, Pratt & Whitney was convicted of using its Canadian subsidiary to sell advanced Z-10 attack helicopters engines to China, along with the software to operate them. "At the same time it was helping China, the company was separately earning huge fees from contracts with the Pentagon, including some in which it was building weapons meant to ensure that America can maintain decisive military superiority over China's rising military might."[10]

The website POGO, The Project On Governmental Oversight, maintains lists of crimes and other violations committed by government contractors.[11] Under 'Import/Export' misconduct there are numerous recent treasonous activities from major corporations, things for which a civilian would be jailed and a soldier shot. Boeing was fined for exporting military technology to Russia and others. Lockheed Martin illegally sold space launch technology to the Chinese. IBM appears again, this time for exporting computers to a Russian nuclear weapons laboratory. Halliburton sold pulse neutron generators to Libya. ITT sold high-tech night-vision technology to China. Northrup Grumman is particularly noteworthy for selling secrets for Inertial Navigation Systems to various countries; shockingly, it sold Russia the software for the inertial guidance system that protects Air Force 1.[12] The Pratt & Whitney violation is also there, listed under P&W's parent corporation, United Technologies.

The Military-Industrial-Congressional Complex

On January 17, 1961, President Eisenhower gave his farewell address to the nation. In it, he warned of the "military-industrial complex," of the col-

---

* The German office urged their staff to use their imaginations—*Fantasie* in German—to come up with a substitute product.

lusion, and even of the conspiracy, between corporations and the military to constantly expand their income and their influence. Eisenhower worried that this collusion threatened freedom and democracy.

In recent years, it emerged that Eisenhower had considered instead warning of a "military-industrial-*congressional* complex." The President removed "congressional" noting, "It was more than enough to take on the military and private industry. I couldn't take on the Congress as well."[13] That is concerning: if the leader of the free world cannot warn us of a looming threat, then perhaps that threat is already too large to stop. We did nothing to the bankers who created the recent Great Recession; they were "Too big to fail and too big to jail," and so they escaped prosecution for recklessly bringing the world to collapse. We must wonder if the modern corporation, along with our own Congress, have grown too powerful to bring to heel.

Increasingly, corporations are not trying to create products that solve problems; they seek to create, even fabricate problems that need their products. They increasingly don't fill needs, they manufacture needs. In the worst traditions of the atrox, one of those manufactured needs appears to be war-for-profit.

Throughout history, wars were started to feed the narcissist's wealth and self-service. The Civil War was fought to protect slavery; critics point out that most of the Southern soldiers were not slave owners, but we can use our insights into the authoritarian personality to explain why that is no counter argument. Greed explains so many of our wars, which were highly profitable for a few: attacking Native Americans to clear land for farming and ranching; invading Haiti, the Dominican Republic, Cuba and Nicaragua to protect profits for the fruit conglomerates; invading Russia in the 1920s and Korea, Cuba, and others later to defend capitalism; deploying troops in the Suez and the Canal Zone to protect shipping interests; attacking Iraq to feed oil profits; and so forth.

The difference now is that war doesn't serve other industries; war serves the war industry, which means there is constant pressure for profit from murder. Government is pressured to deploy and destroy for greed. Much as with the ancient Spartans, there is a need to manufacture conflicts. After WWII, war profiteers fanned the Cold War. When the Cold War thawed and profits decreased, they shifted to terrorism, which too was convenient. The war on terror was fed by Cold War profiteering: we supported the Mujahideen in Afghanistan and then betrayed them when there was greater profit elsewhere. The abandoned Mujahideen became our bitter enemies and formed the foundations for much of the Islamic terror we experience today, off of which the same U.S. industries profit. There appears to be corporate pressure to betray the Kurds in the same way as a guaranteed method to generate more terrorism and war profits. We might wonder how many of the three thousand killed in 9/11, or the hundred thousand civilians killed in Afghanistan, or the hundreds of thousands killed in Iraq, or the untold numbers killed in the destabilization of the Middle East, go back to the activity of war profiteers in the Cold War and since. And now the refugees pouring out of the war-torn countries are fanning racist panics across Europe, which the atrocino uses to undermine egalitarian ideals, foster paranoia and bigotry, which in turn increase right-wing profits. Global arms sales are growing at a healthy clip.[14]

Wars were always manufactured for profit, and the atrox always funded those wars with money extracted from citizens. The problem we face today is that as the atrocino pursues the same strategies; he is not only making a mockery of egalitarian government, he is dismantling it as well. As we will see, he is deliberately drawing us back toward fascist and even feudalist systems. The atrocino has tricked us into reviving our old codependencies, as we sacrifice children, women, and men, and neglect much-needed domestic services, to feed his narcissism.

Psychopathic Media

The duplicity of the atrocino expands to exploit us in all domains. For instance, large corporations increasingly control the media. Currently 80 percent of the books in the U.S. are produced from just five companies, only two of which are American corporations;[15] 90 percent of all U.S. media—books, newspapers, magazines, radio, television, Internet—are produced and controlled by six corporations.[16] Those media empires, in turn, are controlled by just fifteen billionaires.[17] As I am writing this, the Federal Communications Commission is working to revoke Net Neutrality, handing over to corporations control of the Internet infrastructure that was built with citizens' tax dollars, which would enable that handful of people to increasingly block us from seeing the small portion of independent news that remains. Independent news is in danger either way; the few profitable independent media that survive suffer constant wooing from the handful of media plutocrats to sell out.

The atrocino manipulates, acquires, controls, and sabotages modern media. Some of this sabotage is by design, but much of it is simply a byproduct of greed and intellectual sloth.[18] In his slender volume *The Business of Books*, André Schiffrin documents the decline of the book industry. One of the more important trends he relates is that when he and other editors demonstrated that new and daring titles could still be profitable, the overlords were uninterested: they told their employees to stick to accepted patterns.[19] We will return repeatedly to this threat to the modern world: the atrocino, like the atrox, desires control. Progress is a threat to his control.

Media executives often choose to protect their advertising revenues by protecting their advertisers,[20] but it is so much easier to simply cut newsroom staffs so deeply that investigative reporting dies and nothing embarrassing can be produced that might threaten the advertisers and owners. Through it all, the media atrocino will accept advertising money from any source, even from sources that endanger those democratic processes that protect the media itself.[21]

THE NICKEL STRATEGY

At times, I have worked with public service boards and served on one for a few years. Corporations have great advantages over the governments and boards that oversee them. First of all, the relevant oversight body often has to take the word of the corporation: the actual costs, salaries, and efficiencies of the corporation are either proprietary information or buried within volumes of information. In fact, when one of the oversight groups requests more information, it is not unusual for the corporation to respond with a deluge of documents. Even then, however, there is no way to know if the information is accurate or complete.

Second, the legislative bodies and oversight boards change membership constantly, but corporations are long-lived, and managers spend careers working toward their objectives. This allows for the 'nickel strategy': a public service corporation goes in and asks to bill its customers another nickel or so per month for some seemingly reasonable purpose: to keep up with inflation; to cover price increases in raw materials or labor costs; from comparisons to other markets; to respond to increasing regulations; in support of declining revenues; *etc*. The board has to figure out if the request is fair. And it's hard to argue about a nickel. But that nickel might amount to millions of dollars for the corporation.

Every publicly regulated corporation does the same thing, constantly dinging the rest of us for a nickel here and there. On those occasions they are told 'No,' they wait a year or two or perhaps only a few months. When the membership changes in the responsible body, they come back again. Meanwhile, they are lobbying government to appoint more 'reasonable' board members and encouraging the citizens to elect more 'reasonable' officials.

They do the same thing with regulations, constantly chipping away at them. And with each step that they take, they gain, we lose. It is reminiscent of the saw about terrorists: law enforcement has to be right every time, but the terrorist has to be lucky only once. Citizens cannot stop watching the corporation for a moment.

Psychopathic Government

A frequent complaint about duplicitous government targets 'lobbyists.' The complaint is misstated; there are lobbyists for the arts, education, civil liberties, and any number of non-profits. The problem isn't the lobbyists, nor even corporate lobbyists.

The problem is that corporate lobbyists represent the major donors of the same elected officials that they are lobbying. In effect, corporate lobbyists are not advocates, they are enforcers. If elected officials do not vote as the donor's lobbyist requests, the donation in the next election cycle will move to someone more amenable. Accepting such donations is often viewed as dishonest self-service on the part of elected officials. But it is also an ethical dilemma: if the current elected official is ousted, she may be replaced by someone willing to sell out for even worse things.

The courts, including the Supreme Court, have ruled that corporations are people and are entitled to give unrestrained political donations. Somehow, the courts have bizarrely—or as we will see, perhaps maliciously—accepted the argument that these donations do not unduly influence government policy.[22] Which brings up another problem: the same lobbyists and corporations who compromise the legislative and executive branches of government have also assiduously worked to neutralize the independence of the judiciary by influencing judicial elections and by lobbying officials who nominate and appoint judges.[23]

It is obvious that the atrocino's money influences elections and public policy: the narcissist has no interest in anything else. If his donations didn't buy him the government he wanted, he wouldn't make donations. One current example is illuminating: an overwhelming majority of Americans, majorities in both parties, and even a majority of gun owners, want two modest gun protections: universal background checks; and the delegalization of assault weapons. The NRA leadership and the rest of the gun lobby have nevertheless blocked even these modest compromises in favor of corporate greed.[24]

We also see repeated attempts by the atrocino and the authoritarian personality to diminish the republic: by blocking minorities from voting; by manipulating the voter rolls; by gerrymandering districts; by giving an elite minority power over the majority; and by undermining democratic rules in other ways.[25]

Government is slipping away from the citizens, meaning that we are, less and less, a democracy. We are moving toward oligarchy and plutocracy. Or even kleptocracy: our government is being stolen out from under us.[26] Remember Eisenhower's admission that he could not include Congress in the military-industrial complex. That was over fifty years ago, and the situation is much worse today.

Psychopaths and narcissists now control much, perhaps most, of media and government. Through those two, the atrocino is increasingly controlling what remains of our autonomy. Soon David Parker Ray and Adolf Hitler will have tricked us into willingly entering their bondage. Once we do, it will be too late. We think it can't happen here, not in our country, not in the modern world. We are too advanced for that. That is certainly what millions of German Jews, Roma, Poles, and others thought: "It can't happen here."

Disastrous Profits

Every organism is amazing. Even the repulsive housefly is a marvel that does things no engineer could reproduce: it flies with great agility; it moves across landscapes, even vertical landscapes, at a significant fraction of its flying speed; it lands upside down on the underside of surfaces; it finds and refines its own fuel; it makes its own repairs; and it carries onboard machinery to make copies of itself.

But when a lizard grabs it, all that brilliant complexity is reduced to a few hours of sustenance for the lizard.

The same thing happens with the conqueror. Alexander removed fabulous wealth from Persepolis, but it was only a small fraction of the wealth that was in the city, invested in the buildings, the infrastructure, the furnishings, and other possessions. And of course, the wealth was nothing compared to the lives he took. Or to reduce human life to a cold GM-type economic consideration, the wealth Alexander took was small compared to the destroyed investment in educating and training the workers, artisans, engineers, and clerks.

We see the same thing with corporations. By dumping toxins into the environment, corporations save themselves a tiny fraction of the deferred costs of cleaning up the problem, not to mention the extortionary costs in human disease that result. In the recent subprime mortgage crisis, the CEOs collected millions while the world lost trillions, vaporizing hundreds of thousands of dollars for each dollar some CEO put in his pocket. And the military-industrial complex diverts money from education, infrastructure, law enforcement, libraries, arts, parks, and myriad other activities that serve everyone, and drive progress, in order to kill innocent victims around the world and to feed a bloated and grossly overblown military budget. All of these activities net the executives a sliver of a penny on each dollar or even on each hundred dollars. Again, they make millions, the world loses trillions.

If a corporation can make a nickel but it costs the rest of us $1, $100, or $1,000, the corporation will do it. It is not just that they are evil; they are designed to be evil. By law, the corporation has a fiduciary requirement to make every penny it can, however it can, with no concern for the impact on the rest of humanity.

This is one of the practical applications for the earlier discussion of anempathy. The corporation is a large, unfeeling meat grinder, a juggernaut whose greed is never sated. It does not matter how kind or generous the executives, employees, and shareholders might be in person; when they connect together in joint stock, they become a deadly virus, a literal zombie: an unthinking, unfeeling evil that seeks to acquire only more victims and spread its disease. The modern corporation is a vehicle that, if left unchecked, will allow the atrocino to destroy the modern world and to energetically lead us back into feudalism and the Dark Ages. Or even to yet worse times.

Win-Lose

A major problem that arises in dealing with the psychopath/narcissist is that we assume he is like the rest of us. He just wants to be accepted. Our fairy tales and our movies repeat that theme regularly: show the villain some love, acceptance, and fairness, and he will reform his bad ways, forever.

It is a fatal error. We assume that middle class desires will satisfy the psychopath and the narcissist and that problems can be resolved through trust and honest dealing. It is the mistake that Lloyd George made with Hitler.

Like the malignant narcissist and the atrox, the atrocino studies us. He understands what motivates us, and he uses it against us.* We do not understand him, however, and so we offer him win-win offers, solutions which appear practical and attractive to us. He is not interested in fairness, however, and he is certainly not interested in being the equal of people whom he derides as inferior, even negligible. So we are beguiled by his glib flattery and cowed by his aggressive bluster. And he increasingly traps us.

The atrox will take the best offer he can get for the moment, anything from a nickel to the Sudetenland, with no intention of reciprocating or fulfilling his part of the agreement. We fail to see that he is not interested in getting more than he has now; he is interested in getting more than everyone else. We seek win-win, he seeks win-lose. He wants it all.

---

* He studies us personally, but his corporation studies us methodically and even scientifically in order to manipulate us as well. This power is growing to alarming levels; witness Google's internal video, "The Selfish Ledger." Vlad Savov, "Google's Selfish Ledger is an Unsettling Vision of Silicon Valley Social Engineering," TheVerge.com, May 17, 2018, https://www.theverge.com/2018/5/17/17344250/google-x-selfish-ledger-video-data-privacy.

Chapter IX:
The Modern World

Taxes are the price we pay for civilization.
–Oliver Wendell Holmes Jr.

If it weren't for employees and customers, business would be great.
–Don Pippin Jr.

In 1413, Filippo Brunelleschi demonstrated to the Florentine public his discovery of perspective drawing, which allowed for a dimension of realism in art that had been previously unknown. It was one of the highlights of the Renaissance because it was something that the great authorities of the classical world—ancient Jerusalem, Athens, and Rome—had not discovered. It was an immediate sensation.

Discovery is a common thing today, but in the Middle Ages and early Renaissance (as we saw with Vesalius and Harvey), innovation and invention could be shocking, even scandalous. This was by design. When the Roman Empire collapsed in the fifth century, the leaders of the church believed that the end times were near. St. Augustine and other Christian leaders urged the faithful to invest the little time remaining in preparing their souls for the Second Coming. With the Apocalypse at hand, doubt and independent thought were unimportant; there was simply no call for new ideas. Augustine preached that obedience, self-denial, and discipline were all that a Christian needed.

Obedience, self-denial, and discipline, of course, are what the atrox wants from his serfs. It is ironic that these traditions came to dominate so much of Christianity and Western thought. In a radical departure from the exclusive and abusive hierarchy of the atrox, Jesus preached a Gospel of inclusion, compassion, and service, all of which reinforced a culture of egalitarianism. Jesus claimed that the very people whom the hierarchy discounted and discarded, the poor, the weak, the suffering—and most important of all, the children—were the kingdom of God. It was radical theology. As we have seen, Paul injected Roman priorities into Christianity. Constantine and his sons further impressed authoritarian culture onto the church. Then Augustine unintentionally completed the reversion of Christianity from a community of mutual sharing back to an authoritarian hierarchy that eventually came to be a major contender for power, wealth, and narcissism. Christianity left behind its brief experiment with the egalitarian and returned to the exploitive, authoritarian hierarchies of history.

The modern world began to emerge from this captivity in the Renaissance, which centered on Brunelleschi's Florence. Prior to the Renaissance, Florence had suffered heavily in the Black Plague, and the population dropped by over half. This meant that the survivors frequently inherited great resources. It also meant that the farms were able to support more people with more food and that the farmers and craftsmen who survived were able to demand higher wages for their work. At the same time, the humanists' studies of antiquity introduced ideas of more democratic governments, and modest republican reforms followed. Finally, the Medici family of bankers became *de facto* rulers of the city. As bankers, they were more keenly aware of long-term cause and effect in the city, particularly as they were using the more sensitive double-entry bookkeeping.* In addition, they were aware that their clientèle, and therefore their banking profits, derived from strata of society which the traditional nobility ridiculed and ignored. With those, the Medici themselves comprised one of many *parvenus* who proved that noble pedigree was not necessary for power and success and that the common classes could produce wealth, innovation, culture, and leadership that equaled or exceeded that of the traditional nobility. These all worked together to form a more egalitarian community than was present in most of fifteenth-century Europe.

Brunelleschi's studies in perspective added to that emerging Florentine egalitarianism. The visual arts might appear to be of little consequence in the grand scope of history, but in Florence they proved pivotal. First, perspective moved painting from a God's-eye or king's-eye eye view to a *pedestrian* view, one of our 'p' words; so painting and drawing in perspective brought a decidedly egalitarian view to art.†

But Brunelleschi confounded the authoritarian mindset in a second challenge. If a single point could be chosen for the full flowering of the Renaissance, a strong candidate would be March 25, 1436, which was the first day of the New Year in fifteenth-century Florence. On that day, the Florentines consecrated Brunelleschi's greatest design, the Cathedral of Saint Mary of

---

* The Medici bankers were using double-entry bookkeeping decades before Luca Pacioli's seminal work on the subject. Jacob Soll, "Accounted For: The Origins of Modern Finance," *The New Republic*, October 16, 2012.

† Indeed, the concept of perspectivalism became essential to the late nineteenth-century philosophy of Nietzsche and American pragmatism.

the Flower, better known as *il Duomo di Firenze*—the Dome of Florence. It was yet another sensation and a turning point in Western civilization.

In the design, Brunelleschi had produced a new solution for a tricky problem: how to build a dome atop an eight-sided lower structure. His solution, an eight-sided dome with catenated arches, was unprecedented. For the first time, modern people had produced something monumental that was not simply a copy of antiquity and did not just rival the ancients, but something that was irrefutably new and novel, something beyond anything attempted by the architectural and mechanical genius of Greece or Rome. With the completion of the Dome, the Florentines announced themselves as equals to the ancients. It was a major step away from authoritarianism.

• • •

Around 340 years later, the next large step was taken, and the story is perhaps even more remarkable. In 1776, a group of bumptious bumpkins declared their independence and precipitated war with the enormous might of England. They revived a version of the extinct republican government of ancient Rome, which was surely seen as farce by the Europeans. One can imagine peels of laughter drifting across the Atlantic.

That decision, however, further set the stage for the modern world. In a major upset, the hardy colonists prevailed over the superpower that was England. The American Revolution against the English monarchy was ironically aided by the Bourbon kings, primarily to distract their British enemies. The inability of the French nobility to recognize the danger of those Roman-American ideals proved fatal: thirteen years almost to the day after the American Declaration, French commoners rose up in revolt and overthrew the Bourbon kings. The French Revolution eventually disseminated republican ideals—forcefully, as we have noted, by Napoléon—to Europe where in fits and starts, it gradually expanded in geography, scope, and application. Over the next two centuries, the governmental experiments in the United States and Europe led to increasingly egalitarian reforms. The American evolution is illustrative: U.S. democracy began with the vote of landed white men but later added all white men, then all men, and finally included all men and women. Each was a further step toward equality and a further escape from the tyranny of the Old World.

• • •

Then, 169 years after the founding of the United States, WWII ended with the defeat of three vicious authoritarian regimes. But it was also a blow against prejudice and racism inside the United States: Rosie the Riveter demonstrated that women could do men's jobs; the Tuskegee Airmen proved that blacks could out-perform most white fighter pilots; as Japanese-Americans were shuttered in internment camps, their enlisted relatives proved their loyalty by fighting valiantly against their historical cousins; and the efforts of Albert Einstein, Leo Szilard, and Robert Oppenheimer brought the war to an abrupt end, and their contributions, along with those of other Jews in the war effort, gave the world pause and forced the reconsideration of a glib and reflexive anti-Semitism. Then, the photographic evidence and personal histories pouring out from the concentration camp survivors only intensified the growing rejections of prejudice and racism.

The euphoria of victory whisked in two other innovations. The first was the GI Bill, providing college education to men and women who previously had no hope of schooling beyond high school. This eliminated yet more inequalities. But perhaps the most remarkable was the Marshall Plan, which rebuilt Europe and elevated our enemies back to parity with the rest of the world. As noted, the results vastly exceeded the most optimistic predictions. The Plan ushered in the *Pax Americana*, a period of greatly diminished war and an explosion in commerce, technology, health, education, and overall standard of living.

Unfortunately, the seventy years of prosperity since the end of WWII comprise the lifetimes of almost everyone alive, which means that much of the advanced world has forgotten what horror and oppression look like. We tend to take our stability and prosperity for granted, we assume that we can be reckless with our government and our society, and that everything will continue the same. As I have noted, *Hitler ad portas*. We are unaware of what awaits us if we destroy what we have struggled five hundred years to create and have waited ten thousand years to see.

The Modern World

...

The Renaissance and the *Pax Americana* comprised diffuse and multi-faceted social changes involving many countries and cultures. As a result, they are complex and resist simple definition and interpretive agreement. The year 1776, however, represents a well-defined governmental advance based on a brief number of laws and codified principles. As such, it is more amenable to analysis.

Consider that Americans define our fundamental right as freedom. But 'freedom' by itself is a vague term. Freedom can be undesirable: the criminal—or as we have seen, the king—desires total freedom in order to rob us of our wealth, our homes, even our lives. What is war but the complete freedom of the conqueror? So we need a clear prepositional object; we need to specify freedom *from* something. In 1776, we wanted freedom from the King of England. But we escaped him long ago, so from what do we want freedom today?

One popular complaint is that we want freedom from government interference. But government is, by definition, interference; again, without the 'interference' of governmental restraint, the criminal and the conqueror have complete freedom. So government is interference in our finances through taxation; interference in our work through various laws and regulations; and interference in our private lives through the enforcement of personal accountability. To be sure, when government grows large it approaches totalitarianism and tyranny.

But when it retracts too far, society approaches lawlessness. This is why the atrox wants the lawlessness of war and the atrocino wants unbridled, Darwinistic capitalism. But the king and the corporate baron desire temporary freedom only as a means to an end: lawlessness opens up opportunities for the exploitation and subjugation of others and to complete domination.

So the narcissist does not disapprove of law or government. He disapproves of law and government that restrict him and do not permit his exploitation of others. This is why law under the atrox enforces privilege and reduces equality. Conversely, law in the democracy restricts privilege and demands equality.

"We hold these truths to be self-evident, that all men are created equal, that they are endowed by their Creator with certain unalienable Rights, that among these are Life, Liberty and the pursuit of Happiness." We are not literally created equal. Nevertheless, the concept of equality nibbles at the edges of what freedom shoots for. Consider that democracy insists that we should be equal before the law, equal in the ballot booth, equal in the marketplace, and increasingly, equal in our access to education. As we have seen, however, equality is anathema to king and conqueror.

I propose that our desired freedoms in the modern world are still a freedom from the king, but must also be from all *would-be* kings. Democracy should ensure our freedom from the atrox but also from the atrocino. Our liberty is a freedom from their exploitation, privilege, and double standard. I suggest that the modern world does not depend so much on equality as it does on the imperative to be free from mandated *inequality*, particularly the exploitive and subjugating inequality of privilege and the double standard. We seek to be free, not of law, but of laws that penalize the great majority and benefit a small, tyrannical minority. That, I argue, is the essential freedom we seek.

Which brings us back to government interference. The problem with a too-powerful government is that it can become the vehicle for the same inequality we need it to prevent. It is too easy for an elected official, a bureaucrat, or a military officer to grab control of the apparatus and set himself up as the new atrox. In fact, this perhaps is why Marxism has failed. Socialism works fine in the family; for instance, the children do not work, but they often derive the greater share of the family's resources. So the healthy family reflects the maxim, "From each according to his abilities, to each according to his needs." But socialism does not scale up well. Once a government sufficiently powerful to enforce a nationwide socialism comes into being, the inherent centralized power permits some narcissist to grab control and set himself up as dictator. Karl Marx wanted to be free us of capitalist slavers. He never accounted for military and bureaucratic slavers.

We want freedom from subjugation and inequality, which are pretty much the same thing. But to guarantee those freedoms, we need to invest in some entity that is strong enough to stop the atrox without morphing into a new atrox. That is where other freedoms become critical.

Freedom in the modern world thrives under three primary protections, which are themselves freedoms: free elections; free markets; and free expression. Only the third is original to the New World,* but the United States has helped shape them all.

---

* Freedom of expression has traditionally been recognized as originating with John Milton's *Areopagitica*. Milton, however, almost certainly got his ideas from his close friend, the colonial Puritan Roger Williams. Williams's defense of freedom of the press, *Queries of the Highest Consideration*, was published some months before the *Areopagitica*; as Williams used Milton's printer, it seems certain that Milton read *Queries*. Williams, however, also originated the idea of separation of church and state. Williams's intent was not to protect government but the church. As biographer John M. Barry so sharply put it, "when one mixes religion and politics one gets politics." John M. Barry, *Roger Williams and The Creation of the American Soul: Church, State, and the Birth of Liberty* (Viking, 2012).

History suggests that those three are insufficient, however. Each of these three can be perverted to undermine the very law that guarantees them. Dictators have frequently been democratically elected; free markets are vulnerable to exploitation by profiteers; and freedom of expression allows for distortions, lies, and populist inflammations. So it would be helpful if we could find one central idea that unites these, which might add nuance to our understanding and might help as a guide for adjustments as we go.

I propose a rather ungainly word: *feedback*. The *Oxford English Dictionary* states the word first appears in 1923, in *Harmsworth's Wireless Encyclopedia*. Harmsworth simply defines feedback as power transfer from one part of a circuit to another. In biology, however, Claude Bernard and Walter Cannon introduced the concept of 'homeostasis,' the idea that within the organism critical factors such as temperature, pH, and salt content can be maintained within narrow ranges. We now understand that homeostasis is accomplished through a complex system of feedback loops. Feedback loops are also fundamental in artificial intelligence, robotics, and cybernetics, where they are critical to logical behavior.

To our point here, feedback loops also unite the three fundamental freedoms above. Don't do your job in government, you aren't re-elected. Don't do your job in the marketplace, you are out of business. As for freedom of expression, that is the most important, because it provides feedback for everything else: we can inform one another that an elected official or businesser[*] is not doing her job and limit her impact.[†] But as noted, as these three guarantee freedoms to the public, they also free the atrox and the atrocino to game the rules.

In the democracy, the demagogue fans the emotions, makes unreasonable or counter-productive promises, and sabotages rivals in order to win elections. Once in power, he can dismantle democratic protections against monarchy by bribing, intimidating, murdering, jailing, or otherwise eliminating resisting elected officials, judges, and law enforcement.

The rough-and-tumble of free markets provide many efficiencies, but they are also vulnerable to fraud, graft, and monopoly. Monopoly is the worst; it is the economic equivalent of monarchy, it eliminates the feedback of the consumer just as monarchy eliminates the feedback of the citizen. Under both monarchy and monopoly, citizens and customers have no options.

---

[*] 'Businessman' is sexist, 'business person' is clumsy. This is my suggested solution.

[†] With those, the balance of powers in the three branches of U.S. government also targets a system of feedback loops.

There is nothing to restrain costs nor to ensure quality. In a world that is progressing rapidly, both monarch and monopolist do not adapt and improve. They leave themselves and their nations at a competitive disadvantage in the larger world. Both create lose-lose.

And then there is freedom of expression, particularly the freedom of the press and other media. As noted, freedom of expression is a feedback mechanism for all of the others; the ability of people to publicly complain and criticize enforces accountability. But competition and public accountability threaten the atrocino in his drive to empire. So he constantly seeks to influence, control, or own the media and muzzle critics. When that is not possible, he finds ways to discredit the media by publishing contradictory research and misleading anecdotes, by attacking journalists and their sources and by creating confusion in other ways.

Hitler exemplified the suppression of all three freedoms. Although he was democratically elected, he eliminated free elections. He argued for a strong economy and privatized many industries, but he also increasingly placed markets under his control. He used media freedoms to publish his own message, but his critics, particularly those in the press, were regularly assassinated or otherwise silenced even before Hitler became Chancellor. Hitler illustrates why the atrox and the atrocino argue for freedom: he gained power by exploiting freedom, but once in power, he eliminated freedom for others.

So a critical aspect of the modern world, and progress, is feedback, because it restrains monarchy and monopoly. When we debate policy, it might be helpful from time to time to step away from considering how a course of action might affect one or more of our freedoms or other guarantees and reflect instead on how it might affect feedback to those in power.

Feedback is also critical to personal progress. A swift response or reaction from our choices help us learn to make better decisions. One crippling dysfunction that humanity inherits from the narcissism of the atrox, however, is that we often blame the messenger. It is a miniature of the problem with whistle-blowers: when we provide feedback, when we criticize the process or the outcome, it is unwelcome and we are often attacked. We are not viewed as beneficial agents improving the system; to the contrary, no matter how cogent or useful our feedback is, we are regarded as trouble-makers. So when we give feedback to friends, family, and colleagues, they typically do not view it as helpfulness. They view it as betrayal and as a personal assault.

This unfortunate approach is the result of outer class morality dominating middle class morality. The middle class is adamant about personal accountability. Yet members of the middle class often respond to complaint and criticism with an outerclass mindset: they are offended, and they attack the complainer. They blame the messenger, which is allied with blaming the victim: those complaining are typically the victims of the problem.

That resistance to feedback, however, traps the authoritarian system. As we have discussed, to maintain competitiveness, the atrox and atrocino need innovators and inventors. Their narcissism and monopoly, however, require uncomplaining minions. If the king or CEO insists on conformity of thought, they will get no new ideas; but if they allow a culture of critical thinking and innovation, then they open the gate for challenges to their control.

Critical thinking cannot be reliably contained, particularly not in the modern world. As we have seen, authoritarian traditions, supported by the genetic trapdoor, eliminates many objections to the atrox. But education and critical thinking help people to free themselves of their dogmatic traps. As progress accelerates, and as the demand for educated thinkers increases, the number of people willing to challenge, defy—or of particular concern in the digital age, sabotage—the atrox or atrocino grows. It is only a matter of time before a clerk or technician moves beyond analyzing records and equipment and begins analyzing social and legal contradictions. A few mechanical engineers will always mutate into social engineers.

With that, hierarchical promotions in an authoritarian regime are too often based on loyalty and ideological purity. (In business, that 'ideological purity' becomes a zeal for profit over substance.) The better analysts and the more creative problem solvers, on the other hand, will often object to the dishonesties and contradictions, be held back, and their facility for analysis and problem-solving will be restrained with them. This means that under authoritarian hierarchies, innovation and productivity will increasingly lag behind freer and more meritocratic systems.

Seeing his country chronically lag behind, the despot often invests in the football defense. Unwilling to improve his own system, and unwilling to be subjected to criticism for his poor leadership, he will try to sabotage other, more progressive systems; he will, in effect, attack Thebes. The atrox or atrocino sabotages everyone in order to protect his narcissism and privilege. It is another manifestation of the lose-lose mindset of the atrox.

Dancing around the Law

The Founders designed the United States to protect us from the atrox, and they were largely successful. But they were unaware of the atrocino. In eighteenth-century Europe, power was held by the king and the nobles; the

Founders could not predict that transportation, mass production, retail cloning, and mass communication could create the kingly wealth that would appear in the Industrial Revolution. The only subjugation they understood were royal prerogative and slavery.*

The Founders realized, however, that a certain amount of materialistic self-interest could be used to pull the wagon of the republic, and they provided for a free market. They could not anticipate that the draft animals would, step by step, grab the reins.

Government has had some success in restraining the atrocino in the past. As we noted, a truly free market is lawless, and so legislation was gradually promulgated which makes it less free but also less exploitive: anti-trust legislation, truth in advertising regulations, worker protections, food and drug regulations, *etc*. But the atrocino moves faster than government, he adapts and constantly finds new, unregulated ways of making money. He also constantly seeks to outflank government and to circumvent, or even clandestinely break, laws. On top of that, he uses the practices that we covered in the previous chapter to buy our government out from under us. We are increasingly at a loss to protect ourselves.

One of the most draining threats is the recurrent culprit, the military-industrial-congressional complex. U.S. military expenditures are the greatest in the world, larger than those of the next eight nations combined.[1] We maintain almost eight hundred overseas military bases around the world, while England, France, Russia, and China have fewer than forty collectively.[2] Aircraft carriers are ruinously expensive and currently cost the United States about $10 billion apiece. Not surprisingly there are only nineteen in the world, but eleven of them fly the U.S. flag. Nuclear attack submarines cost just under $2 billion apiece, and the U.S. has fifty-four, while the rest of the world has forty.[3] Normal military expenses plus veterans programs consumes about two-thirds of U.S. discretionary government spending, almost $700 billion dollars.[4] And now we find ourselves in wars from which we cannot seem to extricate ourselves.

The atrocino has created great wealth by using our taxes to murder millions. He has commandeered the world's beacon of democracy and turned it into a machine gun for conquest, straight out of the worst traditions of the conqueror. As he perverts our resources in murder-for-profit entrepreneur-

---

* It is an irony that the Founders, in turn, subjugated others through slavery. For all of their intellectual prowess, the Founders nevertheless rationalized their own hypocrisy and lack of intraception. We will see in the epilogue that this original error served as the spark for a conflagration that is bringing the United States perilously close to kleptoplutocracy.

ship, he simultaneously blocks progress: massive over-funding of the military leaves education, healthcare, infrastructure, the arts, and the social safety net all underfunded and shunted aside.

The same is true of other looming problems. While we are distracted with the football mentality, attacking the other political party and struggling in class warfare, the atrocino uses the nickel strategy to enrich and empower himself in a myriad of micro-attacks, whittling away at our protections and our public services as he does. This has come to include even those services that we paid for in advance, such as Social Security. As the atrocino bats out catchwords such as free markets, free speech, democracy, patriotism, illegal immigrants, radical Islam, law and order, socialism, bloated government, nanny state, and entitlement programs, he is quietly buying out our government from beneath us.

He then manipulates it all for personal profit. He raids our tax dollars with impunity, dismantles our protections, diverts funding from children and other vulnerables, extorts us for our medical care, melts down our retirement accounts, plunders our banks, and all the while shifts his taxes onto the rest of us.

So when the atrocino speaks of freedom and the intrusion of big government, when he distracts us through anger media, when he dog whistles on the topics of class and racial warfare, he is tricking us into removing our governmental protections, to his benefit. He wants us to open the gates to the citadel so that he can slip inside and resume his assault and exploitation. He wants to strip us of our freedoms and return us to bondage.

Just as we saw with Hitler, when the atrocino speaks of free markets, he really wants the freedom to reduce competition so that he can more easily climb on top of the rest of us. When he argues for freedom of speech, he is seeking a megaphone to drown out investigative journalists, whistle-blowers, consumer critics, and other dissenting opinions. When he invokes his right to participate in free elections, it is to convince us to select candidates who will grow his power and privilege and decrease our protections. Any time the powerful bark out some fundamentalist catchword, we need to sit back and analyze how it benefits him: his power, his profits, and his narcissism. When it isn't obvious how the atrocino benefits, we should be doubly wary. We must assume he has discovered an angle that we can't yet see.

The atrocino succeeds because we are all potential authoritarian personalities, we all have a tendency to be simplistic, anti-introspective thinkers. He exploits our freedom, our equality, and our justice only so that he might remove them from his path. He abuses equality to achieve inequality.

Trying to pull the authoritarian personality away from his preferred authorities, and to help him to see that modern problems are nuanced without clear answers, and that the goal is a balance among dangerous extremes, will be difficult.

It raises interesting ethical and legal problems. Should we guarantee the atrocino's participation in the democracy if he is striving for plutocracy? Should we protect his activities in the free market when his real goal is monopoly? Should we defend his freedom of speech if he wishes to deny us ours? At what point do we decide that the atrocino is simply screaming 'Fire' in the polling station?

Empathy & Compassion

The psychopath lacks empathy and compassion. Those two, however, are the centripetal emotions that hold community together and encourage trust, equality, and collective action. Our collectivity, however, is a threat to the atrox. If people unite and rise up against his abuses, the atrox will fail, or at the least will lose great resources in the struggle to hold on to power. This will leave him with a weakened state, one that rival conquerors can invade.

And so the atrox and atrocino foment anger, paranoia, distrust, and divisiveness. All of these block our empathy and compassion, and we regress into a state of short-sighted self-interest and interpersonal exploitation. And so we mimic the atrox. If he exhibits psychopathy, we reflect his inability to care. If he is a narcissist, we crush common sense under self-centeredness. If he is a sadist, we pursue the physical and psychological pain of others.

Empathy existed before civilization; it helped maintain the family and the tribe. What our modern ideals of equality and justice aim for is to repulse the culture of atrox so that empathy and compassion may re-emerge. Once it does, those groups and organizations which are more cohesive, tolerant, and honest will enjoy greater cooperation and more rapid progress than those groups which are not.

The Corporation

The work of Babiak and Hare looked at corporate snakes. Their considerations of psychopathy in the workplace, and their insight that modern business is an environment where the psychopath can flourish, are key. Jon Ronson notes, "Capitalism at its most ruthless rewards psychopathic behavior."[5] Others have gone beyond that to argue that the organization itself can be a psychopath.[6] I suggested as much above when I noted that the corporation is anempathetic.

That may still seem dubious, however, because we think of the corporation as a thing and of a psychopath as a person. But in a way, that is the point: the full psychopath is not a complete person; he has aspects that are unfeeling, mechanical, even bureaucratic. To use a science fiction metaphor, the psychopath is a cyborg: part animal, part machine. Everything about him is human except his humanity.

Similarly, the corporation often reduces its workers to cyborg-like status: king and corporation need our work and cleverness to create wealth and power for them, but they wish to extinguish our human connections, strip us of our autonomy and compassion, and convert us into mechanical and bureaucratic automata. We are trained to follow the rules and to consider only the unfeeling economic equations which govern those rules. We become interchangeable bodies which, like our ancestors under the atrox, serve greed and narcissism.

That observation, together with our previous considerations, gives us an explanation of corporate and bureaucratic psychopathy and anempathy: a lack of feedback. The absentee owners, *i.e.*, the investors in the company, are typically disconnected from the outcomes of their ownership. Most investors are unaware of the suffering their investments cause; they focus exclusively on stock prices and earnings. When the investors, particularly the major investors, become aware of the mischief created from their investments, many of them rationalize away the negatives. The first, the lack of awareness, is bureaucratic anempathy; the second, the lack of concern once problems appear, is personal anempathy and facultative psychopathy.

The employees are caught in the same problem; they do not see the harm, or they rationalize it away. Or at least most of them do. As progress accelerates, the CEO is increasingly caught in the double bind of the modern atrox: analytical thinkers will eventually analyze the corruption and exploitation of the system. And then the whistle-blowers emerge and threaten his power.

Evidence of the psychopathy of the corporation is not hard to find. We have seen that the bank crisis created a recession that affected every sector of the economy and caused hardship across the globe, but the CEOs richly rewarded themselves as their victims struggled. Now the same bankers are using their government influence to strip away the recent protections designed to prevent them from repeating the entire catastrophe. Likewise, the car manufacturers rationalized away deaths from faulty designs, Big Tobacco rationalized away smoking deaths, sugar rationalized away the deaths from obesity and diabetes, gun manufacturers rationalize away deaths in school shootings, and the pharmaceutical industry rationalizes away the deaths from the outrageous prices of their medicines. These are the problems currently in the news, but look at any industry, talk to the people who work there, look at the harm created to employees, clients, and the public at large. Anempathetic exploitation is the gravitational black hole that tears at the for-profit corporation. If somehow the corporation is not exploitive presently, it is only a matter of time before it careens in that direction. And in all corporations, the absentee owners miss, blithely ignore, or adamantly deny the havoc created from their investments. They lack information; but often, they lack interest and intraception as well. In their self-service and codependency, they either rationalize away the impact or they rationalize away their responsibility.

Just as the general or soldier need not be a psychopath to slaughter great numbers, neither must the CEO nor the stockholder be a psychopath, narcissist, or sadist in order to defraud, exploit, and economically torture large populations. Both the army and the corporation are designed to perform as ruthless Machiavellians. There are objectives to be met, and the stakeholders are divorced from the outcomes; they are interested only in body counts and balance sheets.

So the CEO, the engineer, or the assembly-line worker may be generous to her friends and her community, but when she goes to work, she changes hats and brains. She becomes like the soldier in warfare. Nowhere in the corporation spreadsheet is there a column for compassion, generosity, nor humanity. There is only greed. The workers unquestioningly feed the never-sated Moloch and rarely reflect on the hypocrisy between who they are and what they do.

And then all of this corporate dysfunction begins undermining the only power strong enough to restrain it. It begins chafing at the democratic constraints which protect the human and the humane: banks, tobacco, car manufacturers, Big Pharma, the military-industrial complex, and virtually every publicly traded corporation constantly work to influence elections, skew the courts, sabotage free media, and block public accountability. At every step, the corporate grinder rasps away at equality, democracy, and human dignity. In order to feed its insatiable and narcissistic greed, the corporation is required to scuff away everyone in an attempt to reduce us to meaningless nobodies.

From the outside of the corporation, we see only the winning and the wealth. We miss the imperial moral nakedness. It is yet another fairy tale. We must recognize the sword for what it is.

Power Disparity

Income disparity is a frequent current concern, but I worry that it misses the larger point. The problem isn't income disparity. In the developed countries, even the poor enjoy luxuries that the kings of France could not imagine.*

The real threat is that concentrated wealth fosters inequality. It creates greatly increased power for the wealthy, which means decreased power for the rest of us. We must remember what drives the narcissist: distinction, separation, and control. Money is simply a means to these as it serves as a badge of status. The real goal is subjugation and degradation of everyone else. The atrocino wants to ensure that the rest of us are securely beneath him, that we submit to his superiority, and that we worship and praise him. He wants absolute power.

He constantly defends his power by reminding us, and showing us, that increased organizational size leads to increased efficiency and lower costs. His argument is seductive and compelling. But we must remember that this is only a short-term efficiency. Increased size moves toward monopoly: it leads to fewer competitors and fewer options. So after a temporary decline in prices, over the long term, the enlarging corporations leads to decreased efficiency and greater cost.

The power, narcissism, and psychopathy of the multi-national corporation drives it to seek ever-greater control, which will eventually, but inevitably, lead to price manipulation and an erosion of market efficiencies. Remember, nowhere in the mission statement or goals of the corporation is there mention of price reductions, market efficiencies, or increasing quality. Nor could any publicly traded corporation have such goals: fiduciary duty enjoins management to pursue price inflation, monopoly, and the cheapest quality whenever possible.

We can see this loss of market efficiencies with OPEC and oil, De Beers and diamonds, Microsoft and software. More recently we see them with Google, Facebook, Netflix, and with manufacturers such as Unilever, Monsanto, and Nestlé. All have proven ruthless in buying out rivals and reducing compe-

---

* Again, we tend to confuse luxury and opulence. The ancient kings could not imagine winter fruits and vegetables (and even in summer or fall in previous centuries, the available fruits and vegetables were greatly limited compared to what is available today in every grocery store), climate control, running hot and cold water, nighttime illumination at the flip of a switch, traveling along smooth roads at seventy miles per hour, music and theatre at the push of a button, and the miracles of modern medicine. Granted, many of the Western poor have uneven and inconsistent access to these things, but even among the poor, it is the rare home without electricity, plumbing, and a television. Two hundred years ago, no one enjoyed such things.

tition and then using their wealth and market position to manipulate prices and exploit us in any way possible.* The corporation uses the free market as a useful but temporary convenience to remove market freedoms, to pull us from equality back to authority, and to eliminate feedback, progress, and governmental protection.

The Nickel Attack

Over the past few decades, the U.S. South has suffered the invasion of the red fire ant, *Solenopsis invicta*—"the unbeatable pipe-eyed [ant]." Fire ants build multiple mounds in open areas throughout the warmer months of the year, and every Southerner of any age has accidentally stepped in the mounds and suffered multiple painful stings on her feet, ankles, and legs. Enough stings, or an allergy to the stings, occasionally prove deadly.

The fire ants are fierce, but despite their scientific name, they aren't unbeatable. There is at least one species of ant that defeats them by waiting patiently at the perimeter of a nest, grabbing and ganging individual fire ants, and tearing them apart one at a time. It is a slow but effective strategy.†

Hornets provide a similar illustration. A few hornets can quickly destroy a honeybee hive. But some honeybees, although smaller and less powerful, can take down hornets by ganging them and killing them one at a time.[7]

Both of these are models of what the atrocino and the modern corporation do within the democracy. The citizens in the democracy are more numerous, and collectively we are more powerful. However, the corporation lurks at the edges, nibbles at our freedoms with the nickel strategy, and slowly destroys our democracy in small increments.

Culture of Conspiracy

Some may object that I am suggesting that the modern world faces a massive conspiracy, that there is an international cabal working together to sabotage government, markets, and public opinion.

---

* Or almost. Microsoft and a handful of similar software firms keep trying, but this book was composed on an Ubuntu/Linux computer with writing software from LibreOffice, a Firefox browser, and the Gimp image manipulator.

† I came across the paper describing this behavior years ago, but I cannot find it in my files, and I have had no luck in finding it again. I have corresponded with several myrmecologists who were not familiar with the paper but expressed interest. I decided to include the description here with the rationale that even if my memory is in error, the strategy still makes the point.

I am.

We must reconsider the word 'conspiracy.' In its origins, the word means to 'breathe together.' That is heuristic; breathing together is something that singers and wind musicians do. So the problem does not have to be a symphony production; a jazz number can be equally effective, and for our metaphor, equally disastrous.

Everything in the symphony is carefully premeditated and rehearsed, while jazz music is more spontaneous. The jazz performers nevertheless all know the tune, and they all recognize their cues. And while the orchestra needs a composer and a conductor to hold it all together, the jazz band needs neither. With or without a guiding hand, both ensembles are still orchestrated, and the result of either is tight coordination.

A pervasive culture of greed works like jazz music; everyone knows the tune, everyone is responding to the other players, and everyone has a good idea of what comes next. The rhythm goes on without benefit of baton. Likewise, market or political collusion do not require correspondence; after ten millennia of human bondage, premeditation is no longer necessary to sap people and progress.

The law requires premeditation for the indictment of conspiracy, but that is a failing in the law. Premeditation is not necessary to ensure that actors are working in concert; more importantly, a lack of premeditation does not mean that the resulting damage is smaller. And damage is the starting point for all of the law: 'injury,' 'jurisprudence,' and 'justice' are all related words. An injury is an injustice. So premeditation might alter the punishment—consider manslaughter vs. premeditated murder—but it should not absolve the crime.

That observation is important, because narcissists acting in concert to grow their power, consciously or unconsciously, deliberately or reflexively, decreases the power of everyone else, which diminishes the democracy. The conspirators injure the three key freedoms. As they attack those, they also gain control over the courts and over the rule of law; which means that there is a decreasing likelihood that the public can stop them.

At each step, an economic conspiracy may add a small burden, the negligible crime of stealing a nickel. But left unchecked, the conspiracy grows and metastasizes, until the atrocino takes the reigns of power, becomes the atrox, and takes us back to subjugation and totalitarianism.

Ignorance of the law is not a defense. Neither is the ignorance of the implications of one's actions; liability remains whether the outcome was intended or not. The middle class is held to this standard. Absolving the atrocino from the results of his actions presents yet another double standard.

The drive to totalitarianism is inherent in the culture of the atrocino. Listen to the politicians as they bat around catchwords, foment distraction and dissatisfaction, and play political football all while doing the bidding of their large contributors. Listen to representatives of any industry: the executives, spokespersons, lobbyists; listen to their rationalizations as they pilfer our pockets and our rights. Listen to the media, built or bought by the profiteers, fanning anger and skating over substantial issues and nuance. Despite the apparent dissonances among them, despite the variations in pitch and volume, at bottom they all conspire the same authoritarian and anti-egalitarian song; they all reverberate with the same rationalized melody: submit. The marching rhythm pulses out constantly until the authoritarian personalities rise up and change the laws to give more and more power to the atrocino. In the end, the 'true believers' put the shackles around their own legs and necks; they create a power shift from the people to the exploiting narcissist. It is a collusion of delusion, a massive, rationalizing codependency.*

The atrocino aggressively denies collusion or malicious intent. First, we must remember that integrity is not his priority, only wealth, narcissism, and privilege. Second, we need to look at the evidence and ignore the chatter. At every point the atrocino works to grab as much as he can and to influence consumers, government, and media to tilt the table in his favor.

And we need to recognize that at bottom, we are dealing with a soulless machine, and one which is insatiable. Where in any corporate strategy is there a stated endpoint; where is the defined point of satisfaction? There is none. Nowhere in the corporate mission statement, nor anywhere else, is there a restraint on greed. Nor could there be, the corporation is a machine for greed. The corporation may change its name, change its products, it will certainly change personnel, and it may even move to another country; but the greed persists. There is no calculus for community, tolerance, or progress. The name is clear: the for-profit corporation exists only for profit.

And more profit after that. Once John D. Rockefeller was asked, "How much money is enough?" He gave the answer for the ages: "A little more." At first glance that is charming, but upon reflection, alarming. A nickel more today, and a dime more tomorrow, and too late we realize that 'a little more' ultimately means 'everything.' And everyone.

---

* There is one possible legal remedy: when a prosecutor sees evidence of markets acting in collusion, even without premeditation, she could publicly announce her evidence, which might be as simple as a lack of price options in a particular market. Once she has announced the pattern, she has made the colluders aware of their concerted action. If they do not begin making changes to ameliorate the situation, then they give the prosecutor evidence that a conspiracy now exists, whether or not it did previously.

So the CEOs of Google, Microsoft, and Amazon may see each other as competitors, but underneath they are conspirators. They want market freedoms today, in order to achieve monopoly tomorrow, only so that they might dispense with market freedoms the day after. Nowhere in corporate or personal ambition is there passion for competition and free markets, nor is there room for them in the long run. The goal is limitless profit, monopoly, and market control.

The atrocinos struggle to return us to economic and political serfdom. The only disagreement among them is whose monopoly will prevail.

Progress

Progress is a fairly new concept. If we took Ramesses II and transported him three thousand years into London or Paris of 1776, he would have been amazed by many things. But very few of them would have been beyond his comprehension. Among those confounding him might have been the magnetic compass, gunpowder, and the telescope. With some explanation and observation, however, he would have probably grasped the concepts behind other major advances since his day, such as movable type, the pendulum clock, and the large sailing vessel.

In contrast, if we were to transport one of the U.S. Founders a mere 240 years into our world today, he would be terrified by a myriad of technologies completely beyond his comprehension. He would be able to understand what he was seeing only after years of explanation and study. Among his bewilderments would be: airplanes, automobiles, helicopters, movies and television, maglev trains, antibiotics, cardiovascular surgery, neurosurgery, electric lights, central air and heat, hot and cold running water, nuclear power, holograms, motion detectors, the electric stove, the microwave, submarines, the aircraft carrier, ceramic knives, computers, four-color desktop printers, plastics, 3-D printing, international telecommunications, space travel, robotics, a multitude of domestic appliances and industrial machines, and canned food. Those are only a sample; adding others makes for interesting dinner conversation.

The point is, for the first ten thousand years of civilization, progress was largely a process of bigger and more complex while technical, commercial, governmental, and social advances were infrequent and generally serendipitous. In the last 240 years however, progress has become a rapid succession of ideas, sciences, and technologies.

That is important because for the first ten thousand years, the atrox ran the world. In the last half millennium, beginning with the Renaissance, the seeds of change were sown. The sapling of democracy began to flower a quarter millennium ago, and the mature tree started fruiting in the industrial and scientific revolution. The orchard grows and expands today. Over the last five hundred years, equality and democratic principles emerged, and the world has increasingly been managed by the 'p' class, the citizens. Once freed of authoritarian control, a culture of equality, freedom, and middle class morality created the modern world.

This is demonstrated by Richard Florida's work on the Creative Class®. As Florida points out, creativity and progress are not the result of governmental or community leadership. Rather, they are the result of a culture of tolerance and inclusion—the opposite of the culture of the atrox's hierarchy. Those who generate the modern world gravitate to cultural centers where there is tolerance for them to experiment, explore, and challenge the status quo.[8]

Florida's research supports our thesis here: the outer classes hold us back. Because they are interested in status rather than progress, they do not produce progress, and in fact they obstruct or even prohibit progress. Progress is a middle class desire that arises spontaneously when there is no narcissist to obstruct it.

Nevertheless, the atrocino perpetuates the fairy tale that the upper classes are better and smarter than the rest of us and that we should follow their wise direction. Unfortunately, too many of us still nod in agreement. We should first keep in mind that his argument benefits him personally; and second the evidence argues against him.

Futurists

Recent years have seen the rise of 'futurists,' people who make strategic predictions about the direction the world and technology might take in upcoming decades. It is an increasingly hopeless undertaking.

The futurist looks at current conditions and the recent past and extrapolates from there. The problem with that strategy is summarized by the brokerage industry's standard disclaimer: "Past performance is no guarantee of future results." When there was a king, the future was fairly predictable. In fact, it was so predictable that there was no need for futurists. The future was going to look pretty much like the past, which suggested it would be bleak.

With the rise of equality, however, and with the expansion of an educated middle class with the time and resources for reflection and experimentation, the number of thinkers has exploded. So we have a few hundred futurists assuming that the future will be an extension of the present while a hundred million scientists, engineers, artists, and social innovators are working to ensure that the future looks nothing like the present. Complicating the picture, each of the latter group spends as much time on her single facet of the future, as the futurist spends trying to consider everything together.

The problem with one or a few people considering the future is the problem with one or a few people directing humanity toward the future. With the movement from authority to equality, humanity moved from serial to parallel processing. Under the king, only one person was really allowed to make radical change, and he rarely did: the atrox conforms to the most conservative definition of 'conservative.' The hierarchy was a self-absorbed, serially processing computer, and the throughput for solving all problems moved ponderously up and down the hierarchy; all processors considered and reconsidered all problems in sequence. So even if the king had been interested in progress, the rate of change would have nevertheless remained low.

But with the rise of the middle class, with diffuse luxury and with the generalized education and leisure that have resulted from our progress, the world has become a vast, serially processing computer. Solutions pour out faster and faster. There is no way the futurist can begin to see the disruptive technologies and innovations that will appear in the next five years.

She certainly can't anticipate what will appear in the next five decades.

RISE & DECLINE OF THE MIDDLE CLASS

We started this chapter with three considerations from history. In the Renaissance, the bubonic plague wiped out enormous swaths of people. Their heirs suddenly became more prosperous and comfortable. Republican ideals gently stirred, and equality allowed more people to contribute to progress. This allowed Europe to take a large step from a feudal structure toward a middle class economy, which over the next few centuries produced an acceleration in innovation, productivity, commerce, and a rise in the general standard of living.

In the colonial United States, a hearty middle class was well-established with a standard of living that was already higher than that of Europe.[9] Except for slave owners and the hierarchies they created—with, of course, slaves at the bottom*—class distinctions were decreased and certainly did not approach that of the European nobility. Our independence from the atroces

---

* Actually, slaves were not quite at the bottom because expendable laborers ranked below them for some considerations. See the footnote on page 86 on the slaves and the Irish in nineteenth-century New Orleans.

of Europe lowered trade barriers, stimulated domestic growth, and retained taxes nationally, all of which fed into local economies and helped the middle class to prosper yet further. The result was a rapidly expanding nation which, over the next 170 years, would come to lead the world. The end of WWII formalized our leadership.

But before WWII came the Great Depression. Much of the public suspected that the industrialists and financiers who had emerged in the previous century had brought the country to ruin and much of the world with it. More, it was believed that they were doing little to speed recovery and that perhaps some of them were interested in holding us in poverty—a charge which, with the considerations of narcissism in these chapters, now seems quite likely. That mistrust of the wealthy led to decades of liberal government,* which protected and fostered workers before and after the war. All of this restrained the atrocino and empowered the middle class. That middle class won the war; then a middle class ethos of equality and cooperation led to the Marshall Plan and the *Pax Americana*, and from that, to an unprecedented period of international peace, innovation, and progress.

When a middle class emerges or grows, everyone benefits.† This should not be surprising. Earlier times lacked not only technology, but also technologists, technology investors, and technology consumers. If we could have given the medieval scholar a modern technical education, it might not have made much difference, certainly not in the short term. Because very few people had much education at all, he would have had almost no one to help him build or implement new technologies. There were no investors to fund new ideas because the wealthy had no concept of what progress is nor of how progress works; they certainly could not understand investing in anything other than control through local monopolies or through conquest (which is basically a drive toward global monopoly). On top of that, very few people had the money to purchase anything beyond basic sustenance. So large technological advances were not feasible even had the knowledge existed to produce such advances.

Parallel processing from the contributions of millions of middle class people is what makes the modern world possible. Consider that no one to-

---

* This includes Eisenhower, explaining why the hard right was disgusted with him; and surprisingly, Richard Nixon, who was as paranoid and narcissistic as any U.S. president has been. But despite his hunger for autocracy, Nixon shrewdly opened trade with China in order to play them off against the Soviets (something a liberal president would have been pilloried for), created the Environmental Protection Agency, and expanded civil rights.

† The same pattern is seen with real GDP per capita.

day completely understands the 747, the federal government, or the Linux operating system (paradoxically, not even Linus Torvalds). These advances are all too complex. A massive middle class, each with focused knowledge of one part of the system and working in a parallel, is necessary to design, build, and maintain great initiatives. But they would still be insufficient, because for each component of a complex system, there is another enormously complex system supporting it. Every component of the 747, even easily overlooked things such as seat materials and in-flight magazines, requires a manufacturer employing another population of designers, engineers, technicians and clerical workers and factories specializing in producing that one aspect. These are supported by yet other complex industries, not just chemists and production engineers, but non-obvious people such as artists, bankers, corporate lawyers, supply-chain specialists, craftsmen, construction companies, furniture makers, computer and telecommunications industries, *etc*. Even the inexpensive pens, pencils, and paper have extraordinarily complex industries supporting them. Then there is the complex role that government plays in supporting and regulating all of those industries: roads, bridges, the Internet, police and fire protections, the military, international trade agreements, the law courts, bureaus for registering and protecting intellectual property, and even funding much of the fundamental research that makes the rest of it possible. And of course, supporting all of these must be an extensive educational effort: schools and universities, libraries, books and journals, on-the-job training, seminars, conferences, and thinkers focused on constant research and development.

To build or produce anything of complexity requires a massive egalitarian effort; and that effort requires yet another enormous complexity. And all of it in turn requires an enormous, egalitarian, middle class population of consumers with sufficient income to purchase enormous numbers of any product once it is on the shelves. A handful of customers won't do; the price drops only once the customer base is enormous. The modern world is impossible without an enormous, prosperous, and well-educated middle class to design, build, market, distribute, sell, purchase, and maintain the products.

The problem is the atrocino is too self-absorbed and too dogmatic to see the obvious, what is all around him: universal education and rising affluence provide him with his employees, his support industries, and his customers, all of which make his wealth possible. But even if he were to realize such things, he might not care. His focus is dominance and win-lose. Again, his focus is not more money *per se*, only on making much more money than everyone else.

Profitable Socialism

A way to approach the transition to the modern world is to consider the 'basic unit' of a system. The goal of the conquering narcissist is dominion, and so his basic unit is the minion. The goal of the corporation is greed, and so its basic unit is the dollar. But the shared goals of the democracy are equality and progress; and so our basic unit is the citizen. Improving the citizen improves the system for everyone. Before the modern period, the peasants and the citizens were of little consequence. Clearly, there are incompatibilities between the atrox or atrocino, and the modern world. What is essential within the democracy is anathema to the narcissist.

For the past ten thousand years and even into much of the twentieth century, the desirable employee was a mindless clerk. That will no longer work. Clearly, a broad, prosperous, and intellectually nimble middle class is essential for the modern world. There are two overriding concerns for producing and maintaining that middle class.

Education is the first. Years ago a bumper-sticker said it well, "If you think education is expensive, try ignorance." If we were to suddenly end all public financing for education, within a decade or two our economy, our innovation, our military might, and our international leadership would vaporize. Without universal education America would decline into a third-world country.

The second concern is healthcare. A helpful metaphor is to view the democracy as a farm. No prudent farmer would ignore the maintenance of his livestock, his crops, nor his machines; they are his basic units; they are all critical to his success. By failing to provide quality healthcare for our citizens, the whole system suffers. We have a shared economic interest in keeping our citizens healthy and productive.

Education, however, is possibly the more important of the two. Without healthcare, we temporarily or permanently lose workers and valuable time without them. The system is less productive and less competitive. In the modern world, however, without education we cannot compete at all. When we empower our citizens through education, they not only provide income for themselves and their families—including producing the excess to pay for healthcare costs—but they also become lifelong learners, better-informed voters, and more active in civic life. Educated and empowered people make superior employees but also superior citizens. Healthcare keeps them at work and provides for a more reliable and predictable workforce.

Cosmopolitan Darwinism

Nations face the pressures of cosmopolitan Darwinism, which is the modern retort to social Darwinism. Competition in the advanced countries requires a highly complex economy with highly educated and highly paid workers. Those countries where the corporation and the narcissist dominate will lose these assets and lose out in market competitiveness.

As noted, quality education is expensive; this is also true of healthcare. The shrewd entrepreneur, however, is not worried about cost, but only ROI. If she can invest a dollar, or a billion dollars, and it is likely to grow at a healthy clip, she should invest it. However, there is no direct profit in educating, protecting, and maintaining a broad middle class. Such contributions produce a longer ROI curve than any modern investor could hazard. In addition, because the benefits from such investments are diffusely distributed, the investor has no guarantee of a return on her money. Granted, there is a risk in all investments, but this one has an even larger risk facing it from the other side: if investments in education and healthcare are not made, the loss of the investment is all but guaranteed. Education and healthcare are our mutual investments; they strengthen our way of life and our economy, as they strengthen all of us. They are the rising tide that carries all ships.

In a related problem, a general level of prosperity is crucial for a healthy customer base, but capitalism nevertheless seeks to reduce costs and wages, which erodes the middle class economy and the customer base with it. So in the complexity of the modern world, there are benefits to capitalism that capitalism cannot provide.

We can see how these two social programs benefit everyone, but only the government can fund and enforce them, through taxation and compulsory, universal education and healthcare. Only government has the power to compel the narcissist and the corporation to pause in their ruthless competitions and force them to sacrifice short-term profits to serve our mutual long-term interests: social, medical, educational, and yes, economic.

It's an interesting paradox: *modern capitalism requires socialist programs.* Without critical socialist services, the capitalist will have no employers, support industries, nor consumers.

Narcissist

The atrocino will argue otherwise, but that is a major point of this book. It doesn't matter what fundamentalism the atrocino and the atrox argue, nor what ideology they convince authoritarian personalities to follow. They may demand that capitalism solves all problems and that unfettered capitalism will solve them quicker. But cosmopolitan Darwinism defines the bottom line. Nations under the sway of corporations and plutocrats who insist that their freedoms allow them to use their money and power without restraint will find their citizens increasingly exploited and subjugated. Those nations will return to feudal economies.

A rising middle class, however, is a threat to the narcissist in two different ways. First, as general wealth increases, his wealth will decrease, particularly in the short term. The relative difference in wealth between him and his employees will decrease permanently, which means that his distinction will diminish in the economic hierarchy, both within the corporation and outside of it in the social register.

But second, a better-educated middle class also threatens the narcissist's prestige in the intellectual hierarchy. So much of the drive of the narcissist is to be seen as unique, with unique talents, and he presents himself as the visionary who directs and designs the future of the company, the man who is responsible for its impact on the larger world. But as the atrocino attempts to dominate and control the organization by preserving the traditional serial computing of the hierarchy, he leaves his company in peril. To remain competitive, the corporation must function more and more as a parallel computer, and there is an increasing drive toward intellectual parity. The corporation increasingly needs fewer minions and more thinkers who can function as critical and innovative collaborators and as intellectual peers of those atop hierarchy. For those narcissists in the executive suites, the attenuated range of incomes is objectionable enough. The even greater attenuation, or the eventual disappearance in the ranges of knowledge, expertise, analysis, and creativity, however, are anathema. If the CEO is not clearly superior, not physically, financially, nor intellectually, it becomes hard to explain how he is superior at all. The modern world is a threat to ten thousand years of narcissistic control. And so the narcissist ignores the realities and presses on in his self-service and dogma.

We previously noted that when André Schiffrin showed his publishing overlords that new ideas and new voices could be profitable, his demonstrations fell on deaf ears and dull minds. That one is particularly important, for a couple of reasons. First, Schiffrin generated the profits before he went to his bosses; why would a strong businesser reject obvious profit? The likely answer is corporate narcissism. Schiffrin was straying from his orders; he was challenging the dogma and the paradigms. By generating solutions that were his own ideas, he was threatening the prestige, power, and leadership of his bosses. He was threatening the hierarcy.

Second, Schiffrin's effort was titled *The Business of Books*. That's concerning, because ideas are the business of books. If the decision-makers in our most intellectual of businesses are impervious to progress, then our prospects are bleak for finding corporations in other disciplines who behave otherwise.

Indeed, other sectors work under the same narcissistic priorities. The atrocino resists any progress. When Detroit was required by sequential laws to make cars safer, more fuel-efficient, and less polluting, at each step senior management adamantly insisted that it couldn't be done, and/or that it would destroy profits. Then the middle class workers, from the engineers down to the assembly-line employees, designed solutions to the problem, and generally produced a rise in profits with them. The oil companies argued for years that alternate energy was not viable, and conservation was pointless. When unstable oil prices hurt their bottom line, however, the scientists, engineers, and production workers, inside the oil companies and out, found ways to make alternative energy and conservation viable, and often profitable. And if books are our most intellectual of activities, computing and telecomm should not be far behind; but we currently struggle against online retailers, social media, and Internet providers, who make the same arguments for self-service and exploitation that traditional industries do: there are no good solutions to these problems. What the atrocino really means is that he is not interested in good solutions. The arguments against him in this, ironically, are economic: in the modern world one path to bankruptcy is failing to design new solutions and failing to identify new sources of revenue.

The weakness in corporate leadership is suggested by a rapidly growing investment strategy: large corporations increasingly seek to buy out new and innovative businesses rather than develop ideas in-house. In effect, they are admitting they are at an intellectual disadvantage to the myriad of innovators out in the 'real' world. The weakness of the large corporation is not an inferior workforce, but an inferior leadership.

Corporations tend to exhibit the same anti-progressive and anti-intraceptive dysfunction in all of their considerations. They fight against laws supporting product quality, providing employee and consumer protections, and requiring corporate accountability. Again, such things are important to the democracy, as they are to the long-term success of the corporation. Nevertheless, the atrocino argues that such things are government meddling and paradoxically warns that they constrict free competition, undermine market efficiencies, and hamper American competitiveness.

The atrocino wants to make money the old-fashioned way: through narcissistic control. He wishes to continue dictating what his employees do and think and to continue designing the market to suit his vision and his bottom line. As Henry Ford said, "Any customer can have a car painted any color that he wants, so long as it is black." Ford later changed his mind, but unwillingly, but only in response to competitive pressures: his rivals began giving customers what they wanted.

The many examples in these pages show that corporate arguments about business and economic concerns are often canards and rationalizations. In examples where the underlying numbers make sense, but which do not conform to narcissism and dogma, the dysfunctional priorities of the atrocino become apparent. The ambition of the narcissist is a two-sided coin with one head and a multitude of tails. The atrocino wishes to elevate himself; but that requires that everyone else must be subjugated and depressed.

Interestingly, this aspect is largely missing from the psychiatric characterizations. Other than the desire to exploit others, the diagnostic criteria tend to omit an essential aspect of the narcissist: denigration. If the narcissist is superior, then everyone else must be inferior, and he must ensure that they remain there. In the typical narcissist, one with no extraordinary position or power, this diagnostic insight may not be obvious. In the ruling narcissist, however, that toxic aspect is critical: inherent to self-promotion is other-negation.

The atrocino wishes to build his wealth with modern citizens and modern infrastructure, and he wishes to live in a country with rich and diverse luxuries and comforts. But he wishes to have all of this at no cost to himself. In effect, he wants the product without the price, an approach he would find risible in his clients or customers. It is an expression of how the narcissist views himself as special and entitled. The strange thing is, throughout civilization, he has often gotten away with it; the rest of us did the king's work for him while he lived in wealth. Today, an increasingly shrinking economic elite still get away with it. No one person produces work worth millions of dollars a year. But the atrocino nevertheless insists that he does, and through subjecting others into an economic hierarchy, he manages to accrue wealth far beyond his individual contribution.

The problem with this exploitive strategy is a matter of simple math. Before the Renaissance, there was not much of a middle class, and so very few people had education, enjoyed time to think and analyze, or even believed that they were free to think for themselves. There was limited wealth, limited education, and limited progress. As the middle class grew, wealth was distributed to more people. That produced a rise in education and an expansion of independent, creative, and analytical thinking. With more thinkers, there were more ideas; and more ideas produced more progress. What holds us back is millennia of codependency with the most evil and dysfunctional people in history.

The Modern World

Both sides of the economic spectrum, of course, are given to simplisticism. Pure socialism will not solve all problems any more than pure capitalism will. We need balance and nuance. We do not need all socialist programs, only *effective* socialist programs. And the effect we should shoot for is the aforementioned fundamental unit of the democracy—citizens. Effective socialist programs produce improved citizens, which means a well-educated, critical, and robust middle class. The optimum we need is a useful balance between competition and cooperation.

The Broad Brush

Some may feel that I have painted with an overly large brush in describing corporate culture. I have not.

If I had read my own comments here a few years prior to publication, I would probably have found them an overreach, too. But occasionally, working on ideas and extending them through the inherent logic of writing produces surprising insights.* When I arrived at the conclusions here, that large corporations were evil entities, and described the intense narcissism of so many of their leaders, I was skeptical. As I looked back over my notes and reflected on my readings and researched further, however, I became more convinced that the indictments were justified.

We noted earlier that we can see the obvious flaws in others' religions and dogma, but we miss the gaps in our own. With that, we considered that for those of us who have escaped our dogmata enough to question what politics, religion, or other ideologies have taught us, the wake-up call is jarring. It's like one of those optical illusions where at first we see nothing and then suddenly a pattern vaults forward which should have been obvious.

When we manage to back out of our fairy tales, we quickly find all around us evidence which contradicts what we formerly 'knew' to be true. We are surprised that we could have missed so many facts and so many apparent and salient contradictions. If successful, this book will extend those experiences. I have jeopardized our popular beliefs about the loveliness and excitement of the past, about kings and conquerors, and about our romantic

---

* Seasoned writers note that any type of writing can have an aspect of 'automatic writing' to it. It is a zen experience, where author and pen, or author and keyboard, merge and ideas come pouring out of powerful subconscious processes. I occasionally write down something and then sit back and am a bit surprised by it; a conclusion materializes that was not foreseen. For some of these ideas, it may require some effort and time, perhaps months, to justify them through conscious logic. When the idea is only later confirmed by logic, it can be impressive but also a bit scary.

notions concerning it all. But as I noted, the surprise is that we are surprised. The evidence was always right there in front of all of us.

We remain blind to yet other problems. The more I thought about the modern corporation, the more I read about the corruption, incompetence, and short-sightedness of corporate management, the more I came to suspect that we are held in exactly the same religio-romantic thrall that blinded us under the king. It is not simply that the large corporation is sometimes evil; it is that it is necessarily evil, it is a soulless predator. Consider that the drive to fame and fortune have not changed; the men who pursue the money and status of corporate management are still those who are willing to sacrifice family, friend, and community to get there. The perverse drive to supremacy and subjugation of the narcissist did not suddenly disappear in the modern world. The same men who are ambitious in war are ambitious in peace, and they remain as ruthless as ever. The carnivorous tiger does not change his stripes that fast. Unfortunately, neither do the herbivorous zebra, okapi, or nyala.* It was not so long ago that we began escaping from the atrox. His cultural and genetic drivers remain, as do ours.

The ancient voices still whisper to us, drawing us into subjugation and sheepishness. Meanwhile, the atrox merely moved to where self-aggrandizement and the control of others is easiest and quickest. So today we defer to the CEO, the investment billionaire, and even the corporate raider in much the same way that we bowed to the king. We appear to be equally blind to the crime and the hypocrisy of the atrocino as we were to the atrox. We permit and even justify the atrocino's outrageous salary, his scandals, his crimes, and his exploitations, all the while assuming, just as we did with the king, that he is our 'better.' He understands the issues and what we really need better than we do.

Of course, he does not. And as we have noted, it is not necessary that the CEO be a psychopath or narcissist, because the corporation, and therefore corporate culture, are both. And so to manage the corporation, the CEO typically behaves as such. So we find ourselves in a world where the corporation exploits us at every point and constantly blocks innovation that would lead to intellectual, technical, economic, or social progress. Inchingly, but unceasingly, it seeks to return us to subjugation.

---

* The tiger is Indian, the three ungulates are African. In trying to make this metaphor, I seemed to find that where ungulates are striped or spotted, the predators tend not to be and vice versa. This was striking in the hyena, where the spotted hyena seemed to correspond roughly with the territory of striped ungulates, but the striped hyenas tend to live outside of those areas. I would guess that some naturalist has noted this pattern before me.

I refer the reader to the definitive treatise on the subject: *Dilbert*.[10] The cartoons may be humorous, but my assertion is not. As fans in the corporate world note, "Dilbert is a documentary." The cartoonist for the strip, Scott Adams, freely admits that he gets many of his best ideas from the personal stories sent in from his readers.

Next, talk to anyone who has worked in a large corporation. Overlook the blunders of management; everyone makes mistakes. Rather, listen to the closed-minded arrogance of it all. Listen to the stories of self-absorbed managers who refuse to listen to customers, clients, suppliers, employees, or even to consider proof and hard research numbers, but who are nevertheless promoted for toeing the corporate line and hectoring his people to meet the numbers. Then try to find someone who has worked in a large corporation who describes any other culture, who describes a large for-profit organization that sincerely listens to employees and customers and is aggressive about problem-solving and innovation.

After that, recall the difficulties we all experience in attempting to resolve problems with any large corporation. Reflect on the time lost simply trying to reach a person, how much longer it takes to speak to someone who can actually resolve the problem, and then how often after all of that, the corporation is simply deaf to complaints or solutions. Then consider how many corporations simply block feedback altogether, refusing to provide a telephone number, email address, or even a postal address for resolving problems.

Finally, imagine an employee, executive, or board member who openly stated within the corporation, even in supposedly humane industries such as healthcare, "I think it would be in the best interest of our customers [or our nation, or our world] if we targeted lower profits to keep our product more affordable." At best it would be met with shocked silence; at worst, raucous laughter. That sums the problem: there is no room in the corporation for the humane and the human. There is no mechanism for weighing any consideration other than profit. Again, when the CEO or the employee sits at her desk, she becomes a Machiavellian predator and serves Mammon alone.

Compare that behavior to the way we live our private lives, consider the sacrifices that so many of us make for our families, our friends, our communities, and our nation. Normal people frequently contribute to, and sacrifice for, the good of others. In our private lives, we serve higher purposes, and we exclude greedy, self-absorbed people. It's a searing irony: we refuse to associate with the kind of people we work for.

The corporation never sacrifices, and like the atrox it eagerly pursues the Deadly Sins. The corporation believes greed is a virtue and that it is the *only* virtue. The corporation profits in peace and profits even more in war. Where does corporate exploitation stop?

No: Where *could* it stop? What defined curb is there to corporate ambition? Where in the charter or the culture of the corporation is there a limit or restraint on corporate rapacity? The corporation is a soulless machine that lives for greed. We should hardly be surprised to find so many other evils emerging from it. There is no place compassion or humanity in the corporation; there is only winning. And for the corporation, winning is profit.

Not humanity. Not country. Not the earth itself. These can all be sacrificed for sufficient profit.

We earlier considered the political convention where the delegates were sure that the economy was terrible even though their own local economies were healthy. This is the reverse of that: almost no one works for a corporation with intelligent and far-sighted leadership, yet we nevertheless assume that corporate leadership is intelligent and far-sighted. The emperor's nakedness is right there in front of us all, but we are still convinced that he is finely adorned. We accept a romantic fantasy which we have never questioned. We must escape our fairy tales.

Queen Victoria

We noted that Genghis Khan was easily one of the greatest conquerors in history. Under Genghis, the Mongols expanded their territories to 13.5 million km². Soon after the death of his grandson Kublai, however, the empire reached a height of 24 million km², about 16 percent of the world's land surface, containing a population of perhaps 100 million people.

Genghis was not the greatest conqueror, however. That title goes to someone we have already considered from the modern period. This conqueror ruled about 35.5 million km² and subjugated over 400 million people.* The most vicious conqueror in history, by far, was a dowdy matron, devoted to her family and friends and beloved by her subjects, even many of those subjects she ruthlessly crushed.

For the cover of this book, I considered adding a Hitler mustache to a portrait of Queen Victoria. I ultimately rejected the concept, in part because

---

* It should also be noted that two of her grandsons, George V and Wilhelm II, her second cousin Ferdinand I of Bulgaria, together with other relatives through marriage and blood, Nicholas II and Ferdinand I of Spain, bear responsibility for much of WWI, in which over eighteen million people died; and of course the end of WWI and the harsh terms of the Treaty of Versailles ensured that the conflict would reignite as WWII. King Leopold of Belgium, whom we have covered elsewhere, was also Victoria's cousin.

the probable outrage would have occluded the point I wished to make: although *grandmother* Victoria was a model of middle class virtue, for her scope of conquest and horror, *Queen* Victoria could be compared to Hitler. Caught between the middle and outer class moralities, Victoria is an apt mascot for our thesis here; she straddled the vicious culture of the atrox and the nurturing culture of the family. She is the clash between antiquity and modernism, the transition from ruthless domination to tolerant equality.

She was able to do both, of course, because her imperial persona lacked a feedback loop. Victoria did not know the extent of the horror, in part because the British became masters at whitewashing and hiding the realities of conquest. We saw this in the Bombardment of Alexandria, the horrors of the Boer War and their torture of children such as Lizzie van Zyl, the cover-up of the annihilation after the Kikuyu Rebellion, and the order from the Secretary of State for the Colonies for the complete destruction of all potentially embarrassing records.

British whitewashing reached a level of parody, however, when confronted with parody. The British government would not allow the comedy troupe Monty Python to use real castles in the filming of *The Holy Grail* because such lampoonery would disrespect the 'dignity' of the castles.[11] We see again that the narcissist brooks no humor. The risible hypocrisy of this posturing should be obvious by now: castles were garrisons for terrorizers, henchmen, and thugs. Their 'dignity' is the antipode of dignity, it is scandalous exploitation and murderous enforcement. It is part of the fairy tale about who we imagine we are and where we believe we came from.

And so on the one hand, the English proved to be tireless workers and pioneers against the mistreatment of workers, of children, of the mentally ill, and even of animals. On the other, they were the historical record-setters in hacking and shooting and blowing people to death all over the world. The paradox is as lancing as the hypocrisy. The English gave us so much of the modern world: the rule of law over royal prerogative, the foundations for much of democracy, the philosophical arguments for pragmatism and moderate politics,* a great many of the seminal advances in science, and a disproportionate share of advances in the industrial revolution. They have nevertheless comprised some the bloodiest butchers in history. The nineteenth-century

---

* Pragmatism is frequently portrayed as an American philosophical movement. The word may have been coined by Americans, and the formalization of the concept may have come from Americans, but I would argue that the basic concepts were already present in the works of Edmund Burke and Bernard Mandeville. In fact, philosophers have a hard time of characterizing Burke's philosophy, I would argue, because there was no philosophy. Burke was already a pragmatist.

English somehow manage to be reactionary progressives and authoritarian egalitarians, simultaneously representing both the best and worst of humanity, the great, the horrible, and the hypocritical, but all of those enlarged and amplified. As such, of course, they represent the facultative and situational psychopathy and narcissism that we have seen with otherwise responsible, respectable people.

Modernity is the result of an emerging middle class. The atrox and the atrocino strive toward a feudal system comprising a few important people, with an enormous majority of exploitable and expendable nobodies. Democracies were designed to restrain and eliminate the atrox. The atrocino, however, is a more recent problem. He has come to control too much of government, market, and media, and he skews power and privilege toward himself and his goals. Our current laws and governmental controls are not equipped to stop the atrocino. If we do not stop him soon, however, we may find ourselves in a new, economic feudalism.

Chapter X:
The Ugly Truth

> *You want the truth?! You can't handle the truth!*
> – Colonel Nathan R. Jessup, *A Few Good Men*

> *All right, but apart from the sanitation, medicine, education, wine, public order, irrigation, roads, the fresh-water system, and public health—what have the Romans ever done for us?*
> – Reg, *Life of Brian*

Much of the early European exploration in the New World can be traced to a single animal: the beaver. Because beavers are prized for their fur and for the high-quality felt made from it, in many parts of North American, the animal was hunted to near extinction. In the early twentieth century, an attempt was made to reintroduce beavers to the Adirondacks. Between 1901 and 1906, about twenty beavers were released. By 1915, the population had grown to an estimated fifteen thousand. If we conservatively calculate that all twenty were released in 1901, then each of the original beaver pairs produced 1,500 descendants over fourteen years, with an annualized growth rate of 120 percent.

The potential for population growth with all living things is large. Even elephants, some of the slowest-reproducing animals on the planet, can potentially reach enormous numbers: over four centuries, a single breeding pair could reach perhaps one billion animals if unchecked. That time frame may seem slow to us, but in biological time scales, four centuries is nanoscopic.

These represent the problem of superfecundity. Natural populations, of course, do not expand at such rates, and in fact, typically do not expand at all. A mature female cat, for instance, can have three litters a year, with four to six kittens each; those kittens will be sexually mature in a year. In seven years, if unrestrained, a single pair of breeding cats could produce 370,000 descendants.

That does not happen. Consider that in the U.S. there are an estimated seventy-five million house cats, and most of them are not spayed or neutered.

If we assume that half are fertile, they could produce about three hundred million kittens per year. They don't produce nearly that many, but conservatively assume they produce only 2 percent of that total, or six million kittens. Only about 1.4 million cats are euthanized in shelters every year, which suggests that most of the offspring die in other ways. There are three major possibilities for an early death: predators (including human euthanasia); microbes; and environmental insufficiency, which primarily means starvation, but also includes exposure and other injuries.

It was the English cleric Thomas Malthus who first pointed out the problem of superfecundity, and he applied the concept to the human condition. If unchecked by predators or disease, humans, like all animals, will overbreed and outstrip our food supply. It does not matter how efficient we become in our food productivity, and it does not matter how much of the earth, the Solar System, or even the universe, that we colonize. If left unchecked, humans will breed faster than we can produce food. We will reach a limit.

Superfecundity is not just a problem; it's a universal law. Much as universal gravitation and all universal forces represent physical laws, universal superfecundity is the first law of biology.[1*] Like other scientific laws, it's inescapable. Humans and all living things exhibit superfecundity, and in so doing, sooner or later we condemn the majority of our offspring to failure and death. Maybe our children will avoid it, maybe even our grandchildren. But if population growth is left unchecked by artificial means, at some point the bill comes due. Once the nutritional limit of superfecundity is reached, many will die. Even those who survive, however, will have a hard time of it. As I noted about the reality of nature in the chapter 'The Breeding Programme,' almost all living things live on the edge, scraping by day to day, with barely enough food and other resources to sustain them. In their hardscrabble existence, most eventually fall over the edge and die a premature death. The brutality is that most of those who die, animal or human, will succumb in childhood, many within the first few weeks of birth.[2]

For those of us in the advanced countries with our extraordinary luxury and our very high childhood survival rates, this is a difficult concept to grasp. It is also unpleasant and most unromantic. If we are to avoid this future, however, we must learn to pursue the brutal intraception and ruthless intellectualism that I introduced in the prologue, and that we have expanded through this book. If we do not find ways to control population growth, we will run

---

* If you do not remember this from your biology classes, fear not, and remember you heard it here first.

out of food and other resources, and we will return to the horrors of the past. Cain will resume slaying Abel, and the atrox will reappear.

We don't realize how close we constantly are to those deadly times nor how easily and quickly we could slip back into a situation where only a minority survive and few die of old age.

The Best Predator

As an emergency physician, I am occasionally asked about which U.S. animal is the deadliest. Sharks? They kill about one person a year. Bears? About the same. Alligators? The same. Rattlesnakes? About one person every four years; other venomous snakes kill fewer. Dogs? Only about thirty people a year die in the U.S. from dogs.

Of course, there are many ways to die. Not all deadly animals are predators, and not all kill their victims the same way or for the same reasons. Snakes kill people, but in this country, they cannot eat them. Like the snake, the black widow spider kills by venom but cannot eat the seven people she kills every year. Then there are animals that kill by allergic reactions. About sixty people die each year from insects: bees, wasps, hornets, and as we noted in the South, fire ants. It may seem strange, but insects are twice as deadly as dogs.

The deadliest animal in the United States, however, is an animal that does not wish to kill and usually dies along with its human victims. Deer kill over one hundred people each year from more than one million collisions with motor vehicles. Even when they don't kill people, however, deer are expensive. At over $3,000 per vehicle collision, deer cost over $3 billion in annual car damage and injury to humans. Germane to our discussions here, they also cost us another billion or so in agricultural damage.

We omitted a likely culprit from our previous considerations: wolves. Wolves are actually quite shy and generally avoid humans. They kill fewer people than snakes. And there simply aren't that many wolves left in the lower forty-eight states. In the nineteenth century, the mainland might have supported a half-million wolves. Today, a little over five thousand remain, perhaps 1 percent of their previous numbers.

Ironically, wolves are the reason that deer are so deadly. Wolves hunt a wide variety of animals, but deer are among their favorite prey. Previously, wolves and other large predators such as bears and wildcats kept deer populations under control.

People began hunting wolves and other large predators partly out of safety concerns but also for livestock protection. Wolves and other carnivores eat cows, horses, pigs, chickens, and anything they can catch. And previously deer were, in effect, part of our livestock; one hundred years ago, they were a large portion of the American diet.

Today, however, few people hunt deer, and almost no one hunts as a primary source of nutrition. So deer face fewer predators: there are fewer wolves and other large carnivores, and people today hunt them less. Not surprisingly, their numbers have exploded. That's why they are killing us now. They're everywhere.

That would seem to be a good thing for the deer. It is not. Without predators, the deer are worse off. If biological success is surviving and reproducing, then as we noted in Chapter IV, that success is an illusory thing, because it is always temporary. Populations may briefly expand, but then a deadly feedback loop kicks in: predators will expand along with the prey and keep the population in balance. If that does not happen, however, then the population will outstrip its food supply and begin starving.

The latter is what is happening with deer. Today, there are some forests where the wolves have been hunted to extinction and deer hunting has been made illegal. So the deer strip away the grasses and shrubs and all of the seedlings. That is critical: without seedlings, there are no future trees. The forests become much like a city with no children. It may appear lovely, populated only with graceful and polite adults, but without children, there is no future. So without predators, not only do deer starve and/or succumb to disease, they also bring down the forests with them.

What is the best way to manage expanding deer populations? Even PETA agrees that predators are necessary. PETA objects, however, to human predators, arguing that humans harvest only trophies.

I suspect PETA is in the thrall of their own fairy tales and romantic myths, one where the animal hunters (*e.g.*, the 'king' of the jungle and the 'noble' wolf) are good, while human hunters are evil. First of all, most hunters butcher the deer they kill and eat the meat. Even if that were not the case, however, human hunting is still better for the deer than starvation and disease. And often, better than wild carnivores: death from a well-placed bullet comes more quickly and less painfully than from a pack of wolves. Beyond that, it really makes no difference either way. If trophies are taken and the carcass is abandoned, exactly the same carnivores will feed on the corpse, and the remains will sustain the ecosystem in exactly the same ways. The wolves and other carnivores, however, would be doubly benefited: they get the food but avoid the dangers of the chase.

The point is that predators are necessary to keep prey in check. But that brings up a biological confusion. Because of its Victorian traditions, biology is heavily invested in the concept of competition in the struggle for existence. Cooperation and mutual benefit have begun attracting research attention only over the past few decades.

To my mind, the earlier traditions have blinkered much of our thinking. Consider, which of the following would be the superior predator?

1) A predator that diminishes the number of its prey.
2) A predator that has no impact on population numbers.
3) A predator that assists its prey and expands its numbers.

Obviously, the best predator is one that helps itself by helping its prey. If a predator does not behave in this way, it will quickly lose out to predator-prey systems where both benefit.

It's a disturbing insight: prey need predators as much as predators need prey. Without predators, disaster befalls the entire population, perhaps irrevocably: populations which outstrip their food supply typically crash and risk going extinct.

I propose a second biological law, the law of universal predation. All living things, or at least all large living things, require predators to avoid population crashes, and possible extinction.*

The Superpredator

This brings us to a new consideration. We are the predator that hunts all other predators. We slay the shark, the bear, the lion, and the eagle. We hunt the whale, the elephant, and the hippopotamus. We level forests, divert rivers, and demolish mountains. We also split the atom, plumb the ocean bed, and send our mechanical minions across the vault of space.

So where is the predator that prevents us from overbreeding and from outstripping our food supply? What animal keeps human populations healthy? What predator hunts the superpredator? Clearly, only one animal can hunt the superpredator: another superpredator.

Moralists have pondered war, and its causes, throughout civilization. In

---

* In full disclosure, I am not quite as confident about this law as I am of the previous one, and I'm still thinking about it. For instance, some microbes and a few other tiny animals can go into a state of organic suspension for years without need of water or nutrition. These species cannot easily crash and may not need a predator.

previous chapters we have provided another reason for war: the malignant narcissism of the conqueror. That, however, is what ecological behaviorists call a 'proximate' explanation. It is an explanation that, while true, stops short of the fullest understanding.

Every selected behavior or trait has an 'ultimate' explanation. There is no limit to the number of proximate explanations, but all ultimate explanations are singular: there is only one, and it remains the same for understanding all biological problems. We considered the law of universal superfecundity and the law of universal predation. Here we reach another biological law, the law of ultimate biological meaning. The ultimate explanation for any selected behavior or trait is that it left more reproducing offspring than any competing behavior or trait. If the behavior or trait does not leave more reproducing offspring, then it will lose out to the behavior or trait which does.

Traditionally war has simply been viewed as the victor gaining more resources and the loser dying and disappearing from the gene pool. But we need to reconsider the situation through the lens of the foregoing: the best strategy is the one where predator and prey sustain each other. The law of ultimate biological meaning suggests that human groups who go to war leave more reproducing offspring than those who do not. Given that, it appears that we go to war because we need predators. Without predators, we overpopulate, starve, crash, and risk the whole population.

Humans hunt one another. We considered this in the child's game of hide and seek and in the apparent human adaptations for fleeing quietly without stopping for days. We hunt each other, just as we hunt deer and rabbit. And as we have seen, just as the tiger does, the hunter spares no one, not the women, not the children, not the babies. We hunt everyone. Theologians tell us that God is a loving creator. If so, Mother Nature is a remorseless bitch.

War is not exclusive to humans. Various primates, ants, and other pack animals engage in warfare. But war is distinct to social animals simply because war is the struggle of social groups. Individuals fight, social groups war. And most, if not all, social mammals have a leader, an alpha.

The alpha is the origin of the atrox. But evidence suggests that the ancestral alpha was very different from the modern atrox. Many pre-civilization groups appeared to have been small tribes: cohesive, egalitarian packs consisting primarily of relatives. They lacked the social stratification and the military-style hierarchy of the atrox. Nor could they afford a large hierarchy: the psychopath and the narcissist would have been ruinous in a small group where efficiency and communal contribution are essential. An anecdote from the Inuit is illustrative. Occasionally within a tribe a man is identified as *kunlangeta*, someone who is shiftless, dishonest, and a womanizer. Eventually, one of the other men will force him to go fishing with him. Once out of sight, the offender is pushed off the ice.[3] There are not enough resources to support exploiters.

Once excess appears, once there is a settlement with food or other stores, it attracts raiders, and an arms race appears: stopping the raider requires larger settlements, which requires larger invading armies, which requires the settlements to invest in more defenses and maintain their own armies, which requires the invaders to invest in machines and heavier assault weapons. These excalations were the likely opening for the psychopath, the narcissist, and the sadist to pursue their desires and dominate.

From that arms race, however, the modern world eventually emerged. As repulsive as the conqueror is, he brought us to this point; he forced humanity into civilization. For several of the conquerors in Chapter II, we began by noting their contributions. They viciously slaughtered and subjugated vast populations for their narcissism, but they nevertheless brought slow progress to the world.

As we have seen, the atrox did not intend to do this; he had no interest in progress, only control and privilege. Much like the modern dictator wants thinkers who will not think too hard about him and his decisions, the ancient king needed thugs who would control the peasants but not aim their thuggish activities on him. But he is living by the sword. When the atrox empowers his lieutenant-nobles and grants them access to their own resources, it is only a matter of time before they challenge him. The atrox increases his power by reducing the power of everyone else, but the reverse is also true, the lower rungs of the hierarchy gain power by reducing the king's. With limitations placed on King John, some power and decision-making moved a step down the societal ladder, which was a small progress. The *Magna Carta* would seem to be a minor change; it was quickly violated, and it was hardly democracy. But it was a first step toward reducing the atrox. With each successive step in the Anglo-American power lineage, lower groups, each in turn, were also able to step up and grab more power. And at each step, more autonomous actors participated and were able to contribute to prosperity and progress. At the same time, the arms race rewarded the slightly more innovative culture, offensively and defensively. Superiority gradually shifted from brute force to analysis and innovation.

Ancient Rome demonstrates the power of intelligence, technology, and cohesion over simple might: when compared to their Germanic adversaries, Roman armies often fought with fewer troops, and individually, their soldiers were physically smaller on average. The Romans nevertheless unfailingly prevailed over the northern tribes because of intelligence, technology, and discipline. At least the Romans prevailed until the Varian Disaster at Teutoborg Forest. That defeat is also telling: the German tribes were finally successful, not because they were larger, but because they fought smarter. Under the direction of Arminius, they adopted Roman-style tactics and planning. Intelligence and coordination slowly win out.

Progress is a matter of numbers, of how many people are sharing in power and luxury, which enables them to design more solutions. As power diffuses down the hierarchical ladder, the atrox becomes weaker, and progress accelerates.

• • •

The atrox did not lead us into horror; he simply took us along a different path through horror. Because until only the last moment of history, and except for only a handful of people today, all life is horror. Mother Nature slaughters millions, our tribal ancestors slaughtered millions, and the atrox slaughters millions. Neither Mother Nature nor the atrox desire progress. It is just that blind trial and error produce beneficial advances. Neither Mother Nature nor the conqueror could see that their bloody progression through history was slowly, creepingly, equipping humanity with the tools to rebel and escape. So despite the eons of suffering and oppression, gradual progress occurred. The modern world emerged.

Modern progress began coming into its own in the early Renaissance and with the roots of the scientific revolution. Even here, however, the horror of the atrox was key: much Renaissance science dealt with various problems of weapons and war machines.

So that is the ugly truth. Without the horrors of the atrox, we would still be neolithic peoples with minimal, primitive technology, struggling to eke out a precarious living in a wild world.

• • •

Where would we be without history's butchers, without Alexander and Athenian culture, Julius and Roman culture, Napoléon and republican ideals? We can say confidently that we would not be here. But when we ask, 'Was it worth it?' we cannot ask those who were starved, tortured, enslaved, and slaughtered over the past ten thousand years. The cost of our progress was easily a billion human lives or more; they're the ones who paid the price for our comfort.

We have modified and modernized the atrox's civilization in order to block his legacy of human horror. Today, life is protected and held paramount, but we must remember that this situation is artificial; it exists only because many people sacrificed everything to create it. Theologians may argue that life is a sacred gift from the Deity, just as the Founders argued that life was unalienable.

But life is protected only if we decide, together, that it is sacred and something to be guarded and cherished. Without a broad alliance of people dedicated to defending one another, the value of human life is just another fairy tale. And the forces arrayed against us are primeval and powerful. As predator and prey, we still have our stripes. If we are to maintain our dream, if we are to avoid collapsing back into horror, then we need to stop more than the atrox. We have to stop the forces of nature. We are not simply fighting to escape ten thousand years of the conqueror; we are fighting to escape four billion years of Malthus and Darwin.

We must recognize and remember the cost of the modern world: the pain, the suffering, the torture, and the death of untold millions. When we see efforts to take us back to narcissistic strongmen and to a culture of force, we must remember the price. And we must recognize that the only thing preventing it from happening all over again is us: our culture, our learning, and our commitment to one another.

OLDER, GENTLER PSYCHOPATH

In 1924, two exceptionally intelligent University of Chicago students, both from privileged, affluent families, kidnapped one of their cousins, a boy of fourteen. They brutally murdered him for no reason other than to prove that they were smart enough to get away with it.

They did not get away with it. Despite their mental superiority, Nathan Leopold and Richard Loeb were quickly identified and tried. The case was billed as 'The Crime of the Century,' and the subsequent prosecution, 'The Trial of the Century.' The pair were defended by no less than Clarence Darrow. It was the first trial in which psychoanalysis was introduced into evidence; Sigmund Freud himself had been retained for the defense and traveled from Germany to analyze the two men. Unfortunately, ill health prevented him from participating.[4] Darrow's closing oration lasted twelve hours and is considered one of his finest legal arguments.

With an IQ of 210, it emerged that Leopold was the leader of the pair, but he also exhibited behavior consistent with psychopathy: he looked forward to the trial and was even curious about his execution. Through Darrow's skillful defense, however, the death penalty was avoided, and both men were sentenced to jail. Loeb was eventually murdered by another inmate, his assailant insisting that Loeb had made sexual advances on him.[*] Leopold, however, became a model prisoner, taught in the prison school, and learned twenty-seven foreign languages while incarcerated. He was paroled after thirty-three years, moved to Puerto Rico, married, and worked as a lab technician for the rest of his career. After his conviction, he lived quietly and had no other brushes with the law.

Leopold illustrates an occasional, odd pattern. Some psychopaths seem to lose some of their exploitative and Machiavellian behaviors in middle age. Thereafter, they may lead a normal or even a charitable life.

Recall that although Ashoka maintained his capacity for viciousness, at forty-four he turned to religion after the Kalinga War and began pursuing charitable works. Similarly, after Constantine converted to Christianity, he was still capable of great violence, but he also became a patron of the church, building basilicas and supporting worship in other ways. He also introduced certain humane practices—humane at least for that time and culture—into the Roman treatment of prisoners and convicts. We also considered Oskar Schindler, who in his mid-thirties suddenly shifted from exploiting the Jews in his sweatshops to protecting and saving them.

Louis IX of France—St. Louis, as he is better known—also led the typical bloodthirsty life of the atrox in his younger days, participating in two crusades and expanding the Inquisition in the south of France. Nevertheless, after he turned forty, in the 1258 Treaty of Corbeil, and in the 1259 Treaty of Paris, he swapped and even yielded French holdings to achieve peace. Willingly yielding anything is atypical of the atrox. Louis also expanded his patronage of the arts and founded what would later become the Sorbonne.[†]

The same pattern seems to appear in the atrocino. Many of the robber barons of the nineteenth century turned to charity in their later lives. Cornelius Vanderbilt, William Duke, Johns Hopkins, and Leland Stanford were

---

[*] In an oft-quoted bit of snarkery, *The Chicago Daily News* reported, "Richard Loeb, despite his erudition, today ended his sentence with a proposition."

[†] It should be noted that these changes occurred after the death of Louis's mother, Blanche. She had held the regency in Louis's early life, and she remained a power behind the throne throughout her life. It is possible that her absence simply allowed Louis to express his own preferences.

cutthroat capitalists who all built eponymous universities. John Jacob Astor founded the Astor Library in New York and funded countless charities. John D. Rockefeller largely designed the modern corporation, and after losing his empire from the Trust-Busters (which paradoxically multiplied his wealth), he then designed the modern nonprofit corporation. The list continues: William Randolph Hearst, Andrew Carnegie, J.P. Morgan, Henry Ford, and John D. MacArthur were all ruthless businessmen who turned to charity in later life.

There are numerous others. The relative virtues of each of these men is the purview of the biographer. Great wealth, however, is not accumulated through refinement and polite requests. These were hard-nosed, sharp-elbowed businessmen who had no compunction about steamrolling rivals or exploiting employees and customers. It is entirely possible that some of their later philanthropy was simply fashion. Perhaps it was just another narcissistic display of wealth, one in which none of them wanted to be outdone by the other.

Nevertheless, this pattern across kings and capitalists warrants further consideration by historians, mental hygienists, and criminologists. If later in life the atrox and the atrocino do move away from psychopathy toward normalcy, and even toward real philanthropy, then it suggests two interesting possibilities. First, the recurring pattern across the atrox, the atrocino, and the malignant narcissist suggests that at least some of this behavior is genetic. Second, if it is genetic, then it would appear that this shift is the product of selection, which means it generates biological efficiency, and we would want to identify the ultimate meaning. Actually, we would want to identify the ultimate meaning of both behaviors: the atrox greedily and lethally accumulates land, power, and wealth early in his career; later in his career, he becomes nurturing and generous toward the same people he exploited to acquire his wealth and power. We can see how this shift might comprise a superior strategy and how it might make his kingdom and his descendants more compet-

---

* As I have reflected on this possibility, a few things disturb me. One is that, since the dawn of civilization, there have been perhaps one hundred thousand, or even one million, successful kings and equivalents distributed over ten thousand years. Those may seem large numbers to the layman, but for the evolutionist, they are quite small. They don't seem to constitute a sufficient population, nor time span, for selective processes to produce such a complex pair of age-related behaviors. On the other hand, if the genetics of the atrox do not produce these behaviors *de novo*, but draw on variations already present in the gene pool; and if the genetics is really a matter of simply switching the brain centers for empathy on and off; then it would probably be enough. James Fallon notes that he seemed to have a normal emotional life as a child, and oddly enough, one aspect of his empathy remains: he becomes very emotional about handicapped children. His experiences suggest age-related functions. It would be interesting to look at head scans of aging psychopaths and see if there are shifts in brain center activity in any of them after forty.

itive when compared to either neolithic hunter-gatherers or kingdoms where the king left behind only exhausted populations. It suggests that in tandem, the two behaviors may be selected.

Of course, the atrox would probably give very different explanations for his philanthropy. He might state he does it to attain heavenly immortality or even worldly immortality through fame. He might state that it makes him feel good. He might say it is good for business. Or as we noted, he might do it for the attention, to feed his narcissism. The atrox's perceived reason does not matter. Military, economic, and genetic selection will choose the best solution.

When useful ideas appear in government, society, business, or in any human activity, they often spread slowly and lurchingly. This is true for general advancement: progress and egalitarian ideas began reappearing a half-millennium ago, but today only a minority of the world lives in comfort within egalitarian and democratic states. The great majority of the world still awaits these advances, and there are many parts of the globe where people lack even rudimentary utilities and remain the chattel of the rich and powerful. Innovation may suffer a lag time before it expands and penetrates everywhere.

Advances also need time to evolve and become institutionalized. For instance, the U.S. Founders thought they had created an egalitarian system. We know now that they had not. It was a slow path to adding unlanded white males, then African-American males, and then women to the system. It is not finished; the atrocino and his supporters work to block the vote of those who disagree, particularly minorities and other 'undesirables', and they game the system so that a wealthy white minority can control much of government. There was a lag between the declaration of democracy and the realization of democracy, and then there is a further lag before democratic ideals become institutionalized as custom and culture.

That lag is a time of great instability and danger. While the middle class struggles toward egalitarian ideals, the atrocino and his disciples sap at the fortifications of the law and of decency. The delay between vision and progress, and then progress and habit, is dangerous. As the Nazis showed the world, a minority of authoritarian personalities can take advantage of disaffection and chaos, or even foment them, and flip the slow-moving democratic turtle on its back.

We need to be clear about how the atrocino works, we need to recognize the threat he poses, and we need to realize that the slow work toward democracy, equality, and justice is far from complete. If we do not watch diligently and continue the work, our way of life can easily fall apart.

Epilogue: Response

> *On some great and glorious day*
> *the plain folks of the land will reach their heart's desire at last,*
> *and the White House will be adorned by a downright moron.*
>
> –H. L. Mencken

> *We cannot teach people anything.*
> *We can only help them discover it within themselves.*
>
> –Galileo Galilei

In the prologue, I noted that we would use scientific approaches to analyze historical and social patterns. My efforts proved more prescient than I realized at that time.

In 1975, the biologist R.D. Alexander presented an idea he had been toying with. He had been wondering what a mammal might look like if it lived in a colony similar to that of ants or bees. He speculated that such a mammal would be largely subterranean, probably a rodent, living near a concentrated and easily harvested food source. From that, he postulated such colonies might be located in a region with large wet-dry shifts, because plants in such conditions concentrate water and nutrients underground, and he pointed out that east Africa supplied the necessary conditions. He also suspected that snakes would be a major predator and so the mammals might have a soldier caste for defense of the colony.

After the talk, someone approached him and informed him that research was underway in east Africa on precisely the animal he proposed: the naked mole rat.

Compared to predicting black holes or time-space dilation, Alexander's prediction might seem minor. But physicists are aided by overarching formulas and mathematical analysis which help them 'see' such things. Alexander was simply sitting back and thinking about the problem.

In the waning days of writing this book, I was pushing hard toward my publication deadline, and I was surprised to identify a similar vindication for my ideas here. I have laid out a very aggressive charge against the corporate leader. I have argued that in his narcissism, the atrocino would *deliberately* destroy modernity to serve his greed, vanity, and dogmatism. I worried, however, that I had gone too far out on the limb. I would have liked a rock-solid example to point to.

It worried me. I grew up in Louisiana, with a bawdy house that passes for government. I constantly saw the mismanagement of state leadership, which kept the state near the bottom of national rankings for almost every important indicator of public prosperity.* Some of that was narcissism and corruption, but much of it was simply self-perpetuated ignorance and sloth.

A recent governor, however, aggressively slashed social programs and education, and his actions appeared to carry a malicious intent. His apologists would point out some of this was necessary. For instance, in Louisiana only healthcare and higher education aren't constitutionally protected, and there was a budget shortfall to be addressed. Those two areas of funding were simply victims of the budgetary pressures.

However, one of the first things the governor did in office was to slash Louisiana's income taxes, which precipitated the cuts. Reducing taxes might seem to be simply good conservative policy, except for the fact that Louisiana income taxes were already well below the national average; and he slashed them as analysts were predicting a looming, massive drop in state revenues. So the governor created an environment that required cuts, knowing full well that higher education, healthcare, and other social programs would be injured, perhaps irrevocably.

There were even stranger aspects. The governor had previously served as one of the state's top officials in higher education, overseeing most of the state's colleges and college students. He was cutting the same institutions he had led, and he understood the implications; he was not acting from ignorance. Finally, as he made these cuts, he warned college administrators not to complain. The president of the largest college complained anyway and was quickly fired. The implication was that the governor wanted the cuts to go through. Then reports began emerging from the governor's inner circle that his intent was to ensure that only students from upper middle class families would be able to afford a college degree.

As the Louisiana governor was doing this, governors across the U.S., all from the same political party, were simultaneously working to slash higher education, healthcare, and other social programs in their own states. Their actions appeared coordinated and even orchestrated. It seemed that some malice was afoot.

---

* For most of my life, in rankings for education, poverty, health, or economy, Louisiana was regularly forty-ninth. We claimed that the state's unofficial motto was "Thank God for Mississippi." Mississippi, however, has passed us up.

Epilogue

Then, like R.D. Alexander, I found my rats.

Some time back I had purchased Nancy MacLean's *Democracy in Chains: The Deep History of the Radical Right's Stealth Plan for America* but had not yet found the time to read it.[1] In my final weeks of writing, I happened across it on my bookshelf and opened it for a few minutes of bedtime reading.

I did not get sleepy. MacLean had stumbled across the files of one of the most secretive movements in the U.S. today, a conspiracy of plutocrats and ideologues working to sabotage the country in just the manner I have described in the preceding chapters. It was a Keystone Cops moment: despite all of their decades of stealth, despite their arrogance and belief in their inherent intellectual superiority, they had stupidly left all of their early records in their former headquarters, completely unprotected. MacLean walked through the front door and hit the mother lode.

Their files documented an attempt to recast America in the mold of a Latin American kleptocracy. Specifically Chile: the central, foundational figure for this ongoing attempt to reverse modernity was the late economist and Nobel laureate James McGill Buchanan, who helped Augusto Pinochet write the Chilean constitution.

With Buchanan's help, Chile was converted from a budding democracy into a kleptoplutocracy (there is really little difference between the two; either the plutocracy or the kleptocracy will inevitably morph to comprise the other).

One of Buchanan's central dogmata was 'economic liberty,' and the Chilean constitution placed economic freedom above democracy and personal liberty. We have seen that the atrox and atrocino argue for freedom, but it is an artful dodge, as they really desire the freedom to strip others of their freedom. In this case 'economic liberty' really means 'political inequality'; it is a bastardization of the Golden Rule: he who has the gold writes the rules. Economic liberty is yet another shrewd camouflage that hides the true desire of the atrocino: inequality, hierarchy, subjugation, and exploitation; or as we have come to understand it, narcissism.

The Buchanan and Pinochet protections for wealth over democratic processes were so strong, however, that modern Chileans seem to have no practicable way to re-enter the modern world. The moneyed interests have a stranglehold on government. It is not clear how Chile can rewrite her constitution through any means short of another political or military strongman, one possibly installed by open revolution. Of course, in that transition, there is a good possibility that the strongman will set himself up as yet another dictator and write a constitution that only creates new problems and no progress. Chile would be plunged back in the 1920s.

Despite the obvious failings of Pinochet's government, with the torture, assassinations, and jailings; the illegalization of opposition parties; the elimination of a free press; rampant corruption; the nationalization of many private industries; and the financial convulsions that have sent the Chilean economy sliding off the charts; despite all of these, the Cato Institute, the Heritage Foundation, and other of the plutocrats' thin-clients celebrate Chile as an "economic miracle."[2] Which, in their eyes, it is: although Chile now teeters on the brink of implosion and collapse, the wealth of the kleptoplutocrats has been preserved, and so the effort was a resounding success.

Narcissism can be seen all through this American cabal, even before the plutocrats arrived with their stacks of cash. Buchanan and his colleagues were chased from several universities because of their insufferable arrogance. Then when they found that elected officials and the public lacked the "strategic courage"[3] to see the brilliance of their ideas, they shifted to anti-democratic strategies. They used just the tactics we have discussed here: they began by deliberately employing dissimulation and anger-mongering to distract the public and elected officials. To help them in this, they commented that, "The emerging Internet, for its part, 'appears especially well suited for rumor, gossip, and talk of conspiracy.'"[4] Of particular interest to our examinations here, they also recognized "how vulnerable humans are to hardwired drives that resist reasoned evidence."

As these ideologues and plutocrats began undermining the basic constructs of democracy, they also began buying elections and politicians with them, objecting to the balance of powers, sabotaging voter rights and equal protection, packing the courts and indoctrinating sitting judges, working to overthrow public education, dispensing with Social Security, Medicare, and all other aspects of the federal social safety net.

It is telling that when Buchanan died, the plutocrats and power mongers who had commandeered his ideas and abused his academic prestige did not even bother to attend his memorial service. At first glance, that seems to be nothing more than tastelessness. I think it is a metaphor for the priorities of the atrox, the atrocino, and the authoritarian personalities who follow them: people, mutual respect, and personal contribution are unimportant to the narcissist. Others' lives are unimportant to him in war; they are merely vehicles to acquire money, power, and fame. There is no reason we should think that any of that would change in peace.

This brings us back to the ideology of the atrocino. The plutocrats attempting to model the U.S. after the failed Chilean attempt at 'economic liberty' are, paradoxically, poor businessmen. Their insistence on ideology is a product of their simplistic world view: rather than recognize that the free market is useful and produces many efficiencies, but like everything else has its limitations and flaws, these plutocrats subscribe to a fundamentalism which leads them to insist that the free market is *perfect*. It will solve all problems. This thinking leads the atrocino to make bad decisions for himself, for his businesses, for his nation, and for the world.

These kleptoplutocrats prove their hypocrisy with their own choices: not one of them has moved his headquarters to Chile. Chile does not have the workers, the consumers, nor the diverse luxuries of an advanced nation; it never occurs to the plutocrats that equality and general prosperity are not obstacles to progress, but the vehicles of it. This American cabal nevertheless fatuously, and seditiously, works to move Chile, whole cloth, to the United States.*

The failure in their logic is easy to see, but their dogmatism and narcissism lead them to ignore the most obvious economic evidence and to pursue poor business decisions. General prosperity brings progress and wealth. Inequalities, whether of government participation, education, or wealth, bring decline and decay. These 'titans' of industry blindly subscribe to antiquated social ideas because they support antiquated business ideas.

Democracy in Chains is a case study for our deliberations here. MacLean provides us with evidence that the atrocino would happily sabotage his own country, or the entire world, in order to promote his wealth and distinction.

And to enforce his ideological vision. We earlier suggested that perhaps zealotry and dogmatic ideology should be considered as psychiatric diseases. The cabal exposed in *Democracy in Chains* supports that idea, particularly when dogma is driven by narcissism. Together, the two can produce a bizarre spiral, a tailspin: as we saw with Hitler, the authoritarian can also become his own authoritarian personality. He can become enamored of his ideas and will blindly follow his own rationalizations, particularly when they also reinforce his arrogance and narcissism.

Consider that Pol Pot did not consciously wish to make his country worse. He insisted that, with time, a purely communist state would produce the superior condition. But his fervent ideology, his firmly locked intellectual trapdoors blinkered him to the shortcomings and failures of his approach. He was unable to see the illogic, and the lack of humanity, in the horror he created.

---

* But without the brown-skinned Spanish speakers, of course. Notice that racism appears repeatedly in this book. As we noted earlier, 'us vs. them' is the most primeval of class distinctions, and so different body and facial types, language, clothing, and culture are the prehistoric valuations that we perpetuate and which almost definitely have a genetic component supporting them.

This can also be seen in the antebellum South. Slave owners, along with their white followers, blindly rationalized away the decline of Southern competitiveness; they ignored the weaknesses of their neo-feudalist society and argued instead that their society was the superior one. That blindness proved their undoing.

Woven into the South's demise was a historical precedent and parable. Classical ideals had shaped the emerging United States, but in defiance of those egalitarian traditions, the South worked to retreat into aristocracy. But as the South rejected Roman ideals, it duplicated Roman economic decadence. In a midway mirror of reflected irony, the Romans were blinded by their own self-serving ideology: just like all conquerors, the Romans were convinced that their conquest and domination over other peoples was just, fair, and even pre-ordained; and that it was their right to rule others.* And just like the antebellum South, the Romans believed in their sacred right to enslave others.

The two traditions converged over technical progress, or the lack of it. Many of the machines that emerged in the Middle Ages, that paved the way for the Industrial Revolution and that gave the North a decided advantage in the Civil War, originated with ancient Roman designs. The Romans, however, had never seriously pursued their own technical innovations because it was easier and cheaper—in the short term, at least—to use slaves instead.

The South also found it was easier to use slaves and saw no reason to invest in expensive new technologies, even if the machinery might prove more efficient and profitable in the long run. When the war broke out, these handicaps precipitated several crises. For one, the antebellum South produced much of the world's cotton but had no weaving mills. So the South could not make uniforms for its own troops nor canvas for tents and other coverings; raw cotton had to run blockades to get to England, and the finished cloth had to cross the same blockades to return. There was limited mass manufacturing of other kinds as well, and in particular there was a dirth of railroads. The war proved what peacetime commerce would have taken decades to show: the South's blind devotion to self-service, and the ideology of slavery, held it back.

Blind ideology is damning. As we have seen repeatedly, dogmatic concerns often drive the atrox and the atrocino to foment war, create economic pandemics, and pursue human exploitation, all of which create human suffering. Given that, how can we exclude zealotry and ideological fanaticism from our psychiatric considerations?

---

* And to our continuing thesis, those the Romans subjugated often agreed that their imperial masters were just and fair. To our more recent thesis, that assessment from the subjugated was not entirely in error: note the quotation introducing Chapter X and see Clifford Ando, *Imperial Ideology and Provincial Loyalty in the Roman Empire* (University of California, 2013).

Epilogue

• • •

In popular usage, 'left' and 'right' have come to mean the same thing as 'liberal' and 'conservative,' respectively. This is a critical mistake.

The U.S. Founders certainly used the words 'liberal' and 'conservative,' although they had somewhat different meanings at the time. But in their deliberations they would not have understood 'left' and 'right.' Those concepts appeared only a couple of years after the Constitutional Convention, during the French Revolution. In the Estates General, those early meetings leading up to the decapitation of the French monarchy, the nobility and the clergy sat to the *right* of the presiding member; the anti-monarchists, the republicans, sat to the *left*.*

It is important to maintain the distinctions between liberal and left-wing, and conservative and right-wing, because we too quickly assume that the right represents tradition. This approach misses the central significance of both the American and French Revolutions and of modernity. The right represents authority and the exclusive, vertical hierarchy. The left, however, represents the inclusive, egalitarian approach of both revolutions. It is the mobility vs. the nobility.

In contrast to those terms, however, 'conservative' means to keep things the way they are or to return them to how they recently were. 'Liberal' is derived from the Latin word for freedom; in this case, the liberal is free to experiment and change things. The fact is that all of us must be overwhelmingly conservative. We do things the same way across the globe as people have done since the beginning of civilization or even the beginning of life. We eat, dress, sleep, raise families in much the same way our ancestors did; we carry on banking and commerce as people have done for centuries; and we look to our Constitution and other traditions for guidance about resolving modern political, social, and economic problems. Conservatism is essential for the continuity of life.

But 'liberal' is essential for the modern world. All progress is necessarily liberal because progress requires the freedom to experiment and the freedom to change. So the problem is not *whether* to be liberal or conservative, only *when* to be liberal or conservative, because the two positions are clearly unattached from any permanent ideology.

Consider that today's conservatives base many of their beliefs on the eighteenth-century American Revolution. But the men who carried out the Revolution were quite liberal, even radical, in their day. Modern Christians

---

* The right is the favored seat, as evidenced by the name 'Benjamin': 'son at the right hand.'

who proudly invoke the traditions of the Puritan Pilgrims would be viewed by those Pilgrims as anathema; and there are few conservatives today who would happily suffer the Pilgrims' rigidity and intolerance. That insight can be taken backward in jumps: the Pilgrims would have rejected the beliefs of the Inquisition; and the Christians of the Inquisition would have rejected the beliefs of the Christians before Constantine; and it is not clear how any of them would have felt about the Christian teachings before the destruction of Jerusalem, because the ideological tensions between the early Apostles and Paul are not completely understood today. On top of that, as conservative as the early Christians might appear today, they were quite liberal when compared to their Pagan neighbors around the Mediterranean.* Dostoyevsky pointedly lampoons these inconsistencies in *The Brothers Karamazov*: Jesus returns during the Inquisition, and the Church authorities sentence him to death. The Grand Inquisitor then explains to Jesus where he is wrong.

If that sounds ludicrous, there are powerful people in religion and politics today who loudly and frequently, but dishonestly, boast of their Christianity. Their hypocrisy is easy to identify: they studiously avoid any teachings of Jesus that address Christian obligations to the weak and the poor and ignore these humane concepts in their actions, public statements, and policy proposals.

They also demonstrate the problems with 'right-wing Christians': Jesus taught a peaceful doctrine of inclusion, tolerance, and equality. Given that the right-wing hierarchy is built on *ex*clusion, *in*tolerance, and *in*equality, it is not clear how right-wing Christians can be Christian at all. So right-wing Christians are often necessarily hypocritical because they are literally trying to serve two masters, Jesus and the authoritarian leader, roughly correlating with Jesus's teachings about 'God and Mammon.' The right-wing Christians cannot see this, of course; they are blinded by our ten thousand years of inherited oppression under the atrox.

We can see a similar conservative-to-liberal shift in politics. Consider that in the United States, many Republicans express their admiration for President Kennedy. While he was President, however, many conservatives loathed him. The fact is, Kennedy was liberal for the 1960s, but his views have become conservative over the ensuing sixty years.

---

* It was the early Christians who began replacing the scroll with the codex/book. Part of that was because the book was more portable, which made it available for sharing and bringing to meetings, which were egalitarian activities. Books were also easier to hide from the authorities. One of the reasons, however, was that the early Christians saw themselves as the moderns, rejecting the conservatism of both Rome and traditional Jews.

Epilogue

A salient example is the contemporary Republicans who proudly boast that they belong to the party of Abraham Lincoln. Lincoln, however, represented the liberal voices of his time, as Republicans were originally the liberals and Democrats were the conservatives. That shift gives us a grating contradiction today: as we noted above, many of the Republicans who boast of their association with Lincoln simultaneously work to block African Americans from voting and to suppress them in other ways. In essence, they work to return African Americans to political inequality and force them back toward economic servitude.

Communism also illustrates the problem of left-right vs. liberal-conservative. In most Western countries, the communist is liberal and the capitalist is conservative. In Russia, China, and other countries, today's communist may be the conservative and the capitalist the liberal.

So conservative and liberal are not a set of core ideas, but moving targets and fluid political positions; because, of course, with time some of what is new and suspect today will become old and trusted tomorrow. And as progress accelerates, liberal and conservative will become even more unstable and inconsistent. In comparison, however, the egalitarian ideals of the left, and the hierarchical oppression of the right, are constant and durable. We either think for ourselves or we submit to someone who thinks for us.

These distinctions take us back to an earlier problem, that of the so-called 'left-wing authoritarians.' The phrase is an oxymoron; to be left-wing is, by definition, to be anti-authoritarian. As for 'right-wing authoritarians,' that is a redundancy. For the same reason, there cannot be right-wing egalitarians; and 'left-wing egalitarians' is yet another redundancy.

There can, however, be liberal or conservative authoritarians and liberal or conservative egalitarians. Fascists are conservative authoritarians but modern communists can be liberal authoritarians.* Liberal egalitarians, are simply those who accept ideas from almost anyone. Conservative egalitarians might represent something like the Dutch: they might be personally conservative and resistant to change but tolerant of those who think otherwise. And the fully egalitarian conservative might be a Burkean: when Edmund Burke first proposed conservatism, he did not describe a fierce reactionary recalcitrance. Instead, he was advising people to take a pragmatic, skeptical, test-it-first approach to new political ideas.

---

* *Das Kapital* was published in the late nineteenth century, and the October Revolution was in 1917, both over a century ago. So in Russia or China, communism is the way things have been done and is conservative. In the United States, communism would be a significant change and so it is liberal.

The central conclusion, however, is that within modern democracies—which means within the modern world itself—there is no place for the right. There is no place for someone who defers to others, who blindly follows a more powerful leader and who then compels others to follow as well. The modern world is based on equality, inclusion, and independence of thought. Without those, progress and modernity itself disappear.

As for the liberal authoritarians, we find that they are really not all that different from the conservative authoritarians. If we view liberal vs. conservative as a bell curve, what we find is that the tails strongly resemble one another. Authoritarianism trumps all policy preferences. To adapt from John M. Barry, "When you mix change with authoritarianism, you get authoritarianism." Which should be no great surprise; the point of authoritarianism is that no one thinks but the authoritarian leader.

Liberal and conservative right-wingers only disagree about which authority will be blindly followed. In effect, they are no different from the soldiers of France fighting the soldiers of England. In their struggles from Hastings to Waterloo, both comprised authoritarian personalities following an authoritarian ruler. They simply fought over which side wins; in earlier times of chronic shortage, that really meant which side survives. And to our point here, neither the historical French nor English were interested in dialogue, fairness, or progress. That is why until recently, there was very little dialogue, fairness, or progress. At the political extremes, adherents of either position tend to be inflexible, intolerant, militant, and in our key diagnostic, humorless.*

Radicals on the left and right both pursue similar tactics and goals. Both engage in clever sophistry in an attempt to oppress, embarrass, and coerce the other. They both insist that their freedom of speech permits them to gag the other. They argue that a 'fair' government should crush the rights of the other. They rationalize that democratic inclusion should limit, or even exclude, the other. Both use modern protections as convenient paths to eliminating modernity itself. It gives a new insight to the term 'polemic.'

How should we respond to the atrox and the atrocino? That, perhaps, is our mistake; we focus on the authoritarian leader. The authoritarian is typically too far gone, either genetically, culturally, or habitually; he is lost in his psychopathy and narcissism. He may be the initiator of our problems, but he is not the problem itself.

---

* In this metaphor, the 'left' wing oddly ends up in the middle of the liberal-conservative bell curve. This is not surprising: if the left is maximally, or at least optimally, inclusive, then it will embrace the middle and much of the two tails. The left wing also sits there with the 'middle' class morality of cooperation and accountability.

We are. In current politics, it is emerging that about one-third of the population are inflexible, right-wing conservatives who fight change and, when given the proper authoritarian figure, will suddenly contradict everything they said they previously stood for. They follow their demagogue irrespective of obvious hypocrisies, lies, and betrayals from the leader they support. Given that, we must suspect that about one-third of the population are right-wing liberals, those who assertively follow a demagogue who demands some change which counters the right-wing conservatives. They also blindly follow their leader and ignore contradiction, dishonesty, and dissimulation.

We must focus our energies on both sets of authoritarian followers, liberal and conservative. They are the key to creating equality and progress; they are key to healing our world because they are the part that is trapped. Although we probably cannot change the fully genetic psychopathy of the atrox or the atrocino, there is still humanity in their followers. If we can reach that humanity, if we can recover the innate open-mindedness and logic that is inherent to all healthy people, then they will become allies, participants, and contributors in progress. And with that, if they change, then the atrox and the atrocino become much less important, because they lose their power.

But we have to be savvy, even Machiavellian about how we deal with the portions of our world who are entrenched. Attacking them only drives them to dig deeper, which serves the atrox. We have noted that the atrox is a manifestation of pure evil. One of the historical manifestations of evil is that it sows discord and confusion. It is right there in Cain and Abel but also in the Tower of Babel. When we begin fighting, we all become even more authoritarian and more entrenched. And so the anti-authoritarian response cannot be the same as the authoritarian response.

We noted that the Marshall Plan was arguably the high point of civilization. In that response, we stopped attacking our enemies, and we healed them, elevated them, respected them, and included them. It turned out to be an accelerant poured on the dimly glowing embers of the modern world. It was the conterintuitive response, but it succeeded wildly.

This is why the left vs. liberal and right vs. conservative distinctions are so important. Our liberal leaders, by and large, are not leftists; they, like the conservative leaders, too often pursue confrontation and calumny.[*] If we are to

---

[*] By and large, I have avoided naming contemporary figures in this book, but one name stands out at this point: U.S. Senator Bernie Sanders. It is ironic that in a country where so many insist that the United States is a Christian nation, but then ignore the central concepts of Christianity, that perhaps the most 'Christian' of our leaders—i.e, the person who pursues humanity, peace and reconciliation—is ethnically Jewish and often accused of being an atheist.

pursue equality and inclusion, then we need to *practice* equality and inclusion. We need to attempt a peacetime Marshall Plan with our political enemies.

The solution is easy in concept: listen, include, be patient. But it is much harder in application. If we are to rehabilitate humanity from our millennia of physical, verbal, sexual, and intellectual abuse, then we are going to have to turn for help to the people we ridiculed at the beginning of Chapter III: psychiatrists, psychologists, and their allies. They have experience in helping the authoritarian personality recover. They must be the ones to teach the rest of us how to heal one another. But we must be prepared for a lot of work, because it will take a long time to change these light bulbs.

With that insight comes another important caveat. Both liberal and conservative authoritarians, absorbed with their narcissism, wish to sit off in some power center, direct the rest of us to implement the solution, and then boast that this is progress. That is an inadequate strategy. People are animals from small tribes; not surprisingly, we best help each other one-on-one or in small groups. As we noted, it is the atrox who counts only the discounted lives. At the head of a column, or in the front of the cheering crowd, there is no meaningful, lasting human commitment; there are no humane bindings. We only really change another person at the personal level and with a personal commitment.

• • •

When students today recite the Gettysburg Address, few of them are aware that it was a lightning rod when Lincoln delivered it. His critics accused him of attempting a political sleight of hand: by stating, "a new nation, conceived in Liberty, and dedicated to the proposition that all men are created equal," he was not only rejecting slavery, he was also arguing that the Declaration of Independence was our central document, not the Constitution. This is because at that time the Constitution did not guarantee equality.[5]

The South did not want equality; that was the cause of the war. The many northerners whose wealth depended on southern cotton didn't want equality. None of the rapacious nineteenth-century commercial and industrial barons who exploited their workers wanted equality. And so, as we have seen, the powerful used the law to circumvent the purpose of the law: they argued that we are not a nation of equals.

As the atrocino works to exploit us, he will often enlist fundamentalist arguments; he will argue the text, the rules, the law. He invokes the fundamental in order to distract us from the foundation. He cites the law to avoid the values and the goals which the law was designed to protect, the benefits which make the law necessary. The preceding paragraph presents the problem well: What is a democracy if not a nation of equals? But the law does not always protect equality, nor prevent inequality.

Similarly, consider 'checks and balances.' The Founders wrote in a number of checks and balances in the Constitution in order to restrain a potential atrox from grabbing too much power. But beyond the problems they foresaw, they wrote no Constitutional guarantee that there should *be* checks and balances. So what happens when the checks and balances are violated in a way that the Founders did not anticipate? What happens when a Senate leader abuses his position as a check on the President, to ensure that balance and fairness are eliminated? This nation was specifically designed to prevent anyone from holding the kind of power that King George had. Should the courts rule only on the law while ignoring the central concepts and values that made the laws necessary?

There are other examples. But we must remember that it is the bureaucracy which runs on disembodied rules, as do the hierarchy, the military, the theocracy, the machine…and the psychopath. Simple predators, from the virus to the shark, also follow mindless rules. But for humans, we travel in ruts, not on rails; we do not have to follow blind rules. Instead we pursue morals, values, and goals. These higher goals must always overrule the rules.

Strict legal interpretation should not be used to circumvent the reason for our laws.

Through the Emancipation Proclamation, Lincoln furthered the cause of equality even though the Constitution at that time did not guarantee it. Several Amendments addressed that problem; perhaps the most important was the Fourteenth Amendment, guaranteeing equal protection under the law. It was written to protect the freed slaves but was quickly commandeered by the wealthy and their allies on the federal bench to protect corporations.

The large corporation is toxic. It has no loyalty to any person, nation, nor virtue: it will sacrifice people within and without the organization, casually discarding not just their careers, their health, and their homes, but also their lives; it will drain the assets and resources of the country that fostered and nurtured it, rapaciously exploiting all legal protections, then sell out the nation's secrets and security, spend its profits undermining the order of the larger society, and then flee to another country; and there is no evil it will not pursue for sufficient profit. Like all soulless systems, the corporation has no core values. Any benefit it creates is a lucky side effect of greed.

All groups have faced threats since the beginning of life. Among those we face today, however, one of the most severe is the large corporation. From the Fourteenth Amendment and into today, the corporation has argued it is a person, and the authoritarian personalities throughout our government have increasingly agreed, handing more and more of the henhouse to the fox.

There are good reasons that the corporation should be entitled to certain protections, particularly property rights and equal standing before the court. But they do not remotely resemble citizens. Their loyalties are no different than foreign nationals, particularly those from hostile countries. Foreign nationals may not vote, and neither may the corporation, for the same reasons: they have no loyalty to the country. Foreign nationals are prohibited from participating or interfering in our government, and the corporation should be likewise constrained.

If this nation is to survive, it is imperative that we construct a separation of corporation and state.*

• • •

Economics has long been called 'the dismal science.' I question whether it is truly a science. Science assumes that reality—and therefore Truth—is universally consistent and is valid at all times and to all observers.

When we consider economics from that viewpoint, we can immediately see problems. Sure, we all need food, clothing, shelter; those are universally true; they are amenable to scientific analysis. But what equations are there for calculating value beyond that? The truly important things in one person's life may not be remotely important to the next person. Once we get beyond a few basics, once we leave the animal-like needs of the neolithic hunter and step into the abundance of choices inherent in modernity, then scientific, universal truth tends to dissipate. That may seem minor, but I argue that it is central.

I suggest that economics isn't. The word 'economics' comes from the Greek οἶκος (*oikos*, 'house,' from which we also get 'ecology') and νόμος (*nomos*, 'rule'). Taken together, they mean 'the management of the home.' It does not mean, as we might assume, the management of the business, of the marketplace, nor ironically, even the management of the economy. Economics isn't.

When the businesser speaks of economics, she is referring to the accumulation of hard cash, or assets which produce it and/or which are fungible with it. That isn't the management of the home: no good homemaker only watches the budget. But that is what the 'good' corporation does, not only

---

* This has been proposed as a potential 28th Amendment: https://www.change.org/p/support-a-28th-amendment-for-the-separation-of-corporation-and-state.

in managing business, but also in attempts to manage government and the whole world. Which is another example of the fatal flaw in the corporation. We started this chapter looking at corporate sappers who wish to turn the United States into a kleptoplutocracy and to force us to submit to their economic bondage and conform to their ideological ambitions. The corporation has no other view of the world beyond money, and the atrocino has no view of humanity beyond the control and dominance money commands.

Next, no parent raises her children by calculating cost vs. earnings. Most children eventually produce an ROI, but it is paid to the next generation and to the community as a whole. The parent gets little of it. Pursuing an expenditure with no clear, self-serving profit flies in the face of standard business practices; but raising children is exactly that sort of 'poor' investment. Even staying within a budget isn't paramount for the family. The good parent will sacrifice everything and go into ruinous debt to advance, protect, or save the life of even one of her children. This is another decision with no traditional ROI. The same applies to many family decisions.

True economics, *eueconomics*, the management of the home—and by extension, the management of the community and the nation—flies in the face of commercial economics. The things that are of the highest importance to normal, healthy people are deliberately excluded from traditional economics. Traditional economics serves the atrocino's narcissism, greed, and dysfunctional priorities. From Alexander to Hitler to the corporation, traditional economics serves the worst of humanity, it destroys, parasitizes, and otherwise undermines eueconomics.

I propose that there are at least three non-fungible axes in the management of the home and of life. The first is material assets: money and items exchangeable with it. Second are aesthetic experiences, activities which bring us 'enjoyment', a completely ephemeral and individual product. Finally there are salvational strategies, those things which serve some deity and which bring hope of an afterlife. I am not necessarily advocating the salvational—nor could I, there is poor agreement among the religious about its characteristics and even its existence—I am merely considering how people invest/divest their money and time in ways that escape traditional economic analysis.

The first economic axis is the bio-financial; it is the value of activities and products which, at least at their foundation, served survival and reproduction. Economists and biologists often use the same mathematical, statistical, and game-theoretical models for these interactions. It is tempting to correlate this with traditional economics, with the economics of the corporation, but as we have seen that would be an error. The homemaker and the CEO do not focus on the same things and for reasons noted above in Chapter IX: the ROI curve is too long, and the benefits of biological strategies may be too diffusely distributed for the traditional investor to pursue them. On this first axis, resources are not only acquired; they are also exchanged and invested, which are typically not possible on the other two axes. But if one were to propose some exchange and investment value on the other two axes, the relationships would escape any hard analysis and would therefore, again, exceed science.

The second, the aesthetic axis, is the attempt to derive enjoyment from life. The economist can assign a price to such things based on what the average person might pay for them, but the norms and trends go well wide of anything resembling science or universality. For some people, modern art is a waste of canvas, wood, and paint, while others will give fortunes—and occasionally, even their lives—acquiring or protecting important works. I myself have traveled to France many times, in part for the cuisine; but I have at least one friend who complains that French cooking is inedible. I have also known people who spend a great deal of money traveling abroad to attend the opera, while other friends would pay good money to *avoid* the opera. That one is particularly telling, that the same experience can have both a positive and negative value. This may even be true within the same observer, depending on her mood or other conditions: a glass of wine might be delightful on a Saturday night and repulsive on a Monday morning when one is focused on goals and deadlines. Likewise, a week in solitary confinement is an extreme punishment for the prisoner, but the constantly interrupted scholar might find it a delightful holiday. As for that, the concept of extreme aesthetic luxury for the scholar—and perhaps even their idea of Paradise—might be the minimalist entertainment of a few books, some paper, and pencils. The cost of these few items is negligible compared to the joy they provide the scholar; the ROI is incalculable. Even if the scholar produces Nobel-caliber work, the monetary value is often incalculable, as the ideas simply float out into the intellectual sphere with no clear profit.

And in all of the preceding considerations of aesthetic value, once consumed, an experience has absolutely no monetary value nor any clear return on investment to any consumer. Where is the science in these things? Where is a universal economic valuation? The economist can certainly calculate production costs and what the enthusiastic consumer might pay for such things, but there is no consistent monetary value for many types of experiences. The aesthetic aspect of life is not consistently fungible with the material.

The third, salvational axis is an attempt to reach some definition of godly approval. People such as Augustine of Hippo, Thomas à Beckett, and Katherine Drexel gave up their fortunes in pursuit of Paradise. Many other people, from religious martyrs to radical terrorists, even give their lives in the same pursuit. Further confusing the picture, there are a wide range of valuations of Paradise: we have seen conquerors who would slaughter vast numbers in pursuing religious zeal; the aforementioned who give all of their possessions or their lives; those who simply tithe; and finally, there are religious adherents who believe that salvation is free and universal. Such varied valuations, from the price of millions of lives, down to free and universal access, completely escape economic analysis. And either way, economics is impotent here. We can't know the real cost, because we can't verify who receives godly approval, we can't know who gets to Paradise. We can't even prove Paradise exists. So we certainly can't agree to any value of it.

The salvational axis is also non-fungible with the other two. Some sacrifice the entire material axis for salvation, while others deny themselves enjoyment and aesthetics (anti-aesthetic ascetics, as it were). Once again, the economist can identify no clear profit nor investment potential in the salvational axis.

The point to all of this is that economic calculations are useful to the material producer, but they are of widely inconsistent utility to the aesthete, and of no value whatsoever to the believer. All of these taken together show traditional economics is of limited help for making the intensely personal decisions, and for normal people, the most important decisions, about how to manage our homes, our communities, and our lives.

There is no place in the corporate spreadsheet for anything but money and those items which are fungible with money. The atrocino nevertheless coerces us to map all three axes onto the first axis alone. This is not surprising; money is not just his power, it is his pleasure and his religion. And so he works to convert the meaning of home, family, and community into a dominated financial hierarchy conveniently compressed beneath him. It reflects the unification delusion.

The atrox killed us and turned us into slaves and minions to serve his narcissism. The atrocino attempts to squeeze us back into that historical subjugation, to serve him, his power, his ideology, and his narcissism. Traditional economics serves the king.

The Six Branches of Government

We are taught in school that the Founders established three branches of the federal government: the executive (the President); the legislative (Congress); and the judiciary (the courts, particularly the Supreme Court).

As the federal government grew, two things happened, and two unofficial branches of the government emerged. The first was the bureaucracy, which we can think of as the fourth branch of the government. This component was small for a long time; during the Civil War, Lincoln's presidential staff comprised two secretaries, and visitors could drop in to visit with him without an appointment. Over the course of the twentieth century, however, the federal workforce grew rapidly, particularly with the expansion of the military in WWI and WWII. After WWII, our economy expanded dramatically, and several additional things happened: We retained a large standing military to deal with the Cold War; We began investing in social welfare; And we needed accounting and enforcement to administer it all.

The problem is, the resultant bureaucracy becomes a power unto itself, and one that can, in some ways, exceed all other branches. One example is the military and the insatiable rapacity of the Pentagon, as manifested in the Military-Industrial Complex; by omitting the role of Congress in it, Eisenhower tacitly admitted that it was already too large. A very different example is the IRS, which can disregard basic Constitutional protections, seize our property without due process, and has wide latitude to invade our privacy in ways that the rest of government may not. Then there is the intelligence apparatus, which can become toxic: J. Edgar Hoover knew the darkest secret of every major elected official, and he did not hesitate to threaten them with releasing those secrets. Through mechanisms like these and others, the federal bureaucracy slowly elbowed up to the table with the other three branches of government.

The second faction to emerge, the fifth branch of government, is the corporation, along with its ubiquitous lobbyists.* As the U.S. government expanded, and as corporate wealth multiplied over much of the same period, ruthless business interests have increasingly sought to gain wealth in the same way conquerors did: by plundering the rest of us. Increasingly, kleptoplutocrats have perverted our government to increase their profits. As we have seen, the corporation pursues this strategy with little or no concern for the health of the citizen, nor the nation; just as with the conqueror, the corporation will freely sacrifice our lives for profit and narcissism.

---

* It is a myth that Ulysses S. Grant coined the word 'lobbyist'. Hiring people to represent the powerful may be new, but self-serving interests have sought to influence power since the first king emerged at the stirrings of civilization.

Epilogue

There are two general themes to this book. The first is a historical and biological theory about why we blindly follow demagogues and their ideologies; why, given our ability for logic and analysis, do we look at slick con-men, and their various dogmata, and turn off our intellectual powers?

The second theme is that these men, and the prejudices we inherit from them, have held us back for almost all of civilization. Once we get rid of the bullies, however, once we topple the political, ideological, and economic strongmen, we gain peace and prosperity. Once we have those two, then innovation and genius spontaneously emerge. That, I would argue, is what our government was trying to do: to stop the bullies. Freedom is the freedom from oppression and suppression. It is the freedom to try new ideas, and to experiment.

The resultant innovation and genius, however, have forced governments around the world to foster economic and intellectual competitiveness. Because progress was relatively slow in 1776, the U.S. Founders barely understood this aspect. They implemented intellectual property laws, but little beyond those. And so our government contains no fundamental guarantees for aspects of government that are essential for progress and competitiveness: education, health, general prosperity, and leisure. And so the atrocino and his authoritarian followers argue loudly that these should be done away with.

They argue against modernity. They fatuously argue for the medieval and the feudal, and for national collapse.

So the world faces new threats to modernity, home-grown threats. Hitler has morphed, he has become the narcissist atop the corporation and the bureaucracy. He is prising open the gates and has thrust a foot into the citadel of human cooperation and advancement. We do not see that we are in danger of losing everything we care for: our communities, our friends, and most of all, our children.

There are no effective checks and balances against the two more recent branches of the federal government. We have no Constitutional protections from these two, from the powerful bureaucracies and lobbies, and from the evil that controls them.

Or at least there hasn't been.

I propose that there is a sixth branch of government. In reality, it is really the first branch: We, the People.* We have always been here, of course, but our ability to express ourselves in ongoing ways is only beginning. Powerful, elite

---

* Note that this is from the Declaration of Independence, not the Constitution. Once again, our laws should serve our ideals. When those priorities are reversed, our system of justice slides toward an anempathic and exploitative machine, and something that is easier for the atrocino to abuse.

forces are trying to force us backward toward a non-democratic state, one where power, wealth, and prerogative are concentrated into fewer and fewer hands. In order to work unopposed in their efforts to dismantle our protections, they neutralize dissent through distraction and provocation. Currently, the national dialogue is one dominated by anger, which benefits the authoritarian leader. We must stop playing ideological football and start working toward pragmatic, inclusive solutions.

It is not enough for us to express outrage, to stand back, and complain. Our attentiveness and engagement are the only escape from the rapidly-tightening shackles. It is critical that the first branch of government step up and assert our power; we must roll up our sleeves and get to work. Because when all of the other checks and balances begin to fail, then we must be the final check. Only we can restore balance.

We are the last feedback in the system.

Thank you for reading this,
I hope you have found it worth your time.
If so, please consider writing a review at your
favorite on-line book retailers.

—Joseph N. Abraham MD

NOTES:

EPIGRAPH

1. H. Munro & Nora K. Chadwick, *The Growth of Literature*, vol. I (Cambridge, 2010), xix.

2. W. H. Auden, *Collected Poems*, ed. Edward Mendelson (Modern Library, 2007), xxx.

3. *Troilus and Criseyde*.

PROLOGUE: FANTASY AND HORROR

1. Jim Steinman and Dean Pitchford, "Holding Out for a Hero," Columbia Music, 1984.

2. "The Massacre at My Lai," *Life* 67, no. 23, December 5, 1969.

3. Hannah Arendt, *Eichmann in Jerusalem: A Report on the Banality of Evil* (Penguin, 1963).

4. Charles Darwin, *The Descent of Man and Selection in Relation to Sex* (Murray, 1888).

5. Joseph N. Abraham, "*La Saboteuse*: An ecological theory of sexual dimorphism in animals," *Acta Biotheoretica* 46, no. 1 (1998): 23-35.

CHAPTER ONE: KINGS

1. Eugen Weber, "The Sixteenth Flora Levy Lecture in the Humanities: Some Ups and Downs of History," in *Explorations: The Twentieth Century*, vol. X, 2004. https://explorations20th.wordpress.com/2012/10/04/the-sixteenth-flora-levy-lecture-in-the-humanities-some-ups-and-downs-of-history/ Later published as: E. Weber, "The Ups and Downs of Honor," *The American Scholar* 68, no. 1 (Winter 1999): 79-91.

2. Terence Hanbury White, *The Once and Future King* (Penguin, 2011); John Ronald Reuel Tolkien, *The Lord of the Rings* (Houghton Mifflin Harcourt, 2012); Mario Puzo, *The Godfather* (Penguin, 2005); Brad Grey, David Chase, James Gandolfini, et al., *The Sopranos: The Complete Series*, HBO Home Video, 2008.

3. W. Harrison, *The Description of England. The Chronicles of England, Scotland and Ireland* (Henry Denham, 1587), 238.

Chapter 2: Conquerors

1. "Never think that war, no matter how necessary, nor how justified, is not a crime." Ernest Hemingway, "Foreword," *Treasury for the Free World*, ed. Ben Raeburn (Arco Publishing, 1945), xii.

2. Between 4,194,200 and 4,851,200 according to Gerald Reitlinger, *The Final Solution* (Sphere Books, 1961). Between 4,871,000 and 6,271,500 according to Norman Davies, *Europe: A History* (Harper Perennial, 1998).

3. Two million dead, one million unaccounted for. William L. Shirer, *The Rise and Fall of the Third Reich* (Random House, 1960). Or 3.9 million according to Boris Urlanis, *Wars and Population* (University Press of the Pacific, 2003).

4. Jose M. Ortiz, "The Revolutionary Flying Ambulance of Napoleon's Surgeon," *U.S. Army Medical Department Journal* (October–December 1998).

5. Étienne-Louis Malus de Mitry, *L'Agenda de Malus: souvenirs de l'expédition d'Egypte, 1798–1801* (Paris, 1892), 135. Quoted in Dwyer, Ibid.

6. Dwyer, Ibid.

7. F. Bernoyer, *Avec Bonaparte en Égypte et en Syrie, 1798–1800: dix-neuf lettres inédits* (Les Presses Françaises, 1976), 147. Quoted in Dwyer, Ibid.

8. Jacques-François Miot, *Mémoires pour servir à l'histoire des expéditions en Egypte et en Syrie pendant les années VI, VII et VIII de la République française* (Paris, 1814), 145. Quoted in Dwyer, Ibid.

9. P. Browning, *The Changing Nature of Warfare: The Development of Land Warfare from 1792 to 1945* (Cambridge University, 2002), 47. Quoted in Dwyer, "'It Still Makes Me Shudder,'" 383. Dwyer also notes several other historians who reject the horrors of Napoléon.

10. Report from César Berthier, SHAT, Armée de Naples, C-5, 4 (August 1806), 23. Quoted in Dwyer, "'It Still Makes Me Shudder.'"

11. M. de Tascher, *Notes de campagne, 1806–1813* (Châteauroux, 1932). Quoted in Dwyer, Ibid.

12. As one historian darkly quipped, "It was *Beja vu*." Observador Portugueze, *Historico e Politico de Lisboa*, November 27, 1807. English translation, *Quarterly Review* 4, no. 7 (Murray, August & November 1810): 20.

13. I. Fletcher, *The Lines of Torres Vedras 1809–11* (Osprey Publishing, 2012), 25.

14. Nuno Valério, coord., 'Quadro 2A—População portuguesa em diversos períodos,' *Estatísticas Históricas Portuguesas*, vol. I (Instituto Nacional de Estatística, 2001), 31. I used the change in population between 1776 and 1811.

15. A. Zamoyski, *Moscow 1812: Napoléon's Fatal March* (Harper Collins, 2005).

16. Lavaux François, *Mémoires de campagnes*, 159. Quoted in Dwyer, "'It Still Makes Me Shudder.'"

17. An estimated 38 percent of the French males born between 1790 and 1795 died in the Napoléonic Wars. David Gates, *The Napoleonic Wars 1803–1815* (Random House, 2011).

18. *The Library of History Vol. VIII, Diodorus Siculus*, Loeb Classical Library Edition (Harvard, 1963).

19. Xenophon, *Annabasis*, Book II, XXIV.

20. Xerxes, "who aimed at nothing less than the total extirpation of the Greeks." Rollin, C. *The Ancient History of the Egyptians, Carthaginians, Assyrians, Babylonians, Medes and Persians, Macedonians and Grecians*, vol. 1 (Philadelphia: W.W. Woodward, 1879).

21. Diodorus, XVII: 70-71 and Curtius, v. 20, 22 say that Alexander delivered Persepolis to his soldiers to pillage and that he ordered a general massacre of the inhabitants. Plutarch, XXXVII "a terrible slaughter was made of all the prisoners. A letter written by Alexander himself is still extant, in which he orders that they should all be put to the sword."

22. Ibid.

23. Victor D. Hanson, *Wars of the Ancient Greeks* (Harper Perennial, 1999).

24. This number, however, disagrees with the size of the Achaemenid Empire, three footnotes up. Michael Grant, *The Hellenistic Greeks: From Alexander to Cleopatra* (Weidenfeld & Nicolson, 1990).

25. Philip changed Cleopatra's name to Eurydice, which was the name of his mother, to legitimize her as queen. John Williams, *The Life and Actions of Alexander the Great* (J. & J. Harper, 1830).

26. "This is the man who was preparing to cross from Europe to Asia, and has been overthrown in passing from one couch to another." Plutarch, IX.

27. Plutarch, *Life of Alexander*, 9 and 10 says that she was cruelly put to death by Olympias during Alexander's absence. Justin, ix. 7; xi. 2 states that Olympias first slew her daughter on her mother's bosom and then had Eurydice hanged; while Alexander ordered the death of Caranus, the infant son of Philip and Eurydice. Pausanias, viii. 7 says that Olympias caused Cleopatra and her infant son to be roasted on a brazen vessel. Cf. Aelian, *Varia Historia*, xiii. 35.

28. "She was exacting from him a heavy house-rent for the ten months," (The Greeks used the lunar calendar, and so pregnancy was calculated as ten months). Arrian, *Anabasis*, 7.12.6. E. J. Chinnock, transl., *The Anabasis of Alexander, or, The Affairs and Conquests of Alexander the Great* (Hodder and Stoughton, 1884). Original Source, George Grote, *History of Greece*, 69; Plutarch, *Life of Alexander*, 25-39; Arrian, *Anabasis*, vii. 12, 12. "He was wont to say, that his mother exacted from him a heavy house-rent for his domicile of ten months."

29. From the Behistun Inscription. Kenneth Dover, *The Greeks* (University of Texas, 1995).

30. William Woodthorpe Tarn, *Alexander the Great*, Vol. 1 (Cambridge University, 2003).

31. "He afterwards captured Bessus and tore him asunder, by bending down the tops of trees and tying different parts of his body to each, and then letting them spring up again so that each tore off the limb to which it was attached. Alexander now had the corpse of Darius adorned as became a prince." Plutarch, *Life of Alexander*, xliii. Alternately, Quintus Curtius Rufus says Bessus was crucified in the place where Darius III had been killed, and Arrian states that he was tortured and then decapitated at Ecbatana.

32. Ibid.

33. Appian, *Gallic Wars*, 4.1.

34. Caesar, *Commentaries on the Gallic Wars*, 4.15 and 29.

35. Ibid., 1.12, 1.53, 2.10

36. Appian, *Gallic Wars*, 1.

37. Plutarch, *Caesar*, 22 .

38. Ibid., 15. Also see Pliny, *Natural History*, Book VII, chapter XXV.

39. Estimated population of Gaul in AD 14, at the death of Augustus; adding back in the two million victims and slaves gives eight million. Or 5.75 million: C. McEvedy and R. Jones, *Atlas of World Population History* (Penguin, 1978); 5.8 million: Bruce Frier, "Demography," In *The Cambridge Ancient History: Late Antiquity, Empire and Successors, AD 425-600*, Vol. 14 (Cambridge University Press, 2000).

40. Appian, *Gallic Wars*. 2

41. Exodus 32:27-28

42. Numbers 31:17-18.

43. Joshua 8.

44. Joshua 10, 11.

45. 1 Samuel 18:27.

46. In his analysis of 1 Samuel 27:11, Ellicott concludes that these tribes were allies; but it is nevertheless an assumption. Charles J. Ellicott, *Ellicott's Commentary on the Whole Bible* (Whipf and Stock, 2014).

47. 1 Samuel 27:8-9

48. 2 Samuel 1:15

49. Homer, *The Odyssey*, Book XXII, Samuel Butler, transl. (Longmans, Green, And Co., 1900).

Notes for Chapter 2: Conquerors

50. Thucydides, *History*, 1.126.
51. Ibid., 5.89.
52. Ibid., 5.116.
53. Ibid., 2.27 and 4.57.
54. Ibid., 3:36-50.
55. Ibid., 1.114
56. Ibid., 7.29
57. Xenophon, *Hellenica*, 2.1.30-31.
58. Plutarch, *Lycurgus* 13.5-6, "This is a fine tuition-fee which thou art getting from the Thebans, for teaching them how to fight, when they did not wish to do it, and did not know how." Thanks to Josiah Ober and Mark Pyzyk for their help in identifying the original quote and source.
59. 2 Isocrates iv and xii, *passim*.
60. Thucydides, *History*, 4.80.
61. R. G. Chase, *Ancient Hellenistic and Roman Amphitheatres, Stadiums and Theatres: The Way They Look Now* (Peter E Randall, 2002).
62. There are well-known plates from François Mazois showing schematics of the reliefs. Mazois, François, *Les Ruines de Pompéi* (Librairie de Firmin Didots Frères, 1838).
63. Anthony Everitt, *Cicero: The Life and Times of Rome's Greatest Politician* (Random House, 2003).
64. To his credit, his army died fighting, and Catiline's body was found in the vanguard.
65. Everitt, *Cicero*.
66. Sallust, *The Jugurthine War*, 91.
67. Livy, *The History of Rome*, 28.20.
68. Ibid., 28.22.
69. Tacitus, *Histories*, 3.33.1.
70. Josephus, *The Wars of the Jews*, 6.401-4.
71. Ibid., 6.420.
72. 300,000 according to T. Wilhelm, *A Military Dictionary and Gazetteer* (L.R. Hamersly & Company, 1881); 400,000 according to *Putnam's Home Cyclopedia* (G.P. Putnam & Co., 1852).
73. Appian, *The Mithridatic Wars*, 12:58.
74. Plutarch, *Life of Lucullus*, 11:6.

75. Lewis Naphtali, *Roman Civilization*, vol. 2, *The Roman Empire* (Columbia University Press, 1990).

76. Edward Gibbon, *The Decline and Fall of the Roman Empire*, vol. 2 (Viking Press, 1952).

77. Ibid., vol 1.

78. Herodian, 4.9.1-4.9.8

79. Thomas Paine, *The Age of Reason*, ch. VIII.

80. A. Cameron and S. Hall, eds., *Eusebius' Life of Constantine* (Clarendon Press, 1999).

81. William Manchester, *A World Lit Only by Fire: The Medieval Mind and the Renaissance-Portrait of an Age* (Back Bay Books, 2009).

82. Aurelius Victor, *Epitome de Caesaribus*, 41.12. Another tradition has her stripped naked, bound in the mountains, and exposed to wild animals. John Chrysostom, in *Ep. ad Phil. Comm.*, 4.15.5 (Migne, PG LXII, 295).

83. Ammianus Marcellinus, *Roman Antiquities* 19:12:9-16.

84. C. G. Herbermann, *The Catholic Encyclopedia: An International Work of Reference on the Constitution, Doctrine, Discipline, and History of the Catholic Church*, vol. 4 (The Encyclopedia Press, 1913).

85. Henry Charles Lea, *A History of the Inquisition of the Middle Ages*, vol. 1 (Macmillan, 1906); D. C. Parquin, *Souvenirs de commandant Parquin* (Paris, 2003). Quoted in Dwyer, "'It Still Makes Me Shudder.'"

86. Manchester, *A World Lit Only by Fire*.

87. Robert J. Knech, *The French Religious Wars, 1562–1598* (Routledge, 2014).

88. Except where noted, this section on the Crusades comes from Amin Maalouf, *The Crusades through Arab Eyes*, Random House, 1984.

89. Ibid., 39.

90. Thomas Asbridge, *The First Crusade: A New History* (Free Press, 2005).

91. J. M. Robertson, *A Short History of Christianity*, no. 24 (Watts & Company, 1902).

92. Angus Maddison, *The World Economy: Historical Statistics, Statistical Appendix* (OECD Publishing, 2007).

93. Ferdinand Mount, *The Tears of the Rajas: Mutiny, Money and Marriage in India 1805-1905* (Simon and Schuster, 2015).

94. George Carter Stent, quoted in Peter Havholm, *Politics and Awe in Rudyard Kipling's Fiction* (Aldershot, Ashgate Publishing, 2008).

95. Mike Davis, *Late Victorian Holocausts: El Niño Gamines and the Making of the Third World* (Verso, 2002).

96. Donal Lowry, *The South African War Reappraised* (Manchester University Press, 2000).

97. J. H. Balme, *To Love One's Enemies: The Work and Life of Emily Hobhouse Compiled from Letters and Writings, Newspaper Cuttings and Official Documents* (Columbia University Press, 2012).

98. Ibid.

99. A.C. Doyle, *The War in South Africa: Its Cause and Conduct* (George Newnes, 1902).

100. Balme, *To Love One's Enemies*.

101. L. Ryan, "Settler Massacres on the Australian Colonial Frontier, 1836–1851," in Dwyer and Ryan, *Theatres of Violence*.

102. B. Madley, "Tactics of Nineteenth-Century Colonial Massacre: Tasmania, California and Beyond," in Dwyer and Ryan, *Theatres of Violence*.

103. Henry Saxelby Melville, *The History of the Island of Van Diemen's Land, from the Year 1824 to 1835 Inclusive* (Cambridge University, 2011).

104. D. L. Shelton, *Encyclopedia of Genocide and Crimes Against Humanity* (Macmillan, 2005).

105. M.E. Chamberlain, "The Alexandria Massacre of 11 June 1882 and the British Occupation of Egypt," *Middle Eastern Studies* 13, no. 1 (January 1977).

106. G. Behrman, *The Most Noble Adventure: The Marshall Plan and the Time When America Helped Save Europe* (Simon and Schuster, 2007).

107. John Mason, *History of the Pequot War, The Contemporary Accounts of Mason, Underhill, Vincent and Gardener* (Hellman-Taylor, 1897).

108. William Bradford, *Of Plymouth Plantation, 1620–1647* (Houghton Mifflin, 1912).

109. B. Madley, 'Tactics of Nineteenth-Century Colonial Massacre: Tasmania, California and Beyond,' in Dwyer, *Theatres of Violence*.

110. "Eye Witness," *San Francisco Bulletin*, Mar 13, 1860, quoted in John Alden Mason, *The Language of the Salinan Indians*, vol. 14 (University of California, 1918). "Eye Witness" was later identified as Bret Harte. George Stuart, *Bret Harte, Argonaut and Exile: Being an Account of the Life of the Celebrated American Humorist, Author of 'The Luck of Roaring Camp', 'Condensed Novels', 'The Heathen Chinee', 'Tales of the Argonauts', etc., etc.* (Houghton Mifflin, 1931).

111. A.L. Hurtado, *Indian Survival on the California Frontier*, vol. 35 (Yale University, 1988).

112. J. W. Schultz, *Blackfeet and Buffalo: Memories of Life Among the Indians* (University of Oklahoma, 1962).

113. B. Tovías, "A Blueprint for Massacre: The United States Army and the 1870 Blackfeet Massacre," in Dwyer and Ryan, *Theatres of Violence*.

114. Rob Harper, "Looking the Other Way: The Gnadenhutten Massacre and the Contextual Interpretation of Violence," *William and Mary Quarterly* 3 (2007): 64.

115. Derrick Jensen, *A Language Older Than Words* (Chelsea Green, 2004).

116. "Testimony of Robert Bent," *United States Congressional Serial Set*, Issue 1279, U.S. Government Printing Office, 1867.

117. Helen Hunt Jackson, *A Century of Dishonor: A Sketch of the United States Government's Dealings with Some of the Indian Tribes* (Roberts Brothers, 1885).

118. Edward Sylvester Ellis, *The Life of Kit Carson: Hunter, Trapper, Guide, Indian Agent, and Colonel USA* (New York Publishing Company, 1889).

119. D. Svaldi, *Sand Creek and the Rhetoric of Extermination: A Case Study in Indian-White Relations* (University Press of America, 1989); and S. Hoig, *The Sand Creek Massacre* (University of Oklahoma, 2013).

120. Bob Couttie, *Hang the Dogs: The True Tragic History of the Balangiga Massacre* (New Day Publishers, 2004).

121. Committee for the Review and Restoration of Honor for the No Gun Ri Victims, *No Gun Ri Incident Victim Review Report*, Government of the Republic of Korea, 2009.

122. Daisaku Ikeda, *Buddhism: The First Millennium* (Independent Publishers Group, 2009).

123. John S. Strong, *The Legend of King Aśoka: A Study and Translation of the Aśokāvadāna* (Motilal Banarsidass, 1989).

124. W. Geiger, ed., *The Mahāvamsa, or, The Great Chronicle of Ceylon*, vol. 63 (H. Frowde/Oxford University, 1912).

125. The critical word is an obscure term, *kitika*; see note in Strong, *The Legend*, 211, which draws on Franklin Edgerton, *Buddhist Hybrid Sanskrit Grammar and Dictionary*, vol. II, *Dictionary* (Yale, 1954).

126. Laurence Austine Waddell, *Historical Description of Ashoka's Hell, Report on the Excavations at Pātaliputra (Patna): The Palibothra of the Greeks* (Bengal Secretariat Press, 1903).

127. Strong, *The Legend*.

128. Ven. S. Dhammika, "Rock edict XIII," in *The Edicts of King Ashoka* (Buddhist Publication Society, 1993).

129. Strong, *The Legend*.

130. Beni Madhab Barua, *The Ajivikas* (University of Calcutta, 1920).

131. G.K. Nariman, *Literary History of Sanskrit Buddhism* (Indian Book Depot, 1923).

132. Strong, *The Legend*.

Notes for Chapter 2: Conquerors

133. Susan A. Niles, *The Shape of Inca History: Narrative and Architecture in an Andean Empire* (University of Iowa, 1999).

134. Kim MacQuarrie, *The Last Days of the Incas* (Simon and Schuster, 2008).

135. Pedro Sarmiento de Gamboa and Clements Robert Markham, *History of the Incas*, no. 22 (Courier Corporation, 1998).

136. Mark Cocker, *Rivers of Blood, Rivers of Gold: Europe's Conflict with Tribal Peoples* (Vintage, 1998).

137. John Hemming, *The Conquest of the Incas* (Macmillan, 1970).

138. Colin Clark, *Population Growth and Land Use* (Springer, 1977). Colin McEvedy and Richard Jones, *Atlas of World Population History* (Penguin, 1978), 152-56.

139. John Man, *Genghis Khan: Life, Death, and Resurrection* (Random House, 2010). To be fair, it is possible that the Mongols destroyed many households where the inhabitants escaped, leaving more people per household. Everything in this section makes that unlikely.

140. Weatherford, *Genghis Khan*, "conservative scholars place the number of dead from Genghis Khan's invasion of central Asia at 15 million within five years" noting that "even this more modest total…would require that each Mongol kill more than a hundred people." Others have also suggested that some of the numbers are exaggerated.

141. Donald R. Morris, *The Washing of the Spears: A History of the Rise of the Zulu Nation Under Shaka and Its Fall in the Zulu War of 1879* (Da Capo, 1998).

142. Elizabeth A. Eldredge, *The Creation of the Zulu Kingdom, 1815–1828: War, Shaka, and the Consolidation of Power* (Cambridge University, 2014).

143. Charles Rowden MacLean, "Loss of the Brig 'Mary' at Natal, with Early Recollections of that Settlement and among the Caffres," *The Nautical Magazine and Naval Chronicle* XXIV, no. 3 (March 1855).

144. Morris, *The Washing of the Spears*.

145. Candice Millard, *Hero of the Empire: The Boer War, a Daring Escape, and the Making of Winston Churchill* (Anchor, 2017).

146. Andrew Rice, *The Teeth May Smile but the Heart Does Not Forget: Murder and Memory in Uganda* (Picador, 2010); Bernard Tabaire, "The Press and Political Repression in Uganda: Back to the Future?" *Journal of Eastern African Studies* 1, no. 2 (2007); Alicia C. Decker, *In Idi Amin's Shadow: Women, Gender, and Militarism in Uganda* (Ohio University, 2014); Priscilla B. Hayner, *Unspeakable Truths: Confronting State Terror and Atrocity* (Routledge, 2010).

147. Barbara Demick, *Nothing to Envy: Ordinary Lives in North Korea* (Spiegel & Grau, 2009).

148. Although the course manager later prevaricated, saying the reported score was how Dear Leader had scored against par. The lie is certainly smaller in that expla-

nation, but still outrageous. Josh Sens, "The Real Story Behind One of the Most Fabled Rounds in Golf," *Golf,* Wednesday, June 1, 2016.

149. Cindy Boren, "Kim Jong-Il: A Sporting Life (with golf, bowling, soccer and basketball interests)," *Washington Post,* December 19, 2011.

150. Leo Hickman, "Kim Jong-Il: Ten Things You Never Knew," *The Guardian,* December 19, 2011.

151. David Chandler, *Voices from S-21: Terror and History in Pol Pot's Secret Prison* (University of California, 2000).

152. Elizabeth Becker, *When the War Was Over: Cambodia and the Khmer Rouge Revolution* (Public Affairs, 1998).

153. Frank Smith, *Interpretive Accounts of the Khmer Rouge Years: Personal Experience in Cambodian Peasant World View* (Center for Southeast Asian Studies, University of Wisconsin-Madison, 1989).

154. Alexander Laban Hinton, *Why did they kill?: Cambodia in the Shadow of Genocide,* vol. 11 (University of California, 2004).

155. Becker, *When the War was Over.*

156. Sydney Schanberg, "The Enigma of Khmer Rouge Purpose," *Saturday Review,* August 23, 1980. Quoted in Karl D. Jackson, ed., *Cambodia, 1975–1978: Rendezvous with Death* (Princeton, 2014).

157. Becker, *When the War was Over.*

158. Sterling Seagrave and Peggy Seagrave, *Gold Warriors: America's Secret Recovery of Yamashita's Gold* (Verso, 2003).

159. Caroline Elkins, *Imperial Reckoning: The Untold Story of Britain's Gulag in Kenya* (MacMillan, 2006).

160. Ibid., 366.

161. Ian Cobain, Owen Bowcott, and Richard Norton-Taylor, "Britain destroyed records of colonial crimes," *The Guardian,* April 17, 2012, 19.01 EDT. https://www.theguardian.com/uk/2012/apr/18/britain-destroyed-records-colonial-crimes.

162. Some scholars have begun using 'she' instead of 'he' for generic considerations, in part to rectify millennia of preferring the masculine. In this case, however, the substitution adds insight. If I may lapse into mild sexual stereotyping—or perhaps archetyping—the consideration of the individual and the particular is more associated with a feminine viewpoint, while the aggregate and generic tend to be more masculine and more like the conqueror.

163. Eugen Weber, "Antisemitism, Holocaust and Genocide," in *Studies in Contemporary Jewry: X: Reshaping the Past: Jewish History and the Historians,* vol. 10, ed. J. Frankel (Oxford University USA, 1994), 301.

164. R. I. Simon, *Bad Men Do What Good Men Dream: A Forensic Psychiatrist Illuminates the Darker Side of Human Behavior* (American Psychiatric Association, 2009).

CHAPTER 3: PSYCHOPATHS

1. James Fielder, *Slow Death* (Pinnacle Books, 2013), 47; Tom Philbin, *I, Monster: Serial Killers in Their Own Chilling Words* (Prometheus Books, 2011), 174.

2. Alfred Hitchcock, *Psycho*, Shamley Productions, 1960.

3. Ronald Schouten, James Silver, and Jim Silver, *Almost a Psychopath: Do I (or Does Someone I Know) Have a Problem with Manipulation and Lack of Empathy?*, (Hazelden Publishing, 2012), 24.

4. Dr. Cleckley's family has generously published the text of the fifth edition to be used free of charge for non-profit, educational use. Available at http://www.cassiopaea.org/cass/sanity_1.PdF.

5. S. O. Lilienfeld and B. P. Andrews, "Development and preliminary validation of a self-report measure of psychopathic personality traits in noncriminal population," *Journal of Personality Assessment* 66, no. 3 (1996): 488.

6. Paul Babiak and Robert D. Hare, *Snakes in Suits: When Psychopaths Go to Work* (Harper, 2006).

7. Martha Stout, *The Sociopath Next Door* (Broadway Books, 2005).

8. James Fallon, "The Mind of a Dictator," Oslo Freedom Forum, May 10, 2011, https://oslofreedomforum.com/talks/the-mind-of-a-dictator.

9. James Fallon, *The Psychopath Inside: A Neuroscientist's Personal Journey into the Dark Side of the Brain* (Penguin, 2013).

10. Insight TV, "What Makes a Psychopath?" SBS Network, Australia, June 3 2014, https://www.youtube.com/watch?v=kXMnc2Xjj-o.

11. Jeremy Seal, *A Fez of the Heart: Travels around Turkey in Search of a Hat* (Pan Macmillan, 1995).

12. Matsui Minoru, *Japanese Devils* (Center for Asian American Media, 2001).

13. Bob Tadashi Wakabayashi, "Reviewed Work: Japanese Devils by Matsui Minoru, Oguri Ken'ichi," *The Journal of Japanese Studies* 28, no. 2 (Summer 2002): 430.

14. R. Christie and F.L. Geis, *Studies in Machiavellianism* (Academic Press, 1970); R. Christie, and F. L. Geis, "How devious are you? Take the Machiavelli test to find out," *Journal of Management in Engineering* 15, no. 4 (1970): 17.

15. Phil Harris, Andrew Lock, and Patricia Reese, eds., *Machiavelli, Marketing, and Management* (Taylor & Francis U.S., 2000); Antony Jay, *Management and Machiavelli: Discovering a New Science of Management in the Timeless Principles of Statecraft* (Jossey-Bass, 1994).

16. Mark Brown, "John le Carré on Trump: 'Something seriously bad is happening,'" *The Guardian*, September 7, 2017 18.28 EDT. https://www.theguardian.com/books/2017/sep/07/john-le-carre-on-trump-something-truly-seriously-bad-is-happening.

17. Francis Ford Coppola, *The Godfather, Part III*, Paramount Pictures, 1990.

18. Amanda Brickell Bellows, "How the Civil War Created College Football," *New York Times*, January 1, 2015, 4:51. https://opinionator.blogs.nytimes.com/2015/01/01/how-the-civil-war-created-college-football/

19. Erich Fromm, *The Heart of Man* (Lantern Books, 2011).

20. Eric Hoffer, *The True Believer* (Harper & Row, 1951).

21. E)) Mike W. Peng, *Global Business* (Cengage Learning, 2016), 4.

Interlude: Genetics, Eugenics, Genocide

1. "100 Million Dieters, $20 Billion: The Weight-Loss Industry by the Numbers," *ABC News*, May 8, 2012.

2. Edward O. Wilson, *Sociobiology: The New Synthesis* (Harvard, 1975).

3. Shirley Telles, Meesha Joshi, Manoj Dash, P. Raghuraj, K. V. Naveen, and H. R. Nagendra, "An evaluation of the ability to voluntarily reduce the heart rate after a month of yoga practice," *Integrative Physiological & Behavioral Science* 39, no. 2 (2004): 119; Herbert Benson, John W. Lehmann, M. S. Malhotraf, Ralph F. Goldmani, Jeffrey Hopkins, and Mark D. Epstein, "Body temperature changes during the practice of g Tum-mo yoga," *Nature* 295 (1982): 21.

4. Barack Obama, *Dreams from my Father* (Crown/Archetype, 2004).

Chapter IV: The Breeding Programme

1. Molly Hennessy-Fisk, "Battered bull rider struggles for eight seconds of fame," *Los Angeles Times*, August 6, 2014.

2. Jared Diamond, *Guns, Germs and Steel: The Fates of Human Societies* (W.W. Norton: 1999).

3. J.J. Saunders, *The History of the Mongol Conquests* (Routledge & Kegan Paul, 1971), 174.

4. G. Barraclough, ed., *The Times Atlas of World History* (Times Books, 1979).

5. Lawrence W. Marvin, "Atrocity and Massacre in the High and Late Middle Ages," in *Theatres of Violence: Massacre, Mass Killing and Atrocity throughout History*,

eds. P. G. Dwyer and L. Ryan, vol. 11 (Berghahn Books, 2012).

6. Colin Tudge, *The Time Before History* (Simon and Schuster, 1997), 256.

7. Eva Botkin-Kowacki, "Common Swifts Airborne Life: Eat, Sleep, and Mate without Touching Earth," *Christian Science Monitor*, October 27, 2016.

8. Price T. D., J. Wahl, and R. A. Bentley, "Isotopic Evidence for Mobility and Group Organization among Neolithic Farmers at Talheim, Germany, 5000 BC," *European Journal of Archaeology* 9, nos. 2-3 (2006): 259-84.

9. Martha Stout, *The Sociopath Next Door* (Broadway Books, 2005).

10. J. Kagan, D. Arcus, N. Snidman, W. Y. Feng, J. Hendler, and S. Greene, "Reactivity in Infants: A Cross-National Comparison," *Developmental Psychology* 30 (1994): 342-45; Xinyin Chen, Paul D. Hastings, Kenneth H. Rubin, Huichang Chen, Guozhen Cen, and Shannon L. Stewart, "Child-Rearing Attitudes and Behavioral Inhibition in Chinese and Canadian Toddlers: A Cross-Cultural Study," *Developmental Psychology* 34, no. 4 (1998): 677; J. Philippe Rushton, "Ethnic Differences in Temperament," *Personality and Person Perception Across Cultures* (1999): 45; Yueh-Ting Lee, Clark R. McCauley, and Juris G. Draguns, *Psychology* (Ehrlbaum & Assoc., 1999).

CHAPTER 5: THE NOBLE CLASSES

1. William Golding, *Lord of the Flies* (Penguin, 1983).

2. Ken Albala and Trudy Eden, eds., *Food & Faith in Christian Culture* (Columbia University, 2011), 62.

3. Lucien Bély, *Histoire de France* (Éditions Jean-Paul Gisserot, 1999), 70.

4. Sir Wilfred Thomason Grenfell, *Adrift on an Ice-pan* (Houghton Mifflin Company, 1909), 21. Basil Miller, *Wilfred Grenfell: Labrador's Dogsled Doctor* (Zondervan, 1948).

5. Simon Sebag Montefiore, *Stalin: The Court of the Red Tsar* (Vintage, 2007).

6. "Stalin's Last Crime, Robert Siegel talks with Jonathan Brent," *All Things Considered*, National Public Radio, April 8, 2003, 12:00 AM ET.

CHAPTER 6: PRIVILEGE & THE DOUBLE STANDARD

1. Eugen Weber, "The Sixteenth Flora Levy Lecture in the Humanities: Some Ups and Downs of History," *Explorations: The Twentieth Century* X (2004). Later published as E. Weber, "The Ups and Downs of Honor," *The American Scholar* (1999): 79.

Chapter 7: The Authoritarian Personality

1. Thomas Strentz, "The Stockholm Syndrome: Law Enforcement Policy and Ego Defenses of the Hostage," *Annals of the New York Academy of Sciences* 347, no. 1 (1980): 137; Michael Adorjan, Tony Christensen, Benjamin Kelly, and Dorothy Pawluch, "Stockholm Syndrome as Vernacular Resource," *The Sociological Quarterly* 53, no. 3 (2012): 454.

2. L. C. Gjerde, N. Czajkowski, E. Røysamb, R. E. Ørstavik, G. P. Knudsen, K. Østby, S. Torgersen, J. Myers, K.S. Kendler, T. Reichborn-Kjennerud, "The Heritability of Avoidant and Dependent Personality Disorder Assessed by Personal Interview and Questionnaire," *Acta Psychiatrica Scandinavica* 126, no. 6 (2012).

3. Theodor W. Adorno, Else Frenkel-Brunswik, Daniel J. Levinson, and R. Nevitt Sanford, *The Authoritarian Personality* (Harper Brothers, 1950).

4. Gareth Norris, *The Developing Idea of the Authoritarian Personality: An Historical Review of the Scholarly Debate, 1950-2011* (Edwin Mellen, 2012).

5. Eric A. Zillmer, Molly Harrower, Barry A. Ritzler, and Robert P. Archer, *The Quest for the Nazi Personality: A Psychological Investigation of Nazi War Criminals* (Routledge, 2013).

6. Bob Altemeyer, *Right-Wing Authoritarianism* (University of Manitoba, 1981).

7. G. R. Watson, *The Roman Soldier* (Cornell University, 1969), 119.

8. John Jay Osborn, *The Paper Chase* (Whitston, 2003).

9. E. L. James, *Fifty Shades of Grey* (Arrow, 2012).

10. Wilfred Trotter, *Instincts of the Herd in Peace and War* (Fisher Unwin, 1921).

11. Dirk R. Van Tuerenhout, *The Aztecs: New Perspectives* (ABC-Clio, 2005), 131.

12. Alice Goffman, *On the Run: Fugitive Life in an American City* (Picador, 2015).

13. Andrew Stuttaford, "The Nazis' Supernatural Obsession," *The National Review*, October 2, 2017.

14. Greg Mitchell, *The Campaign of the Century: Upton Sinclair's Race for Governor of California and the Birth of Media Politics* (Random House, 1992), 570.

15. Ronn Torossian, "Hitler's Nazi Germany Used an American PR Agency," *Observer.com*, December 22, 2014.

16. Patricia S. Churchland, *Touching a Nerve: Our Brains, Our Selves* (W.W. Norton, 2013).

17. Leo McCarey, *Duck Soup*, Paramount Pictures, 1933.

18. Bruce Bradley and Dennis Stanford, "The North Atlantic ice-edge corridor: A possible Palaeolithic route to the New World," *World Archaeology* 36, no. 4 (2004): 459.

19. Michael Grunwald, "GOP Delegates Say the Economy Is Terrible—Except Where They Live," *Politico*, July 19, 2016.

20. Neil deGrasse Tyson, Twitter, @neiltyson, June 14, 2013, 7:41 AM.

21. Anahad O'Connor, "How the Sugar Industry Shifted Blame to Fat," *New York Times*, September 12, 2016.

22. Fernando de Rojas, *Celestina*, transl., Margaret Sayers Peden, Act 4, Scene 5 (Yale University, 2012).

23. Noam Chomsky, *The Chomsky Reader* (Pantheon, 1987).

24. "Those Were the Days," ©1979, Tandem Productions, all rights reserved.

25. Paul Bogart, "Two's a Crowd," *All in the Family*, Tandem Productions, 1978.

26. Robert Harris, *Fatherland: A Novel* (Random House, 2006).

27. Ward Moore, *Bring the Jubilee* (Wildside, 2009); Harry Turtledove, *The Guns of the South* (Del Rey, 2011).

28. Philip K. Dick, *The Man in the High Castle* (Penguin UK, 2012); William Overgard, *The Divide* (Jove, 1980).

29. R. H. Stein, *The Method and Message of Jesus' Teachings* (Westminster John Knox, 1994), 13.

30. Robert F. Jones, "Bang! Gotcha! You're Dead," *Sports Illustrated*, October 19, 1981, 64.

31. Margaret Heffernan, *Beyond Measure: The Big Impact of Small Changes* (Simon and Schuster, 2015); Thomas Petzinger, *The New Pioneers: The Men and Women Who are Transforming the Workplace and Marketplace* (Simon and Schuster, 1999).

32. "Slavery, as we shall afterwards show, dishonors labor; it introduces idleness into society, and with idleness, ignorance and pride, luxury and distress. It enervates the powers of the mind, and benumbs the activity of man." Alexis de Tocqueville, *Democracy in America* (Penquin Classics, 2003).

33. General Baron Antoine Henri de Jomini, *Life of Napoleon*, transl. H.W. Halleck (Andesite, 2017), 104; Philip Dwyer, *Napoleon: The Path to Power 1769-1799* (Yale University, 2008).

34. "Il est un devoir dont il semblera cruel même de parler. Un général en chef doit faire fusiller trois hommes, pour sauver la vie à quatre ; bien plus, il doit faire fusiller quatre ennemis, pour sauver la vie à un seul de ses soldats. Mais, d'un autre côté, les agents autrichiens et les prêtres qui cherchèrent à faire soulever la Lombar- die rent fort bien. Et plût à Dieu qu'en 1814 et 1815, on se fût conduit ainsi en France contre les Prussiens, Autrichiens, Russes, etc. A Pavie, la clémence eût été un crime envers l'armée ; elle lui eût préparé de nouvelles vêpres siciliennes; le com- mandant de la garnison française de Pavie fut fusillé ainsi que la municipalité. Pour calmer Pavie, Napoléon y avait envoyé l'archevêque de Milan, ce qui est plaisant." Marie-Henri Beyle Stendhal, *Vie de Napoléon: Fragments: Oeuvres Posthumes de Stendahl* (Calmann Lévy, 1882), 153.

Chapter 8: The Atrocino

1. Myron Levin, "Engineer's Memo Returns to Haunt GM," *Los Angeles Times*, April 30, 2001.

2. General Motors Corp. v. Mcgee, 837 So.2d 1010, District Court of Appeal of Florida (4th Dis., 2002).

3. Grimshaw v. Ford Motor Co., Civ. No. 20095, Court of Appeals of California (4th Ap. Dis., Div. 2, 1981).

4. Daniel Kadlec, "WorldCon," *TIME*, July 8, 2002, 28.

5. Alan Deutschman, "Is Your Boss a Psychopath?" *Fast Company* 96, no. 7 (2005): 44.

6. Louise Story and Eric Dash, "Report Shows Bonuses Paid by Bailed-Out Banks," *New York Times*, July 30, 2009.

7. Michael Dobbs, "Ford and GM Scrutinized for Alleged Nazi Collaboration: Firms Deny Researchers' Claims on Aiding German War Effort," *Washington Post*, November 30, 1998, A1.

8. Charles Higham, *Trading with the Enemy: An Exposé of the Nazi-American Money Plot, 1933-1949* (Delacorte, 1983), 67.

9. Ibid., 46.

10. Zach Toombs and R. Jeffrey Smith, "Pentagon Contractor Caught Illegally Selling Military Technology to China," *The Atlantic*, July 6, 2012.

11. https://www.ContractorMisconduct.org/

12. "US Department of State Directorate of Defense Trade Controls, David C. Trimble, Proposed Charging Letter," March 14, 2008, http://pmddtc.state.gov/compliance/consent_agreements/NorthropGrummanCorp.htm.

13. Melvin A. Goodman, "Eisenhower's Neglected Warning," *ConsortiumNews.com*, January 16, 2011, https://consortiumnews.com/2011/011611b.html.

14. Zachary Keck, "Report: In 2018, Global Defense Spending Will Reach Highest Level Since Cold War," *The National Interest*, December 23, 2017, http://nationalinterest.org/blog/the-buzz/report-2018-global-defense-spending-will-reach-highest-level-23763.

15. Thad McIlroy, "What the Big 5's Financial Reports Reveal About the State of Traditional Book Publishing," *BookBusinessMag.com*, August 5, 2016, http://www.bookbusinessmag.com/post/big-5-financial-reports-reveal-state-traditional-book-publishing/.

16. Ashley Lutz, "These 6 Corporations Control 90% Of The Media In America," *BusinessInsider.com*, June 14, 2012, http://www.businessinsider.com/these-6-corporations-control-90-of-the-media-in-america-2012-6.

17. Kate Vinton, "These 15 Billionaires Own America's News Media Companies," *Forbes*, Jun 1, 2016.

18. Ken Auletta, *Backstory: Inside the Business of News* (Penguin, 2004).

19. André Schiffrin, *The Business of Books: How International Conglomerates Took Over Publishing and Changed the Way We Read* (Verso, 2001).

20. "The Guardian View on Journalism and Advertising: Selling the News Short," *The Guardian*, February 20, 2015. There is also journalistic payola: Jon Christian, "These are the People Paying Journalists to Promote Brands in Articles," TheOutline.com, January 18, 2018, https://theoutline.com/post/2978/these-are-the-people-paying-journalists-to-promote-brands-in-articles.

21. Farhad Manjoo, "A Villain Dangerous to Ignore: Online Ads," *New York Times*, February 1, 2018, B1.

22. Adam Winkler, "'Corporations Are People' Is Built on an Incredible 19th-Century Lie," *The Atlantic*, Mar 5, 2018.

23. Paul Rosenberg, "GOP's Court-Packing Spree: It's Only the Beginning," Salon.com, December 3, 2017, https://www.salon.com/2017/12/03/gops-court-packing-spree-its-only-the-beginning/.

24. Sarah Zhang, "Why Can't the U.S. Treat Gun Violence as a Public-Health Problem?" *The Atlantic*, Feb 15, 2018; Alan Berlow, "How the NRA Hobbled the ATF," *Mother Jones*, Feb. 11, 2013, http://www.motherjones.com/politics/2013/02/atf-gun-laws-nra.

25. Paul Rosenberg, "There's No Such Thing as a Victimless Billionaire: Inside the Shadowy Voter Fraud Conspiracy that's 'Still in Progress.'" Salon.com, September 5, 2016, https://www.salon.com/2016/09/05/theres-no-such-thing-as-a-victimless-billionaire-inside-the-shadowy-voter-fraud-conspiracy-thats-still-in-progress/.

26. Alex Kotch, "Tax Forms Reveal Koch Brothers Spent Millions to Shape State Politics in 2017," Truthout.org, February 25, 2018, http://www.truth-out.org/news/item/43637-tax-forms-reveal-koch-brothers-spent-millions-to-shape-state-politics-in-2017; "In her memoir, Riva Levinson, a managing director at the firm from 1985 to 1995, wrote that when she protested to [Manafort] that she needed to believe in what she was doing, Manafort told her that it would 'be my downfall in this business.'" Franklin Foer, "The Plot Against America," *The Atlantic*, March 2018.

Chapter 9: The Modern World

1. "List of Countries by Military Expenditures," Wikipedia.org, retrieved December 12, 2017, https://en.wikipedia.org/wiki/List_of_countries_by_military_expenditures.

2. David Vine, "Where in the World Is the U.S. Military?" *Politico*, July/August 2015.

3. "World-Wide Nuclear-Powered Attack Submarines," GlobalSecurity.org, retrieved December 21, 2017, https://www.globalsecurity.org/military/world/ssn.htm.

4. Jasmine Tucker, "The President's 2016 Budget in Pictures," National Priorities Project, https://www.nationalpriorities.org/blog/2015/02/09/presidents-2016-budget-pictures/.

5. Jon Ronson, "Strange Answers to the Psychopath Test," *TED2012*, March, 2012, https://www.ted.com/talks/jon_ronson_strange_answers_to_the_psychopath_test.

6. Mark Achbar and Jennifer Abbott, *The Corporation*, Big Picture Media, 2003.

7. "Hornets from Hell," NatonalGeographic.com, retrieved February 3, 2018, https://video.nationalgeographic.com/video/bees_vs_hornet.

8. Florida has a number of important books exploring this trend, the first of which is Richard Florida, *The Rise of the Creative Class—Revisited* (Basic Books, 2014). For more on Florida's work, visit his website, CreativeClass.com.

9. Harry Dent, "U.S. Economy: From 1776 to 2014," Economy & Markets, July 4, 2014, https://economyandmarkets.com/economy/u-s-economy-from-1776-to-2014/. Note that this graph is logarithmic. So the change in slope after 1776 and after the Great Depression are actually much steeper, and in fact, are not straight lines but accelerations.

10. Scott Adams, *Dilbert*, United Media, 1989–2011, Universal Uclick: 2011–present.

11. David Morgan, "Pythons celebrate 'Holy Grail' 40th anniversary," CBS News, April 25, 2015, https://www.cbsnews.com/news/pythons-celebrate-holy-grail-40th-anniversary/.

Chapter 10: The Ugly Truth

1. Nancy Scheper-Hughes, *Death Without Weeping: The Violence of Everyday Life in Brazil* (University of California, 1992).

2. Martha Stout, *The Sociopath Next Door* (Broadway Books, 2005).

3. Daniel M. Rudofossi, *Cop Doc: The Police Psychologist's Casebook—Narratives From Police Psychology* (Routledge, 2017).

Epilogue

1. Nancy MacLean, *Democracy in Chains: The Deep History of the Radical Right's Stealth Plan for America* (Penguin, 2017). Also see, Erica L. Green and Stephanie Saul, "In Deals for Donations, Conservatives Influenced The Hiring of Professors," *The New York Times*, May 6, 2018, A10.

2. Ibid., 166.

3. Ibid., 143.

4. Ibid., 224.

5. Garry Wills, *Lincoln at Gettysburg: The Words that Remade America* (Simon and Schuster, 1992).

Image Credits:

xvii-xviii: My Lai Massacre, photos by Ronald L. Haeberle for the U.S. Federal Government.

xx: SexSel Proliferation of theories, by author.

6: Tyburn Triple Tree drawing, hanging, and quartering; *Execution of Edmund Campion, Alexander Briant, and Ralph Sherwin*: engraving by Giovanni Battista Cavalieri. From Richard Simpson, *Edmund Campion: A Biography* (John Hodges, 1896), 436.

8: *Portrait of Henry VIII* by the workshop of Hans Holbein the Younger, 1537-1547, from Wikimedia.org.

11: Imperial Coronation Egg with Coronation Carriage by Fabergé, from Wikimedia.org.

11: Elizabeth's Coronation Carriage, Courtesy Crochet.david via Wikimedia.org.

12: Charles and Diana's Carriage, Courtesy Elke Wetzig/CC-BY-SA via Wikimedia.org.

13: *Coronation Portrait of Queen Elizabeth II of the United Kingdom*, by Herbert James Gunn, 1953-1954, from Wikimedia.org.

22: Chehel Minar, Courtesy GerardM via Wikimedia.org.

32: Plates from François Mazois showing schematics of the reliefs, from François Mazois, *Les Ruines de Pompéi* (Paris: Librairie de Firmin Didots Frères, 1838) via archive.org.

43: Countries England has not invaded, by author.

45: Lizzie van Zyl, from Wikimedia.org.

49: Alexandria after bombardment, 1882, from Wikimedia.org.

56: Balangiga Massacre cartoon with title "KILL EVERYONE OVER TEN," appearing in the *New York Journal* on May 5, 1902.

58: Flag of India with Ashoka Wheel, from Wikimedia.org.

71: "Hands of Lingomo and Bolengo," picture captured by Alice Seely Harris and John Harris, from Wikimedia.org.

72: "Nsala of Wala in Congo looks at the severed hand and foot of his five-year old daughter, 1904," and "Mutilated Children from Congo," from Mark Twain, *King Leopold's Soliloquy: A Defense of His Congo Rule* (Boston: P. R. Warren Co., 1905), via Wikimedia.org

87: *Nuremberg Rally*, via Michael Leventhall, Greenhill Books.

154: *Lion capital of Ashoka*, from Wikimedia.org.

211: *Cupola del Brunelleschi*, Courtesy of sailko via Wikimedia.org.

Index

A

Achaemenid Empire, 21
Adams, Scott, 239
Adorno, Theodor, 158-60
Aegina, Greece, 30
Agger, Robert, 105
Alesia, Battle of, 64
Alexander, 15, 17, 20-24, 38, 47, 85, 112, 128, 147
Alexandria, Egypt, 20
Allain, Mathé ix
Altmeyer, Robert, 160
America First party, 201
American Psychiatric Association, 92
American Revolution, 211, 261
Amin, Idi, 67, 86
amphitheaters, 37
Amritsar Massacre, 47
Amun-Min, 128
Andrews, Brian, 94
anempathy, 115-16, 125, 221
anti-intellectualism, 120-21, 174, 177, 184
Anti-Social Personality Disorder (ASPD), 92. *See also* psychopath
Aquinas, Thomas, 178
Aristotle, 152
Arminius, 137
Ashoka, 58-59, 85, 112, 252; Ashoka's Hell, 59, 85, 167
Astor, John Jacob, 253
Atahualpa, 60-61
Atatürk, Kemal Mustafa, 101
Athens, Greece, 28-29, 31
Augustine of Hippo, 270
Australia, 46
Aztecs, 167

B

Babiak, Paul, 94-95, 199-200, 220
Balangiga Massacre, 56
Barber, Bernard, xxi, 174, 176-77
Barclay, McClelland, 88
Barry, John M., 264
Battle of Marathon, 28
Battle of the Thirteen Sides, 63
Bayeux Tapestry, 34
Beckett, Thomas à, 270
Bedriacum, Battle of, 36
Beria, Lavrentiy, 147
Bernard, Claude, 215
Bibighar Massacre, 44
Bloody Angle, 164
Boeing, 202
Boer War, 44-47, 241
Bonaparte, Napoléon. *See* Napoléon
Boudica, 136
Bradley, Omar, 153
British East India Company, 116
Brunelleschi, Filippo, 209-11
Buchanon, James McGill, 257
Buddhism, 58-59
Burke, Edmund, 263

C

Caesar, Julius, 15, 17, 24-26, 64, 111
Calabria, Italy, 19
California, 52-53
Caligula, 37
cannibalism, 42, 67, 87, 102
Cannon, Walter, 215
Capac, Huayna, 60
Capone, Al, 1-2, 5, 108
Caracalla, 37-38, 110
Carnegie, Andrew, 253
Carré, John le, 108
Carroll, Lewis, 83

Carson, Kit, 55
Catena, Paulus, 113
Catiline, 32-34, 85, 132, 158
Charles IX, 2
Chase Bank, 202
Chehel Minar, 73
Chile, 257-59
China, 61, 64, 67; Civil War, 70
Chivington, Colonel John, 54, 56
Chomsky, Noam, 187
Christianity, 26, 39, 51, 114, 150, 209-10, 262; advent of, 3; intolerant sects of, 39-41; Virtues of, 152-53
Christie, Richard, 105-7, 110
Civil War (American), 74, 203, 260, 272
Cleckley, Herv, 89-92, 94-96, 109
Cleitus the Black, 23, 147
Clovis I of France, 1-2, 5, 41
Coca Cola, 202
Cold War, 203-4
Colorado, 54
Colosseum, 32, 34
communism, 114, 263
Congo, 70
Constantine, 39, 147, 150, 209, 262; and Christianity, 150, 252
Constantius II, 40
Córdoba, Spain, 19
Cosmopolitan Darwinism, 233
Council of Nicaea, 40
Creative Class®, 228
Crusaders, 41-42
cult of personality, 3, 68, 79, 101, 114, 142, 146-48, 162, 165, 178, 185

D

Dahmer, Jeffrey, 87, 111
Darius, 21, 23
dark pentad, 115, 126
dark tetrad, 111-12
dark triad, 109-11
Darrow, Clarence, 251
David (King), 27
De Beers company, 223
Dewey, Thomas, 195
Diamond, Jared, 129
domestication, 128, 147, 161, 165
Doyle, Sir Arthur Conan, 46, 48, 160
Drexel, Katherine, 270
Duke, William, 252
Dunlap, Al 'Chainsaw,' 199

E

Ebbers, Bernie, 199
Egypt, 16, 20
Eichmann, Adolph, 157
Eisenhower, Dwight D., 86, 101, 153, 202, 206, 272
Elizabeth II of England, 10, 14
Elkins, Caroline, 71
Emancipation Proclamation, 267
Encyclopedia of Genocide, 73
Enlightenment, 15
Enron, 199
Euripides, 29

F

Fabergé jewelry, 10
Fallon, James, ix, 95-101, 116, 119, 122
fanaticism, 113-14
Fastow, Andrew, 199
Federal Communications Commission, 204

First Battle of the Marne, 164
Florence, Italy, 210; il Duomo di Firenze, 211
Florida, Richard, 228
Football Mentality, 169
Ford, Henry, 198, 201, 236, 253
French: Reign of Terror, 114; Revolution, 211, 261; Wars of Religion, 2, 41
Freud, Sigmund, 251
Fromm, Erich, 112, 154, 159
Fundamentalism, 178-80, 182
futurists, 228-29

G

Gacy, John Wayne, 87
Galen (Roman physician), 176-77
Gambino, Carlo, 108
Gaul, 64; conquest of, 24-25
Gaulle, Charles de, 153
Geis, Christie, 105
Geis, Florence, 105
General Motors (GM), 197-98
genetics, 118-19, 122, 139
Genghis Khan, 61, 63-64, 111, 131, 240; Samarkand, 62
George, Lloyd, 208
Germany, 66, 75-76, 112-13, 172, 190, 201, 151
gerrymandering, 206
Girika (Ashoka's Hell), 59, 85
gladiators, 32, 37
global warming, 183
Goebbels, Joseph, 175
Gratidianus: torture of, 32-33, 112, 133, 158
Great Depression, 189, 230
Great Jewish Revolt, 36
Great Recession, 203
Great Sepoy Rebellion, 44

Greeks, 20, 26, 28
Grenfell, Wilfred, 146, 148
gunpowder, 61

H

Haeckle, Ernst, 114
Hare, Robert D., 91-92, 94-96
Harvey, Sir William, 176
Hearst, Patty, 156
Hearst, William Randolph, 253
Helvetii: Caesar's defeat of the, 24
Henry III of Navarre, 2
Henry VIII, 9-10, 78
Hercules, 3
herd mentality, 163-64, 174
hero worship, 162-63
Hirohito, 242
Hiroshima, Japan, 242
Hitchcock, Alfred, 89
Hitler, Adolf, 15, 66, 76, 88, 112-13, 158, 169, 201, 216
Hobhouse, Emily, 45
Hoffer, Eric, 114
Holocaust, 76-77, 117, 157; deniers, 76, 102
honor, concept of, 149, 151-52
Hoover, J. Edgar, 272
Hopkins, Johns, 252

I

IBM Hollerith, 202
ideological zealotry, 113
Incans, 60-61
indentured servitude, 17
India, 44, 54, 58; retaliations in, 47, 74
Indochina War, 70
Industrial Revolution, 218, 260
Inquisition, 41, 252, 262

Iraq, 101
Islam, 20, 26, 203
Italy, 19

J

Jaffa: siege of, 16-19, 137, 165
Japanese Devils, 122, 160
Jericho, 73
Jerusalem, 36, 39, 74
Jesus, 27, 40, 209
Jewish, 74-75, 114; persecution, 133. See also Holocaust; uprisings, 74
Joséphine (Empress), 19
Judaism, 26. See also Jewish

K

Kalinga, 59; War, 252
Kellerman, François de, 19
Kennedy, John, 76
Kenya, 71
Khmer Rouge, 68, 113, 160
Khwarazmian empire, 63
Kikuyu: genocide, 72; Rebellion, 241
Kim dynasty: 67; Kim Il-song, 67, 148; Kim Jong-il, 67, 139, 147-48; Kim Jong-un, 67
kleptocracy, 206, 257
kleptoplutocracy, 14, 258-59, 269
Korean War, 57
Kraepelin, Emil, 89
Krushchev, Nikita, 148
Kuhn, Thomas, xxi, 174, 176-77, 181
Kulik, Grigory, 147-48
Kulik-Simonich, Kira, 147

L

Labute, Neil, 105
Leakey, Louis, 134
Lee, General Robert E., 74, 79, 101, 108, 111, 125
Leopold (King), 70
Leopold, Nathan, 251-52
Levites, 26
Leyendecker, J.C., 88
Library of Alexandria, 20
Lilienfeld, Scott, 94
Lincoln, Abraham, 54, 263, 266-67, 272
Lines of Torres Vedras, 19
lobbyists, 206, 226, 272
Loeb, Richard, 251-52
Louis IX, 252

M

MacArthur, Douglas, 153
MacArthur, John D., 253
Macedon, Kingdom of, 20, 22
Machiavellian, 104, 109-11, 115, 149; characteristics, 107; egocentricity, 94; in military, 107-8
Machiavelli, Niccolò, 104; *The Prince*, 94, 104, 109
MACH IV, 107, 109, 149, 160
MacLean, Nancy, 257, 259
Macleod, Iain, 73
Madoff, Bernie, 199
Madras Famine of 1877, 44, 165, 170, 185
Magna Carta, 249
Mao Zedong, 60, 113, 148, 160, 162
Marcus Aurelius, 34
Marius, 34-35
Marshall, George C., 101, 153

Marshall Plan, 50, 212, 230, 265-66
Marxism, 113, 180, 214; regimes, 160
Marx, Karl, 214
Maugham, Somerset, 194
McGee trial, 197-98
media, 204-5, 207
Medici family, 210; Catherine de', 2, 41
Mein Kampf, 114
Melian Dialogue, 29
Melos, island of, 29
Melville, Henry, 47
Mencken, H. L., 1
Mengele, Josef, 88, 111
mental health, 81-84, 88, 95, 99, 110
middle class, 230-31, 233-34; morality, 150-51
Midianites, 26
Milgram, Stanley, 155-58, 160
military-industrial complex, 202, 207, 218, 222, 272
'Missing Massacre' of Alexandria, 47, 73
Molotov, Vyacheslav, 147-48
Mongols, 62, 64
Montana Territory, 53
Monty Python, 241
Montgomery, Bernard, 153
Moravian Christianity, 54
Morgan, J.P., 253
mortgage crisis, 199, 207
Moses, 26
Mujahideen, 203
Mustafa, Kemal, 101
My Lai massacre, xix, xvi, 4, 57, 73, 75, 102, 115, 122-23
Mytilene revolt, 30

N

Nagasaki, Japan, 242
Napoléon, 15-20, 62, 74, 196, 211; Beja, 19; Pavia, 196
narcissism, 103-4, 107, 111; malignant, 112
National Rifle Association (NRA), 201, 206
Native Americans, 51-52, 54, 137, 203; Blackfeet, 53; Cheyenne, 54; Heavy Runner, 53; retaliations against, 74
Nazis, 76, 97, 112, 157; art, 88; collusion, 201; compliant behavior, 157; soldiers, 87, 159
Neo-Confederates, 164
Nero, 35, 37, 147
Net Neutrality, 204
New Testament, 27
New Zealand, 46
Nikolai II (Tsar), 10
nobility, 50, 132, 142-46, 149
No Gun Ri, 57, 73
North Korea, 67, 147, 165
Nuremberg: Defense, 157; rallies, 164; Zeppelin Grounds, 87

O

Ohio, 54
Old Testament, 26, 28
Oligarchy, 206
Olsson, Jan-Erik, 156
Olympias (Alexander's mother), 23
Osbert, William 'Longbeard' Fitz, 137

P

Paine, Thomas, 39, 180
Patton, George, 153

Pax Americana, 50, 212-13, 230
Pearl Harbor, HI, 201
Peloponnesian War, 29-31
Peninsular War, 19
Pequot Indians, 51
Persepolis, 21, 24, 207
Persian Wars, 23, 191
Philip (Alexander's father), 23
Philippines, 56, 75
Philistines, 27
Pilgrims, 113, 137, 262
Pinel, Philippe, 89
Pinner, Frank, 105
Pinochet, Augusto, 257-588
Plato, 152
Plutarch, 25
plutocracy, 206, 220, 257
Pol Pot, 68, 111, 113, 259
Pompeii, 32
Ponzi scheme, 199
Pope Francis, 14
popular sovereignty, 15
Portugal, 19
Pratt & Whitney company, 202
propaganda, 88
Psycho, 89
psychopath, 89, 99; criminal, 92, 95; in the workplace, 94, 220; moral, 98, 101
Psychopathic Personality Inventory, 94
Psychopathy Checklist (PCL), 91-92, 94
Puritans, 51-52

Q

Quito, Kingdom of, 60

R

racism, 35, 44, 76, 114, 124; and genetics, 119, 124-25, 164
Ramesses II, 227
Ray, David Parker, 84-86, 112, 171
Renaissance, 25, 209-10, 213, 229, 250; medicine, 190
Reynauld of Châtillon, 42-43
Rhode Island, 51
Richard the Lionheart, 42
Rockefeller, John D., 226, 253
Rojas, Fernando de, 187
Rolls Royce, 202
Rome, 24, 32, 74, 77: civilization, 32; fall of, 20; financial interests, 24; games, 111; inventions, 25
Ronson, Jon, 81, 199, 220
Russia, 19, 66-67, 70, 172, 202-3, 218, 263

S

Saladin, 42-43
Salem witch trials, 51
Samar Island, 56
Sand Creek Massacre, 54, 56
Schiffrin, André, 234
Schindler, Oskar, 97-98, 252
schizophrenia, 93
Schneider, Kurt, 89
Scythopolis, 40
Second Punic War, 35
Seneca, 81, 147, 161
serial killers, 84, 86, 88
Servile Wars, 37
Shaka (Zulu), 65-66, 87, 111, 158, 161, 163
Shakespeare, William, 105
Shkreli, Martin, 201
Sicarii revolts, 36, 74

Index

Siemens company, 202
Simon, Robert, 77
Skilling, Jeffrey, 199
slavery, 17-18, 25, 54, 86
Smith, Adam, 180
Smith, General Jacob H., 56
social Darwinism, 44
socialism, 182, 214, 219, 237
Socrates, 152
Soissons, Battle of, 1
Solutrean hypothesis, 177
Soviet Union, 66
Sparta, 31, 139, 162, 203
Spartacus, 136
Spencer, Herbert, xix
Spotsylvania, Battle of, 164
Stalin, Joseph, 66, 113, 147-48, 160, 165
Standard Oil, 201-2
Stanford, Leland, 252
St. Augustine, 209
St. Bartholomew's Day Massacre, 2, 41
Stockholm Syndrome, 156-57, 178
Stone, Michael, 86, 88
St. Rémy, 1
St. Valentine's Day Massacre, 1-2, 5
Suez Canal, 48
Sulla, 34, 147; Reign of Terror, 32, 35
superfecundity, 243-44, 248
Symbionese Liberation Army, 156

T

Talheim Death Pit, 135
Tamerlane, 131
Tascher, Maurice de, 19
Task Force Barker, xvi, 123. *See also* My Lai Massacre

Tasmania, 46
Theatre of Marcellus, 32
Thebes, 31; uprising, 21
The Iliad, 28, 151
The Mask of Sanity, 89-90
The Prince, 104, 109
Third Reich, 113. *See also* Nazis
Thompson, Hugh, 57, 122-23
Titus, 36-37, 39, 74
tobacco, 183, 201
Tocqueville, Alexis de, 195
Torquemada, 85, 111, 113
Toy Box Killer, 84-85
Treaty of Corbeil, 252
Treaty of Paris, 252
Trojan War, 28
Troy, 29, 73
Truman Defense Committee, 201
Truman, Harry S., 110, 201
Tuol Sleng prison, 69
Turkey, 101
Tyburn: 'triple tree,' 136
Tyre, Siege of, 21, 23

U

Uganda, 67
unification delusion, 180-81

V

Vanderbilt, Cornelius, 252
Victoria (Queen), 43, 116, 241
Victorians, 43-44, 116; colonists, 52; massacres, 47

W

Wagoner, Richard, 198
war for profit, 203-4
Washington, George, 101

Weber, Eugen, xxi, 1, 9, 76, 124, 151-53
Williams, Roger, 51, 113
Wilson, E.O., 119
Wiyot Massacre, 52
WorldCom, 199
World War I, 164, 272
World War II, 88, 102, 172, 212, 272

Z

zealotry, 113-15, 186, 259-60
Zhemchuzhina, Polina, 147
Zimbardo, Philip, 156; experiment, 160
Zulu (nation), 65, 87, 111, 158
Zyklon B, 75
Zyl, Lizzie van, 45, 241

www.ingramcontent.com/pod-product-compliance
Lightning Source LLC
Chambersburg PA
CBHW070750230426
43665CB00017B/2317